WORLD
SHOPPING
GUIDE

PUBLISHER'S NOTE

WORLD SHOPPING GUIDE

WHAT TO BUY WHERE –
BY THOSE IN THE KNOW

PRION

First published in Great Britain 1997 by
PRION BOOKS
32-34 Gordon House Road, London NW5 1LP

Copyright © Prion Books 1997

ISBN 1 85375 239 8

**Edited by Roy Weaver, formerly of the British
Diplomatic Service, and Catherine Young, former
Chairman of the British Diplomatic Spouses
Association**

Consultant Editor: Gerri Gallagher

Cover by Design Revolution
Typset in Sabon
Printed and bound in Great Britain
by Creative Print and Design, Wales

INTRODUCTION

The British Diplomatic Spouses Association is a support group for all spouses of serving and retired Diplomatic Service officers. It was created as the Diplomatic Service Wives Association in 1965 at a time of tremendous transformations in society as well as in the Service. Conditions were changing, generally getting more difficult and dangerous and it was felt that the 3000 wives were facing problems which had to be addressed centrally. Thirty years on it had grown in strength and the scope of its activities is much wider. The Association deals with issues such as employment and training, but never loses its focus on how to improve daily life.

Better information on all matters is one of the principal aims of the Association. Moving from one country to another can become less traumatic if one is well prepared and we try and share as much as we can of each other's experiences.

The great worldwide shopping experience may have started long before the Diplomatic Service Wives Association but it was often undertaken by domestic staff. Nowadays most of us have to fend for ourselves from day one in a foreign country, using foreign (often disjointed) words to buy foreign goods. We all make splendid mistakes: what I took to be spice for a stew in the south of Damascus was in fact powder to soothe a skin rash, to be diluted in the bath. It is a miracle not more diplomatic dinners turn into mass poisonings!

We live in an age where we assume everything can be found anywhere. This is very very far from the truth. We have all known the frustration of hunting for ever for what anyone would consider as basic toiletries. The positive side is the feeling of pure joy when a perfect little gem suddenly appears on a shabby stall...

This venture has shown that some spouses have taken shopping to a real art. Instead of waiting idly for their work permit to be eventually issued, they take up the challenge of the local shops and markets and will soon take enthusiastic visitors to their favourite haunts.

It is right all this experience should be shared beyond the Association's membership which is scattered in a number of outstations around the world. That experience is reflected in the variety contained in the individual entries. Naturally, the personal experiences upon which they are based may show some inequality of treatment place by place (despite the editor's best efforts)! This, however, should not be taken as affecting the shopping worthiness or amount of interest of a particular place. I sincerely hope that the efforts of all our contributors, who have spent a great many hours in some cases to send the most accurate picture of their posting, take the hassle out of your travelling and only leave you the joys of discovery.

CATHERINE YOUNG
*former chairman, British Diplomatic Spouses
Association*

HOW TO USE THE WORLD SHOPPING GUIDE

WHAT IS THE WORLD SHOPPING GUIDE

The *World Shopping Guide* is an informative A-Z companion to shopping in over 200 countries and cities across the world. Aimed at the business visitor in a hurry and the newly arrived resident, it gives practical advice on what to buy and where, where to eat, currency, tipping and security information for each location. The book has been compiled by 250 members of the Diplomatic Spouses Association and reflects in-depth knowledge of every location listed.

HOW COUNTRIES ARE ARRANGED

The countries are arranged alphabetically. Each entry gives general information on the country and then usually deals with at least one city, in most cases the capital. However, for the bigger countries other important cities are also listed, again in alphabetical order.

Some points to note are: Hong Kong is listed as a special administrative area under China, Scotland is listed under the UK, Hawaii is listed under the USA entry and Goa is listed as a city under India.

THE COUNTRY ENTRIES

Each country begins with a short introduction, which provides bullet point information on the following areas:
The **Language** spoken in each country; the **Currency** used and the most up-to-date exchange rate against the British pound; the opening days and hours of Banks and Shops; the availability of **Cash Points** and **Credit Card** use; **Duty free** available; whether to **tip** or not and how much.

Some entries naturally list more of this information than others but the individual contributors have tried to be as thorough as possible.

The entry continues with some general information on the location, such as the day-to-day cost of living, what sort of clothes are available, details of the main shopping streets, advice on local specialities and information on English language bookshops and publications.

Finally, each entry has three sub-headings, which give information on **Eating and Drinking, Transport** and **Security**.

The information covered includes the cost of eating out and advice on where to eat, what public transport is available and any necessary security precautions which should be taken in a location.

AFGHANISTAN

KABUL

Language **Pushtu**
Currency **Afghani. Rate of exchange fluctuates**
£1=7430, Mar 1997

The Foreign Office advises against all travel in Afghanistan in view of the extremely volatile situation there. Personal security dangers are real and travellers are most unlikely to get into Afghanistan even if they want to. It is much easier and far better to get some genuine atmosphere among the refugees now living in Quetta or Peshawar, where authentic Afghan ethnic foods and souvenirs are easily obtainable.

Traditionally the main things worth buying have been karakul (Persian lambskin from which coats and hats can be made), carpets, embroidery, lapis lazuli, marble, carvings, metalwork and pottery. There are also collectors' items like Turkoman and nomadic jewellery, old coins, knives and guns. Note that Afghan coats can start to smell unpleasant if not properly cured.

Old Kabul was highly geared to the tourist trade. However the continuing civil war has taken its toll: not only have many buildings been destroyed or damaged and shops closed, but the availability and prices of almost all goods are extremely unpredictable.

ALBANIA

TIRANA

Language **Albanian**
Currency **lek (Lk) of 100 quindaka.**
£1=207, Mar 1997
Banks **bring cash dollars and change at banks or**
American Express bureau in town centre
Shops **0800–1300, 1500–2000. Street kiosks and**
vendors early till late; market in morning,
some vendors stay late
Tipping **increasing**

The main shopping area is in the city centre, where the markets and street traders are to be found. Western products are becoming more and more freely available from the small food shops and kiosks which have sprung up along the main streets. There is even a simple supermarket which stocks basic articles, mainly imported from Greece. Small shops are opening up with cheap Turkish and Chinese made clothing. The only Western-style clothes shop is Benetton, catering mainly for the casual market. Shopping can also be done in most of the major hotels.

Things worth considering to bring back include carpets, copperware, filigree work and embroidery. The quality though is not always very good.

British daily newspapers are sometimes available on the day following publication. The Sundays are generally available on Monday. An English-language newspaper, the *Balkan News*, is available weekly. The *Herald Tribune* is available daily.

EATING AND DRINKING

There are twenty or so Western-style restaurants in Tirana – Italian, French, German, Chinese and of course Albanian which displays a marked Balkan/Turkish influence. Albanian wine, the red in particular, is passable and inexpensive although quality is inconsistent. Local brandy and raki can be tried. Only imported lager-style beers are available. Bars have popped up along the side-streets offering coffee and canned drinks. It is inadvisable to eat snacks (ice-cream, chips and hamburgers) from street vendors as their hygiene leaves a lot to be desired.

TRANSPORT

Albania has trains that run very slowly and overcrowded private buses whose road-worthiness is questionable. Both are relatively cheap. Taxis are available in the major towns and the fare is bargained before the journey starts.

SECURITY

Due to over 40 per cent unemployment and an average salary of less than £30 per month, Westerners are targets for attack through petty theft and mugging. The normal precautions need to be taken about walking alone at night. Tipping has not been usual in the past but this is changing as Western influence increases.

The outbreak of civil unrest in early 1997 should deter tourist travellers.

ALGERIA

ALGIERS

Language **Arabic**
Currency **Algerian dinar (DA) of 100 centimes.**
  £1=92, Mar 1997. Exchange rate set by
  government; not convertible
Banks **Sat–Wed 0800/0900–1500/1600**
Bargaining **yes**
Tipping **common in addition to service charges;**
  10 per cent in restaurants, 10 dinars per bag for
  airport porters

Because of the high security threat to foreigners, the Foreign Office advises against travel to Algeria.

The cost of living is high and import of consumer goods is controlled. Most locally produced items are of poor quality. It is wise to carry a couple of decent plastic carrier bags with you; those which shops supply are normally of poor quality and often charged for. Some knowledge of French is useful.

The main shopping area centres around the Rue Larbi Ben M'hidi, Place de la Grande Poste and Rue Didouche Mourad in which there is a branch of the official arts and handicrafts organisation, SNAT, with branches also in Boulevard Kohammed Khémisti and Rue Maitre Ali-Boumendjel. These shops provide a useful overview of what might be available elsewhere and the sort of prices you should aim at in bargaining. Best buys include carpets and rugs, if you know what you are doing. But only buy an item because you like it, not as an investment. Tuareg items are usually expressly made for the tourist trade.

Books in English for both adults and children are unobtainable.

EATING AND DRINKING
There is a reasonable number of good restaurants in and around Algiers, but in terms of value for money they are expensive. They mostly specialise in Algerian or French dishes, but there are also some Vietnamese/Chinese restaurants. Local delicacies include couscous, *burek* (minced meat), *merguez* (spicy sausage) and some rather sweet cakes. For local dishes and good fish try Restaurant le Berry or Restaurant-Café d'Angleterre, both in Boulevard Mustapha Ben Boulaid.

There are a number of good value restaurants in the area around the Places des Martyrs, Emir Abdelkader and Port Said. Beer and Algerian wine are normally available, but there is rarely any choice of brand and they are expensive.

TRANSPORT
Buses are irregular, overcrowded and rarely used by Europeans. Taxis, although numerous, are sometimes impossible to get, particularly at peak hours. They normally only stop at fixed points in town to collect customers who queue.

ANDORRA

The main – practically only – industry of this tiny country and its capital Andorra la Vella is selling duty-free electronic and other goods to the seven to eight million tourists who pass through every year. Few of them stay any time in the country and there is a large number of shops along the main road between the French and Spanish frontiers. Andorra has no currency of its own and French and Spanish currencies are in use. As ever with so called duty-free offers, make sure that you are getting exactly what you want and that the price converted into your own currency represents a real bargain compared with home.

ANGOLA

LUANDA

Language **Portuguese**
Currency **kwanza (Kz) of 100 lwei. £1=8650, Mar 1997**
Banks **use cash US dollars**
Credit cards **American Express, Visa, Access**
Shops **1400–1600 Mon, 0900–1600 Tue to Fri,
    0900–1200 Sat**
Duty-free **cigarettes and drink at hard currency
    shops up to twice UK price**
Tipping **theoretically illegal, but small gifts in kind
    (cigarettes, etc.) normal practice**

Banditry is common, even in Luanda itself, mainly in the early evening and at night. Because of this, the Foreign Office advises against visiting Angola.

The main fact of everyday life in Luanda is that the local currency has a black market rate of many times the official rate. This makes local shopping with kwanzas impossibly expensive. Because of this there are few conventional shops in the city, mainly large open-air markets where goods are sold at high black-market prices. Everything in the way of consumables has to be imported. Virtually everything is in short supply or erratically available and no brand names can be guaranteed at any time. Shopping can be difficult, but most basics can be found although often at a price and after some shopping around.

There is a branch of Benetton in Rua Major Kanyangulo. Clothes are available in the local shops, but they are often of inferior quality. Attractive wax-print fabrics (made in the Netherlands or Dubai) are available in the local markets.

There are supermarkets in the town centre such as Intermarket in Rua de Joao Barros and Jumbo in Avenida Deolinda Rodrigues. There is an enclosed market for fruit and vegetables and other sundry items at Largo do Kinaxixi. There is also a noisy market which sells herbs and spices at Avenida N'Gola Kilwanji in Sao Paulo. Both markets are closed on Mondays. The markets are a source not only of local atmosphere but also of fresh fruit and vegetables, although the supply is erratic and seasonal. Avocados, melons, passion fruit, limes, mangoes, papayas and pineapples can all be found in season.

There are some quite good souvenirs or gifts available. The main post office in Largo F. Cunho da Cruz sells souvenir stamps in booklets or loose in envelopes. Cuban cigars can be obtained in the Rua Guevara from the white building 200 metres above the intersection with Avenida Lenin. Hand-painted tiles are to be found in the Rua Dr A. Barca opposite the road exit from the Intermarket. A good place for local arts and crafts is Futungo Market 17 kms south of Luanda, open Saturday and Sunday. Otherwise try Espelho da Moda in Rua Major Kanyangulo or Bazaar Okapi in Rua Rei Katyavala.

South African wines, spirits, liqueurs, soft drinks and fruit juices are available in the supermarkets although the supply is not always dependable. There is an interesting fish market on the Ilha where garoupa, corvinha, gambas and lobster can be bought.

EATING AND DRINKING
Eating out is generally limited to a few restaurants and hotels.
Portuguese cuisine is the nearest you get to a local speciality.
Restaurante Cervejeria A Petisqueira in Rua Jaoa Monteiro is
excellent, crowded,and closed on Mondays. Restaurante
Monte Carlo in Rua Commandante Kwenya is slightly expen-
sive, but serves good Portuguese and seafood. Restaurante
Mexicana in Rua Cabral enjoys a pre-independence setting.
The Hotel Navio Westminster is a boat moored on the Ilha.
For inexpensive coffee, cakes and sandwiches try the
Pasteleria Primor in Rua dos Enganos: nice terrace.

TRANSPORT
There are no regular taxis and the buses are infrequent, overcrowded, unhygienic and not recommended.

ANGUILLA

Language **English, Creole**
Currency **East Caribbean dollar (EC$) of 100 cents.**
  £1=4.2, Mar 1997
Banks **0900–1400 Mon–Thur**
  0900–1400,1600–1800 Fri
Credit cards **accepted at most hotels, restaurants**
  and tourist shops
Shops **0800–1600 with break for lunch**

Anguilla is a small island only 35 square miles in area and
quite expensive, catering mainly for the up-market tourist
trade. Almost everything is imported, even most of the local
gifts and souvenirs. For the serious shopper the island of St
Martin is only seven miles away and easily accessible in 20
minutes by ferry boat. St Martin offers duty-free shopping,
although food is liable to duty when imported to Anguilla.

 Although The Valley has most of the island's local stores
and supermarkets, gift shops are scattered throughout and
most hotels also have their own shops. The Drug Store in The
Valley has T-shirts and other small gifts as does The T-Shirt
Shop just a few minutes walk away. Road Bay has The
Anguilla Craft Shop at Stoney Ground.

 There are local daily newspapers such as the *Chronicle* and
the *Daily Herald* published in St Martin which have some
international and local news. There is another newspaper the

Light which appears weekly in Anguilla and has entirely local coverage.

EATING AND DRINKING

Beer, liquor and cigarettes are obtainable locally at reasonable prices. Restaurants are very good but expensive and hotel dining rooms are reliable. Fish and seafood, including spiny lobster, is good and chicken is plentiful. Ripples Restaurant at Sandy Ground is recommended.

TRANSPORT

There is no public transport. Taxis can prove hard to find when needed and are expensive to use.

ANTIGUA & BARBUDA

Language **English**
Currency **East Caribbean dollar (EC$) of 100 cents.
£1=4.2, Mar 1997**
Banks **0830–1200 Mon to Thur, 0830–1200,
1500–1730 Fri**
Tipping **10–15 per cent service charge in hotels and
restaurants; government fixed rates for taxis;
airport and hotel porters expect small tips**

The cost of living is very high because nearly everything is imported. The small resident population cannot justify shops having the range of goods one would normally find in a larger country. In general the range of clothing available is limited except for casual clothing and beachwear and is much more expensive than in Britain. For women there are local ready-made clothes, usually of indifferent quality and style. Attractive imported clothes are available at boutiques and hotel tourist shops but are very expensive. There are sandals of reasonable quality.

There are now glitzy cruise-ship facilities and a casino at Heritage Quay in St John's, where the shops are filled with expensive items supposed to be duty-free but in practice rarely convincing bargains. The traditional shopping centre lies near by, around St Mary's Street. The market offers a hint of genuine local atmosphere. Basketware and woodcarvings plus of course the inevitable T-shirts are available everywhere including on the beaches.

There are four local English-language newspapers identified with the various political parties and largely devoted to local politics. British Sunday newspapers and *The Economist* are usually available on Monday morning.

Eating and Drinking

Eating out is expensive. There are only a few really good restaurants, at which it is advisable to book beforehand and to be ready to eat by 2100. Fish is particularly recommended and Booker B's off Long Street is as good a place as most to try flying fish. There are other decent restaurants on Redcliffe Quay.

Transport

Public transport is limited, but the number of taxis has increased with the expansion of the tourist industry. They are expensive, and uncertain timekeepers. They have no meters and it is advisable to establish a price before beginning a journey by knowing the official rates which are displayed at the airport in the baggage arrival hall.

Argentina

Buenos Aires

Language **Spanish**
Currency **Argentinian peso (ARP). £1=1.64, Mar 1997**
Banks **0900–1900 Mon to Fri**
Credit cards **all major cards accepted in shops and restaurants; a fee may be charged**
Shops **0930–1930 Mon to Fri, 0930–1300 Sat; malls stay open later**
Tipping **5–10 per cent in restaurants**

Buenos Aires offers a range of individual and distinctive shops. There are no large chain or department stores, except for C&A which has just opened three small outlets, but there are many shopping malls around the city housing small individual stores offering wide ranges of goods such as clothing, shoes, handbags and other leather accessories.

Basically everything is available, but prices are high especially for better quality goods. Many commodities are made by subsidiaries of European or American firms. Argentine women are extremely smart and fashion conscious. Ready-made clothes and materials can be bought, often under famous labels, but they are usually made locally and are of lower quality than British-made articles. It can be difficult to find women's clothing larger than a UK size 14. Few locally made beauty products have not been tested on animals.

The main shopping streets are in the central area including the Calle Florida, which is pedestrianised. There is the Galerias Pacifico shopping mall as well as many smaller shops offering good quality leather goods and crafts. The Avenida Santa Fe is another famous shopping street.

For an excellent selection of handicrafts go to Kelly's at Paraguay 431 or any of the other shops in the same street. Artesanias Argentinas at Montevideo 1386 is also good and is a non-profit-making organisation. At weekends there are craft markets at Plaza Francia, Plaza Belgrano and Plaza Dorrego, and on Thursday and Friday there is the Feria del Cabildo in the courtyard of the old town hall on Plaza de Mayo.

Local specialities include all types of leather goods, alpaca, picture frames in the local metal known as peltre, silver maté pots (maté is the local equivalent of tea), wooden craftwork from the north-west of the country and jewellery made from the local silver and the local semi-precious stone called rodocrosita. There are also excellent wines at excellent prices: for those with a sweet tooth an absolute must is *dulce de leche*, a runny caramel confectionery available in tubs: Alfajores are chocolate-covered biscuits containing *dulce de leche*. Branches of the Havana shops sell both of these last two items. Good quality fur and leather coats and leather suede jackets can be bought although, apart from nutria or seal and other local furs, they are not cheap.

English-language publications include the daily *Buenos Aires Herald*. Foreign newspapers are available at kiosks in the centre of town. Books in English can be bought from shops such as Yenny in the Design Centre, but they are often triple the UK price.

EATING AND DRINKING
Beef, as one would expect of Argentina, is a staple food. There is ample opportunity to dine out. Best areas for restaurants are the Design Centre at Pueyrredon 2501, the newly developed Puerto Madero docklands area and Costanera Norte. *Parillas* (grill restaurants) are worth trying.

Ice-cream lovers will like the Freddos chain of shops. Coffee fans will find many roasts and blends available. Fruit juices and squashes tend to be sweet, as does the local ginger ale. Although the local gin is slightly sweet, it is almost as good as the UK product, though the locally blended whisky is far inferior to the Scottish. Argentina is the world's fifth biggest wine producer and there are excellent reds and whites available. Trapiche chardonnays are highly thought of.

TRANSPORT
The Buenos Aires public transport system is extensive, relatively cheap and usually crowded.

There is a fairly extensive bus service, both in the city and in the suburbs. The underground, although not as extensive as in London, is cheap and fairly clean. Taxis are cheaper and far more abundant than in London.

SECURITY
Bag snatching is not uncommon. Avoid ostentation and take care, particularly at night.

ARMENIA

YEREVAN

Language **Armenian**
Currency **dram of 100 couma. £1=760**
Banks **take cash US dollars**

Armenia is in the early stages of its post-USSR economic development and sees its major consumer export potential in its excellent cognacs and mineral waters.

Meals are cheap, even in the larger hotels. But quality is variable.

Women in particular are advised to take care in Yerevan at night.

ASCENSION ISLAND

There is no local taxation or duties, but everything is imported and prices are on average 25 per cent higher than in the UK.

There is only a limited supply of goods available locally.

Fresh fruit and vegetables are never in plentiful supply. Apart from two shops run by NAAFI, there are some very small shops selling T-shirts and one or two other basic clothing items. The things sold in the gift shops are usually made in Hong Kong, Taiwan or Korea. The Islander newspaper is published weekly by voluntary effort.

There are numerous walking trails and at nineteen locations the Ascension Heritage Society has set up letter boxes containing a visitors' book and a recording stamp to use on maps, first day covers etc.

There are no hotels, cafés or public bars on the island, but there are several clubs and visitors are always made welcome. There is no public transport or taxi service.

AUSTRALIA

Language English

Currency **Australian dollar (AU$) of 100 cents.
£1=2, Mar 1997**

Banks **0930–1600 Mon to Thur 0930–1700 Fri
some open Sat morning**

Credit cards **most accepted**

Cashpoints **yes**

Shops **0900–1730 Mon to Thur 0900–2100 Fri
0900–1700 Sat 0900–1800 Sun (city centres only)**

Refunds **yes, with receipt; time limit of a week
unless goods faulty**

Sales **mostly genuine**

Duty-free **tax-free shops in all cities (take passport
and air ticket); discount stores may be cheaper for
electrical goods**

Tipping **not customary, but leave small change for
taxi drivers; 10 per cent in restaurants where no
service charge**

Import/export restrictions **quarantine regulations
apply to animal products, which will be destroyed
on arrival (including leather goods newly
purchased in India and South-east Asia and
flowers); evasion risks fine or imprisonment.
Permission needed to export articles more than 30
years old**

The day-to-day cost of living is much like that in the UK, although public transport is cheaper. Good quality merchandise such as clothing tends to be a bit more expensive than in the UK, although a wide range of reasonable casual clothing is available. There are some excellent lines of smart casual wear such as Sportscraft, Aywon, Nouvelle Nouveau, etc. which are not too expensive especially in the sales. Contact lenses are cheap and UK prescriptions are accepted.

Gifts and souvenirs available include the usual boomerangs, fluffy kangaroos and koalas or outback and aboriginal items including landscapes, didgeridoos and even investment art. There are a few places selling goods such as batiks, carvings, paintings and pottery which display some artistic influence.

Other ideas for gifts and souvenirs include Akubra hats and Drizabone jackets, moleskin trousers, sheepskin rugs and Tea Tree Oil products such as soap, handcream, etc. and Vegemite.

Items of jewellery, and opals in particular can be good buys.

The cost of eating out is comparable to that in the UK. A feature of many restaurants is BYO (bring your own) wine. Licensed restaurants tend to be more expensive than BYO and wine will rarely cost less than $15 a bottle. Clubs are also highly recommended. The price of food is heavily subsidised by the "pokies", as the one-arm bandits are known. Australian wines and beers are both excellent and reasonably priced.

CANBERRA

Canberra has a population of only about 300,000 people and does not offer the range of shops that is found in the larger cities. People used to big cities will miss the busy streets and choice of shops and stores.

Canberra has four shopping precincts which house the main chain stores. These are Canberra Centre and Westfield Shopping Centre at Belconnen in the north, and Woden Plaza and Tuggeranong Hyperdome in the south. Manuka is an attractive shopping area, the Chelsea of Canberra. It has boutiques and speciality shops, open-air restaurants and cafés. The vegetable markets in Fyshwick Market, Belconnen Market and Tuggeranong Market are a feast for the eyes. Fresh produce can be bought there from Thursday to Sunday.

There are branches of the department store David Jones in Canberra Centre and Woden Plaza. Another department store,

Grace Brothers, is in Canberra Centre, Belconnen and Tuggeranong. These are smaller versions of the stores in Sydney, Melbourne, Perth, etc.

Canberra abounds in local arts and crafts. Artists have stalls in the local markets. Gorman House Arts Centre is in Ainslie Avenue, Braddon and has a market each weekend. The Old Bus Depot Markets in Wentworth Avenue, Kingston, are open on Sunday. Australian arts and crafts are also available from Australian Choice on the ground floor of the Canberra Centre, Everything Australian on the top floor of Belconnen Mall and the National Trust Gift Shop in Old Parliament House.

The following galleries specialise in paintings and other Australiana for collecting or for gifts – Southlands Gallery in Mawson Place, Mawson; Beaver Galleries at 81 Denison Street, Deakin; Solander Gallery at 36 Grey Street, Deakin, Bungendore; Woodworks at Kings Highway, Bungendore, Cuppacombalong Craft Centre at Nass Road, Tharwa and Roberts Gallery at Barton Highway, Gungahlin.

There is a huge selection of wooden bowls and other wooden articles at the Bugendore Woodworks, half an hour from Canberra. Hansons in Civic has duty-free opals. At Federation Square Ginnindera there are Aboriginal artefacts, boomerangs, and paintings – check that the cheaper ones are authentic and not made in China. For soft toys go to Australian Choice in Canberra Centre. The cheaper toys in tourist shops are made in China. Britches in Furneaux Street in Manuka stocks all sizes and styles of Akubra hats and Drizabone jackets. R.M.Williams in Canberra Centre has moleskin trousers, the Australian working gear. For sheepskin rugs and Ugg boots try the Shearing Shed, Kingston, the Wee Jasper Workshop, an hour away from Canberra via Yass or Mortel's Sheepskin Factory in Wollongong Street, Fyshwick. Tea Tree Oil products such as soap and handcream are available at health shops and supermarkets, as is Vegemite, as Aussie as you can get.

British newspapers can be bought at the larger newsagents in Kingston and Manuka. The weekly international editions of the *Guardian*, *Telegraph* and *Express* are more widely available. There are excellent speciality bookshops at the National Library, National Gallery and the Botanical Gardens. General bookstores can be found in the shopping malls.

EATING AND DRINKING
Canberra boasts a wide selection of take-aways and eating houses offering everything from the traditional pie and chips

and Kentucky fried chicken to ethnic restaurants or establishments. There is a vast range of prices with a three-course meal with wine at an average restaurant starting at around $30 a head. The Telstra tower on top of the Black Mountain nature reserve offers stunning views some 25 to 35 kilometres each way and an expensive revolving restaurant for those celebrating. An average three-course dinner would cost about $55 to $60 a head. The Oak Room at the Hyatt Hotel is a top-price restaurant, about $80 a head. Other top of the range recommended restaurants include the Lobby, Fringe Benefits and the Boat House. Middle price range restaurants would include all the Italian and ethnic eateries. Robertos in Manuka, Bellucis in Dickson and the Ottoman, a Turkish restaurant in Manuka are all excellent. Canberra clubs offer great value for money. Out-of-town visitors can sign the guest book and enjoy the facilities. Recommended are the Hellenic and Southern Cross Club in Woden, the Canberra Yacht Club and the grander Canberra Club in Civic.

TRANSPORT

Buses are the only form of public transport in Canberra. They provide frequent and regular services during the day, but not later in the evening. Bus tickets can be purchased in the form of a credit card for 10 rides at newsagents. Taxis are plentiful and satisfactory. Fares are reasonable and charges are metered.

BRISBANE

It is not over-cynical to suggest that Brisbane's main claim to fame is as the home of Castlemaine lager. The city has had the reputation of being something of a backwater, despite numbering over one million inhabitants. It sprawls somewhat and is unexceptional. Shopping is adequate and the main shopping area is for the most part coverable on foot. A wide range of good quality clothing is available, some of it expensive, but locally made casual clothing is available at very reasonable prices. The range of goods is comprehensive and only specialist or designer requirements may be difficult to find. Many goods are imported from Europe or the Far East.

The town centre lies in the triangle between Central Station and the loop of the river. Queen Street is the traditional heart of the city. It has a pedestrian precinct which includes the Myer Centre, a large shopping mall with fashionable shops and several eating places. There is a wide range of shops, department stores and supermarkets of varying quality. There are several large new shopping complexes all under cover and fully air-conditioned with free parking facilities in the suburbs. Eagle Street runs off Queen Street and there is a market there next to the river on Sunday which is quite good for arts and crafts.

Those looking for more atmosphere and excitement will gravitate to Fortitude Valley, the area around Brunswick Street station just one stop from Central. There is a wide ethnic mix including Irish and Chinese in the shops and eating and drinking places. On Saturday there is a flea market in Duncan Street Mall. South of the river, the area around Vulture Street and Boundary Road is similar in atmosphere with several reasonable eating places.

The usual national and international newspapers are widely available and there are plenty of standard bookshops, such as Dymmocks in Queen Street.

Late night shopping is until 2100 on Thursday in the suburbs and on Fridays in the city. Shops close at 1600 on Saturdays. Sunday trading is increasing and Sunday open markets are popular.

EATING AND DRINKING

There is a wide range of eating places in Brisbane from fast-food outlets to smart restaurants where the cuisine approaches international standards. Apart from the choice offered by the Myer Centre, Petrie Terrace has up-market pretensions. "Bring your own" wine restaurants are considerably cheaper and popular. Try the Fortitude Valley and Vulture Street/Boundary Road areas.

TRANSPORT

It is possible to travel by public transport for shopping. Taxis are plentiful and satisfactory. They are fitted with two-way radio systems and can be booked by telephone.

DARWIN

Darwin has a strong Aboriginal influence and a relaxed life-style, perhaps necessitated by its climate. Practically all commodities have to be brought from the south. The cost of freight is high, so the cost of living is appreciably higher than in other state capitals. Most things are available, but supply is variable. There is a wide selection of casual clothing in local shops and supermarkets.

The centre of town is around Smith Street and its mall in the area between the harbour and the Botanical Gardens. Around the harbour itself you will find some souvenir and gift shops as well as eating places. There is an extensive air-conditioned shopping complex at Casuarina in the northern suburbs, about five miles from the centre. There is a Saturday morning market at Parap Road.

For arts and crafts, worth trying are the Framed Showcase and Raintree Galleries, respectively on Stuart Highway and in Knuckley Street near the mall. Almost next door to the latter is Blazez, also worth trying.

British newspapers are not available in the shops. Some popular British magazines are available from newsagents. There is a good selection of books, although they are costly, available for example from Bookworld in the Smith Street Mall.

EATING AND DRINKING

There are many good eating places of all types. Seafood can be particularly good. If you want to treat yourself, go to Christo's at Stokes Hill Wharf on the harbour, Rock Oyster in Mitchell Street in the centre or Holtze Cottage in the Botanical Garden.

There are plenty of bars, as befits a town with Darwin's reputation for hard drinking.

TRANSPORT

The bus service is excellent. Taxis are plentiful and can be called by phone, although one should be prepared for a wait. Fares are metered and are not unduly expensive.

MELBOURNE

There is good shopping available in the main central area, City Centre. The Southgate shopping complex next door to the Victoria Arts Centre is very popular and is good for general shopping, crafts and souvenirs aas well as food outlets. The Victoria Arts Centre itself has a very good gift shop and there are a couple of good restaurants there. Chinatown is the place to go for ethnic shopping and restaurants. Queen Victoria market is large and entertaining.

Big department stores offer a complete range of shopping and the best opportunity for window and comparative shopping. In central Melbourne the major department stores are Myers, David Jones, Daimaru and Georges.

There is good shopping too in many suburbs near the city centre, each with its own distinctive atmosphere. Try for example Acland Street in St Kilda, Chapel Street in Prahran, Bridge Street and Swan Street in Richmond and Brunswick Street in Fitzroy.

A limited range of British newspapers and periodicals is available from newsagents. Weekly international editions are widely available as are locally produced newspapers. Bookshops carry a wide range of British hardbacks and paperbacks.

EATING AND DRINKING
There are many restaurants in the areas already mentioned to suit all tastes and pockets.

TRANSPORT
The suburbs are served by trams, buses and electric trains. All forms of transport are crowded during peak periods, but fares are generally lower than in London. Taxis are plentiful and are computer or radio controlled.

PERTH

Perth is a beautiful small city, very clean, tidy and orderly. Its tiny central area is around the pedestrian precincts on Murray Street, Hay Street and London Court with its many shopping malls, restaurants, food courts and coffee bars.

There are several small boutiques with excellent lines of smart and inexpensive casual wear and a couple of department stores, Myers and Aherns.

British newspapers are not generally available. There is a very good supply of books, but prices range from 50 per cent to 85 per cent above those in the UK.

EATING AND DRINKING
Perth has a wide range of restaurants from the ethnic cheerful to the sophisticated with prices to match. The area for more up-market eating places is concentrated in Northbridge, a few blocks north of Murray Street. In James Street are restaurants such as Vino Vino and Fishy Affair. In Lake Street are The Plum and Emperor's Court. At the intersection of the two streets is Botticelli's.

TRANSPORT
Bus and train services exist, but they are not always frequent or convenient for use outside commuter times. There is an efficient taxi service.

SYDNEY

Many British people will scarcely experience the feeling of being abroad when they are in Sydney, although the cost of living overall is perhaps a little higher than at home.

Centre Point houses the Sydney Tower with revolving restaurants and coffee shops together with several shopping arcades. Close by are lots of other arcades and shops including the Strand in Pitt Street, which is an interesting old building. David Jones, useful for comparative shopping, is in Centre Point. It connects with Grace Brothers, another large department store, which in turn connects with the Queen Victoria Building (QVB), a famous landmark now converted into a shopping mall with a series of speciality small shops. QVB boasts of being one of the most beautiful shopping centres in the world. It is directly connected to the Town Hall station.

In all these centres there are large department stores and numerous speciality shops where serious shopping can be done as easily as window shopping. Practically everything can be found here including clothing, leather goods, food courts and souvenirs. Numerous duty-free shops are found in the area particularly along Pitt Street, George Street and Castlereagh. Duty-free shopping in Sydney is considered by some to be the cheapest in the world, but it pays to know your prices beforehand and to make comparisons. Goods ordered at duty-free shops in town are collected at the airport on departure. There are several chain stores for clothing along the lines of C&A, such as Sussans and Sportsgirl. Woolworths in George Street and Coles and Franklins are lower-range department stores.

Paddy's Market in Chinatown is worth a visit for the ambience and is not far from Town Hall and Central stations. Darling Harbour can be reached by monorail and has a huge shopping complex housing many speciality shops (lots of souvenirs) and a food court. The Rocks, adjacent to Circular Quay, is the old part of Sydney with numerous cafés, pubs and restaurants as well as a small market on the lines of Covent Garden and art galleries. Australian crafts of unusual type can be found here. The most selective souvenirs are found in the Rocks, but try George Street and Pitt Street for leaner pockets.

A little further afield is Double Bay, a 10-minute ride on the Watson's Bay Ferry. This is one of the fashionable areas of Sydney with continental-style cafés and label boutiques. Mosman is similar, best reached by ferry and definitely worth a visit. Bondi Junction is the large shopping area of Bondi Beach. Manly, another suburb by the sea, is also in the northern harbour area.

There are no problems in finding English-language books. The *Sydney Morning Herald* is the main local daily.

EATING AND DRINKING

Sydney has many restaurants ranging from unpretentious cafés to international class restaurants. A dinner in a modest restaurant with Australian wine would cost about $30-$40 a head. Community Clubs such as the RSL (Returned Servicemen's League) allow free temporary membership to visitors. Restaurants are highly subsidised from slot-machine "pokies" gambling and can be surprisingly good. The RSL in Petersham has weekend seafood specials with platters including lobster, oysters, calamari, scallops and prawns for just $22 for two. Hotels often offer reasonably priced buffets. Food courts in shopping centres and malls have a wide variety of fast food at very reasonable prices. Liverpool Street, a short walk from Town Hall station, has a few Spanish restaurants including that inside the Sir John Young Hotel. Doyles in Circular Quay and Watson's Bay are the most famous of Sydney's fish restaurants. Those wishing to try unusual foods such as kangaroo and emu need to keep an eye open: they tend to be seasonal, but are usually well advertised.

Late night shopping in Centre Point is on Thursday, and shops are open on Sunday from 1000 until 1600.

TRANSPORT

There is plentiful public transport including trains, subway and buses. Unlimited daily travel tickets are available. Harbour ferries are more expensive and more pleasurable: 10-ticket discount cards are available. Taxis are reasonable and easily available day and night.

SECURITY

Sydney is a fairly safe city although sensible precautions need to be taken, particularly in areas such as Kings Cross.

AUSTRIA

VIENNA

Language **German**
Currency **schilling of 100 groschen. £1=19, Mar 1997**
Banks **0800–1230, 1330–1500 Mon to Fri, late night Thur to 1730**
Credit cards **accepted in larger shops**
Shops **0900–1200, 1500–1730; closed midday Sat except for first Sat in month and all Sats in Dec**
Refunds **unlikely in smaller shops**
Sales **Jan, mid-Jul to Aug; regulated by government**
Tipping **maximum 10 per cent; in restaurants include tip in payment rather than leaving on the table**

The cost of living is significantly higher than in the UK. Quality, styling and choice of clothing and footwear is excellent, but there is very little in the middle price range. There is a particularly good choice of specialist items such as snow or hiking boots, skiing and mountaineering equipment, and warm winter clothing.

The main shopping area is in the first district in the pedestrian precinct around the Kärntnerstrasse, Stephansplatz, Graben, Kohlmarkt and Freyung. This is expensive and famous for its luxury items such as up-market clothing and jewellery, including all the designer labels. The area between Stephansplatz and Schwedenplatz is good for books and antiques as well as clothing. There are also good antique shops around Bränerstrasse, Dorotheergasse, Spiegelgasse and Plankengasse. Mariahilfestrasse is more down-market, but widely popular.

The Naschmarkt off the Linke Wienzeile is the largest open-air market with a variety of exotic produce and specialist foods. There is a flea market at the Naschmarkt every Saturday morning from 0600 to 1200, with a vast array of junk and antiques. There is a Christmas market in the Inner City and an Easter market on the Freyung.

Shopping City Süd is vast. There is a free bus service to it on the hour from the IKEA bus stop opposite the Opera.

Among suggestions for gifts and souvenirs are local craft items such as scented candles, embroidered linens, woodcarvings and crystal. Spice posies make popular gifts. Try the Handarbeitsboutique at Mariahilfestrasse 141 or Österreichische Werkstätten at Kärntner Strasse 6.

Trachten and dirndl make good and practical traditional souvenirs and are available from Loden Plankl at Michaelerplatz 6, Kettner at Seilergasse 12 and Leben mit Tradition at Seilergasse 10.

Also not cheap, but again excellent quality, is jewellery. Michaela Frey has become an international name and is at Gumperdorferstrasse 81.

A number of bookshops sell English books and paperbacks including the British Bookshop in the City Centre. Books and magazines are expensive. British daily newspapers usually arrive the same day.

EATING AND DRINKING

The most expensive restaurants are relatively cheaper than their counterparts in London and good cheap restaurants are very competitive. Burggasse and Spittelberggasse have good small restaurants. Many restaurants are closed on Sunday and booking is advisable.

Among the better restaurants are Steirereck at Rasumofskygasse 2, Zum Kuckuck at Himmelpfortgasse 15, Zum Laterndl at Landesgerichtstrasse 12, Alte Backstube at Langegasse 34, Piaristenkellar at Piaristengasse 45 and Hietzinger Bräu at Auhofstrasse 1.

There are many *Heuriger*, or wine bars, in Vienna. Apart from drinking wine, customers help themselves to food from a buffet. This makes for an enjoyable and reasonable traditional night out.

Every visitor must spend some time in a typical coffee house. The Café Mozart at Albertinplatz 2 was made world-famous by the film *The Third Man*. Try also Central at Herrengasse/Strauchgasse, Dom at Stephansplatz 9, Landtmann at Dr Karl-Lueger-Ring, Frauenhuber at Himmelpfortgasse 6, Hawelka at Dorotheergasse 6 or Dommayer at Dommayergasse 1.

Among konditoreis, Demel at Kohlmarkt 14 is expensive as is Sacher at Philharmonikerstrasse 4, world famous for its Sachertorte. Ice-cream lovers must try Tichy at Reumannplatz.

High-quality Austrian wines are not cheap, but there are many reasonable ones for everyday drinking available at a good price. Local brandy and liqueurs such as Slivovitz, Marillengeist and Enzian are reasonable.

Transport
There is an extensive and efficient public transport system
based on the tramway network, bus routes, the Stadtbahn, the
U-Bahn and the Schnellbahn (a fast suburban railway) Tickets
can be bought in advance at tobacconists and at some stations.
Multiple, weekly and other concessionary tickets are available.
Taxis are relatively inexpensive and not too difficult to find
except in rush hours.

Azerbaijan

Baku

Currency **manat of 100 gopik. £1=6000 manat, Mar**
1996
Banks **take undamaged pre-1988 US dollar notes**
and change at hotels or street-corner kiosks
Shops **1000-1200, 1400 to late evening**
Bargaining **worth trying, particularly for carpets; 30**
per cent discount possible
Duty-free **at airport; limited**
Tipping **not necessary**
Export restrictions **export of manat prohibited;**
caviar and carpets may risk confiscation at airport

Things are changing quickly in Baku, as in most of the countries
of the former Soviet Union. The cost of living has been cheap
if one is prepared to accept what is available on the local
economy. As the range of imported goods increases, so does
the cost of living. The opening of Benetton and Levi shops are
indications for the future. A Turkish built and owned supermarket and several well-stocked smaller ones have recently
opened: so standards of butchery for example and of overall
freshness are changing.

Any shopping will give the visitor a feeling for the prevailing atmosphere. The area around Fountain Square is good for
shopping. There are carpet shops in and around the old city
in the area of the Maiden's Tower and one or two shops selling souvenirs and caviar. For souvenirs try Hurriye Bike at 12
U. Hajibeyov or the shop in the Maiden's Tower.

Caviar and carpets are the best buys. However, export of
these articles is often claimed to be illegal. Caviar is available
spasmodically and in season, although the gourmet shop at

the Hyatt nearly always has it – at a price. The best is sold in glass pots with prices ranging between US$10 – 30 per 100g. jar. That served in restaurants or available in the market is seldom of good quality and often poor. Remember that caviar must be kept cold or it will congeal.

Azerbaijan International is an English-language magazine published quarterly in California and available in hotels. As yet no other English-language publications are regularly available.

EATING AND DRINKING

National restaurants in Baku all basically provide the same food. A traditional middle-eastern hors-d'oeuvre consists of many different cold dishes. Main courses include grilled fish and a variety of kebabs. Desserts mostly consist of fruit with occasional sticky cakes and pastries. Locally available drink includes vodka, local cognac and champagne and a growing variety of imported beers. Recommended restaurants for national food include the Mugham Club and the Izmir. Ethnic cooking has arrived and includes Indian, Chinese, Cajun, Tex-Mex and a steak house.

TRANSPORT

Taxis are cheap and can be hailed easily at most times. They are available at the airport; the normal fare into town is US$10. Try to pay in manats: you will pay a lot more if you use dollars. The average fare in town for foreigners is about 10,000 manats and double that in the evening. Public transport consists of a very cheap underground metro, crowded buses, creaking trolley buses and trams, few of which go where you want.

SECURITY

Security generally is good, although handbag snatching is not unknown and street crime is on the increase in all cities.

BAHAMAS

NASSAU

Language **English**
Currency **Bahamian dollar (B$) of 100 cents.**
£1=1.57, Mar 1997. Tied to US dollar, which
circulates freely
Shops **0900–1700 Mon to Sat**
Tipping **15 per cent service charge in hotels and**
restaurants, further tipping optional; 15 per cent
to barmen, taxi drivers, hairdressers, porters and
casino croupiers

Nassau is expensive by UK standards. Most food and consumer goods are imported, mainly from or via the USA and local prices can be up to 50 per cent higher than they are there. For this reason many Bahamians and expatriates shop regularly in Florida (one hour's flight away), but there is a wide range of food products available locally.

The traditional centre around Bay Street is flourishing. It still has its street traders and the colourful straw market, but the area is now geared to the cruise ship and other tourist traffic. Its old warehouses are now converted into shopping centres. Elsewhere on New Providence there are numerous American-style shopping malls with well-stocked stores.

For women a few shops offer a fair selection of fashion lines including many designer labels and fashionable shoes from Italy and the USA. Marks and Spencer, British Home Stores and Mothercare offer a limited range. Some imported men's clothing is available including sports shirts, trousers, shorts and swimwear.

For those not interested in buying any internationally labelled consumer goods there is little in the way of gifts and souvenirs other than the usual tourist merchandise such as conch shells or T-shirts.

EATING AND DRINKING

As an up-market tourist centre, Nassau naturally offers a wide range of restaurants and bars to suit most tastes and varying from high quality and expensive to relatively modest and good value, including local Bahamian cuisine. Good quality local seafood is readily available and local beer is also good. Spirits and cigarettes are cheaper and wine about the same as in the UK.

TRANSPORT

Public transport (medium-size buses) is run by private enterprise and vehicles stop on demand. Taxis are numerous and readily obtainable.

BAHRAIN

Language **Arabic, Farsi**
Currency **Bahraini dinar (BD) of 100 fils. £1=0.6, Mar 1997**
Banks **0750–1200 Sat to Wed, 0750–1100 Thur**
Credit cards **yes**
Cashpoints **yes**
Shops **0900–1250, 1600–1900 Sat to Thur, except in Ramadan; bazaars 1800–1200,1530–1800 Sat to Thur**
Refunds **rare**
Sales **Jan/Feb and Oct; good for expensive clothing**
Bargaining **essential in souks, ask for discounts in shops**
Duty-free **at airport, both departure and arrival; cheaper than discounted prices in town**
Tipping **hotels and restaurants 15 per cent in addition to 10 per cent tax; taxi drivers 500 fils**

Bahrain is expensive and not recommended for serious shopping, unlike other areas of the Gulf. Gold, watches, sports equipment and perfumes are all cheaper than in the UK, but more expensive than in the United Arab Emirates, Saudi Arabia and other states in the area, although there are stories of one individual negotiating 40 per cent off the UK price of a Tag Heuer watch in the Sheraton Complex.

Those wanting a bit of colour and to see how the locals shop can try the souk. Other more modern main shopping areas are the Yateem Shopping Centre and the Sheraton Shopping Complex. There are several new complexes opening. All of these are within a three-mile radius and within easy walking distance of the main hotels, with the exception of the Meridien. There are plenty of well-known names around such as J. C. Penney, British Home Stores, Next and Mothercare as well as Woolworth and Truworth from South Africa, but all are expensive. The international designer shops such as Max Mara, Betty Barclay and Gucci tend to congregate at the

Sheraton Complex. The Arab boycott of Israel has eased, but Marks and Spencer and a few other goods are still not available. The Levis on sale are copies with the same name. Most music cassettes and video cassettes will also be pirated.

Gold is still sold in the souk at the price of the day for one gramme. It is 18 or 22 carat, usually very shiny and not always to European taste. There is a good gold shop in the Yateem Centre called Al Zain. The Sheraton Complex has good gold shops. You can still pay less for jewellery than in the UK, although stones are not cheap. The once famous pearling industry is defunct, although there are plans to revive it.

Silk carpets are not necessarily cheaper because they are prized by the locals, and old carpets are not easy to find. You might be lucky, however, and find perhaps an Iranian Qashqai at a good price. Expect to pay about BD150 upwards for a large carpet.

There is a good Crafts Centre with pottery, rugs, stained glass and a blacksmith, and some Shia villages sell pottery and raffia work. There are also things to buy in the Museum Shop – the museum is tourist attraction number one, so is well worth a look. There is a government tourist shop at the beginning of the souk at Bab al Bahrain. Other possible souvenirs include little trinkets like Indian jewellery, David Roberts lithographs of the Middle East or perhaps even Russian boxes! Other local specialities include Arabic perfumes from the souk and dates.

Anyone who can bring high quality materials from home can take advantage of cheap tailoring and copying to a tolerable standard. Good imported materials are now also available. Shakar in the souk is reliable. A man's jacket with two pairs of trousers will cost about £90 and dressmakers will charge from £10-£25 to make a dress, for example.

Most British national newspapers are available on the day following publication but are double the UK price. Magazines are also expensive. The *Gulf Daily News* is a quick read and costs only 50 pence. There is a fair range of both hardback and paperback books, but again prices are high.

EATING AND DRINKING

There are plenty of restaurants in hotels and outside serving a range of cuisines, and some serve alcoholic drinks. Fish, shrimps, lobster tails, Lebanese food, Arabic food of any type, sharwarma sandwiches (chicken) – similar to doner kebabs in the UK, but much better – are all worth trying. The best French restaurant in town has been the Versailles at the

Regency Intercontinental, where a three-course dinner with wine will cost about £30 per head. The Meridien has an excellent lunch buffet in the coffee shop for £12 – four courses including Lebanese mezze, with a superb view. Otherwise try Chicos for Italian food, the Sheraton for a weekend brunch with jazz on Friday or The Hash House for Thai food.

Alcohol is available in special shops, but it is expensive, and best bought at the duty-free shop at the airport. Otherwise the places to buy alcohol are BMMI (between the Diplomat and the Holiday Inn hotels, African and Eastern branches of which are scattered all over town), or National Hotels. Soft drinks are produced locally. Most brands of cigarettes, pipe tobacco and cigars are readily available and cheap.

TRANSPORT
Public transport is not recommended. Taxis are plentiful and not expensive. Fares are metered.

BANGLADESH

DHAKA

Language **Bengali**
Currency **taka (Tk) of 100 poisha. £1=68, Mar 1997**
Banks **payment at hotels must be made in convertible currency**
Credit cards **not widely used, but accepted in major hotels**
Cashpoints **Standard Chartered have recently installed the first**
Bargaining **at all markets. Cut asked price by at least half and negotiate upwards**
Tipping **in restaurants, at the discretion of the customer**
Export restrictions **permission from the Department of Archaeology required for the export of all antiques, statues and other works of art. Get and keep receipts**

The main exports include clothing, leather goods and tea. Import controls have been relaxed increasing the range of goods available, although prices reflect tariffs, which are sometimes high.

The main shopping areas are DIT1 (Dhaka Improvement Trust 1) on South Avenue and DIT2 on Gulshan Avenue. The former has a very large area for selling produce and is good for local atmosphere. The latter has several craft and gift shops.

Particularly recommended for local crafts such as brass and leatherwork are Ideas at 25 Gulshan Avenue South and Kumudini at 97 Gulshan Avenue. The Salesian Sisters at 105/1/a Monipuri Para are known locally for their fine embroidered linens. St Josephs School of Industrial Trades at 32 Shah Sahib Lane is good for wood and metalwork. There are a number of brass shops on South Avenue near Mymensingh Road, while silver and goldsmiths are to be found at the Silver Market in Islampur in Old Dhakha.

There is a wide selection of materials including silks and safari-suit material for those thinking of having clothing made, which can be done quickly and at a reasonable price. The tailors cannot use patterns and either copy clothes from originals or use drawings or magazine pictures. Tailors and dressmakers include Barber Ali at DIT1.

There are few bookshops, but the Sheraton Hotel bookshop stocks books on Bangladesh.

EATING AND DRINKING

The choice of restaurants has improved and there are now several Chinese, Korean, Indian and Thai restaurants. The Sheraton Hotel Vintage Room is very good, but expensive. The regular Wednesday lobster evening at the Sonargaon Hotel Karwan Sarai restaurant is highly recommended. With the exception of the hotel restaurants, prices are reasonable and you may take your own alcoholic drinks. Corkage is not normally charged. Sea fish is considered safer to eat than river fish.

Recommended restaurants include Moghal at 18 Kemal Ataturk Avenue, Banani for Indian food, Pana Garden at 2 Abbas Garden, Mohakali or Royal Orchid at 60 Gulshan Avenue near DIT1 for Chinese cuisine and Seafood Centre at 76, Gulshan Avenue for Thai and seafood.

Local soft drinks contain a lot of extra sugar to conform to local taste, but otherwise they are made under licence from the major companies with water that is safe to drink. Pepsi, Coke, Miranda, Fanta Orange and Sprite are all available. Polar ice-cream is good quality.

TRANSPORT

Buses are not generally used by expatriates. 'Baby taxis' (scooter-engined) and bicycle rickshaws are inexpensive. Taxis are available at the main hotels and airport. Prices should be agreed before starting the journey.

SECURITY

Markets are full of beggars and children asking for baksheesh.

BARBADOS

BRIDGETOWN

Language **English**
Currency **Barbados dollar (BD$) of 100 cents.**
  £1=5.15, Mar 1997. Freely convertible
Traveller's' cheques **universally accepted, also**
  US dollars
Credit cards **universally accepted**
Cashpoints **available at the Royal Bank of Canada or**
  Barclays, accepting most credit cards
Shops **0900-1700 Mon to Fri, 0900-1300 Sat**
Refunds **yes, with receipt**
Duty-free **large selection of duty-free goods**
  available, take ticket and passport when shopping;
  better in town than at airport
Tipping **most hotels and restaurants add 10 per cent**
  service charge, but an additional tip usually
  expected; small tips appreciated by taxi drivers

Barbados is one of the most popular holiday destinations in the Caribbean. There is a variety of local shops offering a wide range of local and imported goods. From large department stores and shopping malls to supermarkets and mini-marts, there is something for every taste and budget. The main shops of interest to visitors are located in and immediately around Broad Street in Bridgetown. Shops include Cave Shepherd and Harrisons while shopping malls include Da Costas Mall, The Norman Centre and Mall 34.

Duty-free goods available include jewellery such as Colombian emeralds, crystal, china, perfumery, cosmetics and clothing.

For atmosphere, the best places are the Cheapside Market, Fairchild Street Market or Pelican Village. Swan Street has numerous small shops and street vendors offering a range of local crafts and fresh fruit.

Local souvenirs include T-shirts, mahogany carvings, shell crafts and artwork. A particularly good example of the latter is the range offered by local artist Jill Walker whose island-wide Best of Barbados shops are particularly recommended. Other ideas are leather sandals, stamps, melamine trays and coasters, swimwear, pottery or rum. Daphne's Sea Shell Studio is in Congo Road, St Philips.

Shopping areas on the south coast include Quayside Centre, Hastings Plaza and Chattel House Shopping Village at St Lawrence Gap, Christchurch. On the west coast are Sunset Crest in Holetown and Speightstown.

There are two local English-language daily newspapers. British newspapers (expensive) are available the day following publication. A good range of English-language books is available at the Cloister Bookshop in Hincks Street or the Cave Shepherd department store in Broad Street, both in Bridgetown. Books are expensive. Most adult books available are not literary.

EATING AND DRINKING

There is a wide range of restaurants of varying quality and price serving Bajan cooking, plentiful seafood and international food including Chinese, French, Mexican and Italian. For the brave there is the local hot pepper sauce. Other local delicacies include flying fish, pudding and saise, fish cakes, soursop ice-cream and coconut cream pie.

The locally made rum and Banks beer are worth sampling. Tours can be arranged of the Mount Gay and Cockspur rum distilleries as well as Banks' Brewery.

TRANSPORT

There is an island-wide bus service operating a regular schedule which is sometimes used by tourists. Taxis are plentiful.

SECURITY

Security is generally good and there is little or no hassle, but women unaccompanied by men are pestered.

BELARUS

MINSK

Language **Russian**
Currency **Belarus rouble (BRBL). The currency is
    not transferable**
Traveller's cheques **take cash US dollars or German
    marks**

The centre of the city is around the Prospekt Francyska
Skaryny. The main market is in the north-eastern part: it has
lots of produce and local atmosphere.

Handicrafts and works of art are available from the shop
at the State Museum of Art in the city centre. Recommended
gifts and souvenirs include ceramics, woodcarvings and the
highly coloured boxes which are a local speciality.

EATING AND DRINKING
Mushroom hunting is a national pastime and this is reflected
in the local cooking. There are plenty of places to eat of varying
quality. The Westfalia in the Hotel IBB Minsk is recommended.

SECURITY
Street crime is not uncommon.

Belgium

Brussels

Language **Flemish, French, German**
Currency **Belgian franc of 100 centimes £1=56, Mar 1997**
Credit cards **major cards accepted by most large shops**
Cashpoints **yes, plentiful**
Shops **0930–1800 Mon to Sat; many tourist shops also open Sun; smaller shops often close at lunchtime for up to two hours**
Sales **Jan and Jul, offering genuine bargains**
Tipping **restaurants and bars include a percentage in the total bill as a tip; compulsory 20 per cent tip is included in taxi fares**

Brussels is a cosmopolitan city with a superb central shopping area. Its heart is the beautiful Grand'Place and just around the corner are the Galeries Royale St Hubert, Europe's oldest covered shopping galeries, lined with designer shops, bookstores and other expensive outlets. Also close to the Grand'Place are shopping centres such as the Galeries du Centre, Galerie Saint Honoré and Galerie Agora. English is widely spoken, particularly in the main tourist areas.

The Rue Neuve is popular and vibrant. As well as fashion boutiques there are well-known department stores such as Mothercare and Marks and Spencer. The Virgin Mega Music Store is at the Place de la Monnaie. W.H.Smith is located near by at Boulevard Adolphe Max 71 – 75. City 2 at Place Rogier is an indoor shopping mall with an Innovation department store next door.

The Boulevard de Waterloo with the nearby Galerie de la Toison d'Or, Galerie Louise and Avenue Louise constitute the most exclusive area for jewellery, fashion, shoes and leatherware. All the well-known designer names are represented here: Delvaux on the Boulevard de Waterloo is recommended for its handbags. The neighbourhood around the Rue Antoine Dansaert is also very up-market.

The area for arts and antiques is in the Sablon near by. Every Saturday and Sunday there is an antiques market in the Grand Sablon Square. There are also antique shops in the surrounding streets. A few streets away in the Rue Blaes is the flea market, which is less expensive and caters for all tastes. Further down the hill is another flea market at the Place du Jeu de Balle which is open daily, but is best at weekends. The Antiques and Design centre in the Place de la Chapelle is also worth a visit.

Two recommended Sunday markets are the Place Bara by the Gare du Midi which specialises in foods and the caged bird market on the Grand'Place itself. There is also a market at Place du Châtelain each Wednesday afternoon for gourmet foods. The daily flower market on the Grand'Place is expensive but worth a look.

The Woluwé Shopping Centre is situated to the south-east of the city and everything you need for a comfortable day's shopping and sustenance is under one roof. A host of well-known international and Belgian names are represented there. The centre is easily reached by metro from the city.

Local specialities are many, but the most popular are lace, chocolate, cheese, wine and seafood. All can be purchased in and around the Grand'Place. The best-known chocolate outlets are Neuhaus and Godiva.

Patchwork and quilting are very popular in Belgium and there are many specialist shops including Handmade at Marché au Charbon 102, L'Idée Fils in Rue Marché aux Herbes and Schlieper at Chaussée de Charleroi 149.

Apart from W.H.Smith, other booksellers offer English-language books at significantly marked-up prices. The *Daily Telegraph* costs about £1 and many other newspapers and magazines are available.

EATING AND DRINKING
Brussels has something like 2,000 restaurants with a choice of every conceivable cuisine. There are many places where you can eat well and at reasonable cost. The Rue des Bouchers (just off the Grand'Place) offers a variety of gourmet food in a delightful relaxed atmosphere. Particularly appealing is the way in which fresh fish and vegetables are displayed outside the restaurants to attract customers.

Belgium is also famous for its beer. Once nearly every village had its own brewery and many still survive. There is a colossal number of different kinds of beer, but in Brussels Gueuze is the most common. Wheat beers, Trappist beers and fruit flavoured beers are all superb.

TRANSPORT
Public transport is relatively cheap and in the centre there is plenty of it. Most journeys are charged at a flat rate within the

Brussels administrative area. On tram, bus or metro a single ticket, *un directe*, can be bought. *Une carte* is valid for 5 or 10 journeys. Be sure to validate your ticket at the start of the journey. It is difficult to hail a taxi in the street. They prefer to operate from the taxi-ranks. Fares are metered.

BELIZE

BELMOPAN/BELIZE CITY

Language **English, Creole**
Currency **Belize dollar of 100 cents. Tied to the US**
 dollar: US$1=BZ$2
Banks **take cash US dollars**
Traveller's Cheques **dollar denominated**
Shops **0800–1200, Mon to Sat, reopening about**
 1300 except on Wed. Closing times vary

The largest town, main commercial centre and principal port is Belize City. Belmopan lies some fifty miles south-west of Belize City. It is minute and unlikely to attract the independent traveller. A wider choice of shopping is available in Belize City. Those who can will shop in Miami, where generally what costs £1 in UK cost $1. Products produced locally are reasonably priced, but anything imported suffers a heavy import tax. Hence the paradox of a poor country and high prices.

In Belmopan there are no boutiques; though some places stock some clothes, no store carries a wide range of styles or sizes. In Belize City, in the area around Albert Street, there are several boutiques stocking clothes from the USA with bright colours and synthetic materials prevailing.

There are tailors both in Belize City and in Belmopan who can make casual clothes quite cheaply. There are several small women's wear shops in Belize City which carry a limited and small stock, but which can make acceptable casual clothes. Swimwear can be bought in Belize City or Ambergris Caye, but it is expensive and there is not a great choice. Shoes and sandals can be bought in Belize City. Prices tend to be higher than in the UK and the quality is often not so good.

For gifts and souvenirs the choice is rather touristy, but the wooden items such as carvings and bowls are very nice. T-shirts are sold everywhere and for every occasion; quality is generally good.

There is an extremely limited choice of books, at high prices.

EATING AND DRINKING

In Belmopan the choice of restaurants is limited. The most popular is the Bullfrog Inn, which has a good if somewhat limited menu. Belize City has a selection of moderately priced restaurants which offer a reasonably wide selection. Some of these specialise in local dishes such as chicken, rice and beans. The standard of cleanliness in some can leave much to be desired. In Belize City there are several well-known chain hotels such as the Radisson, Biltmore and Ramada with reasonably good restaurants.

Locally made rum and beer are of quite acceptable quality and are reasonably priced.

Excellent papayas, mangoes, oranges, grapefruit, limes, bananas and avocado pears are available in season and are inexpensive.

TRANSPORT

There is no public transport within Belmopan. There is a bus service between Belmopan and Belize City in the morning and afternoon and also services to the other main towns. Fares are cheap. There are taxis in Belize City and Belmopan.

SECURITY

Sensible personal security measures should be taken: do not for example walk alone at night.

BENIN

COTONOU

Language French
Currency CFA franc. £1=945, Mar 1997

Benin is best known for its colourful appliqué tapestries. These are to be seen everywhere, including the main market. Particularly recommended is the Artisan Centre opposite the Hotel de l'Union on Boulevard St Michel.

Visitors should be vigilant at all times. Mugging is not uncommon in Cotonou.

BHUTAN

THIMPHU

Language **Dzongkha, Nepali, English**
Currency **ngultrum. £1=58, Mar 1997 (at par with Indian rupee)**

Tourism is restricted as a matter of policy and therefore expensive. Most visitors will come to Bhutan through India, where shopping opportunities are far greater.

BOLIVIA

LA PAZ

Language **Spanish**
Currency **boliviano ($B) of 100 centavos.**
  £1=8.4, Mar 1997. Aligned with US dollar,
  US$1=$B5.25
Banks **0900–1200, 1400–1650 Mon to Fri**
Traveller's cheques **dollar denominated accepted**
Shops **0900–1200, 1400–1800 Mon to Fri; some open 0900–1200 Sat**
Tipping **token only where 10 per cent service charge added; at airport; not in taxis**

There are a few department stores and several markets where hygiene is generally poor. You can find almost everything including spirits, wine and cigarettes on the thriving black market.

Some shops offer excellent alpaca wool products such as sweaters and other items at prices much cheaper than in the UK. It is also possible to buy leather goods of good quality and to have jackets or shoes made to one's own design at reasonable cost. Local dressmakers and tailors will make a good job of your imported materials if you are staying any length of time.

Bolivian artists and sculptors produce high quality work and there are frequent exhibitions.

Books in English are expensive and the choice is very limited The *Bolivian Times* is a weekly newspaper and currently

costs less than US$1. British newspapers are not on sale.
American periodicals such as *Time* and *Newsweek* can be purchased.

EATING AND DRINKING

There are several reasonable restaurants in La Paz. French,
German, Italian, Swiss, Argentinian, Chinese, Mexican and
Japanese cuisine are available as well as local cooking.
Moderately good meals can be had in the Hotels Presidente
and Plaza. There are some good German-style patisseries.

Good beef is cheap and plentiful. Maté infusions are commonly drunk after meals as well as tea and coffee. These are
not addictive and may be made from mint, camomile or coca
leaves. There are good fruit bargains in the street markets, but
hygiene is generally poor.

Well-known spirits and imported liqueurs are available at
reasonable price. Bolivian and Chilean wines are also available; the quality is variable. Mineral waters and mixers (Coca
Cola, soda water, lemonade, ginger ale and tonic water) can
also be bought reasonably as can Pilsener-type beer of good
quality.

TRANSPORT

Public transport is abundant and consists of single-decker
buses (*micros*), minibuses, communal taxis (*trufis*) and ordinary taxis. Service is poor and buses are in any case slow and
uncomfortable. Taxis are more expensive and scarce at night,
but radio-taxi services are available at a cost of less than £1
around the centre.

BOSNIA-HERZEGOVINA

SARAJEVO

Language **Serbo-Croat**
Currency **dinar of 100 paras, but Deutschmark is in
common use. Traveller's cheques and credit cards
not accepted**
Tipping **10 per cent in restaurants and bars**

The Foreign Office advises against any travel which is not essential.

Little is available locally and conditions are subject to sudden change. The limited supplies available are sometimes pre-war stock and often poor quality. The cost of food fluctuates greatly depending on supply, but is generally higher than in the UK.

There are a number of restaurants still operating in Sarajevo, although they tend to close early. They offer mainly local cuisine (ie. meat-orientated) and other than pizzas and the occasional frozen fish, vegetarians are not catered for. The standard is quite good, but there is not much variety. The local speciality, *cevapci* – a kind of kebab – is excellent and cheap. Typical prices for a meal out would be main course DM10 – 20, bottle of wine DM30, beer DM5. There are numerous bars around town usually serving coffee, local beer and soft drinks.

BOTSWANA

GABERONE

Language **English**
Currency **pula (BTP) of 100 thebe (pronounced taybay). £1=5.7, Mar 1997**
Banks **0800–1700 Mon to Fri, 0800–1200 Sat**
Credit cards **all major cards accepted**
Shops **0800–1230, 1400–1700 Mon to Fri, 0800–1300 Sat**

Gaberone is a small town with quite a number of shops, but with limited and, at times, expensive stock. The major centres in South Africa, by contrast, have a wealth of shops and are much better for serious shopping.

The Mall is the original pedestrian shopping precinct and is located in the centre of town. It has most things you will need in the way of shopping. The African Mall lies to the south behind the President Hotel, off Independence Avenue on Merafe Road. There are now also several suburban shopping areas with a good range of basic services such as the Nyerere Drive Shopping Centre, the Kagiso Centre/Broadhurst Mall on Segoditshane Road and the spanking new Kgale Hill

Shopping Centre.

There is an increasing number of women's boutiques offering cotton dresses, although the selection is not wide. Everyday clothing is available at reasonable cost at the South African owned Woolworths chain (there is a shop at Market Square in the Broadhurst Industrial area), which is equivalent to Marks and Spencer in the UK. Safari suits are available locally at very modest prices. Diamonds are also a good buy if you know what you are doing.

For crafts and souvenirs go to Botswanacraft in the Mall near the President Hotel or else the Bushman Craft Shop or Ditso Curio Shop, both in Broadhurst. Basketry can be quite elaborate and artistic. Other things worth looking out for include bow and arrow sets, ostrich-egg jewellery, leather goods, woodcarvings, particularly of animals, and pottery and ceramics. On Saturday morning small vendors set up shop in the square of the Mall.

South African newspapers are available on the day of publication. The Botswana Book Centre is recommended for books.

EATING AND DRINKING

Hotels such as the President and Gaberone Sun on Nyerere Drive offer a range of restaurants. There are recommended places also in the African Mall such as the Taj or the Park. In the Broadhurst North Mall are Mama's Kitchen and Kgotha.

TRANSPORT

There are taxis subject to telephone booking. Combies on the street are crowded, but get you from A to B. The city is quite dispersed, so some walking is necessary. The road surfaces, either tarmac or dirt (there are a few pavements around), are very hard on shoes.

SECURITY

Sensible personal security precautions are necessary.

BRAZIL

Language **Portuguese**
Currency **real of 100 centavos. £1=1.67, Mar 1997**
Banks **0800–1700 Mon to Fri, 0800–1200 Sat**
Traveller's cheques **take dollar cheques and cash**
Credit cards **major cards, e.g. American Express**
Cashpoints **yes, 24 hours with some UK cards, 10 per cent charged**
Shops **usually 1000–2000, some early closing Sat, some Sun opening**
Refunds **possible for genuine complaints, with receipts**
Sales **regular, with genuine reductions and some outstanding bargains.**
Bargaining **in markets; fixed prices in shops, but ask for discounts for cash**
Duty free **Rio airport, much cheaper than in town; $500 per person allowed on arrival and departure**
Tipping **10 per cent in hotels and restaurants in addition to service charge; 10 per cent to taxi drivers in Brasilia; US$1 to airport porters; small tips to barbers, hairdressers, shop porters and unofficial car-park attendants**
Export restrictions **certificate from Patrimonio Historico required for antiquities**

Most of the consumer goods available are of local manufacture. It is hard to generalise about price levels, but they tend on the whole to be much higher than in the UK or USA. Quality is variable, but is improving. Imported goods are very expensive. Brazil is one of the world's major shoe-producing countries, but all the most interesting products are for export.

There are numerous boutiques which sell attractive up-to-the-minute fashions, but few designer or specialist outlets. Prices are sometimes high and occasionally the workmanship is not perfect. In addition, Brazilian fashion tends to be somewhat transitory and value for money is poor unless purchases are made during the sales. Cotton casual wear is readily available, often at prices lower than in the UK, and the quality and finish have improved in recent years.

Good quality, modern costume jewellery is very popular. Other recommended souvenirs include *cachaça* (sugar-based alcohol), T-shirts, coffee, semi-precious stones, arts and crafts and John Somers pewter.

Local varieties of gin, vodka, whisky, brandy, Martini and Campari are readily available and comparatively cheap. Opinions as to quality vary. Try a *caipirinha*, a local drink made from cachaça, crushed limes and added sugar. Then buy a bottle of cachaça to enjoy the same drink at home.

Good locally manufactured spirits are available in the supermarkets at reasonable prices. Locally made Teacher's whisky (all the ingredients except the water are imported from Scotland) is very good, but expensive. Brazilian coffee is good, as is local beer. All types of soft drinks (with the exception of ginger ale) are available.

The only daily newspaper published in English is the *Daily Post*, American owned and published in Rio. British and American books are on sale at something over twice the UK price. Magazines and periodicals are also available at inflated prices.

Some knowledge of Brazilian Portuguese is desirable to make shopping easier.

BRASILIA

Brasilia lacks any bustling centre. There are no picturesque little streets from which one can gauge the atmosphere of the city and few bars or cafés with much character. It is so spread out and the pedestrian is so poorly catered for that to walk anywhere is virtually out of the question. Congestion is increasingly frequent in shopping and business areas where insufficient car parking has been provided. There is little available which is not available elsewhere with better choice and often cheaper prices. Those travelling to this still young city will find a selection of souvenirs from everywhere else in Brazil representing the history and interests of this enormously diverse country.

The main central shopping malls are Conjunto Nacional and Liberty Mall near the central bus station and Venancio 2000 adjacent to the hotel district. Another mall, Park Shopping, is 10 kms out of town. The central markets are the Hippy Market, weekends only, under the television tower, which features arts and crafts from all over Brazil, Feira do Paraguai near the sports stadium with imports from Paraguay of all descriptions, the Guara Market, a little further out than Park Shopping, the only real market with produce and other wares.

There are few local specialities available which are not better value elsewhere in Brazil. An exception is precious and semi-precious stones. Recommended for good quality stones, loose or in a setting of your own choice, are J. R. Stones at Centro São Francisco at Eqs 102/103, Bloco A, Lojia 72 or Schunks Gems at SHIS QI 15, Chacara 62. The Hippy Fair has a vast selection of items from all over Brazil – sarongs, T-shirts, lacework, hammocks, etc. The soapstone copies of various distinctive modern statues in the city are nice souvenirs and are available for about £2 each from the pavement stalls at the edge of the Hippy Fair.

A very limited selection of English-language newspapers and magazines, usually American, is available at the airport and the bus station. Some English-language books, all more expensive than in the UK, are available at Casa do Livro at Sds Ed Venancio VI, Loja 3/17 or at Livraria Solidar at Conjunto Nacional, Loja 16.

EATING AND DRINKING

Virtually any type of cuisine is available in numerous restaurants, often very expensive and of varying quality. Recommended for *churrasco*, Brazilian barbecue, is Spettus at SHS Q 5, Bloco E. Recommended for *feijoada*, traditional beans and meat, is the Naoum Plaza Hotel at SHS Q 5, Bloco H 1.

TRANSPORT

The only shopping areas within walking distance of the hotel area are the Hippy Fair at weekends and Venancio 2000. Public transport is not satisfactory and cannot be relied upon. Buses are very crowded for most of the day. Taxis are plentiful and fairly well controlled by the authorities. Radio-taxi services are available and generally reliable, albeit expensive.

SECURITY

Personal security is good, but take extra care in markets and busy areas. There is rarely any serious hassle with beggars.

RIO DE JANEIRO

There are several shopping malls and centres including the Barras Shopping Centre on the Avenida das Americas, Latin America's largest with two and a half miles of boutiques, stores and leisure areas. Ipanema and Copacabana have shopping areas within easy reach of most hotels which have boutiques and small arcades. H.Stern on Visconde de Piraja in Ipanema is the world's largest jewellery store and a must for the serious shopper. Amsterdam Sauer next door is smaller, but still worth looking at. There are colourful outdoor markets (*feiras*) with a wide variety of foods, herbs and flowers ranging from the familiar to the exotic. They take place daily in all areas of Rio. There are also two large indoor markets.

Bright, attractive cotton beach wraps (*cangas*) are widely available near the beaches and from street vendors and are good value. Bathing gear is plentiful, varied and multicoloured but it can be more expensive than in the UK and women's swimsuits tend to be very briefly cut.

The Hippy Fair on Praça General Osório in Ipanema is the best place for regional art and craft souvenirs. Stalls sell a smaller range of similar goods every evening along the Avenida Atlantica in Copacabana. Legep on Avenida das Americas in Barra is an out-of-town specialist in everything connected with semi-precious stones. Cerâmica at Petropolis is one hour out of Rio, but is well worth the visit and the drive is a lovely one.

Two-day old copies of the *Daily Telegraph* and other British newspapers are available at stands on all major streets for £4 or so. There are few English books in the shops.

EATING AND DRINKING

Eating out ranges from the cheap and cheerful through the ever-available steak and chips or pasta and excellent seafood restaurants to the expensive international restaurants. Nearly all open late and stay open until the early hours of the morning.

For a taste of Brazil try Majórica at Rua Senador Vergueiro 11 in Flamengo or Porcão at Rua Barão da Torre 218 in Ipanema. For *feijoada* try the Caesar Park Hotel in Ipanema on Wednesday and Saturday or Casa da Feijoada at Rua Prudente de Morais 10.

Give *caipirinha* a try at Acadamia da Cachaça at Rua Conde Bernadotte 26.

TRANSPORT
Buses are fast, frightening and overcrowded, but cheap. They are also a hunting ground for pickpockets and bag snatchers. Taxis are numerous and inexpensive and the metro system is excellent, although limited.

SECURITY
The malls are very safe, but be very aware especially in Copacabana and at the Hippy Fair. Be careful about wearing anything which is or which looks expensive.

SAO PAULO

A city growing fast – perhaps too fast for its own good. Orientation is difficult, which makes the underground system useful.

The Praça da República is the hub of old Sao Paulo. There is a good market every Sunday. Stay in this area for atmosphere, shopping and value. The shopping malls tend to be expensive.

The *Daily Post* is available and some English-language books and periodicals, albeit at high prices.

Public transport, apart from the underground, is unusable.

BRUNEI

BANDAR SERI BEGAWAN

Language Malay, English
Currency Brunei dollar (B$) of 100 sen. £1=2.27, Mar 1997. Fully interchangeable with Singapore currency
Banks 0900–1500 Mon to Fri, 0900–1100 Sat
Credit cards major cards accepted in hotels and stores
Cashpoints Hong Kong Standard Bank and Standard Bank, at shopping centres
Shops 0930–1700 Mon to Sat; supermarkets and dept stores 1000–2000/2200 Sat and Sun
Bargaining in markets and small shops; not supermarkets and new shopping centres

There is no income tax in Brunei, and several important commodities such as petrol are subsidised from the rich oil and natural gas resources to keep the prices low. The country imports nearly all of its requirements, including 90 per cent of its food. The serving of alcohol is forbidden and there are no bars (even in hotels) which will do so, although there is a black market offering goods at inflated prices. Non-Muslim visitors are allowed to bring a small quantity of alcohol into Brunei for their own consumption. The allowance varies and it is advisable to check with the airline. A customs form must be filled in at the airport for all alcohol carried into the country. To the east of the town centre, in Jalan Residency, is the Brunei Art Centre which includes a shop selling a few local craft items. There is some silverware and samples of the traditional hand-woven sarongs are also for sale here, together with a small selection of basketware. Another place to buy souvenirs is David Bujang's Borneo Primitive Art Shop at 32, Simpang 462 Kampong Sungai Hanching, Jalan Muara. Here you will find a wide range of arts and crafts from the whole island of Borneo.

The Yayasan Centre is a new shopping precinct in the business district offering a wide range of goods. Other shopping centres are Centrepoint/Jalan Gadong, the Seri Complex and Jalan Muara. The Yaohan and Hua Ho department stores offer a wide range including clothing and sports, electrical and household goods. A limited selection of fashion clothes is available within the department stores and can be found in some of the small boutiques in the Yayasan Centre. There are talented dressmakers to be found in most shopping areas.

There is an open-air market selling fresh produce near the water village (Kampong Ayer) and a larger market behind Centrepoint. Both are worth a visit to experience the local atmosphere.

The local English-language newspaper is the daily *Borneo Bulletin*. The *Singapore Straits Times* is flown in daily. Books are available from Booker International in Centrepoint. Books and English magazines are expensive.

EATING AND DRINKING

There are many good restaurants serving Chinese, Thai and Malay food. On Jalan Sultan there are a few cafés serving traditional dishes, rice and curries, at very reasonable prices. The hotels have good restaurants and in the Yayasan Centre both the Italian restaurant and Deli France are excellent. There are many Chinese restaurants including Lucky in the Seri Complex, which has excellent food and is reasonably priced.

Tenaga is a good Indian restaurant near Centrepoint.

TRANSPORT
There is very limited public transport. More buses are being introduced. All transport runs to a loose timetable. There are two types of taxi: the main taxi service does not cruise the street for passengers. Taxis must be picked up at the airport, at the rank at the bus station in central Bandar or called to a hotel or an address. This takes time and a price should be negotiated when ordering and confirmed before setting off. There is also a limited number of CTS taxis restricted to the capital area. They operate on a fixed charge (B$3) to any location within the town area (negotiate if the journey takes the taxi outside the zone). Water taxis are popular, particularly for sightseeing around the traditional Malay Water Village and the river system leading out of this village. It is necessary to bargain fares for these trips.

BULGARIA

SOFIA

Language **Bulgarian**
Currency **lev of 100 stotinki. £1=2550, Mar 1997**
Banks **0800–1200 Mon to Fri, 0800–1100 Sat**
Traveller's cheques **no–take cash dollars**
Credit cards **major cards accepted in some shops,
    hotels and restaurants**
Shops **0800/0900–1300, 1600–1900 Mon to Sat**
Refunds **unlikely**
Bargaining **in markets; fixed prices in shops**
Duty-free **limited range at airport; prices similar to
    city centre**
Tipping **waiters, porters, taxi drivers, hairdressers:
    10 per cent**
Export restrictions **Bulgarian currency may not be
    exported; icons and other works of art require
    export certificate**

Shopping in Sofia is an experience – but not a very exciting one. It can also be time-consuming and frustrating. Goods are not always available and when stocks do come into shops they sell out quickly. But queueing for food and other everyday goods is not the problem it once was. Comfortable footwear is a must as the pavements are uneven and sometimes dangerous.

The situation in the Former Yugoslav Republics determines to an extent the convenience of life in Bulgaria, since most direct links with Western Europe lie through Serbian and Croatian claimed territories. By Western standards there are as yet few attractive shops and many everyday items are still unavailable or in spasmodic supply. The rate of inflation remains high (but is reducing) and prices are changing rapidly. Shops, consumer services of all kinds and leisure facilities are simple but improving. Western, mainly German, produce available in supermarkets and other shops is sometimes near or past its sell-by date.

The main shopping area consists of Vitosha Boulevard, Graf Ignatiev and other near-by streets. There is also an open-air market around the Alexander Nevski Cathedral. This is a good area for looking for antiques. Best buys include wine and nuts, but also lace, woodcarvings, paintings, old weapons and watches, kilims, pottery and old musical instruments.

British newspapers and books are available from major hotels such as the Sheraton and Intercontinental, but they are expensive.

EATING AND DRINKING

Eating out has improved over recent years and almost every day more cafés, restaurants and pizzerias are being opened. Bulgarian wine is good and inexpensive, a definite must for any interested visitor. Local beer is strong, both in flavour and in alcohol content, and inexpensive.

TRANSPORT

In Sofia there is a good and very cheap, but often overcrowded, tram and bus service. Discounted travel cards are available. Taxis can be hired from ranks in the centre of the city or ordered by telephone, but they are sometimes scarce. Pirate taxis are common, but there is often a demand for fares to be paid in hard currency, particularly at the airport. Visitors staying in central hotels will be able to walk to most of the shopping areas.

SECURITY

The usual personal security precautions should be taken, especially in the area near the central railway station.

Burkina Faso

Ougadougou

Language **French**
Currency **CFA West African. £1=945, Mar 1997**

Recommended gifts and souvenirs include masks and other woodcarvings, embroidery, leatherware, pottery and woven goods.

The city centre is on and around the Avenue Nelson Mandela. Just to the south of this and across from the Hotel Central is the market. The Artisan Centre is on Avenue Dimdolobsam.

Visitors should take sensible personal security precautions, especially after dark.

Burma (Myanmar)

Rangoon

Language **Burmese**
Currency **kyat (K) of 100 pyas. £1=10.25, Mar 1997**
Banks **tourists must exchange $300 into foreign exchange currency vouchers at the airport. Otherwise money is exchanged in official kiosks in town or at Bogyoke Aung San Market**
Credit cards **accepted only in the Gem Emporium and in larger hotels such as the Strand**
Shops **hours variable, generally opening 1000, closed Sun**
Bargaining **yes, but not everywhere**
Tipping **not common practice in Burma, but becoming less unusual in Rangoon and other major tourist centres. The tourist hotels add a 10 per cent service charge plus 10 per cent government tax to their bills**
Import/export restrictions **a strict watch is kept on cameras and other similar items–what comes in must go out**

Burma is famous for its rubies, sapphires and jade, and arrangements can be made to purchase jewellery with foreign exchange, which confers the right to export it. The Gems Museum and Gems Mart are in Kaba-Aye Pagoda Road. If you buy gems on your credit card you will be reimbursed for false stones. Stones bought in Burma are not, however, necessarily cheaper than in the UK, and frequently jewels that have been exported illegally from Burma to Bangkok are cheaper there. Lacquerware is attractive, expensive if paid for in kyat, but reasonable if purchased through a "dollar shop". Silk (usually in the form of *longyis* unmade up, (i.e. two and a half metres) is beautiful. The colours and ikat designs are expensive, but worth it. A softer silk can be found at better rates at Inle Lake. The *longyi*, the traditional dress worn by women, is popular as a souvenir. Men wear checked cotton and women a variety of colours and designs with an *angyi* blouse. There are also paintings and watercolours by local artists at very reasonable prices. There are a number of galleries in the Golden Valley area and hotels also hold exhibitions. A marvellous range of basketware from tables to table-mats is available at places like Bogyoke Aung San Market. Orchids are available all year round and are stunning.

Scott Market, now renamed Bogyoke Aung San Market, is probably the best-known market, and is conveniently situated in the centre of town. It is open on Sunday, but closed on Monday and although it opens at 0800 none of the stores is properly open until 1000. The market sells everything from gift cards by local artists to materials and souvenirs such as lacquerware both antique and modern, silverware to basketware, puppets, mother of pearl, Shan bags and pyongi umbrellas – even Timberland jeans at knock-down prices. You can change foreign currency into kyat with shopkeepers who are government-authorised money-changers. Geared towards tourists, prices tend to be high and some shopkeepers now refuse to bargain at all. There are several other markets including the Chinese and the Indian markets which are worth exploring. They tend to close by midday. Augustine sells Burmese antiquities behind the Burma Seafood Restaurant in Insein Road. There are antiques and rattan stalls on the airport road and shops near the Shwedagon Pagoda selling old basketware and Buddhist memorabilia of various quality, but prices are high. One can get by with English in the main towns of Burma.

Mandalay, the last royal capital of Burma, is still the cultural capital of the country and famed for its pagodas and temples. It is also a centre of traditional crafts such as ivory and wood-carving, silk weaving, gold leaf, silverware and stone masonry.

The other traditional craft centres on the tourist route are Inle and Bagan.

No British papers or periodicals are on sale locally. Photocopied English-language books are available from roadside stalls in town at absurd prices. Hotels sell a limited range of easy-readers.

EATING AND DRINKING

Facilities for eating out are improving. Standards of hygiene in local restaurants may leave something to be desired, but many new hotels are opening to international standards. The Golden View Restaurant situated under the Shwedagon serves Chinese and Burmese cuisine and gives a memorable evening to visitors with its floor show and dancers (watch out for the magician in wellies). The Ashoka at 77 Pyidaungau Yeik Road is the best and most expensive Indian restaurant in town. The newly refurbished Strand Hotel is a must to look at, but the food is expensive and perhaps just a little disappointing on occasion. Most tropical and exotic fruits are available in season. The new hotels all have coffee shops and locally grown coffee is delicious.

TRANSPORT

Buses can be fairly old and are rarely if ever used by foreigners. There are many new taxis available which are relatively inexpensive. If you are unlucky enough to find a taxi without a working meter, negotiate the fare before starting.

CAMBODIA

PHMOM PENH

Language **Khmer**
Currency **riel. £1=3590, Mar 1997**
Banks **take dollar notes, acceptable particularly in
tourist areas. There is a black market**
Tipping **not mandatory but welcome. Best buys
include Buddhas, carvings, coins, gold and silver,
as well as sarongs**

A good place for gifts and souvenirs is the Central Market.
The O Russei Market is a couple of hundred metres away
down Achar Heamcheay. Away to the south near Keo Mong
Boulevard is Tuoi Tom Market. There is an Art School outlet
at 19th and 184th streets.

EATING AND DRINKING
Eating out is cheap. Fish can be good. Local beer is reasonable.

SECURITY
The capital is reasonably safe, but crime is increasing, particularly after dark.

CAMEROON

Language **English, French**
Currency **CFA franc. £1=945, Mar 1997. At
fixed parity of CFA100 to the French franc. Only
Banque des Etats de l'Afrique Central accepted:
Banque des Etats de l'Afrique Occidental are not
legal tender**
Traveller's cheques **French franc denominated;
French currency easily exchangeable**
Credit cards **Visa accepted in tourist hotels and
restaurants**
Shops **0830–1230,1430–1700 Mon to Fri; some close
afternoon, most close 1230 Sat**
Bargaining **in markets**
Tipping **5–10 per cent in restaurants and cafés**
Export restrictions **more than CFA500 forbidden;
control of export of antiquities and some artefacts**

Recommended buys include woodcarvings and masks in particular, jewellery and semi-precious stones, bronzes, basketware and leatherwork. Gold jewellery is attractively priced.

Local produce is reasonably priced with a wide variety including tropical fruits. There are plenty of bars of varying standard. Imported drinks are expensive, but local beer (including Guinness brewed by Guinness in Douala) is excellent and cheap.

Some French is useful for shopping.

Sensible security precautions are necessary. Violent crime is not uncommon, especially in the large cities.

YAOUNDE

Prices for imported goods are higher than in the UK, though locally produced goods are often cheaper. Most of the decent clothing available in the shops is French and expensive. There are several good but expensive supermarkets selling mainly French goods. Local shop prices for cigarettes and spirits, but not wine, are reasonable.

The shopping and commercial centre situated in the Avenue du President Ahmadou Ahidjo and surrounding streets is run-down and unattractive. The big Central Market is near by and at the end of Avenue Kennedy is a Centre d'Artisanat with an interesting selection of local crafts. This is a good street not only for shopping but also for lingering in the cafés.

Hachette has a branch in the Avenue John Kennedy. This and La Bouquinerie sell French books and a few paperbacks in English at a price. British newspapers can be obtained, but again, at a high cost. French newspapers and magazines are on sale as well as *Time*, *Newsweek* and *The Economist*. There are some locally published English-language periodicals.

EATING AND DRINKING

Some local styles of cooking are an acquired taste, but there are several good restaurants with prices varying from the reasonable to the very expensive.

TRANSPORT

Taxis, usually very old and in poor condition, are cheap and abundant, but the fare must be agreed before getting into the car, expecially for exclusive hire. There is no public transport service in Yaounde.

DOUALA

The economic capital and largest city in Cameroon, lacking perhaps beauty and class, but not vitality. It can be justly proud of good hotels, a wide variety of restaurants and shops as well as a busy night-life.

Due to the rising crime rate and ten years recession Akwa, the old heart of town for business and night-life along Boulevard de la Liberté, is less in favour for shopping and browsing. The administrative quarter, Bonanjo, around Place du Gouvernement or the residential area Bonapriso, south along Avenue de Gaulle have more to offer.

The Crafts Market has now been relocated on to Avenue de Gaulle. After long bargaining you can buy Cameroonian traditional art or African beads. Receipts are necessary to avoid difficulties at Customs and random export duties when leaving. Buying so-called antiques is a sure way of being cheated. They are all too often recently and expertly made in Foumban.

More specialised quality shops worth a visit include Couleurs Exotiques, Rue Tokoto in Bonapriso, or the long-standing Ali Baba in Rue Gallieni opposite the Wouri Cinéma in Akwa. On sale are good selections of traditional wood-carvings, beads and other pieces of colourful jewellery.

There is just one bookshop in Bonapriso, Rue Batibois, selling international newspapers and French books only.

British newspapers and some magazines can be obtained at the local bookshops or hotels. The major local newspaper, the *Cameroon Tribune*, publishes daily in French and weekly in English.

EATING AND DRINKING

There are a number of good restaurants, some offering quality African/Cameroonian dishes and others providing excellent Vietnamese, Chinese and Cambodian cuisine. Prices are high by UK standards. Wines are varied but expensive. Best areas for eating out are Bonanjo and Bonapriso. Le Touristic in Boulevard de la République is popular. For French-style patisserie and tea-rooms try Chococho off Njo-Njo street in Bonapriso and Délices in Akwa on Avenue de la Liberté.

TRANSPORT

City buses are not recommended for Europeans. Taxis are usually hired on a seat-by-seat basis, but can be taken for the journey. Bargain before setting out except for local journeys for which there are fixed prices.

SECURITY

Certain areas of the city such as Akwa are dangerous to walk around. Care must be taken if visiting the market where a high incidence of theft is reported.

CANADA

Language **English, French**
Currency **Canadian dollar (C$) of 100 cents. £1=2.1 Mar 1997**
Banks **1000–1500/1600 Mon to Thur, 1000–1800 Fri**
Traveller's cheques **in Canadian dollars**
Credit cards **all major cards accepted**
Cashpoints **yes**
Shops **hours variable; few open before 1000**
Refunds **yes, within 14 days, with receipt; rebates from provincial sales tax and Services Tax (GST) at major stores**
Sales **genuine reductions on quality goods**
Tipping **10–15 per cent in restaurants, bars, taxis; C$1 per bag to airport porters, minimum C$2**

Consumer prices are generally a little higher than in the UK, but frequent sales mean that good quality casual clothing can be bought cheaply. European styles and fashions are considerably more expensive than in the UK and the selection of designs much more limited. Some well-known British brands - Aquascutum, Burberry, Morlands and Jaeger, for example - are available, but the clothing itself is not always made in the UK and is more limited in range and much more expensive.

Outdoor sports, winter and children's clothing can be bought comparatively inexpensively, with regular promotional events during which prices are often cut dramatically. Winter clothes in particular are best bought locally, since European versions can be inadequate for local temperatures. On the whole fur coats are much cheaper in Canada than in the UK. Women who have difficulty in finding shoes in narrow fittings will find a better selection in Canada. Winter boots are a good buy.

North America is *the* place for sports and leisure wear. Every shopping mall has a big selection and large reductions in price occur during each season.

Some ideas for gifts and souvenirs are – maple syrup, available in every grocery store; Felix and Norton Biscuits Gourmet; excellent quality Canadian cosmetics from MAC (Make-up Art Cosmetics), available in larger stores such as Ogilvy and The Bay; outdoor clothing for winter such as down anoraks, available in all department stores, fur hats and coats, for the feet, snow boots by Sorel or fashionable Caterpillar boots at prices lower than in the UK and sports clothing and equipment, including Bauer skates.

Hardback books are the same price as in the UK, but considerable markdowns occur once the paperback version is issued, and shops offer year-round bargains. Paperbacks tend to be cheaper than in the UK.

OTTAWA

Ottawa is a relatively small and comfortable capital divided by the canal into Upper Town around the Parliament and Lower Town around Sussex Drive. The central area, north and south of the east-west axis of Wellington and Rideau Streets, is manageable for the most part on foot.

In Upper Town, Sparks Street Mall is a popular area full of boutiques and tourist shops. The Bank Street promenade stretches from Gladstone Avenue to Wellington Street. The L'Esplanade Laurier shopping centre is situated at the corner of Bank Street and Laurier Avenue. Antiques Row is at 1185, 1181 and 1179 Bank Street South with over 50 dealers open seven days a week.

In Lower Town, the Byward Market between York and George Streets is a busy market offering farm-fresh produce and other speciality and gourmet foods with neighbouring boutiques and eating places. It is the oldest continuously operating outdoor market in Canada.

To the south of the centre, the area around Somerset Street from Bronson Avenue to Preston Street is known as Chinatown. Little Italy is centred around Preston Street from Carling Avenue to Somerset Street. Somerset Village on Somerset Street between Bank Street and O'Connor Street houses some restored Victorian buildings with an array of trendy boutiques and eating places.

There are many shopping malls throughout the city. They are ideal for winter shopping, they are warm and everything is under one roof. The main malls are Bayshore (west), Rideau Centre (city) and St Laurent and Orleans (east). Within the malls are department stores such as The Bay, Eatons and Sears.

EATING AND DRINKING

Eating out can still be cheaper than in the UK, but the better restaurants can be very expensive, particularly for alcohol. The range of restaurants in Ottawa is wide, but the overall standard is not particularly high. Apart from Chinatown and Little Italy, there are some reasonable restaurants in the Byward Market area such as the Old Fish Market Restaurant at 54 York Street. Hull, on the Quebec side of the river, has a number of very good French restaurants, some are expensive, but all offer good value.

TRANSPORT

There is an extensive and efficient bus service which is subsidised and its use encouraged by the city government. Taxis are always obtainable, but usually have to be phoned for. They are not allowed to cruise, but can be picked up at a few hotels.

EDMONTON

Edmonton has little claim to fame other than being the capital of Alberta, gateway to the Rockies, the most northerly city in North America and home not only to Molson beer, but also to the world-famous and world's largest West Edmonton Mall. Some tour operators even admit that the Mall is the best, perhaps the only, reason for visiting Edmonton.

The city centre is largely the area around Jasper Avenue and Sir Winston Churchill Square: it can be covered on foot in normal conditions. Shopping facilities are designed for maximum comfort and convenience, particularly for winter shopping. In the heart of the city the Edmonton and Eaton Centres incorporate a wide range of stores in enclosed complexes connected via overpasses and subways with other major stores and facilities in the area.

In the suburbs there are a number of large enclosed shopping centres including the West Edmonton Mall with over 800 shopping outlets as well as leisure displays and other entertainments. It can be reached by bus from Jasper Avenue.

Some British retail stores such as Marks and Spencer and W.H.Smith have branches in Edmonton. British newspapers and periodicals may be purchased, but they are expensive. A recommended bookshop is Greenwood's on 82nd between 103rd and 104th.

Eating and Drinking

Eating out is a popular if expensive pastime. French, German, Italian, Swiss, Mexican, Chinese, Japanese, Korean and Ukrainian establishments are available and the standard of cuisine is generally agreeable. The best general area for the visitor to cover is Old Strathcona which lies on 82nd Avenue between 102nd and 105th Streets. On 82nd Avenue itself are for example the Strathcona Gasthaus and Veggies. In the city centre on Jasper Avenue The Silk Hat at 10251 is well worth a try.

Transport

Edmonton has a better than average (by North American standards) public transportation system. Bus services are generally good and there is a flat fare. Tickets can be obtained on the bus (correct fare only) or bought in advance in booklets of ten. A light rail transit service is being extended. Taxis usually respond quickly to telephone calls and provide a reliable service in all but the worst weather, but you cannot rely on picking up a cruising taxi.

MONTREAL

Most shops, department stores and malls are concentrated along Sainte Catherine Street, Montreal's main street which is comparable to Oxford Street in London. There you will find department stores such as The Bay, Eaton's and Ogilvy as well as Marks and Spencer, HMV and the Body Shop. Another department store is Holt Renfrew in Sherbrook Street. This and Ogilvy are best for designer labels such as Versace.

The main shopping malls are Place Ville Marie on René Lévesque Boulevard, Promenade de la Cathédrale and Cours Mont Royal on de Maisonneuve Boulevard and Eaton Centre and Place Montreal Trust on Sainte Catherine Street. These malls are all interconnected and are collectively described as the "Underground City". The whole complex is mostly situated under office buildings and incorporates metro stations. Here you will find all kinds of shops and boutiques selling everything you can think of, ranging from Aquascutum through Benetton down to Dollarama.

Specialist shops worth the detour include Alexandor in Peel Street for fur hats and coats. Sportsexperts in Sainte Catherine Street offers a good range of skates.

A wide range of British newspapers and magazines is available at bookstores and kiosks, including branches of W.H.Smith. They are expensive.

EATING AND DRINKING
Some restaurants allow customers to bring their own wine.

TRANSPORT
The streets are safe, unlike those of some North American cities, and public transport is excellent. There is a standard fare for a single trip anywhere in the city by metro or bus. Taxis are plentiful and can be hailed in central areas. They are more expensive than elsewhere in North America, but cheaper than in central London.

TORONTO

The shopping facilities – heated in winter and cooled in summer – are abundant and efficient.

The city centre is contained within an area approximately one mile square centred around the north-south axis of Yonge Street. The area features large underground shopping plazas and multi-storey malls such as the Eaton Centre at Dundas and Yonge. To the south, the Harbourfront area has been redeveloped to offer various attractions including an antiques market and a crafts centre, as well as a host of fashionable shops. Chinatown lies just to the west along Dundas Street as far as Spadina Avenue.

A little further afield are two fashionable and expensive shopping areas, Yorkville and The Beaches. Yorkville is to the north of the centre, just north and west of the junction of Bloor Street and Yonge Street. The Beaches is east of the centre, on Queen Street.

British newspapers, magazines and books are available in Toronto in many bookstores. Lichtman's stores thoroughout Toronto have a good selection of British newspapers available the day after issue in the UK.

EATING AND DRINKING

Toronto has excellent restaurants of a wide enough variety and quality to suit all tastes and pockets. At the bottom end are the food malls and fast-food outlets. The Old Fish Market in Market Street is good for fish.

TRANSPORT

Toronto has an overlapping and interlocking urban transit system of subways, buses, streetcars and trolley buses. It is possible to reach almost anywhere in the centre of town by public transport. A single system with free transfers (including between subway and buses) operates thoroughout the city. The system is busy at rush hours, but not to the same extent as London's. Taxis are abundant and can be summoned by phone.

VANCOUVER

Vancouver is a beautiful city with its centre in a mile or so square on the peninsula around Robson Street. Eaton's is on Robson Street itself while The Bay is just one block north on Georgia Street. At the eastern end, at the neck of the peninsula, lie Gastown and Chinatown. Gastown, in the area around Water Street, is a fashionable area popular with tourists and somewhat reminiscent of London's Covent Garden. Chinatown is in the area around East Pender Street and offers the predictable range of shops and eating places. The whole Gastown/Chinatown area is packed with boutiques and galleries as well as plenty of more down-market places.

Granville Island is just to the south of the centre across Granville Bridge. Like Gastown, this is a relatively recently developed area. As well as its shops and galleries there is a market daily from Monday to Saturday which is good for arts and crafts and food.

The standard range of national and international newspapers is available from kiosks and hotels. Good bookshops include Duthie's in 919 Robson Street and Blackberry Books on Granville Island.

EATING AND DRINKING

There are numerous restaurants and fast-food outlets at all levels of quality and price. Eating out can still be cheaper than in the UK and it is easy to take a young family out for a meal. The better restaurants can be expensive, particularly for drinks. Apart from Chinatown, there are several reasonable restaurants on West Broadway, south of the centre.

TRANSPORT

Public transport is readily available and in all cases suitable. There is a standard bus fare for all in-town journeys, though a monthly pass is available. The service is good, expecially during rush hours. Taxis can be ordered by phone. They cannot be hailed on the street, but can be found at designated cab ranks.

CAYMAN ISLANDS

GEORGETOWN

Language **English**
Currency **Cayman Islands dollar (CI$). £1=1.39, Mar 1997. Linked to US dollar at US$1=CI$.83, Nov 1996**
Credit cards **major cards accepted**
Shops **0900–1700 Mon to Sat**
Duty-free **yes, but rarely a bargain**
Tipping **15 per cent where no service charge**
Export restrictions **anything made from turtleshell will be confiscated on departure**

Prices of imported goods are higher than in the US or UK because of the high import duties levied, although there is no income tax or excise duty. Local produce includes some tropical fruits and excellent seafood.

Cayman lives on its tax-haven status which has made it rich and Georgetown a modern commercial centre. Many tourists will see only West Bay, referred to locally as Seven Mile Beach, just north of Georgetown. There is shopping in Georgetown, in the hotels and on the beach, but there is nothing especially recommended among the usual range of T-shirts, conch shells and other tourist souvenirs. Turtleshell items should not be purchased since the species is by international convention officially endangered.

There are three good bookshops on the island, but the choice is nowhere near as varied as in the UK although the quality of books is quite good. There are two local newspapers. The *Caymanian Compass* is the national daily which does not cover international affairs in any great depth however. The weekly *New Caymanian* is similar. Two- or three-day-old copies of British newspapers can be bought in the supermarkets at inflated prices. Bookstores and filling stations stock a good supply of magazines, but these are usually American versions of the magazines seen in the UK.

EATING AND DRINKING

There is a wide variety of good restaurants and bars, mostly in the Seven Mile Beach area. Almost all restaurants offer a wide range of seafood, including conch, and other meals cooked in regional styles. Recommended are the Almond Tree just north of Georgetown and the Cracked Conch in Selkirk Plaza.

TRANSPORT

There is a public transport system, but it is not entirely reliable. Taxis are numerous and safe. Fares are fixed officially, but confirm the fare before starting.

CENTRAL AFRICAN REPUBLIC

BANGUI

Language **Sangho, French**
Currency **CFA franc. £1=945, Mar 1997**

The Foreign Office advises against travel unless absolutely necessary. There is increasing lawlessness, especially in Bangui itself.

The town has traditionally provided a welcome haven for trans-African travellers. In its compact centre are to be found all sorts of French food imports, at a price, as well as real patisseries with coffee.

Diamonds are the country's biggest export, but the standard traveller will probably be content with malachite.

CHAD

NDJAMENA

Language **French**
Currency **CFA franc. £1=945, Mar 1997**

The small city centre is not without its comforts. There is a reasonably good market for tourist trinkets and a fair amount to eat and drink. Travellers are advised to be vigilant at all times.

CHILE

SANTIAGO

Language **Spanish**
Currency **Chilean peso (CHP). £1=661.79, Mar 1997**
Banks **0900–1400 Mon to Fri**
Credit cards **major cards accepted in most supermarkets, shops, petrol stations and hotels**
Shops **0800–1200, 1600–2000 Mon to Fri, 0900–1300 Sat**
Tipping **10 per cent in restaurants if no service charge; tips expected by waiters and porters**

There are heavy taxes on imported goods, particularly luxury items. Chileans have a very sweet tooth, so some drinks and jams, etc. may have a high added sugar content. As well as meat, fish, vegetable and flower markets, most districts have local street markets on certain days selling country produce.

Some knowledge of Spanish is essential.

Main shopping is in the area immediately around the Plaza de Armas and includes pedestrianised streets such as Paseo Ahumada and Paseo Huérfanos. Immediately on the other side of the river is Calle Pío Novio, which is quite good for crafts, as is the Bellavista area.

Woollen clothing can be a good buy. Fur jackets, although not of the best quality, can be bought at a reasonable price locally. Local shoes are excellent value and can be quite stylish, but larger sizes can be hard to find. Leather handbags are good, as is lapis lazuli jewellery. Cassette tapes can be cheaper than UK prices, but may well be pirated.

Easter Island carvings are popular, as are items produced by Indian craftsmen such as ceramics, silver and weaving. For your gifts and souvenirs try Huimpalay in Huérfanos.

An increasing number of bookshops sell books in English, but at roughly twice UK prices. Try Feria Chilena del Libro in Huérfanos.

EATING AND DRINKING

There is an almost inexhaustible choice of good restaurants and bars serving a wide variety of dishes. There are excellent fish restaurants in the Central Market at the northern end of Ahamada on Avenida Balmaceda. Beef and dairy produce is also good. There are plenty of other places in the town centre and in Pío Novio or in Providencia.

For many spirits, apart from whisky, prices are not much more than in duty-free shops. Local wines are excellent and prices reasonable. Local champagne is of good quality and cheaper than French champagne in the UK. Local imitations of sherry and port are poor, but imported items are available at prices cheaper than in the UK. Locally made vermouths are also of good quality. The best-known local spirit is pisco, a clear grape spirit which is the base of a pisco sour (pisco, lemon juice, icing sugar and egg-white). There are several brands of bottled beer, both lager-type and a more heavily malted variety. The former is also available on draught.

Cigarettes are of a reasonable standard and much cheaper than imported makes. A limited selection of cigars is available, generally cheaper than in the UK.

TRANSPORT

Public transport in central Santiago is remarkably good. The modern metro (two lines) is efficient, rapid and cheap although limited in scope. Buses are plentiful, cheap, filthy and liable to break down. They stop anywhere and everywhere without warning and can be very crowded at rush hours. Taxis are reasonably cheap and plentiful. Even during rush hours they can usually be obtained without difficulty. Both the metro and the buses have flat-rate fares although bus fares can vary depending upon the journey and type of bus used.

SECURITY

Personal security is less of a problem than in other Latin American countries.

CHINA

Language Chinese
Currency renminbi (RMB) and yuan (Y). £1=Y13.21, Mar 1997
Banks take US and Hong Kong dollars; small amount of RMB can be imported. It is illegal to change money except at authorised banks and hotels. Visitors must complete and retain Bank of China and Customs declaration forms
Shops 0900–1900, including Sun
Bargaining yes, in local markets
Export restrictions nothing dated before 1795 may be exported

Chinese shoe and clothes sizes are different from Western ones and can cause problems. Shops seldom have fitting rooms. Many of the clothes in the markets carry designer labels, but they are often seconds, fakes or of poor quality. Silk and cotton fabrics are readily available and Chinese tailors are good and inexpensive. Ready-made clothes for large foreigners are few and far between. The quality is not of a very high standard, but it is improving all the time. Local woollen goods are available, but vary in quality. Cotton fabrics may shrink easily. Good quality articles, including cashmere, are available in the international hotels, but are quite expensive. Silk underwear tends to be on the small side and again is expensive.

Chinese toys for children are not always of good quality and tend to lose their paint. They are often unlikely to be up to UK safety standards.

One novelty is the resident doctors in many traditional pharmacies who feel your pulse and then prescribe herbal medicine.

There are many shops selling antiques and other artefacts

though nothing dated before 1795 can be exported. This rule has been applied rather flexibly to objects of small value by the Cultural Relics Bureau. Keep all receipts so that the Bureau can supply the necessary red seal. The Bureau has an office in the furniture department of the main Friendship Store in Peking. Best buys in antiques include porcelain (especially blue and white), calligraphy, paintings, jewellery and jade, old costumes and furniture.

Chinese cuisine is world famous, but the wines and champagne are generally not up to European standards. Mao Tai is a fiery liqueur and an acquired taste. Local bottled and tinned beers, mineral water and soft drinks are cheap and good.

Muggings are increasing in the main cities, as are instances of sexual harassment on trains and in places in Southern China.

BEIJING (PEKING)

Wangfujing is proud of its modern, up-market image while Qianmen Dajie and Dashalan, south of the Mao Mausoleum, retain some of the atmosphere of bygone Beijing. Dongsi, too, retains some traditional-style architecture as well as offering a wide variety of shops. Xidan is popular with the locals.

New is the Zhaofeng Market, across the road to the north-west of the Kempinski Hotel. There is also the Liangma Market across the street from the main entrance of the hotel. There are street markets for clothing, etc. at Sanlitun and Ritan Park. Beware of pickpockets and examine all goods carefully for quality.

Well-known international designer labels are found in the boutiques in the shopping mall of the Palace Hotel. There are modern supermarkets now in the basements of the largest hotels such as the Holiday Inn Lido and Lufthansa Centre.

The major government antique shops are in Liulichang. Rong Bao Zhai is perhaps the best known. Also popular is Huaxia at 12 Chongwenmennei Dajie and also at 293 Wangfujing, which has an extensive stock of merchandise to offer. Other places to shop for antiques are Hongqiao Market near the north entrance of the Temple of Heaven, Chaowai Market north of Ritan Park and the Jinsong Market on Sanhuan Nanlu, the South Third Ring Road. Yanxiang Philatelic Centre in the Yanxiang Hotel on Jiangtai Lu sells rare and current Chinese stamps.

Old carpets are widely available at places such as the Qianmen Carpet Factory at 44 Xingfu Dajie or at the Yihong

Carpet Factory at 35 Juzhang Hutong, both in Chongwen.

Silks are are also available widely and some recommended outlets are the Beijing Silk Store at 5 Qianmen Dajie, the International Silk Boutique at Building 4, Block 2, Anhuili in Chaoyang, New World Silk Store at 118 Wangfujing or Yuanlong Silk Store at 55 Tiantan Lu.

European-style good quality duck-down anoraks and long coats are popular buys at very good prices in the Friendship Store or in the markets. Fur-lined gloves are also useful.

Several well-known English-language newspapers and magazines are on sale in hotels, as are small supplies of paperbacks.

EATING AND DRINKING
There is an increasing number of good restaurants offering a wide variety of Chinese regional dishes and international cuisines. They are generally inexpensive, but not all provide menus in English. Some international fast-food outlets have branches in Beijing.

TRANSPORT
Taxis are fairly easy to obtain and prices are metered and reasonable, but they become scarce after 2100. Taxi stands can be found at all the major hotels and by larger commercial buildings. Buses and trolley buses provide transport for the general public. Fares are very cheap, but overcrowding and wooden seats make for an uncomfortable ride. An underground train system serves most of the city. Stations have their names in Roman letters Cycling is popular in China and bikes can be rented at many hotels.

SECURITY
Beijing is still relatively safe, although petty crime is increasing

SHANGHAI

Shanghai is the richest and most cosmopolitan city in China. Its main shopping streets are Nanjing Lu and Huai Hai Lu, tree-lined boulevards relatively Westernised in style and always busy. They offer a mixture of department stores, shops, places to eat and cinemas. A gentle stroll along Nanjing Lu from the Bund to the Shanghai Centre (about one hour) will take you past the Peace Hotel (Heping Binguan) with the First Department Store on the left, then to the Shanghai Art Gallery and the Antiques and Curios Shop. The Old Town is south of the Peace Hotel, off Zhongua Lu just as it deviates from Zhongshan Lu. Heavily restored to a splendour it may never formerly have enjoyed, it contains an old market and the Yu Yuan Bazaar, a good place for handicrafts and other gifts and souvenirs. For those interested in collecting antiques and porcelain there are many little shops selling such things. The adjacent Yu Yuan Garden is a restful and interesting oasis which offers a welcome contrast to the bustle of the Old Town. (A visit to the Tea House where the Queen took tiffin in 1986 provides a talking point.) But the best overviews and opportunities to do some comparative and window shopping are provided in Nanjing Road, particularly by the Antiques and Curios Shop at 694 and the First Department Store at 830. Several shops specialise in arts and crafts, such as pottery and basketware. Almost next door to each other in Nanjing Road are the excellent Duoyunxian at 422 for calligraphy and the Jewellery and Jade Store at 438.

The Shanghai Silk store at 592 Nanjing Dong Road is well worth a look. Down-filled anoraks can be purchased at reasonable prices.

The *Financial Times*, *The Economist*, *Time*, *Newsweek* and other international magazines are on sale in hotel bookshops. These shops also sell a limited number of English paperbacks.

EATING AND DRINKING

There is plenty of scope for eating out with places catering for both Chinese and Western food as well as two "English pubs". International hotels have reasonably priced coffee shops as well as more expensive French, Italian and Japanese restaurants. For those who like Chinese food the Mei Long Zhen (Nanjing Xi Lu), Lao Zheng Xing and Xin Ya (Nanjing Dong Lu), Lao Fan dian (Fuyou Lu) and Lao Ben Zai (Hankou Lu) are recommended.

TRANSPORT

Taxis are plentiful (except of course when it rains) and have meters. They can be booked by telephone and there are also taxi stands. Buses and trolley buses provide cheap transport for the general public. Fares are very cheap indeed but the buses are uncomfortable and crowded. There is a one-line underground system where the fares are very cheap.

SECURITY

Shanghai is still one of the few cities in the world where visitors can wander around in comparative safety, but beware of petty theft. The biggest problem is local touts wishing to change money.

HONG KONG

(SPECIAL ADMINISTRATIVE AREA)

Language **English, Chinese**
Currency **Hong Kong dollar (HK$) of 100 cents.
    £1=12.41, Mar 1997**
Banks **0930–1500 Mon to Fri, 0930–1200 Sat**
Credit cards **widely accepted**
Cashpoints **plentiful; most international cards
    accepted**
Shops **1000/1030–1800 or later, all week except at
    Lunar New Year; market opening times vary**
Refunds **only if goods are faulty or misrepresented;
    not at markets or factory outlets**
Bargaining **ask for lowest price**
Duty-free **at airport; alcohol and perfumery cheaper
    than in supermarkets**
Tipping **normal practice; most restaurants add 10
    per cent service charge. Round up fare for taxi
    drivers. HK$10 for hotel porters, etc.**
Import/export restrictions **none on currencies;
    certificates needed for antiques costing over
    US$1,000 and/or more than 100 years old. Import
    licence from country of residence required for
    ivory products**

Hong Kong is a free port apart from certain duties on items such as alcohol and perfumery. It is the proverbial shopper's paradise and many visitors actually try to "shop till you drop", although it is unlikely that the short-term visitor will get to know more than one particular area really well. Although some of the traditional skills are disappearing and factory outlets are much less numerous, there are still plenty of things worth considering to bring back such as silk shirts, electronic equipment, spectacles, tailored suits and jewellery. It is best to deal only with reputable establishments and to shop around: it is a good idea to know discount prices back home. Clothes should be unwrapped and examined carefully. Sizing can be confusing and larger sizes difficult to find, so always try on if you can: some shops, especially in the markets, have a no-try-on policy.

On Hong Kong Island there are huge shopping complexes at Pacific Place in Queensway, City Plaza in Taikoo Shing, Causeway Bay, Princes Building and Landmark in Central District. Scattered amongst these malls are markets, local shops, supermarkets, street traders and hawkers. On Kowloon side the huge Harbour City complex near the exit of the Star Ferry has over 500 shops and a mass of restaurants. Nathan Road houses hundreds of shops and Granville Road off to the left has many clothing outlets selling every imaginable kind of sports wear, jeans, cotton sweaters and quite a few designer "over runs" selling for a fraction of their retail price. The New Worlds Centre in Salisbury Road, Kowloon has more than 250 stores, bars and restaurants. The Regent Hotel Shopping Arcade in Salisbury Road has several boutiques, and many other hotels have shopping arcades.

Many of the malls are very glitzy and all the top designer names are represented. Chanel, Versace, Valentino, Gucci and Armani, to name but a few, jostle for space with Marks and Spencer, Body Shop and Burberry. The large Japanese department store Seibu in Pacific Place has many shops within shops, as well as an extensive and extremely well-stocked food hall in its basement. It might be compared with Harrods for the diversity of its goods. Lane Crawford has several branches in Central District, Pacific Place and Ocean Terminal (Kowloon) and carries a vast range of designer clothing, leather goods, shoes, houseware and glassware.

The Wing-On Department Stores and China Products and Emporiums (located all over the island and the New Territories) are crammed full of Chinese merchandise including food and medicine, silk clothing, bedding, ceramics, jewellery, cloisonné ware, artefacts, Buddhas and bric-à-brac. China Arts and Crafts at the Ocean Terminal is particularly good. Prices are fixed.

Every area has its market. Stanley Market on the south side of the island is renowned for silks, cottons, linen and lace bedding as well as evening wear, sportswear, denims, swimsuits, silk ties and scarves. There are also prints, paintings, Chinese curios, leather handbags and luggage in profusion. Wan Chai Market covers the spectrum from fruit and vegetables to clothing, curios, books, watches, towels, furniture and materials – a real Aladdin's cave which gives the visitor a taste of local market life at its most colourful. Western Market near Sheung Wan, easily reached by tram, is good for materials. The Night Market in Temple Street on Kowloon side is fun and open from 2000 to 2300. Li Yuen Street East and Li Yuen Street West are in Central (the Lanes) and stalls offer everything from dress fabrics and leather accessories to sweaters and children's wear. It is open generally from 1000 to 1900. Jardine's Crescent in the centre of Causeway Bay is good for women's and children's wear, cosmetics and accessories. Further down the street are flower stalls, herbalists and the fruit and vegetable section. The best time to visit is between 1100 and 1830. Cat Street, off Hollywood Road in Central, is now a flea market offering expensive trinkets and bric-à-brac, but the surrounding area is still Hong Kong's antique quarter where you can find traditional Chinese furniture, wall scrolls, paintings and porcelain as well as goods from other Asian countries. In Kowloon, Tung Choi Street is often called Ladies' Market since it specialises in inexpensive local women's fashions, jewellery and accessories. It is open daily from 1200 to 2230. The Jade Market, located under the flyover near Kansu Street in Yau Ma Tei, deals in all varieties of jade with wide-ranging prices. It is a good place to pick up a few pieces of jade as souvenirs, but for serious buying always take an expert with you. The Jade Market is open daily between 1000 and 1530.

Local specialities are legion, but silk clothing of every imaginable kind is considered a good buy. Bespoke tailoring remains reasonable, although it is no longer as attractively priced as it once was. A locally made-to-measure suit is slightly more expensive than a ready-made lightweight suit from Austin Reed. The Suit Factory in the second floor off Nathan Road has off-the-peg suits for men and women, with alterations free. The Pedder Building in Pedder Street has several floors of good clothes shops such as Shopper's World Safari.

Getting spectacles made up is recommended, as it is usually quicker and cheaper than in the UK. Most opticians will test your eyes free on the spot. The Optical Shop has branches all over Hong Kong, including Princes Building, Landmark and Pacific Place. Melbourne Optics is in Melbourne Plaza.

Be sure you receive a completed guarantee for cameras,

and keep a receipt. Ensure also that any electrical equipment you buy is compatible with your own electrical supply.

There are six English-language newspapers avilable in Hong Kong, including the *International Herald Tribune* and *USA Today International*. The *South China Morning Post* is the leading locally published English language newspaper.

EATING AND DRINKING

It would be a shame to come to Hong Kong and not sample some of the local cuisine. A well-balanced Chinese meal comprises the five basic tastes – acid, hot, bitter, sweet and salty. Textures should vary between dry and sauced and crisp and tender. A good rule of thumb is to order one dish per diner, plus one soup.

TRANSPORT

Public transport is cheap and plentiful. Trams are the cheapest mode of transport. You enter from the back and pay when you get off at the front. The cost is posted and you will need the correct change. There are also three large public bus companies and a modern underground railway, fleets of minibuses and innumerable taxis. Fares on public transport are lower than almost anywhere else in the world, but buses and trams are very crowded in the rush hour and travel can be an ordeal in summer. Taxis are cheap by UK standards.

SECURITY

The tourist shopper can expect a high level of personal security, but beware of pickpockets and thieves in crowded streets and markets and on public transport.

NOTE

This was written before the return of Hong Kong to China from British rule, in July 1997.

COLOMBIA

BOGOTA

Language **Spanish**
Currency **Colombian peso (COP)**
  £1=1700, Mar 1997
Banks **0900–1500 Mon to Fri**
Credit cards **accepted**
Shops **0900–1230, 1430–1830 Mon to Sat**
Tipping **10 per cent in restaurants, 1–2,000 pesos at airport**

Colombia is the world's largest supplier of emeralds and second biggest producer of coffee. It also produces large quantities of gold, copper and other minerals. Exports of cut flowers and bananas are also an important part of the economy.

The streets (calles) run from east to west, carreras from north to south. Calle 1 is the city centre and numbers increase as you go north. Carrera 7 and the Autopista Norte are the main north-south roads.

Shopping in Bogotá is not much different from shopping in any large, bustling, modern city, and exploring can be fun. Colombians are very clothes-conscious. Hand-made leather and suede jackets, skirts, handbags, shoes and boots are attractive and reasonably priced and can be custom-made. Locally manufactured woollen wraps are cheap and of good quality. There are many shops offering a full range of good quality and stylish clothes at prices comparable to those in the UK, although larger sizes might be difficult to find. Medellin's textile industry makes good fabrics and there are up-market local fashion designers.

There are several shopping centres such as the Centro Comercial Andino at Carrera 11 No 82, the Unicentro at Carrera 15/calle 127 and the Hacienda Santa Barbara at Carrera 7a/calle 116. At Usaquen Park in the north of Bogotá there is a flea market called Los Toldos de San Pelayo each Sunday from 1000 to 1700 offering a wide range of handicrafts, food and other wares.

Recommended specialist outlets include Artesania El Zipa for handicrafts in Unicentro, and Galeria Cano y Accesorios Cano for jewellery in Hacienda Santa Barbara and Unicentro.

There is one local English-language newspaper, the *Colombian Post*, published weekly.

EATING AND DRINKING

Restaurants are plentiful and various cuisines are available, considerably cheaper than in London, but without perhaps the same ambience (it helps to be able to speak Spanish). A reasonable three-course meal without drinks should cost little more than £14, although drinks may well double that. Wine is expensive and choice is limited.

For local cuisine try Casa Vieja at Cra 11 No 89 – 43. El Teatrino at Cra 14 between 93 – 93a has wonderful scallops. Casa Brava at Km 4,5 via la Calera has international cuisine and spectacular views of Bogotá.

There is a wide range of tropical fruit, although quality is sometimes poor. Local varieties of herbal tea are available, although ground coffee is cheap and plentiful. Locally-manufactured cigarettes and cigars are cheap, but of poor quality. Imported cigarettes are widely available, but more expensive.

TRANSPORT

Good walking shoes are recommended for traipsing around the city because the pavements and roads are uneven and pot-holed.

There is a service of municipal and private buses. They are often crowded, dirty, badly maintained and recklessly driven. They are also havens for thieves and pickpockets. Their use is not recommended. Taxis are fairly easily obtained except in rush hours, heavy rainstorms or late at night, but can suffer from similar problems to the buses. It is always safer, where possible, to telephone for a radio taxi.

SECURITY

The old centre of town is relatively safe during the day but dangerous at night. Common-sense precautions against muggers and pickpockets should be taken at all times throughout the city. Shopping centres are generally safe. Credit card fraud is commonplace.

CONGO

BRAZZAVILLE

Language **French**
Currency **CFA franc. £1=944.65, Mar 1997**

Brazzaville is reasonably well provided with shops, and most
essentials in the way of foodstuffs are available. The food is
imported from France by air and is therefore very expensive.
Shortages occur from time to time. The range of shopping is
much wider in Kinshasa, on the other side of the Congo River.

Reading matter in English is very difficult to find.

EATING AND DRINKING
There are good resturants in Brazzaville with a variety of
cuisines and prices.

TRANSPORT
There is no suitable public transport, but taxis are plentiful,
cheap and reliable.

SECURITY
Public order should never be taken for granted in Brazzaville.
With the exercise of common sense and continual vigilance there
is no undue hazard to personal security, although particular care
needs to be taken at night.

COSTA RICA

SAN JOSE

Language **Spanish**
Currency **colon. £1=360, Mar 1997**
Credit cards **widely accepted**
Tipping **not necessary where 25 per cent tax and
service charge added**

In the city centre as well as in the suburbs there are shopping
centres, numerous supermarkets and local markets. Imported
goods are expensive, partly because import tariffs run from 5
to 20 per cent. Virtually everything is available, although
items sometimes go out of stock and larger sizes in clothing
can be hard to find. Most Costa Ricans who can afford it do
their serious shopping in Miami.

Wooden items such as salad bowls, jewellery boxes and
various other ornaments as well as the models of the oxcarts
traditionally used for transportation are usually adequately
made and good value. Ceramics and jewellery available

include reproductions of pre-Columbian artefacts. Other items include ponchos as well as embroidery and basketware. There are also good quality leather shoes, bags and belts at reasonable prices.

Travellers going on to the famous craft centre of Sarchí may prefer to leave their souvenir shopping until then, but there are several places recommended for gifts and souvenirs in San José. Try La Galeria at Avenue 1 corner of Calle 9; Michelle on Avenida Central opposite Cine Capri; Novedades Típicas, north of Auto Mercado in town; El Caballo Blanco by the park in Moravia; La Botija at Avenida Central 2, Calle 1; Galería PreColombina, just south of Hotel Balmoral; Joyería Rodrígues in Gran Hotel Costa Rica or India House at Avenida 2 Calles 5 – 7. It is now illegal to sell pre-Columbian objects.

A very limited supply of English books is available locally, usually the best-seller variety, but they are expensive.

EATING AND DRINKING

There is a reasonable choice of restaurants. Such culinary tradition as there is tends to rely on steak and seafood. For local produce try Cocina de Leña in the El Pueblo shopping centre or Restaurant Poás at Avenida 7, Calle 3 and 5. A nice coffee house with good food is El Cuartel de la Boca del Maite at Avenida 1, Calle 21 and 23. Many restaurants offer good value set meals at lunchtime.

Beer is good and cheap as are the cigarettes. Local rum is excellent, as is the liqueur Café Rica. Costa Ricans do not pay much less for their coffee, despite being huge producers. The best is exported anyway. One or two places have some good stuff and, although not cheap, it can make a nice gift since Costa Rica is synonymous with coffee. Avoid the fancy gift wrappings though, and go for somewhere simple like the supermarket.

TRANSPORT

There are bus services in town which are cheap and frequent, but sometimes crowded. Taxis are available and reasonably priced. Pirates are risky at night, particularly for women.

SECURITY

There is some street crime, even in daylight in busy city streets. Certain areas of San José are best avoided altogether. Do not attract undue personal attention and be wary of money changers.

COTE D'IVOIRE SEE IVORY COAST

CROATIA

ZAGREB

Language **Serbo-Croat**
Currency **Kuna. £1=9.70, Mar 1997**

Despite the recent war, Zagreb still manages to function reasonably enough.

Trg Jelacica marks the centre of town and the Nama department store is on the adjacent Ilica. The main market is at Dolac, but there are other good ones at Trg Britanski and near the Cibona Tower on Trg Tresnjevacki.

The country has traditionally been known for its plum and other brandies as well as for handwork including lace and embroidery. Also worth looking at are jewellery, carpets, tapestries, carvings and ceramics.

Food is of a fair standard and cheap.

Public transport is good.

CUBA

HAVANA

Language **Spanish**
Currency **Cuban peso of 100 centavos. £1= 1.55, Dec 1995. US dollars are widely used**
Banks **0830–1200, 1300–1500 Mon to Fri, 0830–1030 Sat**
Traveller's cheques **dollar denominated, not American Express.**
Credit cards **Visa, Access, Mastercard; not American Express**
Shops **1000–1700 Mon to Sat; some Sun morning opening**
Bargaining **at markets and stalls; fixed prices in shops**
Duty-free **hard currency shops**
Tipping **not essential, but leave spare change for taxi drivers**

For the foreigner, everything from hotel and restaurant bills to shopping and taxis is paid for in US dollars. There is no need or even opportunity to use the local currrency. Cubans use a mixture of US dollars and coins and their own convertible dollars and coins. They are interchangeable within Cuba, but the latter are useless elsewhere.

Cuba is in a state of economic crisis and its shops reflect this. It is expensive and difficult, for example, to find good clothes in Havana and the selection is limited. Cheap but poor quality casual clothing can be found in the hard currency shops. Tourist souvenirs and gift items are also limited. In some shops it is impossible to examine goods without assistance from a sales person. Keep your receipts and be prepared to have your goods inspected on leaving a shop. You may also be asked to hand in shopping bags when entering a shop.

The shops likely to be of most interest to visitors are located mainly in the larger hotels such as the Melia Cohiba in central Havana and the Commodore in Miramar. Both of these have a branch of Benetton, but there are no US or UK retailers around. There are a few open markets which might appeal to the visitor, the best being the artisan market two blocks west of the Melia Cohiba Hotel on the Malecon. Sunday is usually the best day to visit. Here you can buy locally made dolls, hats made from palm leaves, decorated wooden boxes, varnished shells and jewellery. These are also found on stalls in the main tourist areas such as around the cathedral in Old Havana. The second-hand book market is on the Plaza de Armas outside the Palace of the Capitanos Generales in Old Havana.

Cuban cigars are world famous, but can be very expensive, even in Havana. Rum at about US$ 5.75 a bottle for three-year-old white rum is good value. There are many cocktails to be made with rum, well worth sampling during your visit. The Daiquiri according to local legend was invented at the Floridita Bar on Calle Obispo in Old Havana. Cuban coffee is good and inexpensive. Other possible souvenirs or gifts are T-shirts showing the Cuban flag or Che Guevara or the *guyabera* shirt. This is a traditional Latin American tunic-style open-necked shirt, short-sleeved for daytime and long-sleeved for the evening, which can be bought in the international hotel shops and other shops for foreigners.

There are no English-language newspapers or books available, apart from a weekly English edition of *Granma*, one of the main local newspapers.

EATING AND DRINKING
Cuba's past links with Spain, China and West Africa have influenced the cuisine, but really Havana is not a gourmet's city. *Congris*, a rice and black bean dish, is popular with Cubans. A well-known restaurant in Old Havana is the Bodequita near the cathedral. Also worth mentioning is the buffet restaurant in the Melia Cohiba, which is expensive, but often serves good quality food unobtainable in other parts of the city. The recently legalized *paladares* are restaurants run as a family business in people's own homes. There are so many of these that it is best to ask at your hotel for ideas. It is worth trying the seafood dishes available at most restaurants. Lager-type beer is brewed locally and is very good.

TRANSPORT
There is poor and deteriorating public transport. Buses are wholly inadequate for daily needs. Some taxis are available outside the tourist hotels and in sightseeing areas and provide the only realistic option for getting about.

SECURITY
There are beggars, especially around the cathedral area. Bag snatching and other street theft is not uncommon, particularly in Old Havana.

CYPRUS

NICOSIA

Language **Greek, Turkish, English**
Currency **Cyprus pound (C£) of 100 cents. £1=0.81,
    Mar 1997. Not traded internationally. The Turkish
    lira is used in Turkish Cyprus**
Banks **0830–1200 Mon to Sat, and 1530–1730
    in tourist areas**
Credit cards **accepted in hotels and large shops; not
    in garages**
Cashpoints **some, taking Visa**
Shops **0830–1300 Mon to Sat, 1430–1730 in winter,
    1600–1900 in summer, except Wed and Sat**
Sales **yes, with genuine bargains**
Bargaining **10 per cent discount sometimes possible**
Tipping **10 per cent service charge in hotels and
    restaurants, plus tax; additional tip appreciated
    but not expected. Same for taxi drivers**
Import/export restrictions **import of agricultural
    products strictly controlled**

The area around Archbishop Makarios Avenue and
Stasikratous Street, the parallel street behind it, is known for
its attractive and rather expensive boutiques selling designer-
label clothing and shoes as well as silverware, fine porcelain
and imported oriental cloth.

Ledra Street plus the narrow streets in the old city especially in the well-known neighbourhood of Laiki Yitonia, is a
renovated eighteenth-century enclave of particular interest to
tourists who want a taste of Cypriot culture. Here local artisans and craftsmen display their wares along cobblestone
lanes. This and much of the shopping area of old Nicosia is
now pedestrianised.

In Eleftherios Venizelos Square there is an open market
every Wednesday which sells mainly fresh vegetables, fruit and
flowers from the villages. It is particularly colourful and worth
a visit.

Apart from the designer labels, which carry a 70 per cent
import tax, there are many familiar names such as Marks and
Spencer, Body Shop, British Home Stores, Richard Shops,
Mothercare and Laura Ashley; Boots products are sold in ZAKO.
All are, however, much more expensive than in the UK.

Lefkera lace, pottery, jewellery, silver, old maps of Cyprus, icons and copper are all recommended as gifts and souvenirs. Cyprus Handicrafts and Souvenirs is at 20 Regaenis Street. For jewellery, Ioannou Nicos is at the Cyprus Hilton, and Stephanides Jewellers is at 23 Archbishop Makarios Avenue.

Both contact lenses and spectacles are cheaper than in the UK. Tennis racquets, clothing and shoes can also be bought more cheaply locally. The cost of having a suit made to measure is C£45 plus the cost of material. Good quality cloth is available locally.

There is a good selection of English language books available at prices almost 50 per cent more than in the UK. The English-language *Cyprus Mail* is published daily except Mondays. The *Cyprus Weekly* and *Cyprus Today* are published on Fridays. Copies of the British national daily newspapers are available in Nicosia on the day following publication at about double UK prices.

EATING AND DRINKING
Prices of meals out are reasonable. There is a good selection of restaurants serving everything from local mezze to international cuisine, but standards vary. For local fare try Date Club at 2 Agathon Street, Kalymnos at 11 Princess de Tyras, Latsi Fish Tavern at 1 Av. Pavlos Street, Plaka Tavern at 8 Makarios III Square and Scaraveos at 4 Nicokreon Street. Local wines and brandy are cheap and there are two good local beers, Keo and Carlsberg. Specialities include Halloumi cheese, local coffee which is quite strong, and brandy sour, a long drink very popular in summer. Cigarettes made locally sell more cheaply than corresponding brands in the UK.

TRANSPORT
The main shopping streets are within walking distance of most major hotels. Bus services are not easy for foreigners to use. Taxis (usually ordered by telephone) always use meters and are generally reliable.

SECURITY
Street crime, pickpocketing and begging are almost unknown in Cyprus.

CZECH REPUBLIC

PRAGUE

Language **Czech**
Currency **koruna (Kcs) of 100 haleru.**
  £1=46.40, Mar 1997
Banks **0800–1400 Mon to Fri**
Credit cards **increasingly widely accepted**
Shops **0830–1200, 1400–1800 Mon to Fri,**
  0830–1200 Sat
Tipping **10 per cent in restaurants**
Export restrictions **antiques and works of art require**
  receipts for Customs examination and export
  permits where appropriate

Shopping in Prague is in the process of being revolutionised. Most goods, including the big international names, are now available, and queueing is almost a thing of the past. But still low-heeled shoes are needed for walking in the cobbled streets and suitable boots for wearing in the snow. The Czech language is difficult, but German is widely spoken.

The main central shopping area stretches from Wenceslas Square north to Narodni and Na prikope. In the Old Town the centre is around Starometske namesti. Parizska is a favourite for up-market shopping. Shopping centres offer a quick and convenient overview of what is on offer. Pavilon is on Vinohradska and Koruna Palace is at Na prikope/Vaclavska namesti.

Porcelain and crystal are popular buys as gifts or souvenirs and widely available. The same goes for wooden toys. Other popular buys are garnets, books and CDs. Winter boots, gloves and hats of reasonable quality and price are also available. Consumables such as smoked meats and vodka always make acceptable gifts.

EATING AND DRINKING
Czech beers such as Pilsener Urquell and Budweis (Budvar) are world renowned and there also several Prague brews such as Staropramen to be sampled in haunts such as U Flekii.

Some local wines, particularly white wines, are good and reasonably priced even in restaurants. A good area for wine lovers is Michalske in the Old Town.

There is more to Czech cuisine than dumplings or cold

meats, as a visit to V zatisi in Lillova or Parnas at Smetanovo nabrezi will demonstrate. U sulerii in Palackeho is an international restaurant which is different in that the customers cook the food, mainly meat, themselves.

TRANSPORT

The public transport system is good, reliable and cheap although at times crowded. There are buses and trams and an expanding metro system with a system of uniform fares which are very cheap by British standards. Taxi fares are also reasonable.

SECURITY

Basic personal security precautions, mainly against petty street crime, are required, particularly in the tourist areas of Prague.

DENMARK

COPENHAGEN

Language **Danish**
Currency **krone (kr.) of 100 ore.**
  £1=10.36, Mar 1997
Banks **0930–1600 Mon–Wed, 0930–1800 Thur,**
  0930–1600 Fri
Shops **0800/0900–1700/1730 Mon to Thur,**
  0800/0900–1700/2000 Friday, 0800/0900–1300/1400
  Sat
Sales **twice yearly, good bargains**
Duty-free **large stores operate VAT-free scheme**
Tipping **service charge of 15 per cent on hotel and**
  restaurant bills; no further tip expected, but leave
  small change; tip is included in taxi fares

The overall cost of living is higher than in the UK and Copenhagen ranks among the world's most expensive cities. Bargains are therefore extremely few.

The central shopping area of Copenhagen can be covered on foot for the most part and much of it is traffic-free. This includes the main thoroughfare known as Strøget which is in fact five consecutive streets running from Rådhuspladsen to Kongens Nytorv. This area is good both for shops and eating places. It is sensible to take a look at a good large general store such as Illums Bolighus or Magasin while you are in the area, to see the range of what is available.

Denmark is celebrated for its excellent design for table and housewares generally including glass, porcelain and silver. It also produces some very good jewellery. There are good furs and sweaters, as well as leather goods.

British newspapers are generally available in Copenhagen around lunchtime on the day of publication. *The Times* costs kr.18.00, the *Daily Express* kr.14.00, the *Telegraph* kr.9.00. The *Sunday Times* costs kr.32.00. English magazines are also available. Both hardback and paperback books are available, but are much more expensive than in the UK.

EATING AND DRINKING

Restaurants are good, but very expensive. It is worth remembering that most of them have two menus, the ordinary one and the smorgasbord (open sandwiches) list. Good meals can be obtained in unpretentious restaurants and such places seem to be preferred by most Danes. Fish such as herring and gravad laks is excellent. For good fish try Krogs Fiskerestaurant at 38 Gammel Strand or Den Gyldne Fortun at Ved Stranden 18. Illums Bolighus is good for a shopper's lunch.

Wine is rather expensive and drinking beer with a meal is standard practice, even in expensive restaurants, as is only to be expected in the home town of Carlsberg and Tuborg. There are plenty of good bars and several English-style pubs which are popular with younger Danes. Akvavit is a local speciality. Alcohol can be bought in supermarkets, unlike in other parts of Scandinavia. A good place for buying food and drink is Kokkenes Torvehal on Strøget.

TRANSPORT

There is an excellent public transport system which includes buses and both an urban and suburban train system, similar to the London underground. The minimum fare on buses and trains is kr.10.00 a ticket which permits one to travel on buses or trains within three fare zones within one hour. A *Rabatkort* gives 10 separate journeys. Taxis and taxi ranks are plentiful. The tip is included in the fare.

DJIBOUTI

DJIBOUTI

Language **Somali, Afar, French, Arabic**
Currency **Djibouti franc. £1=257, Mar 1997**

An expensive transit point with little to delay the traveller and just about nothing worth buying. Parts of the country remain closed to foreigners. Care is required in the town, particularly at night

DOMINICA

ROSEAU

Language **English**
Currency **East Caribbean dollar (EC$)**
£1=4.2, Mar 1997. French franc also in use

Roseau is an increasingly popular destination for cruise ships. The compact central shopping area is focused on the old market place. The handwoven mats for which the island is best known are by no means cheap, rightly so since they demand a lot of skilled work. Otherwise there is little other than the usual T-shirts and conch shells.

Local fish is good.

DOMINICAN REPUBLIC

SANTO DOMINGO

Language **Spanish**
Currency **peso. £1=22.50, Mar 1997**

Shares the island of Santo Domingo with Haiti, but the main tourist areas, increasingly popular with package trippers, are far away from any trouble spots.

The Calle el Conde is recommended for shopping. The market is on the Avenida Melìa in the old city. The duty-free shops at the Sheraton and other major hotels as well as at the airport accept only US dollars.

Local products available include coral, paintings from Haiti and semi-precious stones as well as cigars, coffee and rum.

ECUADOR

QUITO

Language **Spanish**
Currency **sucre of 100 centavos. £1=6060, Mar 1997**
Tipping **10 per cent; where service charge included, add a little extra for good service. Taxi drivers do not expect tips**

Ecuador is a developing country and you do not find the wide range of consumer goods you would expect to see in a European country. More and more is imported from the States, but prices are high.

There are four main shopping malls: Quicentro, El Bosque, Centro Comercial Iñaquito and El Jardin. The Sukasa department store is to be found at both El Bosque and El Jardin: it is expensive, but has a wide range. Cheaper is the newly opened De Prati at Quicentro. There is a market on Wednesdays and Saturdays where very good quality, although expensive, fruit and other produce is available. This is just opposite Cyrano, a wonderful French bakery which has next door to it Corfu, a shop selling delicious ice-cream. Also in the same street, the Calle Portugal, are a Swiss dairy shop, a German butcher and flower stalls with many exotic blooms.

Local handicrafts such as the Indian-made cardigans in very thick wool are excellent value as are the rugs, woven baskets and T-shirts. The Indian market at Otavalo is a tourist attraction within two hours' drive, as is the neighbouring village of Cotacachi, which specialises in leather goods. Both are good for handicrafts and gifts and souvenirs in general. San Antonio de Ibarra, 20 minutes north of Otavalo, is famous for its woodwork.

In Quito itself the Galeria Latina in the Calle Juan Leon Mera is magnificent, with a wide choice of handicrafts from all over Latin America, but it is expensive. In the same street are other, more reasonably priced shops. Parallel with Juan Leon Mera is the Calle Amazonas, the centre of tourist shopping. Here is the famous Panama hat shop, La Casa del Sombrero. At the southern end of Amazonas on Sunday, in El Ejido park, is a market with paintings and some handicrafts from Otavolo. Another good souvenir shop is Olga Fish in Calle Colon.

British newspapers are not widely available in Quito and English-language books are difficult to obtain. Libri Mundi in Juan Leon Mera has a fair selection of American paperbacks. You can also find some current paperbacks at the Hotel Quito bookshop, but they are more expensive than at Libri Mundi.

EATING AND DRINKING
There is a wide range of good restaurants in Quito offering a reasonably priced night out.

American-type cigarettes of local manufacture are very cheap.

TRANSPORT
Quito is well served by taxis, which are required by law to carry meters. However there are a few which have yet to comply with the law and it is advisable to agree the fare before setting out. Taxis are usually plentiful except during peak hours and heavy rainstorms. There are many bus services, but they are crowded and slow. The new trolley-bus service which runs from north to south of Quito is safe, fast and inexpensive.

SECURITY
The most beautiful part of Quito is the old colonial town, but beware of muggers and pickpockets.

EGYPT

Language **Arabic**
Currency **Egyptian pound of 100 piastres, 1000 milliemes. £1=5.43, Mar 1997**
Banks **0830–1230 Mon, Thur, Sat, 1000–1200 Sun**
Credit cards **Visa, American Express, in exclusive shops only**
Cashpoints **at the Egyptian-British Bank in Zamalek and Heliopolis with Midland card; also at Semi-Rames Hotel, the World Trade Centre and the British Council**
Shops **1000–2000 Mon, 1000–1900 Tue to Sat**
Bargaining **yes, in bazaars and markets**
Tipping **small amounts of "baksheesh" for services; service charge of 12.5–17.5 per cent added in hotels and restaurants**
Export restrictions **on all antiquities**

Ready-made clothing, including casual wear, is produced locally. Although the standard of finish varies, the best is quite good and the prices are much lower than in the UK, e.g. men's cotton shirts for £10 or a suit for £70. The range and style (rather ornate) of women's clothes is not as good as in the UK. Leather jackets, belts and handbags are good buys. Locally made shoes are cheap by UK standards, but will not last as long as British-bought ones.

Reproductions of antiquities are popular as jewellery and as gifts and souvenirs, although not all are particularly tasteful. Egyptian cotton is world famous for clothing and household items such as towels. Prices are reasonable although sizes vary.

Gold and silver can be good buys. Look out also for woodwork, perhaps inlaid – with mother of pearl for example. Leatherwork available includes camel saddles as well as more mundane items. There are countless other possibilities – rugs, carpets and tapestries, spices and perfumes, appliqué, papyrus, brass, copper and bone.

As imported spirits and foreign beer tend to be expensive, most foreigners develop a taste for the local Stella beer.

Despite the efforts of the government, personal security cannot be guaranteed and tourists have been specifically targeted by terrorists.

CAIRO

The main department stores include Chalons and Salon Vert in Kasr el Nil Street, Gettenyo and Rivoli in Mohamed Farid Street, Hannaux in Mohamed Bassiouni Street and Omar Offendi in Talaat Harb Street. There are branches of Benetton, Naf-Naf, New Man and Mobaco (an Egyptian company) in Mohandeseen, Zamalek and the World Trade Centre at which good quality casual clothes can be bought at very reasonable prices, and other clothes shops in plenty.

Cairo's oldest bazaar is the Khan El Khalili. As you would expect, it is very atmospheric and lively. Almost anything can be bought and bargaining is compulsory. Many of the traders close on Sunday. Adjacent to Bab Zuweilya and the Salah Talai Mosque is the Street of the Tentmakers where handmade quilts, cushions and wall hangings can be bought. The Camel Market is in the countryside beyond the north-west of Cairo and operates on Friday mornings; go early, between 0600 and 0800. Attaba is a large covered food market off Sharia el Azhar. The Spice Market is off Ghoureyya Street.

There are several places near Cairo of interest to any visitor looking for handicrafts. Harannayah is good for items such as pottery, ceramics and batik. Another must is the Wissa Wassef School for weaving. Kerdassa is excellent for handwoven cotton and silk rugs, galabeyas and tablecloths.

Carpets and rugs are also available at Wissa Wassef on the road to Saqqara in Harraniyah Village or Aziz a little further on, also at Magda Laurence Oriental Carpets at 3 Ahmed Hishmat Street in Zamalek. There is very good damask at Ouf and Sons in El Mashhad El Hussein Street in Khan el Khalili. Safr Khan in Brazil Street has a good selection of lamps. The Pottery at 165 Sudan Street has some interesting lamp bases.

For leather clothing and other goods go to Badra at 33 Sherif Street, Lumbroso at 19 Talaat Harb Street, the Mipel Handbag Factory at 98 Mohamed Farid Street Sarkis Vartzbedian at 32 Salah Salem Street (better value than the boutique behind the Nile Hilton), The Leather Shop off Michel Lutfallah Street or Vero Chic at 19 Talaat Harb Street.

There are plenty of places at which to buy gifts and souvenirs. Just a few are the Asfour Crystal Factory at 5 Saik el Ahad Street, the Dr Ragab Papyrus Institute at 3 El Nil Street, Miss Egypt at 28 Talaat Harb Street (also in the lobby of the Nile Hilton and Meridien), Mousky Chic in the Nile Hilton, Nomad Gallery at 14 Saraya al Gezira (also in the Marriott Hotel), Prince in Zamalek and the World Trade Centre, Song for Silver in Ismail Mohammed Street or Atlas (also in the Marriott Hotel).

There is a daily English-language newspaper under Egyptian management (the *Egyptian Gazette*) and a weekly newspaper (*Al Ahram*). Some magazines and British newspapers are available, but tend to be rather expensive. Some English paperbacks can be bought locally, at the Al Ahram bookshop, for example. A variety of British and English-language newspapers and magazines are available at news vendors and in Sunny and Alfa supermarkets.

EATING AND DRINKING

Al Omdah in Sharia Al-Gazair is a good place to try *koshari* (noodles and vegetables in a sauce). Back of the Moon at 68 el Marioutia offers traditional Egyptian cuisine at reasonable prices. Bint Al Sultan near the Shooting Club in Mohandeseen is reputedly one of the best Egyptian restaurants. The lobby of the Cairo Sheraton has some of the best Egyptian food in Cairo. Especially good is the *fuul(beans)*. Felfela is at 15 Hoda Shaarawi. The Five Bells at 9 Adel Abu Bakr Street offers Egyptian cuisine at reasonable prices. The Nubian Village in the Meridien Hotel is on the banks of the Nile. There are Indian and Chinese restaurants too.

There are bars in all the major hotels and a scattering of individual pubs catering for Westerners and rich Egyptians such as Pub 28 on Sharia Shaggaret el Dor. But the traditional focus of Cairo society remains the almost exclusively male *ahwa*, serving coffee and *shishas*. Cakes and preserves can be rather sweet.

TRANSPORT

Most of the buses in Cairo are in a dilapidated condition and grossly overcrowded. Taxis are cheap and dirty by UK standards and at times difficult to obtain. Agree a fare beforehand since meters are almost universally ignored. It is not uncommon to share a taxi. There is a single line metro from Heliopolis through the centre of the city to Maadi which is cheap and reasonably comfortable during off-peak hours.

ALEXANDRIA

The main shopping area is in the city centre around Tahrir Square. There are branches of department stores such as Omar Effendi and Salon Vert. International newspapers are widely available in the hotels and at the news stands. There are English-language books at Center Books in Sa'ad Zaghlid Street or Library Mustakbei in Shah Safiya Laghlul Street.

EATING AND DRINKING

There is a limited range of restaurants, serving mostly
Egyptian or Greek-type food. Fish and seafood such as
shrimps are specialities and usually excellent, as is fruit. A
basic meal costs around £8. A more elaborate meal with local
beer or wine might cost £15. Try International Seafood or San
Giovanni in El Geish Road or Samakmak in Ras El Tin Palace
Street.

TRANSPORT

A slow but reliable and cheap form of public transport is the
tram. There is also a motley variety of buses, minibuses and
suburban trains; some are in dilapidated condition and grossly
overcrowded. Taxis are cheap and dirty, but usually easy to
obtain.

SECURITY

Alexandria remains relatively safe for a large city.

EL SALVADOR

SAN SALVADOR

Language **Spanish**
Currency **colon (c) of 100 centavos. £1=14.27, Jan
1997**
Banks **no exchange controls**
Credit cards **accepted in most restaurants and
shops, some supermarkets**
Shops **0800–1800 Mon to Fri, 0800–1200 Sat**
Tipping **10 per cent in restaurants where no service
charge; not expected by taxi drivers, but add a few
colons**

The city centre is clustered for the most part between Calles 1a
and 4a. There you will find a couple of department stores as well
as numerous smaller shops and boutiques. In the suburbs of San
Salvador are modern shopping centres such as Metrocentro and
Metrosur. Many Salvadoreans prefer to do their serious shopping
in Miami.

The best places for buying handicrafts are the Mercado

Ex-Cuartel and the Mercado Nacional de Artesanías. The former is off the 1a Calle Oriente at the corner of 8a Avenida Norte. The latter is about five miles south-west of the city centre on the Interamericana Highway, a little more difficult to get to as well as being slightly more expensive than the Ex-Cuartel. Both are cheaper than shops in the centre.

Recommended items to look for include ceramics, textiles and woodwork, which is particularly attractive if decorated in bright colours in local fashion. Also worthwhile are masks, basketry and embroidery.

Few books are available either in English or Spanish.

EATING AND DRINKING

There is a growing number of good restaurants in San Salvador. The food is mainly steaks, chicken or seafood. There are several bars and restaurants in the Zona Rosa, where the night-life of San Salvador is centred. This is in San Benito, near the Mercado Nacional de Artesanías. The favourite local fast food is *pupusa*, a sort of tortilla. Local beer is good, but the best coffee is exported.

TRANSPORT

Taxis are small, yellow, dilapidated and always available. It is best to have an idea where you are going so that you can advise the driver.

SECURITY

There has been a dramatic rise in violent armed crime since the end of the civil war in January 1992. Avoid ostentation.

ESTONIA

TALINN

Language Estonian
Currency **kroon of 100 cents. £1=21.71, Mar 1997**
Tipping **hotel and restaurant bills include service
charge, but small additional tips welcome**

An attractive small city with shops and eating places already good and improving all the time. A day trip from Helsinki is easily arranged.

The centre of the mediaeval Hanseatic-era Old Town is the square of Raekoja plats (Town Hall Square). This is a good area for shopping for crafts as well as gifts and souvenirs in general at prices which are still reasonable. A general overview of what is available can be gained in the Tallina Kaubamaja department store on Viru väljak about a quarter of a mile east of the Old Town centre.

Favoured items for visitors include ceramics, amber and jewellery, leather and linens.

British newspapers and magazines are still in short supply.

TRANSPORT
The Old Town can easily be covered on foot although transport is quite good. Public transport consists of buses, trolley-buses and trams. Taxis are plentiful and although fares are metered it is wise to agree the fare in advance.

SECURITY
Sensible personal security precautions are necessary.

ETHIOPIA

ADDIS ABABA

Language **Amharic**
Currency **Ethiopian birr (EB) of 100 cents. £1=10.20, Mar 1997**
Banks **0800–1100, 1300–1500 Mon to Fri 0800–1100 Sat. Best exchange rate is at Commercial Bank of Ethiopia**
Credit cards **only at Hilton Hotel and airlines, Mastercard and American Express, not Visa**
Shops **dawn to 2100**
Refunds **difficult to obtain**
Bargaining **yes, except in government and hotel shops; start below half asked price**
Duty-free **at airport and Hilton Hotel; limited supplies but good prices**
Tipping **10 per cent where service charge not included**

Local specialities worth considering are the silver and wooden Ethiopian crosses, silver and gold jewellery, embroidery, leather goods, hand-painted pictures, pottery, rugs, coffee pots and wooden handicrafts. The only clothes available locally are dresses and outfits of local style. These are very attractive, made of various weights of white cotton and decorated with intricate borders of hand embroidery. Some foreign women buy them as evening wear.

The Mercato (or Addis Keteme of Addis Ababa) is a fascinating place and said to be the largest market in Africa. In the two big buildings you can find clothing, Harar cloth (colourful voile shawls) and Ethiopian handicrafts. The numerous individual stalls outside the main buildings are generally better for antique items and jewellery. Care should be taken while walking around Mercato and it is advisable to take a local person with you.

Other main shopping areas and recommended shops are the Piazza located on Adwa Avenue, Churchill Avenue from the Ras Hotel northwards to the roundabout just above the post office where there are five or six shops dealing in local handicrafts, souvenirs and "antiques", in the vicinity of the Ghion Hotel on Ras Desta Street near the Stadium, the Bethlehem Centre on Asmara Road for embroidered handicrafts, place mats, dresses, etc. The Ethio-Craft Centre, a rehabilitation centre for handicapped workers, is situated some distance along the Dessie/Asmara road. They are willing to show you round and articles can be purchased at the centre's shop. There is also a small branch on the Piazza. Alert, another handicapped workers' centre, is on the Jimma Road.

There are English-language newspapers published locally of varying standard. British newspapers are available at the Hilton, but the *Telegraph* costs £3 sterling. A magazine might cost £5 sterling.

EATING AND DRINKING

There is a handful of passable restaurants. The hotels also serve meals. *Injera* and *wot* (sourdough pancakes with a meat or fish sauce) are local foods worth trying, perhaps at the Ghion Hotel or at the Crown Hotel on the Debre Zeit Road. *Tej* (honey mead) and *talla* (local beer) are alcoholic drinks worth trying at one of the local bars.

TRANSPORT

Pavements are primitive, so be prepared to wear very sturdy or expendable shoes. Buses are not recommended. Communal taxis run along fixed routes. They are cheap and may be used if there is no alternative. Regular taxis are expensive.

SECURITY

There are constant encounters with beggars and street vendors. Sensible personal security measures are necessary. Be vigilant at all times, do not attract attention and keep to tourist areas.

FALKLAND ISLANDS

PORT STANLEY

Language **English**
Currency **pound sterling, also Falkland notes and coins**
Credit cards **only in Upland Goose Hotel**
Tipping **expected in restaurants**

A commercial airline route to the Falklands started in June 1996. Shopping is limited, since Stanley is small, but there is no VAT or sales tax so things such as Barbour or Goretex may be cheaper than in the UK.

Try the Falklands Co-op Home Industries in Ross Road, Stanley for knitwear, handicrafts and souvenirs. All items are guaranteed made locally. Attractive Falkland Islands pullovers are good value and all sorts of penguin items are popular. The Philatelic Bureau is in the Town Hall. It has first-day covers and souvenir issues and specialises in the Falklands Islands Dependencies and British Antarctic Territory material as well.

The nearest thing to local newspapers are the weekly *Penguin News* and the weekly, cyclostyled *Teaberry Express*.

EATING AND DRINKING

There is a good selection of wine, beer and spirits at the same price as in the UK and some good, cheap Chilean wines. A limited selection of popular British cigarettes is available more cheaply than in the UK.

There are three restaurants which offer lunch and dinner and two cafés and two pubs for simpler meals. There is also a fish and chip shop.

TRANSPORT
Taxis are available in Stanley.

FIJI

SUVA/NADI

Language **English**
Currency **Fijian dollar (F$) of 100 cents. £1=2.25,
   Mar 1997; freely convertible, no black market**
Credit cards **acceptable at most retail outlets**
Cashpoints **yes**
Shops **0830–1700 Mon to Fri, 0830–1300 Sat**
Sales **not genuine**
Bargaining **yes, in all shops**
Duty-free **at airport, savings marginal; "duty-free"
   shops in Suva and Nadi not really duty-free**
Tipping **not obligatory, a few cents appreciated for
   exceptional services 10 per cent**
Export restrictions **licence needed for all genuine
   artefacts; export of some seashells prohibited**

Fiji is much less sophisticated than its French Polynesia equivalent and to many visitors weaned on South Pacific brochures or tales of Tahiti this is somewhat unexpected. However, the warmth and hospitable nature of most Fijians and aspects of its 300-odd islands more than compensate the traveller. Fiji is not immune from outside influences; Mcdonald's is in Nadi, with another McFiji to be opened soon in Suva.

Nadi (pronounced Nandi) is the site of the international airport and main transit point for tourists, about 190 kms from the capital Suva. Nadi town has hotels with boutiques selling the usual holiday items. Otherwise shopping is largely confined to the main street. Handicrafts and jewellery will usually be of Indian design.

Suva has a fairly well defined if somewhat dilapidated shopping-cum-business area in the centre of town. There is no serious shopping or window shopping on offer. There are good tailors who will make made-to-measure trousers or safari-style clothing in a wool/synthetic or cotton/synthetic mixture for F$60. A safari suit in cotton mixture costs about F$100 whilst cotton/polyester mix shirts are available from around F$15. T-shirts are cheap and cheerful. Shoes and sandals are reasonably priced with a fairly wide selection.

Local handicrafts (baskets, wooden bowls, carvings, table mats and souvenir shells, etc.) are widely available at the handicraft centres located centrally in major towns. Some of the wooden carvings copying Fijian artefacts from the cannibal past are extremely good. Cannibal forks make good salad servers. Local spices make a nice gift or souvenir and are widely available in a range of packagings. Kava is a local drink which can be gift wrapped and will certainly make an unusual present for those who like to try different drinks and who are willing to carry out the preparation instructions. Stamp collectors will wish to visit the Philatelic Bureau in the Ganilau Building.

There are two daily English-language newspapers with reasonable local and international coverage. *Time* magazine (New Zealand edition) and a number of Australian publications are on sale at the better bookshops and at all the major hotels. Paperback books are available, but the choice is limited and prices are at least twice those in the UK.

EATING AND DRINKING

Apart from the hotel restaurants, there are three Chefs restaurants in Nadi, serving European cuisine and the Japanese style Daikoku. The number of good restaurants in Suva is limited. Most restaurants offer value for money, but standards are generally not as high as in Europe, even in the best restaurants. Tiko's Floating Restaurant, a boat moored on Stinson Parade, specialises in seafood. There are several good Chinese restaurants including the Ming Palace on Victoria Parade, the Sichuan Pavilion in Thomson Street, the Castle Restaurant on Queen's Road, the Ocean Restaurant in the Metropole Hotel and the Great Wok in Flagstaff. Otherwise try the Red Lion on Victoria Parade, the Hare Krishna in Pratt Street, the Swiss Tavern in Kimberley Street, O'Reilly's Brasserie in McArthur Street or the Aberdeen Grill at Noble House, Flagstaff. JJs has recently opened near the NBF Building. There is a good selection of wine (mostly Australian), spirits, beer and cigarettes.

TRANSPORT

There are extensive bus services which operate in and between the main towns, as well as widespread taxi services, which are cheap if somewhat primitive. Standards of driving and roadworthiness of buses and taxis vary, but most taxis have meters which actually work.

SECURITY

Normal personal security measures need to be taken. Beware of hassle from "sword" sellers who will befriend you and then hastily etch your name on a carving to put you under obligation to purchase.

FINLAND

HELSINKI

Language **Finnish, Swedish**
Currency **markka (FIM) of 100 penniia. £1=8.10, Mar 1997**
Banks **0915–1615 Mon to Fri**
Credit cards **widely accepted**
Cashpoints **throughout Helsinki**
Shops **0900–1700 or later Mon to Fri, 0900–1400 Sat**
Refunds **VAT refundable to non-EU visitors at certain shops**
Sales **Jan and Jun; good bargains**
Tipping **FIM5-10 per customer to doormen at restaurants and cloakroom attendants at public halls; leave small change at restaurants**

Helsinki is expensive, but offers the visitor comfortable and extensive shopping opportunities within a fairly compact central area. Be prepared in winter for icy pavements, and be sure to dress warmly.

Aleksanterinkatu is one of Helsinki's busiest shopping streets and together with Esplanadi and their cross streets forms part of the original old city centre. In these streets are the leading shops for Finnish design and Finnish and international fashion, as well as shopping centres such as the Kluuvi and Forum. Stockmann, the famous department store, is at Aleksanterinkatu 52. Iso Roobertinkatu is a nearby pedestrian area well supplied with small shops and restaurants. Helsinki railway station has an underground shopping centre with the big advantage of being open on Sunday.

The Itäkeskus Eastern Shopping Mall is the largest indoor shopping centre in Scandinavia, with over 170 shops and restaurants including branches of the leading department stores. It is at Myyrmäki to the east of Helsinki and is easily reachable by metro.

There is a wide range of typically Finnish goods which are suitable for gifts and souvenirs such as glassware, jewellery, ceramics, tableware and wooden articles. In the Kiseleff Bazaar is a shop selling everything connected with the sauna. There is no stigma attached to wearing animal furs in Finland and a good, well-designed range is available, often at a good discount.

For arts and crafts there are several shops in Fredrinkinkatu and Korkeavuorenkatu. Friends of Finnish Handicraft on Yrjönkatu has rugs and other goods. The Kruunhaka area near the North Harbour has many antique shops. Helsinki has eleven bustling market places and three market halls. The beautiful Market Square and Old Market Hall at South Harbour have typical goods such as seasonal berries, knitted goods and reindeer skins. The Hietalahti Market Place and Hall constitute Finland's largest flea market.

The leading bookshop, Akateeminen Kirjakauppa (Stockman's Academic Bookshop), on the Esplanadi has a good stock of English-language books. Prices are almost double UK ones, but there are sale bargains. British newspapers and magazines are available at a few bookshops and at Helsinki railway station. Supplies can sometimes be erratic and daily newspapers are usually one day late. Sunday newspapers are available from the station on Sunday afternoons. *The Times* costs FIM16, the *Independent* FIM16 and the *Sunday Times* FIM30.

Eating and Drinking

There is a superb range of fish, as well as local delicacies such as elk and reindeer available in a wide range of restaurants in Helsinki. Prices can be high especially in the evenings. A modest dinner in a restaurant will cost at least FIM80–200 a head, excluding even the cheapest bottle of wine (FIM120). A two-course meal at a more expensive restaurant can cost FIM 250–350 per head excluding drinks. Dinner in a pub will cost FIM60–90 with a pint of beer costing FIM15–25. The lunchtime smorgasbord is popular at weekends when the larger restaurants charge about FIM100 per head. Local beer and vodka can be excellent.

Transport

Helsinki has excellent public transport. There is a single fare for buses and trams for travel within one hour with discounts for a 10-trip ticket. Tourist day-tickets are also available.

Taxis are obtainable at ranks, by hailing or by telephone. Fares are metered.

FRANCE

Language **French**
Currency **franc (Fr) of 100 centimes. £1=9.17, Mar 1997**
Banks **0900–1600 Mon to Fri**
Credit cards **widely accepted**
Cashpoints **Visa and Access can be used**
Shops **0900–1900, closed all day Sun and Mon morn; some close lunchtime and all day Mon, and all of August**
Refunds **difficult to obtain, but exchange possible with receipt**
Sales **genuine bargains; recommended**
Tipping **10–15 per cent for good service; leave small change in restaurants with service charge Frs2 to theatre and cinema usherettes, Frs3–5 to cloakroom attendants.Taxi drivers expect tips**

Generally speaking the cost of living is higher than in the UK. There is a large selection of clothing and excellent departments in all the big stores as well as boutiques in all price ranges. Apart from clothing there is a wide choice in shoes, leather and jewellery. France is probably the leading producer of luxury goods in the world and as chain stores are less common than in the UK, small individual shops abound and are often worth exploring. There are bargains to be had during the winter and summer sales.

Department stores such as Lafayette or Printemps are to be found in most cities, and designer labels in many boutiques. There are few typically French items which will not be available in fashion shops or supermarkets at home, perhaps at very reasonable prices. Designer labels are well known. So are the wines and other drinks, as well as all the famous cheeses and other foods. Table wines are much cheaper than in the UK and the variety is infinite, but it is impossible to expect vintage wines at cut prices. Export demand has seen to that. So try your local specialist dealer.

It is difficult to recommend mandatory best buys. Buy what you fancy. It is perhaps best to eat, drink and be merry while you are there. Restaurants are generally good and have by law to display their menus outside.

English is spoken in many shops in the tourist area. Personal security is generally good.

PARIS

Paris is a shopper's paradise. Virtually anything you could want is available in Paris – at a price. Shopping is not cheap anywhere in the capital, but the long-time residents have developed coping strategies to deal with the seemingly exorbitant prices asked on the main shopping streets. The "systeme D", where d stands for *se debrouiller* or how to get by is the pride of all Parisians. Everybody has a story to tell about how they managed to get top quality goods at knock down prices. Entire books have been devoted to the subject, and those likely to spend more than a few months in Paris would be well served by a copy of either *Paris pas cher* or *Paris meilleur prix*, both of which outline the best values available in any price category. Not only do they give the cheapest places to buy standard goods, but – Parisians being Parisians – they are full of places to get luxury goods at cut prices as well.

Like most major cities, there is no main area for shopping in Paris, but rather many smaller centres serving the various arrondissements. The main luxury shopping streets are to be found in the 8th arrondissement. They are not great places to find value for money but they are wonderful places to window shop (*leche-vitrine* in French, which translates literally and very graphically as "window licking"). The Rue du Faubourg St Honoré, the Champs-Elysées and the Avenue Montaigne are internationally renowned for exclusivity and style, but they tend to serve wealthy tourists more than the French, who will be right around the corner in streets like the rue de Penthièvre looking for bargains from the same designer names. Miss Griffes (19, Rue de Penthièvre, 75008) has a good selection of haute couture and ready to wear clothing and accessories from top designers like Armani, Chanel, and Valentino. Men's designer clothing can be found at PWS (1, rue de Penthièvre, 75008)

Les Grands Magasins or department stores are a huge part of retail shopping in Paris, and some of the stores are worth a visit as architectural history. The greatest concentration of department stores is just north of the old Opera on Boulevard Haussman, where Les Galeries Lafayette at number 40, Au Printemps at number 64, and Marks & Spencer stores cover several city blocks and offer a huge selection of both established and up-and-coming designer names. Though not technically a department store, Les Halles shopping centre in the middle of town offers many of the same products and services and is perhaps most accessible due to the knot of metro connections which lie beneath it. Just south of Les Halles on the Rue de Rivoli are La Samaritaine and the flagship C&A store. The main left bank department store is Le Bon Marché (22 rue de Sèvres) in the 6th arrondissement, famous for the largest food market in the city.

The BHV (Pronounced Bae-ash-Vae) or Bazar de l'Hotel de Ville (Metro: Hotel de Ville) is located right across the Rue de Rivoli from city hall and is the answer to virtually any house-hold repair, decorating and furnishing problems. Less well known is the warehouse store BHV Entrepot, located just south of the city in Ivry-sur-Seine (101 Boulevard Polvaillant Couturier), where many of the same goods can be found as discontinued or with small defects for 30-50% off the retail price. Household electronics and white goods are particularly well represented at the warehouse store, and come with the same guarantees and service as at the main store.

Flea markets worldwide got their name from the unwelcome inhabitants of the clothes on offer from Parisian ragpickers at the end of the last century. Although the fleas are long gone, the name remains as synonymous for bargain shopping. By far the most famous market is in the St-Ouen (Sat, Sun, Mon – Metro: Porte de Clignancourt), where more than 3,500 vendors operate in several square miles of streets, stands and alleyways. The market breaks down into many specialised areas, and antiques hunters will be best served by the Marchés Biron, Serpette, and Paul Bert found on the streets bearing the same names. Second-hand clothing is found in the Marché Malik and on stands dotted in and around the entire area. Other markets include the boisterous Marché de Montreuil (Sat, Sun, Mon) downmarket Marché de Vanves (Sat, Sun mornings), and smaller markets at Kremlin-Bicetre (Tue and Thur mornings) and Beauveau-Aligré (daily except Mon). Note that another turn-of-the-century profession is also alive and thriving at the markets, where crowds and cramped spaces provide ideal working conditions for pickpockets and con artists.

No shopping guide to Paris would be complete without some mention of Tati (140 rue de Rennes, 75006). Rock-bottom prices provoke mild cases of temporary insanity amongst those rummaging through industrial-sized bins of discontinued clothes, fabrics and just about anything else you can imagine.

For the stout-hearted only.

Half-price tickets for theatre, dance, and concerts are available on the day of performance from the Kiosque-Theatre (Tue-Sat 12-8pm, Metro: Madeleine) and on the mezzanine of the Châtelet-Les Halles Metro station.

Paris is a magnet for people who take their food seriously, and as such is a great place to stock up on cutting-edge kitchenware. La Carpe (14, rue Tronchet, 75008) and Dehillerin (18-20, rue Coquillière, 75001) both provide an astounding assortment of copper pots, cookware, knives and baking accessories. Just down the street from La Carpe on the Place de la Madeleine are the twin temples of French foodaholics. Fauchon (26, place de la Madeleine) and Hediard (21, place de la Madeleine) occupy opposite corners at the north end of the square, and offer unimaginable delights for the discerning palate. Grocery shopping at either won't be cheap, but with so much care taken in preparation and presentation they are worth a visit if only to delight the eye with their artistic arrangements of exotic ingredients.

A classically French shopping experience can be had with a stroll along the left bank of the Seine in the Latin Quarter. *Les Bouquinistes* or booksellers on the Quai de Montebello operate from what look like small green trunks when closed up, but which open into whole worlds of literature and images. The bouquinistes are free to sell what they want and there is no real organisation to the stalls, but collectors of books, postcards, records and pictures will all have a field day sorting through the accumulated collections.

English books can be found at W.H.Smith (248 Rue de Rivoli, 75001) or at Brentanos (37, avenue de l'Opera), not far from the old Opera House. Shakespeare and Co. (37 rue de la Bûcherie 75005) is just a stone's throw from Nôtre Dame on the left bank, and has a huge if quirky and maddeningly arranged selection of new and used books. Be prepared to part with as much as 30-50 per cent more than you would pay in the country of origin. British newspapers can be found on the day of publication at mainline train stations, many newsagents, and in the kiosks that dot the Parisian streetscape.

EATING AND DRINKING

There is a wealth of cafés, bars and restaurants on offer in a city like Paris. Food is an art form in France, and even the most humble of establishments tends to pride itself on the quality of its menu. Not so the fast food outlets of which there are an increasing number scattered throughout the city. If speed and price are the only considerations, most neighbourhoods have a representative of the big international food chains or one of the home grown equivalents. This is the gastronomic equivalent of drinking a soft drink in the home of the world's best wines however, so look for an attractive restaurant instead. Menus are displayed on the outside of the restaurant near to the door so you can clearly see what kind of food you will be getting and at what price. For a longer stay it will pay to invest in one of the many food guides on offer in any of the above mentioned bookstores. Those with only a little time who are seeking an experience of traditional cuisine could try La Coupole (102 Blvd. du Montparnasse), Boeuf sur le Toit (34 rue du Colisée), or Vaudeville (29 rue Vivienne), all of which provide classic French fare at relatively reasonable prices in the centre of town.

TRANSPORT

Public transport is massively subsidised in Paris, and as a result is far cheaper, more convenient, and more comfortable than in London. In central Paris one is never more than about 500 metres from the nearest station, and as it has no traffic to compete with the metro is often the quickest way to any destination. The RER is a light regional railway which intersects with the Metro at strategic points and gives access to distant suburbs as well. For those who prefer to travel above ground the bus network is extensive and reliable with many routes providing stunning views of Parisian landmarks. A metro ticket gives access to all of central Paris on any of the above, but for best value buy tickets in a carnet of 10, or opt for a pass allowing unlimited travel by the day, week or month if you will be staying longer. Taxis are well regulated and relatively cheap.

SECURITY

As in any major city, it is best to avoid certain areas at certain times, but generally Paris is a safe city, and violent crime is rare. Burglaries are common however, and solid doors and locks are essential. Tourists tend to be the targets of street thieves who operate in crowded streets and in the Metro.

BORDEAUX

Most shopping is in and around the Rue Sainte Catherine, Cours de l'Intendance, Place Gambetta and Rue de la Porte Dijeaux.

Bordeaux wines are naturally a popular buy with visitors. There are specialist shops in town or you might prefer one of the bus trips to see the local vineyards organised by the local tourist office. But a decent supermarket might be just the place you are looking for, both for wine and other foods such as cheese. For the latter try also the Marché des Grands Hommes in the square of the same name.

EATING AND DRINKING
The quality of meals in restaurants and hotels at all prices is excellent. Prices are above UK prices, but so is the quality. There is generally good value for money in all but the most luxurious establishments. La Chanterelle in Rue Martignac is well-known and deservedly popular.

TRANSPORT
The bus service is acceptable and fairly cheap. Taxis can be telephoned for or found at a few ranks. Fares are very high.

LILLE

Shopping is concentrated in the Rue Nationale, the Place Général de Gaulle and the neighbouring streets, in Vieux Lille and in and around the Wazemmes Market. The Printemps department store is in the Rue Nationale and there are good quality clothing and other shops in the area. The market is especially lively on Sunday morning and is good for cheaper products of all sorts. Annually during the first weekend of September there is an enormous flea market in the centre of town known as the Braderie de Lille.

Local specialities readily available include chocolates, beer, biscuits, household textiles, furniture, works of art, cookware, kitchenware and glassware. Local arts and crafts such as prints and paintings, carvings, textiles, posters, silverware and all sorts of interior decorative ornaments are to be found in the Vieux Lille area off the Place Général de Gaulle.

La Furet du Nord in Place Général de Gaulle is reputedly Europe's largest bookshop and has a wide choice of British and other foreign newspapers including the *Financial Times* and the *Guardian*, which are printed in Roubaix. The Gare de

Flandres also has two newsagents with British and other foreign newspapers and magazines.

EATING AND DRINKING

Lille is full of restaurants and other places of refreshment, particularly so in Vieux Lille. Local specialities with a Flemish flavour include mussels and chips, *carbonnade de boeuf* (beef cooked in beer) and *potjevleesch* (chicken, rabbit and pork served cold in aspic). Try the Globe Brasserie on the corner of Boulevards Vauban and Liberté, La Tête de l'Art in Rue de l'Arc, La Boucherie in Square Morisson or Le Grizzly Grill in Rue Esquermoise. The more affluent should try L'Huitrière in Place Louise de Bettignies. It has a Michelin star and a business lunch costs Frs260. Although France is famous for the world's best wines, some of its beers from this region, known as bières de garde, are excellent and little known.

TRANSPORT

It is easy to walk from all central hotels to the main shopping areas. For those who need it, the public transport system in Lille is one of the best in France. There are regular local bus services. Two modern metro lines are in operation. Taxis are fairly expensive and not always easy to find, except at the Gare de Flandres.

SECURITY

Personal security is generally good, except for the usual pickpockets in public transport and crowded streets.

LYONS

Bellecour is the centre of fashionable Lyons and there is up-market shopping in the Rue du Président Edouard Herriot between Place Bellecour and Place de Terreaux. Also fashionable is the Rue St Jean across the Saône to the west in the Old Town. Across the Rhône to the east are the Part-Dieu shopping centre opposite the railway station and Les Halles, the wholesale meat and vegetable market. The Brocante Stalingrad in the suburbs is one of Europe's biggest antique hypermarkets.

Lyons has traditionally been a centre for silks and cloths and favourite souvenirs include silk scarves and ties and other high-quality items of clothing and lingerie. A wide range of food and drink is readily available in any supermarket and provides ever acceptable gifts.

The Eton English Bookshop is in Rue du Plat.

Eating and Drinking

Lyons claims to be the gastronomic capital of France and is home to several restaurants starred in Michelin, with Bocuse at the top of the class. Quality food is of course expensive, but you can dine out very well for less than half the cost. Try Léon de Lyons in Rue Pleney in the Old Town or La Tour Rose in Rue du Boeuf.

Transport

Bus and underground services are good. Taxis are not very plentiful and cannot always be hailed. It is often necessary to call for a radio-taxi from one of the many efficient firms in Lyons.

MARSEILLES

The main shopping area in the city centre lies to the east and south of the Old Port in three parallel streets running south from La Canebière – Rue de Rome, Rue St-Ferréol (pedestrianised) and Rue Paradis as well as in the side-streets linking them. The once elegant Canebière itself is now sadly run down.

For atmosphere there is a fish market on the Vieux Port every day and an interesting market off the Rue de Rome specialising in ethnic produce and other items. A much larger street market operates in the Avenue du Prado, the southward extension of the Rue de Rome.

Eating and Drinking

There are cafés and restaurants at all prices both in the centre and in the different quartiers. Some of those with the most moderate prices provide an excellent meal. Country restaurants on the whole present very good value. Marseilles is synonymous with bouillabaisse. Chez Michel in Rue des Catalans is good. But authentic bouillabaisse is expensive and cheaper versions are better avoided in favour of alternative fish specialities. Try the area around the Place Thiers.

Transport

Public transport is generally reliable, with a somewhat restricted but expanding metro system and a good bus network.

SECURITY
Some areas of town are best avoided at night but despite its reputation, Marseilles generally is no more dangerous than other large cities in France.

STRASBOURG

Strasbourg is regarded with envious eyes in many other parts of France, embodying as it does wealth and prosperity and an international atmosphere confirmed by the presence of several European institutions.

Most of the fashionable shops are on the central island of Strasbourg clustered around the Place Klèber. There are several department stores including Printemps, Magmod, C&A and Marks and Spencer. International designer shops are present in abundance and include all the big names such as Chanel, Laroche, Féraud and Lacoste as well as lots of smaller independent boutiques.

British newspapers and periodicals are normally on sale in the city centre, at the Place Klèber or Place Broglié or at the railway station, for example, by midday on the day of publication except Sunday. British books, mostly paperback and at least two and a half times the UK price, can also be purchased in certain bookshops in the city centre. There is a specialist English/American bookshop called The Bookworm at 48 Rue de Pâques, near the Halles.

EATING AND DRINKING
There is a good variety of bars, cafés and restaurants in and around Strasbourg with a heavy emphasis on Alsatian cuisine. Prices may vary from as little as Frs150 per head with wine to more than five times that in one of the more celebrated eating places. Alsatian white wines (which are particularly good value), beers and eaux de vie are of world class in quality and there is a wide variety in the hundreds of restaurants and other hostelries. There are also excellent patisseries and gourmet shops – notably for foie gras – as well as excellent supermarkets.

TRANSPORT
Public transport within the city consists of bus and tram service with a flat fare and free transfers. A reliable taxi service exists, but would-be passengers must either go to a rank or summon one by telephone (they can be booked in advance).

THE GAMBIA

BANJUL

Language **English**
Currency **dalassi (D) of 100 bututs. £1=16.26, Mar 1997. No black market**
Credit cards **accepted in main hotels, supermarkets and restaurants**
Shops **0930–1230, 1430–1900**
Bargaining **normal in markets and at street stalls; start from one-third of asked price**
Duty-free **at airport, but spirits, cigarettes and tobacco cheaper in town**
Tipping **small change to market and supermarket porters; 10–15 per cent in restaurants if no service charge**

The Gambia is largely self-sufficient in produce, but there is very little industry apart from groundnut, beer and soft drinks processing. Tourism is a major industry now and, apart from the Atlantic in Banjul itself, the tourist hotels as well as restaurants and shops are mainly in Fajara and Kololi. There are colourful markets and tourist stalls in Cape Point, Bakau, Koto and Serrekunda which sell locally made clothing, batiks and tie-dyed materials, musical instruments (drums, balaphones and coras), bags, sarongs, jewellery, woodcarvings, masks and sand pictures as well as imported East African artefacts such as woodcarvings, lapis lazuli, malachite, tiger's eye and soapstone. Try Kokotu in Kotu. Safari suits can be made up locally relatively cheaply and reasonably well. Best results are obtained when the tailor has a model garment to copy.

Banjul is a small city laid out on a grid pattern around a central open space renamed 22 July Square after the military coup of that date in 1994. A few of the roads are still not tarmacked, and there are few pavements to walk on. There is a large local market selling virtually everything, including tourist souvenirs. Next to the market are many material stores selling both local and imported cloth – most Gambians wear locally made outfits. There are very few European shops except in the tourist areas some kilometres outside Banjul.

On arrival it is worth exploring Banjul on foot to take in the atmosphere. Gambians are friendly and usually speak English. Life on the streets and in the market is busy and colourful. The African Heritage Centre in Wellington Street offers refreshments and some handicrafts to buy. Jobe's in Box Bar Road sells gold and silver jewellery. In addition there are many street traders selling their wares – anything from hot spicy sandwiches, to sunglasses and beach towels.

Supplies of books, magazines and Western music are minimal and British newspapers arrive only once a week and at a high price.

EATING AND DRINKING

There are numerous bars and restaurants, many of a good standard at reasonable prices. Seafood is plentiful and cheap. Local fish is delicious from white fish fillets (ladyfish, butterfish and sole) to barracuda steaks, prawns and lobsters. The local beef is also of good quality and cheap and is popular in a spicy stew called *benachin*. Chicken and fish can also be used in this dish as well as to make *domeda* (with groundnuts) or chicken *yassa* (marinated in onion and garlic). These Gambian dishes are available at most of the hotels and some of the restaurants. Other restaurants cater for a wide range of different cuisines. There is a good restaurant in Cape Point with a French flavour, a good Indian and several Chinese restaurants. Another popular place to eat, for local or international food, is the Leybato Beach Bar off Atlantic Road on the junction with Kairaba Avenue.

Groundnuts (peanuts) are the Gambia's main cash crop and export item and are fresh and cheap. They are sold by street vendors.

Most Gambians are Muslim and do not drink alcohol. However a good lager-style beer is brewed locally – Julbrew. Wine is reasonably priced. Some locals like to drink palm wine, which is very sweet and sticky, or sweet green tea. There are two soft-drinks factories and well-known brand names and the usual mixers are available. Spirits, cigarettes and tobacco can all be bought considerably more cheaply than in the UK (or indeed in airport duty-free shops), but choice is limited.

TRANSPORT

The public transport system cannot be recommended, though local taxis – usually showing signs of intensive use and limited maintenance and repair – can be used. "Tourist" taxis generally operate from and to the hotels. Establish the cost at the start of the journey.

SECURITY

Although the Gambia has the image of being a dangerous place, occurrences of muggings and robberies are few. The tourist (or *toubab*) will certainly be approached by a "bumster" who will wish to befriend you and show you around. Hotels have started to recognise some of them officially and tourists sometimes prefer to be protected from other nuisances whilst out shopping, etc. Beggars are friendly and do not pester.

GERMANY

Language **German**
Currency **deutschmark (DM) of 100 pfennigs £1=2.71, Mar 1997**
Banks **0900–1300 Mon to Fri, later two days a week**
Credit cards **accepted in larger shops and restaurants, and garages on Autobahn**
Cashpoints **accept international credit cards**
Shops **0830–1230/1300, 1400/1430–1830 Mon to Fri, many department stores till 2030 Thur; 0830–1400 Sat; late opening to 1600/1800 first Sat in month and all Sats in Dec**
Refunds **with receipt, vouchers not cash; not on sale items**
Sales **Jan and Jul; genuine bargains, especially out-of-season sportswear**
Duty-free **at airports**
Tipping **10–15 per cent service charge in hotels and restaurants, but round up bill to next DM5 or 10 10 per cent for services, including porters and hairdressers**
Export restrictions **artefacts over 100 years old need certificate to avoid VAT**

German shopping hours are limited by strict laws. The only exceptions are shops at a railway station, an airport or attached to a petrol station. English is widely spoken in city centre shops.

Prices can be much higher than in the UK, but clothes, for example, can be good value as quality and style are often excellent. Finding small sizes can be a problem, but there are plenty of size 12 and above.

There are many typically German things worth bringing back. At Christmas there are Bethmännchen (small marzipan sweets) or anything from the Christmas markets. Typical German items include Bavarian jackets, wooden nutcrackers or wooden toys, Lebkuchen, porcelain, regional wines or – for the discerning cook – Henckels knives and Kaiser bakeware. Germany stationery and artists' materials, available from all the specialist shops, are expensive but good. Birkenstock sandals are justly world famous for quality and design.

More than 6,000 varieties of beer are offered in Germany, all brewed with malt, hops and water. The fifteenth-century purity law is strictly observed. There is a huge variety of cheap, high quality German wines available. Alcohol and tobacco are less expensive in the German shops than in the UK.

BERLIN

With reunification and its capital status in the new Germany, Berlin is enjoying both a building and a tourist boom.

Berlin is famous not least for its delicate KPM porcelain, which makes an obvious and excellent gift or souvenir for the traveller. There is a shop next to the factory in Charlottenburg and one on the Kurfürstendamm. Every item is handmade and hand-painted so it is not cheap although white, unpainted pieces compare in price to bone china in the UK. Flower shops deserve a special mention for the excellent variety and display on offer. Berliners are reputed to be the biggest spenders on flowers in a country where average expenditure is already high. Shop assistants are always expert in arranging and wrapping the flowers which you have selected, all at no extra charge. Similar service is even found at street stalls.

The main shopping street remains the ever-fashionable Kurfürstendamm which, with its neighbouring side-streets, offers a wide range of quality shops not all too outrageous in price. The Europa Center at the bottom end of the Kurfürstendamm near the church has something like one hundred rather expensive shops. It is easily recognisable even from afar by the revolving Mercedes star on the top of the block. The Ku' damm Carée over the road is another indoor shopping precinct and there is a pedestrianised shopping precinct near by in the Wilmersdorfer Strasse, also good for shopping. The eastern part of the city is changing rapidly: Unter den Linden and the surrounding area is undergoing a substantial overhaul with a range of new shops and restaurants, the new, revived Friedrichstrasse has a branch of Galeries Lafayette as well as a Planet Hollywood restaurant.

Clothes and other shopping is easily done in large centrally located stores such as Peek and Cloppenburg, KaDeWe, Wertheim, Karstadt, Hertie, C&A, Leineweber and Kaufhof. The food floor at the traditional KaDeWe is mind-blowing in the selection which it offers both for food on the spot and to take away – a must for every visitor.

Street markets are very popular, both with locals and visitors, although real bargains are increasingly hard to find. But you might be lucky at one of the *Flohmarkts* (flea markets) in finding a nice piece of old KPM, Jugendstil (art nouveau) or Art Deco. The main *Flohmarkt* takes place every Saturday and Sunday from 0800 to 1530 on the Strasse des 17 Juni, which leads to the Brandenburg Gate. Next to it, a little further along the street, is a crafts market. Those looking for a little bit of ethnic atmosphere might be tempted further afield to the market in the heart of Kreuzberg/Neuköln.

British daily newspapers normally arrive in Berlin on the day of publication. Most German bookstores have a small English section, but the prices are high, often double or triple the UK price. The British Bookshop is at Mauerstrasse 83 – 84, not far from Checkpoint Charlie.

Eating and Drinking

There are restaurants and cafés to suit all tastes. Most reasonable places will provide good basic traditional food at a fair price in comparison with the UK. A simple three-course meal with wine or beer will cost about DM50, dinner at a place with pretensions at least double that. Sunday brunch is popular with Berliners, often with a jazz accompaniment. Traditional-style cafés include the fashionable and famous Kranzler on the corner of the Ku'damm, Café Einstein in the Kurfürstenstrasse (and now also on Unter den Linden) or Café Moehring in the Uhlandstrasse. Pubs include the Zille Stube on Alexanderplatz, Zur Letzten Instanz in the nearby Waissenstrasse or Leydicke in Mainsteinstrasse. The local brew is either Schultheiss or Berliner Kind'l, perhaps with a persiko chaser for the stout-hearted.

Transport

Berlin has a good public transport system with buses, U-bahn (underground), S-bahn (underground and surface railway) plus trams in eastern Berlin. With the exception of "short runs" (three or four stops) when a cheap rate applies, fares are uniform whatever the distance travelled and interchange is possible between different routes and modes of transport within a two-hour period. A single ticket costs DM3.20 and should be validated at the start of the journey. A multiple ticket costs DM11 and gives four journeys. Daily or weekly travelcards are also available. Taxis, which are readily available in most areas, are less expensive than in London.

BONN

Bonn is well known not just as a capital city, but also as an overgrown village, near the home of the first Federal Chancellor Konrad Adenauer and therefore a good place to have the federal capital. Shopping is concentrated in the pedestrian precinct in the centre of the old town, where the visitor will also find Beethoven's birthplace. Everything is there for a pleasant few hours of shopping and eating. The diplomatic quarter in Bad Godesberg, at the other end of the tram line from Bonn's centre is equally compact and comfortable. Shopping in both is good, catering for most needs. Linz, Königswinter and Siegburg which are near by on the other side of the Rhine are also nice centres to walk around (all are pedestrianised), to browse and get the atmosphere. Prices are higher than in the UK.

There is an open-air market at the end of Moltke-Strasse in Bad Godesberg on Tuesday, Thursday and Saturday morning. The Bonn market is open daily on the Marktplatz. There is a large Hertie department store in Bad Godesberg and Hertie, Kaufhof and Kaufhalle stores in Bonn stocking a vast range of food and other goods. There are C&A, Benetton and Body Shop in Bonn. Woolworth is in both Bonn and Godesberg: they sell fairly decent stuff at reasonable prices.

The Birkenstock sandal factory is just across the river in Bad Honnef and they often have sales. Lots of local villages have good pottery, but especially Adendorf (eight potteries on the main road!) betweeen Bad Godesberg and Meckenheim. Children's wooden toys are obtainable from Dora Do at Am Michaelshof 8 in Bad Godesberg or Puppenkönig at Gangolfstrasse 8 in Bonn.

British newspapers, usually delivered on the day of publication, can be bought locally, but are very expensive. Some shops in Bonn stock English books, mainly paperbacks, but at a considerable mark-up. British daily and Sunday newspapers can be bought at Bad Godesberg and Bonn railway stations on the day of publication.

EATING AND DRINKING

Good German wine can be bought at competitive prices and a trip down the Mosel is a must. Try Zum Schwarzen Ritter at Brodenbach or any of the many specialised wine houses. There is a wine festival just about every weekend somewhere in the area from the end of August until the beginning of October. German beer is also excellent, especially the draught from one of the hundreds of local breweries. Bitburger originates not far from Bonn.

Lunch at a reasonable restaurant costs at least DM30 and a dinner from DM40 upwards, exclusive of wines and/or coffee.

In Bonn recommendations include Bayrische Botschaft, in Brudergasse just off the Marktplatz, Zur Lese at Adanauerallee 37 which has nice Rhine views, Le Marron in the Provinzialstrasse with a Michelin star and Pierre et Patrice in Graurheindorferstrasse for French food and German portions. In Bad Godesberg Weinhaus Maternus in Löberstrasse has a Viennese atmosphere, Hotel Cäcilienhöhe has a wonderful view over the Rhine, Das Ännchen on the Ännchenplatz is an old German student hostelry, Wirtshaus St Michael in the Brunnenallee is used by the German Foreign Office for official entertaining and Halbedel's Gasthaus at Rheinallee 47 boasts a Michelin star. Outside town for real German atmosphere try the Sankt Peter at Walporzheim or the Hotel Lochmühle at Mayschoss. The Park Café at Am Kurpark in central Bad Godesberg is typical of a good German konditorei where good coffee and cakes go together.

TRANSPORT

Public transport is good. Tickets for buses and trams are the same. Always have change ready for the ticket machines and stamp your ticket when starting your journey.

Taxis can be found at the main railway stations and other taxi ranks, or can be called by phone.

COLOGNE

This rich and historic city, squeezed between thrusting Dusseldorf and the old federal capital, sprawls impossibly, but its heart is compact and pleasing. The main shopping area running from the beautiful and impressive old cathedral is all pedestrianised and easy to follow. The Old Town is just down the hill towards the Rhine.

EATING AND DRINKING

For wining and dining, and enjoying the local draught beer known as Kölsch, the *Altstadt* (Old Town) is the place. At the top of the market with prices to match is Weinhaus im Walfisch at Salzgasse 13 and Das Kleine Stapelhäuschen at Fischmarkt 1 – 3 is also excellent, but there are plenty of satisfying places more down-market.

TRANSPORT

The transport network of bus, tram and U-Bahn (underground) is excellent and day tickets are available, but in the small city centre the visitor may well not need to make use of any of these.

DÜSSELDORF

Düsseldorf is rich, cosmopolitan and the centre of fashion in Germany. The main shopping areas, Schadowstrasse and Schadow Arkaden, Königsallee and the Altstadt, are all situated centrally only a few minutes' walk from Heinrich-Heine-Allee underground station (U-Bahn). Just one stop away at Nordstrasse there is a further comprehensive range of shops.

Schadowstrasse and Schadow Arkaden offer a typical range of European shops including large department stores such as Kaufhof and Karstadt, a good C&A, Esprit, Habitat, shoe shops galore, a large World of Music, classy confectionery such as Otto Bittner and clothing stores including Leffers or Boecker for women and Peek und Cloppenburg for everyone.

One has only to walk down the Königsallee in the centre of the city to see the top fashions, leatherware and jewellery at enormously high prices. Designer outlets like St Laurent, Dior, Cartier and Chanel, exotic fur fabricators and jewellers jostle with attractive street cafés and pavement artists to offer entertainment and glitzy diversion.

The *Altstadt* or Old Town is a pedestrian area, cobbled and quaint, which offers a wide range of smaller shops such as bakers and innumerable cafes, bars, restaurants and pubs. The open-air market is on the Karl-Platz.

The winter visitor should visit one of the many Advent markets in the centre of town and admire the typical German carved wooden Christmas decorations and perhaps try a glass of mulled wine and a *Reibeküchen* (potato cake).

There are no particular musts to bring back with you.

Perhaps a few chocolates from Bittner, candles and Christmas decorations, wood or glass. If money and conservation are no object, perhaps an exotically styled fur garment from the Königsallee.

British newspapers are available on the day of publication at many kiosks.

Eating and Drinking

Local specialities best consumed while you are there include beer. Numerous local independent breweries offer the typical "Alt" beer – a dark beer served in small, straight-sided glasses. The breweries are old, well established, traditional houses which offer basic food and typical atmosphere – try a *Schweinshaxe mit Sauerkraut* (knuckle of pork with sour pickled cabbage). The breweries are noisy, smoky and jolly places: at least one visit to the *Altstadt* is a must. Apart from the breweries, there are many good restaurants in all price brackets. Worth trying is a typical dessert *Rote Grütze* with vanilla sauce. This is a delicious mixture of red berry fruits.

Transport

Public transport is excellent, punctual and regular. A variety of tickets is available, valid for bus, tram and local train. Validate the ticket when starting your journey. Taxis are plentiful and are metered.

Frankfurt

Frankfurt's major shopping areas are located off the Hauptwache. The Zeil, which runs from the Hauptwache to the Konstablerwache, is lined with all the major department stores: Peek und Cloppenburg, Hertie, Kaufhof, C&A. Adjacent to the Zeil are other shopping areas and pedestrian zones such as Schillerstrasse, Grosse Eschenheimerstrasse, Biebergasse, Steinweg, Rathenauplatz and Goëtheplatz. Schillerstrasse and Goëthestrasse have the more exclusive shops and designer boutiques. Goëthestrasse is one of the most elegant shopping streets in town. The Grosse Bockenheimerstrasse also has some expensive boutiques, but it is famous in particular as Gourmet Alley or the Fressgasse because of its delicatessens, gourmet speciality shops and restaurants.

Out of town there are three large shopping malls that offer nothing you cannot find in the city centre apart from much easier parking. These are the Main-Taunus-Zentrum, the

Nordwestzentrum and the Hessen-Centre.

Hertie and Kaufhof stock most of the items which you would find in a department store in the UK. Large clothing and shoe shops are to be found on the Zeil including H&M and Benneton. Designer shops in Goethestrasse include Guy Laroche, Mondi, Krizia, Jil Sander, Hermès and Luis Vuitton. There is also a Laura Ashley. Yves St Laurent is near by in the Kaiserhofstrasse. Pflöger Delikatessen is in the Fressgasse and is ideal for buying typical German food and drink. The Kleinmarkthalle in Hasengasse is a modern covered market offering a large selection of exotic foodstuffs and is worth a visit even if you do not intend to buy. If you are in Frankfurt just before Christmas, a visit to the Römerberg Christmas Market is a must. Apart from the funfair there are many stalls selling Christmas decorations, toys, hot food and drink.

There is a wide choice of typical gifts and souvenirs to bring back. An *Ebbelwoi-Bembel* is an earthenware jug for apple wine. Frankfurter sausages taste nothing like the pale imitations sold in the UK. Homburg hats come from nearby Bad Homburg. There are Struwwelpeter and Goethe memorabilia.

The British Bookshop in Börsenstrasse offers a good selection of British books and publications although prices are considerably higher than in the UK. The main British newspapers can be bought at any major news stand: some are even printed in Frankfurt. Expect to pay between DM4 and DM5.

EATING AND DRINKING

A trip to one of the many pubs in Sachsenhausen (on the other side of the River Main) is worthwhile, not least to drink the famous *Apfelwein* (*Ebbelwoi*) and for a taste of German cooking. Typical local dishes include *Grüne Sosse* (green sauce), *Rippchen mit Kraut* (pork rib with sauerkraut) and *Handkäs mit Musik* (curd cheese and onions on bread – the music comes later!)

There is a wide variety of restaurants, pubs and hotels to suit all tastes and pockets. To sample typical German cooking you might try the Maingaustuben in Schifferstrasse, Wielandstubb in Wielandstrasse or Schlund in the Eschersheimer Landstrasse – or any of the many cafés in the Fressgasse. The Hauptwache café is a pleasant place from which to watch the world go by while drinking coffee and eating rich German cakes after a morning's shopping.

TRANSPORT

The city centre is so small that the visitor is unlikely to need much in the way of public transport, but there is a good comprehensive network of buses, trams and underground and suburban trains. It is not particularly recommended to use the underground at night alone. Taxis are plentiful, but cannot be flagged down: you must telephone or go to a taxi stand. It is normal to round the fare up to the nearest mark and perhaps add a couple of marks.

HAMBURG

Hamburg, the Venice of the North, is a shopper's paradise. It boasts a wide range of British shops including Crabtree and Evelyn, Daks, Burberry, Mulberry and even a Harrods at the airport. Alsterhaus in Jungfernssteig has a wide range of British merchandise, particularly in its food hall. The citizens of Hamburg are for the most part very fashion-conscious people. Clothing is a little more expensive than in London.

The main shopping streets in the city centre are concentrated in the area of Jungfernstieg, the pedestrianised Spitalerstrasse and Mönckebergstrasse. The latter contains some of the traditional German department stores such as Kaufhof, but also many smaller shops. Some other department stores to be found are Brinkmanns, Alsterhaus, Karstadt, Hertie and C&A. The nearby Jungfernstieg has two shopping malls, Hamburger Hof and at the far end the Gänsemarkt Passage. One of several other malls is the Hansaviertel Galerie Passage in Neuer Wall which connects with Gänsemarkt Passage. At the end of Neuer Wall is the up-market Bleichenhof Passage. There is a market every Thursday morning in Poeseldorf and on Tuesday and Friday in Isestrasse. Eppendorf is an extremely prosperous and up-market district with shopping to match. It has expensive boutiques and antique shops as well as trendy craft places. Karstadt in Eppendorf has a high quality food hall for your consumable gifts and souvenirs.

British newspapers can be bought at most of the larger newsagents in Hamburg and are normally available on the day of publication. Several of the major bookshops in the city such as Frensche in Spitalerstrasse and Colon in Collonaden have many English books, which are, however, much more expensive than in the UK. Second-hand books are available from the English Bookshop at Stresemannstrasse 169.

EATING AND DRINKING

Hamburg has a vast range of eating places ranging from the very rough to the luxurious, both in atmosphere and price. Fish and seafood are specialities. The Alt Helgoländer Fischerstube is at Fischmarkt 4, right on the fish market which is in full swing early on Sunday mornings. Try the extremely up-market Cölln's Austernstuben for its oysters. For typical German cooking try Kanzelmeyer at Englische Planke 8, opposite the Michelskirche, Peter Lembcke at Holzdamm 49, Zum Alten Rathaus at Börsenbrücke 10 or the Ratsweinkeller beneath the Rathaus.

TRANSPORT

In central Hamburg it is best to use public transport. This includes bus, water bus and suburban and underground trains which are for the most part clean and punctual.

Fares are reasonable and tickets are transferable between most forms of city transport apart from the Alster boats. Taxis are plentiful, but relatively expensive.

SECURITY

Areas such as St Georg and parts of the harbour area are best avoided late at night. The famous Reeperbahn is sleazy, but comparatively safe.

MUNICH

Munich is an expensive city, but it has a wonderful atmosphere which makes strolling and window shopping particularly attractive. Be sure to explore the sidestreets as well as the main pedestrian thoroughfares. The main shopping area is centred around the historic Marienplatz and the pedestrian streets which surround it. You will find all the main department stores along Kaufingerstrasse and Neuhauserstrasse. Residenzstrasse and Weinstrasse are more up-market. There are also interesting shops on Sendlingerstrasse and Dienerstrasse and the open-air food market, the Viktualienmarkt, is within easy walking distance of the Marienplatz. Schwabing, the university area, is worth visiting for books, antiques and interesting small shops. Take the U-Bahn to Münchener Freiheit or Giselastrasse. There are two huge sports shops, Sport Schuster and Sport Scheck, which are respectively just off Marienplatz and on Sendlingerstrasse. Dalmayers, a food shop to rival Fortnum and Mason, is on Dienerstrasse.

For tourists, just about everything you can think of is packaged in the blue and white of Bavaria. There are many presents worth consideration. Coats and jackets made from *Loden*, the fine and warm wool in traditional green or in other colours, are available at all department stores and in specialist *Tracht* shops. Traditional *Lederhosen* – leather shorts with braces – or the *Dirndl* – brightly coloured, often floral printed dresses with lacy aprons, petticoats and blouses – are available for all sizes, but make particularly attractive gifts for children. Prices can be high, as this traditional clothing is often bought to last. There are all types of glass, beer mugs with pewter lids, new or antique, sometimes decorated or engraved, robust wine glasses or schnapps sets and *Hinterglasmalerei*, decorative pieces of glass made to hang so that the light shines through them. Beer mugs are also available in ceramic ware: the blue/grey salt glaze is particularly well known, but pottery plates, bowls and jugs in rustic style are also very attractive. Bavaria is famous for woodcarvings ranging from delicate and intricate figures for the Christmas crib to cuckoo clocks and furniture decorated with *Bauernmalerei*, hand painting on wood. Germans love candles which can be bought in all shapes, sizes and colours sometimes perfumed and intricately carved. *Gewürz Straussen* are small posies of spices used as decoration or to scent the room. Tapes and CDs of traditional music as well as consumables such as bottles of Franken wine in the traditional lozenge-shaped bottle called a *Bocksbeutel*, different kinds of schnapps or *Lebkuchen*, traditional biscuits made with spices and honey, are all take-home gifts with a flavour of Bavaria.

EATING AND DRINKING

Bavaria is most famous for its beer and there are six major breweries in Munich that sponsor the annual *Oktoberfest* beer festival, as well as many smaller concerns. *Brezen*, figure-of-eight rolls covered in salt crystals, go well with beer and sharpen the thirst. Of all the sausages available the *Weisswurst* is most typical of Bavaria. *Leberkäse* is a kind of hot meat loaf. A *Hax'l* is a pork knuckle covered in crackling, generally cooked on the spit. Try these and other specialities perhaps at the Spatenhaus on Max Joseph Platz opposite the National Theatre or the Nuremberger Wurstglock'l on Frauenplatz behind the Frauenkirche where the famous sausages are cooked on an open fire. Andechs am Dom is always busy and sells the famous beer from Kloster Andechs. The Rathauskeller (under the Rathaus on Marienplatz) offers typical local food. The Haxnbauer on Sparkassenstrasse specialises in *Hax'l*. In ▪mer beer gardens offer attractive outdoor restaurants. In ▪ the Hofbrauhaus courtyard or the beer gardens in the Englischer Garten. A little further out is the largest beer garden in town, the Hirschgarten just south of Nymphenburg Palace.

TRANSPORT

There is a good transport network of underground, trams and buses covering the city and suburbs. Either buy a day ticket which gives access to all forms of transport or buy a *Streifenkarte* which offers 10 strips which have to be punched at the start of your journey, the number varying with the length of journey. Taxis are metered.

SECURITY

Munich is still a very safe and hassle-free city.

GHANA

ACCRA

Language **English**
Currency **cedi. £1=2950, Mar 1997**
  No exchange black market
Traveller's cheques **accepted with reluctance; take cash sterling or dollars**
Credit cards **accepted in leading hotels and some shops, usually with surcharge**
Shops **hours variable**
Bargaining **expected in markets and at street stalls**
Duty-free **at airport, limited stock**
Tipping **yes, "dash" for all favours and services**

Shopping in Ghana can be an interesting voyage of discovery if you have time to spend going through all the shops and kiosks which form the main type of retail outlet. It is amazing what is available, but if you want one-stop shopping you will be out of luck.

Ghanaians are very friendly and hospitable and pleased to welcome visitors to their country. Tipping, or "dash", is a way of life and used for the smallest of favours. At the vegetable stall the seller will dash you an avocado once you have completed your purchases. The centre of Accra buzzes with humanity. The sprawling main Makola Market in Derby

Avenue has a big material section including locally made screen-prints or tie-dyes, as well as local foodstuffs and other goods. It is worth a visit for interest's sake, but be sure to take a cold drink with you. The UTC store is close by in Commercial Street and could, with some stretch of the imagination, be described as the John Lewis of Accra. Other stores include Kingsway in Kwame Nkrumah Avenue, as well as Adabraka, and Multistores in High Street. Tema Market has fish from the sea and plenty of bargaining. All the leading hotels have small boutiques which stock Ghanaian handicrafts as well as other goods, but they are very expensive.

For local arts and crafts a visit to the Cultural Centre at the end of High Street is a must. Here you will find all kinds of woodcarvings, brass gold-weights and a host of other traditional crafts. The renowned Kente cloth can be found here made up in a variety of clothes, bags and bow ties or sold in lengths. The craft market near by is the ideal place to do your souvenir shopping. The traders like to bargain and it is expected. Roughly half the asking price is right – ask for the best price and come down from there. Best buys are cloth tote bags, Kente bow ties or waistcoats, small wooden carvings, beads (some of which are already made up as necklaces) and the little brass gold-weights and figures. There are many roadside sellers of baskets, woodwork, etc. especially on the airport road.

Ghana was not called the Gold Coast for nothing, and locally made gold jewellery is readily available. Probably the best person to visit is George Hakim in Cantonments Road, on the left as you come south from Danguah Circle. Prices are quoted in US dollars. Payment can be made in sterling or cedis, but not credit cards. Tropical Jewellery, Anabelle Jewellery and Amanda Jewellery are all in Kojo Thompson Road.

The Diamond Marketing Corporation on the fourth floor of Diamond House has Ghana diamonds, gold and silver.

The major hotels stock British newspapers. The Shangri-La has Sunday newspapers on Monday afternoons. The Omari Bookshop, just off the Ring Road in Osu, holds a good stock of English paperbacks as well as books about Ghana. A new bookshop with a large selection of books printed in Europe has opened in Labonne.

EATING AND DRINKING

There is a wide variety of restaurants catering for all tastes. Chez Marie Lou in Cantonments Road has a French style cuisine. Just ʾere is the Dynasty, and the Regal is signposted from the d; both are Chinese restaurants. Also just off the

Cantonments Road is the Haveli, with good Indian food. There are two good restaurants near the airport – La Chaumière is on Liberation Road, near Aviation Road and Bella Napoli is off Volta Street on the corner of Akosombo Road. The main hotels all have restaurants, but be wary of the prices at the Labadi Beach. Most restaurants also serve local dishes such as peanut soup, fish, kebabs, etc. A good meal might cost as little as the equivalent of £15 per head, including beer. Wine is very expensive. Local beer made by Accra Brewery (Club) or Achimota Brewery (ABC) is delicious. Bubra is a draught beer, but beware the alcohol content which can range from 5 to 15 per cent. Locally bottled colas, lemonades, tonics and Schweppes soft drinks are readily available. The local market has an extremely limited selection of cigarettes, all of which are strong, high-tar tobacco.

TRANSPORT

The local *trotros* (minibuses) are not recommended for tourist travel, but there are plenty of taxis, distinguished by their orange front and rear wings, and they are cheap. Agree the price before you get in. From the Labadi Beach Hotel to the Craft Market for example, a distance of about 5 kms, should cost no more than 2,500 cedis, with 200 cedis dash for the driver. All the leading hotels are away from the shopping areas, so travel by taxi will be a must. Some hotels have their own transport and will take guests wherever they wish to go.

SECURITY

Accra enjoys the reputation of being one of the safest capital cities in the world, although obviously undue risks should not be taken.

GIBRALTAR

Language **English, Spanish**
Currency **Gibraltar pound of 100 pence, at par with pound sterling, which is legal tender; Spanish currency also acceptable**
Banks **UK cheques accepted with guarantee card**
Credit cards **all major cards**
Cashpoints **NatWest and Barclays, linked to UK network**
Import/export restrictions **small amount of duty payable on non-foodstuff imports from Spain**

Almost everything is imported, so prices tend to be higher than in the UK. Hi-fi and camera shops are numerous with a wide range of goods, but prices are not cheap and after-sales service is unlikely.

The hub of Gibraltar is Main Street. There are some smart (and expensive) boutiques and various branches of chain stores such as Marks and Spencer, Benetton, the Body Shop, Dorothy Perkins, British Home Stores and Mothercare. Safeway have a very large store, at which cash is available with Switch cards.

A wide range of English books is readily available in bookstores, although at prices slightly higher than in the UK. Try the Gibraltar Bookshop at 300 Main Street. Most British newspapers are flown in daily and are available from mid-afternoon on the day of issue.

EATING AND DRINKING

Eating out costs about the same as in the UK, i.e. a little more than in Spain. There is a wide range of restaurants in Gibraltar of varying standard, some of which are very good. A good meal can be obtained at the Rock Hotel and Whites as well as at the Casino. There are many British-style pubs in Gibraltar, most of which provide food. Fish is a speciality of the area. Most alcoholic beverages and tobacco are much cheaper than in the UK.

TRANSPORT

Buses tend to run half-hourly. Prices are modest. Taxis are readily available, but fairly expensive.

GREECE

ATHENS

Language Greek
Currency drachma (dr) of 100 lepta
 £1=427, Mar 1997
Banks 0800–1400 Mon to Thur, 0800–1300 Fri
Traveller's cheques yes, also Eurocheques
Credit cards accepted in larger shops and tourist
 areas
Cashpoints common in Athens with Visa
 and Access Mastercard
Shops 1000–1400/1430 Mon to Fri, also 1730–2030
 Tue, Thur and Fri, 0100–1600 Sat; tourist shops
 in Plaka open all day and Sun
Refunds rare, but exchanges possible. VAT refunds
 for non-EU nationals possible, but with difficulty
Sales genuine
Bargaining discounts sometimes possible
Duty-free at airport
Tipping 10 per cent normal in restaurants; leave a
 little extra in tavernas for waiters and pot-boys
Export restrictions antiques only from recognised
 antique shops, with receipt

Shopping in Athens can be a delight for those with plenty of
time and money. Much of central Athens is a prime shopping
area and it is claimed that there are more shops there per head
of population than in any other European country. Sometimes
it seems that the rate of mark-up is equally spectacular.

The areas around Omonia Square, Monostiraki and
Kolonaki are particularly full of shops. Some tend to cluster
together in groups of the same type. There are wonderful
materials in the area between Ermou Street and Omonia
Square. Boutiques abound from Omonia to Kolonaki, with
some cheaper ones in Ermou Street. The area around
Monostiraki metro station has touristy T-shirts, beautiful
gold, original leather jackets, handmade jumpers and copies
of museum exhibits. At the Monostiraki end of Pandrossou
Street are handmade sandals. If you want to sample the real
Greece then try the Central Market on Athinas Street. One
side of the street is a fruit and vegetable market, in a building
on the other side is the meat, fish and cheese market.

Some boutiques advertise exclusive designs which, though expensive, certainly will not be found in the local chain store. There are branches of shops such as Marks and Spencer, British Home Stores, Body Shop, Mothercare, Benetton, Natalies and Stefanel, with prices at least a third higher than in the country of origin.

Best buys include handmade women's leather sandals (if you get them from the poet sandal maker in Pandrossou, he will give you a poem as well). Imitation expensive perfumes in ceramic bottles are good presents for teenage daughters and mothers. Hand-embroidered table linen is expensive but beautiful. The famous Flokati rugs are made near Delphi, but are available everywhere. If you are making the trip to Delphi, the village just before you get to the shrine, called Arahova, is where they actually come from (you can bargain for them). Every conceivable item made from leather is available.

The Greek Centre on the first floor at Pandrossou 56/Metropoleus 59 is an excellent gallery with a restful cafe as well. The National Welfare Organisation of Greece has shops at 24a Voukourestiou Street, 135 Vassilissis Sophias Avenue and at the Athens Hilton selling rugs and tapestries, embroideries and other handwork items. If you have room for an urn, Pottery From All Over Greece on Kifissia Avenue in the northern suburb of Maroussi has a very wide selection at reasonable prices. Museums sell copies of their exhibits and some rather nice art books, in English and Greek. English-language newspapers and paperbacks are available at the major hotels and elsewhere, but are costly (apart from the local daily, the *Athens News*).

EATING AND DRINKING

Greece produces a wide range of wines, not just retsina; some are excellent. Small local restaurants (*tavernas*) are common and give good value for money. There are also innumerable better-class restaurants in and around Athens. Gastra at Dimaki 1 has lots of atmosphere, is inexpensive and usually full. Gerofinikas at Pindarou 10 is popular with tourists and locals alike, but not cheap. O Piratis at Tatoiou, Erithrea is an excellent fish *taverna*, also not cheap. Remember that Greece is famous for feta cheese, Kalamata olives (among the best in the world) and baklava.

TRANSPORT

There is an extensive bus and trolley-bus service in Athens, but it is normally crowded during working hours and slow-moving. It is, however, cheap. The metro links Kifissia with the port of Piraeus. Two new lines are under construction. Taxis are yellow and fairly cheap, although you may have to share.

SECURITY
There should not be too many personal security problems or hassle, provided routine measures are taken against pickpockets, etc.

GRENADA

ST GEORGE'S

Language **English**
Currency **East Caribbean dollar (EC$) £1=4.2, Mar 1997**

Grenada is famous for its spices such as nutmeg. Conch and other seafood is good and recommended, as are the local rum and rum punches.

The usual range of tourist souvenirs is available including batiks and T-shirts, woodcarvings and wovenware such as baskets.

Duty-free shopping is available at the harbour for those visitors who can afford it.

GUADELOUPE

GRAND-TERRE: POINTE-À-PITRE

Language **French**
Currency **French franc**

The French influence is reflected in excellent food and wildly expensive imported fashions, but there are markets in the compact centre of Pointe-à-Pitre where local fashions, including cotton hats, and handicrafts are available. There is a market in Basse-Terre on Saturday. The local rum can be wonderful.

GUATEMALA

GUATEMALA CITY

Language Spanish
Currency quetzal (Q) of 100 cantavos.
  £1=9.65, Mar 1997
Traveller's cheques US dollar denominated; take cash
  dollars
Credit cards Visa accepted in most shops, hotels
  and restaurants; American Express not popular
Cashpoints yes
Shops 0900–2000 all week;small shops close
  1200–1500. Closed at Easter. Markets open till
  1700. Exchange possible in larger shops
Bargaining in markets; fixed prices in shops, but
  discounts for cash possible
Duty-free at airport, well-stocked; competitive prices
Tipping 10 per cent to waiters and porters and for
  other services

The overall cost of living compares with that of the UK,
although imported consumer goods are expensive.

Guatemala City sprawls and it can be difficult to find one's
way around.The Plaza Mayor lies at the heart of the first district
(Zona 1) and forms the traditional centre. Shopping is concentrated around 8a Calle and 8a Avenue. The Central Market
lies just to the east behind the cathedral. Zone 9 and particularly Zone 10 are known as La Zona Viva, containing most of
the international hotels as well as small shops and boutiques.

There are several shopping centres around town. In La
Zona Viva for example are Gran Centro Los Proceres (opposite the Hotel Camino Real), Geminis and Montufar. There
are plenty of designer shops in the centres, but goods are
expensive compared with Europe and the US.

Here you can buy handicrafts (*tipicas*), many of which
show the influence of the country's old Maya tradition.
Traditional clothing, for example, is often elaborately embroidered. Naive paintings and ceremonial masks are also popular
for gifts and souvenirs. Other items worth considering include
woodcarvings, leather, metalwork and textiles.

The Ixchel Museum in Zone 10 has a shop with expensive
but good quality arts and crafts. There is also a small Mercado
de Artesania near the airport. Among the hotels, the Camino

Real has some nice shops.

Coffee is available in supermarkets and, gift-wrapped, at the airport.

Antigua, 38 kms from Guatamala City, is a good place for shopping – small, compact and relatively safe. On the Avenida Norte for example is a bookshop with good coffee, a patisserie, an excellent textiles shop and a market for *tipicas*. There is also a massive market for *tipicas* on Thursday and Sunday in Chichicastenango.

Flowers are on sale everywhere at low prices. Florales Orquideas at 14 Calle 8 –13 in Zona 10 is more up-market and specialises in orchids.

Some of the big hotels such as the El Dorado sell British magazines for around £5 a time, as do shops in some of the centres, such as the La Pradera centre in Zone 15. But British books are hard to come by and newspapers almost impossible. A couple of local English freesheets are available in the hotels.

EATING AND DRINKING

Meals at good restaurants are extremely reasonably priced. Such local cusine as there is tends to be Mexican in style. Local beer and rum are good. Spirits and cigarettes from almost any supermarket are cheap compared with UK prices. A packet of Marlboro will cost about 80 pence and a bottle of VAT 69 about £5.

TRANSPORT

There are regular bus services in the capital at a standard fare, which is cheap. The buses themselves vary from new and sound to ancient and unsafe. Use them at your own risk; armed hold-ups are not unknown. Taxis vary from mediocre to poor. There are taxi ranks at all the large hotels, but they are not seen cruising. Taxi fares are expensive and should be negotiated in advance: a journey of about 3 kms should cost Q40.

SECURITY

Basic personal security precautions should be taken, particularly in Zone 1. Try to avoid looking like a tourist or otherwise attracting attention to yourself. Stick to the main streets. Beggars may be troublesome, but are satisfied with very little.

GUYANA

GEORGETOWN

Language **English**
Currency **Guyana dollar (G$) £1=225, Mar 1997**
  Coins rarely used
Tipping **only in hotels and better restaurants, where
  10 per cent is expected**

Georgetown is laid out on a grid system with the main shopping
in and around Regent Street. There are several markets, and
even a couple of department stores, although the range of
merchandise is not extensive. A good choice of handicrafts
includes many displaying Amerindian influences. Although
gold is mined in Guyana it is not recommended you buy unless
you know what you are doing: avoid dealing with street vendors.

The *Guyana Chronicle* is government owned and printed
daily. The independent *Stabroek News* is also published daily.
The *Catholic Standard*, another independent newspaper, is
published weekly. Apart from *The Economist* few British
magazines are imported.

EATING AND DRINKING
There is no gourmet cooking, although the standard is
improving. Local wine made from rice is very poor, but the
rum is excellent. Cheap locally produced mixers are available.

TRANSPORT
The public transport is provided by privately owned minibuses.
They are crowded, uncomfortable and dangerous. Visitors
rarely use public transport, relying entirely on private cars or
taxis. Taxis should be summoned by phone and fares confirmed in advance.

SECURITY
Observe certain simple rules to diminish the risk of being
mugged. Do not carry valuables or more money than you
need. Do not wear expensive jewellery about town. Be alert
for pickpockets.

HAITI

PORT AU PRINCE

Language **French, Creole**
Currency **gourde. £1=25.28, Dec 1996**

Despite recent political upheavals, Haiti is becoming increasingly popular with holidaymakers.

Haiti is particularly famous for its naive-style art, but do not expect it to be cheap. There are also some interesting crafts such as fabrics and woodcarvings. Voodoo drums are popular with visitors who do not mind the problems involved in transporting them back home. The local markets can be a bit too hectic: try rather the artisan shop on Rue 3.

English is widely spoken in tourist areas.

SECURITY

Be sure to exercise sensible security precautions at all times: crime is prevalent and certain areas of the capital are best avoided altogether.

HONDURAS

TEGUCIGALPA

Language **Spanish**
Currency **lempira of 100 centavos. £1=21.22,
   Jan 1997**
Credit cards **Visa and Access accepted in
   most hotels and restaurants**
Tipping **15 per cent service charge normally added
   to bills in restaurants**

Shopping is again becoming difficult owing to the economic situation. There are shortages, and the rate of exchange declines daily. Service is poor in many restaurants and shops. Honduran women take great care of their appearance and visit beauty salons regularly to pamper themselves. Treatments are cheap. Men also visit these parlours!

The centre of town is in and around the Plaza Marazàn

and the adjacent Avenida Miguel P Barahona.

You will be able to get your favourite dress copied for a fraction of what you paid for it originally. Try Carmen Lucas near Iglesia Milagrosa, Elena Hicks in Calle San Pablo or Capellos in Boulevard Morazan. Bortoliny specialises in men's tailoring. Joyería Milla Guirst on Boulevard Marazàn has exquisite jewellery pieces designed and made by the owner.

There are many gift shops in town, but the best place by far to buy gifts and souvenirs is in Valle de Angeles, a 30-minute drive from town. This small, picturesque village has many shops with a concentration of art and craft items from all over Honduras and many parts of Central America. On the way there are beautiful views and some lovely fresh vegetables and house plants at many roadside stalls. Otherwise Galeria Celajes and gift shop is in front of the Hotel San Martin. Galeria Kuskat and gift shop is behind Los Castanos.

Worthwhile gifts and souvenirs include basketry, ceramics, embroidery, leather, traditional musical instruments, textiles and woodcarvings. Paintings in local style can be bought on the Plaza Marazàn.

Foreign English-language newspapers are available at La Colonia supermarket, but not in quantity and expensive. *Honduras This Week* is the weekly local English-language newspaper. Books Village on Boulevard Marazàn has some English books.

Eating and Drinking
There are lots of places to eat. Hondurans like to eat out, and it is not expensive. El Patio has typical Honduran food with fantastic steaks and mariachi music. There are plenty of reasonable cafés and fast-food outlets. Zamorano ice-cream comes from the agricultural college of the same name and is good.

Security
Security declines with the economy. Avoid ostentation and take particular care at night. Do not go to the town centre alone.

Hong Kong see China

HUNGARY

BUDAPEST

Language Hungarian
Currency forint of 100 filler. £1= 283, Mar 1997
Banks 0900-1300 Mon to Fri, 0900-1100 Sat
Credit cards accepted in many hotels, restaurants
  and shops
Shops 1000-1800 Mon to Fri, 1000-1300 Sat. Some
  shops close in Jan for stock-taking; many close all
  Aug
Sales Feb and Aug; excellent bargains
Bargaining only in markets
Duty-free hard currency shops in hotels
Tipping widespread and expected, even when
  service charge added to bills. Tip hairdressers,
  petrol-station attendants, musicians in restaurants
  for special requests; 10 per cent of the bill or 10
  forints for flower delivery or cloakroom
  attendants; at least 10 per cent for taxi drivers;
  20-40 forints for porters at airport, station and
  hotels
Export restrictions strict regulations on import and
  export of forints. Antiques and works of art
  require customs permission. Goods bought for
  forints cannot be exported without approval from
  National Bank. Keep receipts to prove purchase
  with hard currency or credit cards

Shopping has improved dramatically in recent years. Locally
made shoes and boots are cheap, but not stylish and of poor
quality. Most people find the moon boots which are available
at prices cheaper than in the UK useful for snow or when the
thaw sets in.

Skala at XI Schönherz Zoltán/Fehévári utca has the widest
range of goods on offer. Amfora is a well-known name for
glass, pottery or china; there are several branches in town
including V Felszabadulás tér 4.

The flea market is at XIX Nagykörösi út 58. Bargains are
increasingly difficult to find and haggling is a necessity. The
Gellért Market at V Tolbuhin körút, near Szabadság Bridge, is
open daily from 0600.

BAV shops are second-hand stores which buy and sell on

commission and their wares range from good as new to antique. There are several branches. On the whole they are expensive, being geared to the tourist trade, and not of high quality.

Classical records, tapes and CDs are in good supply at reasonable cost. There are annual Hungaraton record weeks in September and October when stalls are set up along the Váci Utca and other shopping areas. Records are sold at up to half list prices.

Konsumtourist is a hard currency shop for souvenirs, etc. which has outlets at the Duna Intercontinental Hotel and elsewhere. There are now two small Marks and Spencer outlets selling women's clothing at prices higher than in the UK. There is a good doll shop at Váci Utca 14.

There are now a few English-language bookshops, and most other shops have a good selection of books in English. Books generally are of a high standard and relatively cheap to buy, including art books. Second-hand English and other books are sold in the state Antiquarium bookshops and can be excellent value for money. Prints and pictures are also good value and framing is good.

EATING AND DRINKING
There are many restaurants and the quality of food is generally good, if a little rich in fat. There are excellent wines and local fruit brandies produced in Hungary and Unicum, the famous local spirit, should be tried at least once. There are also some very good brands of local beer, both bottled and draught.

TRANSPORT
Public transport is reputed to be one of the best and cheapest in the world. Most trams, trolley-buses and underground lines (there are three) run from 0400 to 2400 and there is a standard cost for a single journey. Buses generally run from 0500 to 2300 and are a little more expensive. Tickets are purchased at bus and tram terminals and at tobacconists. Validate the ticket on boarding. If it is necessary to break a journey by taking a different service, a fresh ticket must be bought. One day tickets are available. Taxis are numerous and comparatively inexpensive. They do not cruise for passengers. There are also private taxis.

ICELAND

REYKJAVIK

Language **Icelandic**
Currency **krona (Kr) of 100 aurar. £1=113, Mar 1997**
Banks **0930-1530 Mon to Fri**
Shops **0900-1800 Mon to Fri, 1000-1600 Sat**
Refunds **VAT can be refunded on bills over Kr10,000**
Sales **Jan and Aug; large, genuine reductions**
Duty-free **at Keflavik airport; good range, prices compare favourably with other European airports**
Tipping **not expected and can give offence; service charge added to hotel and restaurant bills**

Reykjavik is a modern town, and the most northerly capital in the world. Be sure to be adequately dressed. Warm and water-proof footwear is essential to negotiate thick, snowy or slushy pavements and one can buy under-shoe spikes to grip the pavement ice. English is widely understood and most under the age of 50 speak it remarkably well.

The oldest part of the town centre is around Austurvollur and Laekjartorg, with newer shops just to the east of this. Most shopping is done in this main town centre area, although there is a fairly large mall a short drive away. There are no good value chain stores like Marks and Spencer.

A surprisingly wide range of household goods is available, but they are almost all imported and very expensive. Scandinavian glass and china cost considerably less in London than in Reykjavik. Similarly, there is a good choice of clothing, but at much higher cost than in the UK. Icelandic sweaters and knitted garments such as scarves can be bought at favourable prices. Other winter clothing such as snow boots can also be good value: insulated gloves and wellingtons, ear-warmers, hats and balaclavas are available. There is widespread interest and ample production and sale of Icelandic paintings. Exhibitions follow each other ceaselessly and are heavily patronised. There are several good galleries in town.

English books and magazines are available in most of the numerous bookshops, but they are particularly expensive.

EATING AND DRINKING

Restaurants are of excellent standard, but expensive, with alcohol exorbitantly priced so few foreigners use them for private entertaining. They can nevertheless be crowded on popular weekend nights. There are some excellent fish restaurants around the port. Be sure to try the local salmon, trout, graflax and caviar. Icelandic export beer is of reasonable quality.

TRANSPORT

The centre of town can be covered on foot, but there are good and frequent bus services. Taxis are reliable, but expensive.

INDIA

Language 15 official languages; Hindi and English most important
Currency rupee (R) of 100 paisa. £1=57.30, Mar 1997. Not freely convertible
Banks 100/1100-1400/1500 Mon to Fri, 1000/1100-1200/1300 Sat
Credit cards Access, Barclaycard, Visa, American Express accepted in larger shops: Diners Club less acceptable
Cashpoints in larger banks, not all accept international cards
Shops 1000-2000, some close for an hour at lunchtime
Refunds exchange sometimes possible
Sales yes, with good reductions
Bargaining expected in markets, bazaars and at stalls; fixed prices in larger shops and stores
Duty-free at Delhi airport
Tipping 10 per cent in hotels and restaurants; Rs10 for other services. Taxi drivers are not tipped
Export restrictions permits needed for gold and silver over Rs100,000 and antiquities over 100 years old

Import of consumer goods is generally allowed now and they are freely available. There are many local items worth considering as gifts or souvenirs – soapstone or marble carvings, gold, leather goods and ethnic jewellery. The choice of fabrics available is wide, from handloom cotton and cotton prints to the finest silks, Kashmir woollens and tweeds. Indian silks are good and though becoming more expensive are by UK standards still comparatively cheap. Inexpensive and good quality cotton clothing is available, such as shirts made for Van Heusen locally by a Coats Viyella joint venture. Local tailors are not expensive and can make passable copies of existing garments. Safari suits, for example, can be made up or purchased locally for £40 to £70. Sandals are widely available at reasonable prices.

Indian carpets of silk and cotton are famous world wide. There are several shops selling beautiful designs. A 10 foot by 8 foot silk carpet will cost about £1,200. A lifelong investment.

Stainless-steel cooking utensils are a great buy at about a quarter of the UK price. For example a large wok-shaped vessel with two handles costs only £7. Many small shops and larger department stores stock hundreds of different items.

Local opticians provide a cheap and efficient service for supplying spectacles and contact lenses. The choice of frames and lens tint is also good. So bring your latest prescription.

International games like Monopoly and Scrabble are much cheaper than in the UK.

Framing is pretty good and very cheap, as is leather binding of favourite books.

Avoid eating salads in restaurants, unless you are sure that they have been properly washed.

There are still rules restricting the consumption of alcohol in public, but there is generally no difficulty in purchasing drinks in clubs, hotels and restaurants. Delhi, for example, is dry on the first and the seventh of the month.

Indian wines and spirits are freely available – at a price. The gin (Booths, made under licence), rum and vodka are acceptable and distillers have now set up a whisky plant near Madras. Imported drinks are very expensive in hotels. The local brand of champagne is very acceptable. The beer is a light, gassy lager (Dansberg or Black Label) and is drinkable. All soft drinks are poor imitations of the real thing, but are acceptable.

There is a vast range of cheap, Indian-made cigarettes on sale. Local brands of cigarettes with British names are cheap, but not of comparable quality to their UK counterparts. It is often possible to obtain imported cigarettes from street vendors.

It is still difficult to browse without hassle in some shops. Apart from the pickpockets and hustlers, India is relatively safe. You will be approached by black marketeers. Do not succumb to temptation.

DELHI

There are a number of popular shopping areas. South Extension on the Inner Ring Road is probably Delhi's most up-market shopping area. There you will find Benetton, Reebok, Lacoste, Nike, Tekson's bookshop, The Heritage Silk Shop, Ebony department store and Gem opticians, as well as numerous shoe shops.

Round the corner on Sri Aurobinda Marg is INA, a large covered market, very atmospheric and good for those wanting to visit a real Indian market. It is closed on Monday.

Santushti Shopping Centre is an up-market shopping area on the edge of Wellingdon Camp (an air-force base), off the roundabout at the Samrat Hotel. It has a number of boutiques. Christina's silk and leather shop is very popular as is the leather handbag shop. Young Fashion sells Lacoste. There is also a nice little restaurant called Basil and Thyme.

Connaught Circus, now called Rajiv Chowk, is a centrally situated, good quality, general shopping area. Nearby on the Baba Kharak Singh Marq are the States Emporia, where each shop sells produce from a particular state. The Shankar Market behind the Hilton Hotel has many fabric shops.

The Khan Market on Lodi Road is a general shopping area which sells a wide range of goods. It is particularly good for books and clothing. The National Cloth House or Delhi Cloth House are recommended for fabrics.

Yashwant Place off Africa Avenue is good for jewellery and all sorts of handicrafts including woodcarvings, brass ornaments and leather. Nearby Sarowini Nagar is an open-air market with just about everything, including saris. The market is closed on Monday.

Phahaganj opposite New Delhi railway station sells incense, perfumed candles, herbal shampoos and local perfumes. Closing day is Monday.

Hauz Khas near the Asian Games village complex is an interesting area with a good variety of shops selling silver, jewellery, leather goods and up-market Western clothing. It also has lots of trendy restaurants. It closes on Tuesday.

Sunder Nagar opposite the Oberoi Hotel is recommended for antiques and jewellery, particularly silver and silver-plated gifts.

Jan Path market includes Cottage Industries, which is particularly recommended for local crafts. As well as Western clothing, there are books, leather goods and most Indian curios. The nearby Palika Bazaar is a subterranean market, not for the claustrophobic.

For antiques such as old furniture, boxes, chests, silver and brass, Sunder Nagar offers a good variety of shops. Otherwise try Goel Exports at S443 School Block, Shakarpur Mehra's Art Palace at M-1 Main Market, Greater Kailash II, The Attic at 180 A/3 Forest Lane, Sainikik Farms, or The Treasure Chest at Maharani Farm, DLF Area, Chattarpur.

For carpets try Obeetees, F45 South Extension 1 (basement), Fabindia, N-Block Market, Greater Kailash I or Shyam Ahuja at Santushti Shopping Centre.

Jewellery can be made to your own design from precious or semi-precious stones. Try Mr Khannak at F-81 Bhagat Singh Market, Bombay Jewellers at 22 Sunder Nagar La Boutique at Sunder Nagar or Nirmal Vijay at A-17 Wengers House, Connaught Place.

Leather handbags and belts are good and cheap. For leather goods try Adamji at X-24 Haus Khas, Christina or Tack at Santushti Shopping Centre.

Cotton towels and sheets are a good buy and much cheaper than in the UK. Try Fabindia, Bed and Bath at E4 South Extension Part II or Bombay Dyeing, a chain found in nearly all markets. Cotton quilts are also good. Those purchased from Anokhi are of a particularly fine quality and sell in their outlets in London for more than four times the price you pay in Delhi.

The Craft Museum at Dilli Haat in Aurobindo Marg and Central Cottage Industries sometimes have ethnic toys. Try Gem Opticians at G-23 South Extension Part I for your frames and lenses.

Suits, shirts and dresses can be made locally more cheaply than buying in the UK, but the tailoring is not always top class. Try Garg Brothers at Khan Market in the back of the Delhi Cloth House. They are good for men's tailoring and not bad for women.

Many books are published simultaneously in the UK and India and there is therefore a wide selection of the best and latest titles in Delhi's many bookshops at prices cheaper than in the UK. Most bookshops stock airmail editions of British newspapers within a day or two of issue, but at high prices. Many local newspapers are in English.

EATING AND DRINKING

The restaurant scene focuses mainly on the better hotels with some good exceptions. Friday and Saturday as well as Sunday lunchtime can be very crowded, so book ahead. For Indian cuisine try Aangan at the Hyatt Regency, Bukhara or Dum Pukht at the Maurya Sheraton, The Frontier at the Ashok Hotel, Copper Chimney at Pamposh Enclave, Greater Kailash I, Kabila at Aurobindo Place in Hauz Khas or Moti Mahal in Malcha Marg and in Old Delhi.

TRANSPORT

It is usually necessary to take a taxi or rickshaw to the various shopping centres. Old Delhi also has very cheap cycle rickshaws, but they are not allowed into New Delhi. Taxis wait at stands. A cruising cab is a rarity. All taxis are metered. Be prepared for the meter to be broken or the driver to have no change.

SECURITY

Delhi is a fairly safe place, although reasonable personal safety precautions are necessary and a certain amount of hassle is to be expected from beggars and hawkers.

BOMBAY

Bombay is large and populous. Although all shopping areas are only a short drive from each other, it could take a couple of hours on a bad day to get anywhere. In addition the government decided a few years ago to replace all English street names with Indian names. However, the streets are still usually referred to by their English names.

Kemps Corner is situated at the centre of several busy roads. There are some good shoe and material shops there, although if you are over a size ten you will have problems. Down the road you come to the sea front. There are many fruit and vegetable stalls in this area as well as several department stores such as In-Style, large by Bombay standards and selling just about everything.

Crawford Market is deep in the Muslim area of Bombay. In the main market are foods and spices as well as dogs, cats and birds. Off the main market are warrens of small roads, each specialising in one particular product such as bathroom fitments, plastic flowers or china. Well worth seeing if you do not mind crowds.

Chor Bazaar is near by and is known as Thieves Market.

If you know anything about antiques this is a collector's paradise, but watch out for some very good copies. Shopping here is time-consuming, dusty, hot, sticky and thirst-inducing.

Colaba Causeway is Bombay's answer to Oxford Street with literally hundreds of small shops selling a variety of goods. Here there is a shop called Cotton World, air-conditioned and one of the few outlets in Bombay which allow you to look at and try clothes without being pestered. The goods are well made, reasonably priced and also fashionable. Colaba is also the place where you will most likely be approached by people selling drugs, black market money changers and saffron sellers.

Fashion Street perhaps sounds more exciting than it really is, but it is still lots of fun to bargain there. Take a taxi to the Bombay Gym – Fashion Street is opposite. It consists of a half-mile row of stalls and many of the items are rejects from clothes made for the UK market. A lot of the clothes wear out very quickly, but one can hardly complain when a skirt might cost only £1.

Most of the main hotels have their own shopping malls, but these tend to be expensive. Benetton, Lacoste, Levi, Reebok, Nike and Mexx are all to be found at Kemps Corner and one or two of them are also on Colaba Causeway.

For local arts and crafts try Contemporary Arts on Nepean Sea Road. You are free to browse. Fixed prices, no bargaining. Cottage Industries is similar, and is not far from the Taj Hotel. It is worth experiencing for the unbelievably time-consuming system for paying for goods. Indian handicrafts can be bought anywhere, depending on your taste. Wooden chests from Chor Baazar, sympathetically restored, are good value at about £100. Small Victorian coffee tables with old tiles on the top are very pretty and start at about £40. Hard bargaining is recommended.

New Earth is near Kemps Corner and sells up-market, good quality bed and table linen. This shop is a must.

One of the best buys to bring back from Bombay is silk made into special occasion clothes. Try Indian Textiles at the Taj Hotel. Prices start at about £10 per metre.

Several shops have had a half-price last-minute sale for the past two years. However, there is a lovely shop in Worli called Shyam Ahuja that has one sale a year and has some excellent reductions in silk items.

There are some good bookshops in Bombay where you can buy English books and magazines at not much more than the UK cover price. Crosswords on Warden Road is a wonderful place to escape the heat on a Sunday afternoon. There are hundreds of books, well displayed. Many novels cost about £2 each and larger specialist tomes, beautifully illustrated, are well below UK prices. Some British newspapers are available the day after publication and there are regular deliveries of the more popular British periodicals, but they are both somewhat expensive. English-language newspapers are published locally, notably the *Times of India* and the *Indian Express*.

EATING AND DRINKING

Several restaurants and shops are to be recommended for their specialities. The best samosas in town are to be found at Café Naiz on Malaba Hill. Chicken Jalfreisi is a must from Quality Restaurant at Kemps Corner. Chicken Dansack comes from the Sir Ratan Tata Centre at the bottom of Hughs Road. There is a stall behind the Taj where servants queue up in luxury cars to collect. It must be good for those brave enough to try. Otherwise there are numerous restaurants of good standard. Bombay is a great place to be a vegetarian.

TRANSPORT

Most large hotels are a taxi ride from the main shopping areas. There are plenty of taxis, but be sure the meter is on when you start the journey. The bus service is adequate, but very crowded.

CALCUTTA

Most visitors will spend their time in the areas of Dalhousie Square and Chowringhee. There are few places they would recognise as shops in Calcutta; most are holes in the wall or stalls in huge covered bazaars like the New Market. Although living costs are low, visitors soon become aware of the almost total absence of anything worth buying and the difficulty of walking around town. The range of consumer goods is limited and quality generally poor.

Locally made suits are just about acceptable since they are relatively inexpensive. Good quality business shirts in cotton or silk can be bought from the Taj Benghal Hotel or from shops in Park Street at half the UK cost, but larger sizes can be difficult to find. Casual shirts in bright colours are even cheaper. Dressmakers are quite good and very cheap although the range of cotton and silk fabrics is restricted. There are plenty of shoes made locally by companies such as Bata and by the Chinese shoe-makers in the market. They are quite cheap but quality is not as high as in the UK.

There are several English-language bookshops in Park Street.

Calcutta seems to be a dumping ground for remaindered books from the UK. There are no antiquarian bookshops, but there are numerous stalls selling second-hand books in College Street and Free School Street. Most are in terrible condition. English is widely and well spoken.

EATING AND DRINKING
The Taj Benghal and Oberoi Grand hotels have good restaurants. The Amber Restaurant is noted for its barbecues and the Zaranj for its gourmet North Indian food. Both are in Chowringhee.

TRANSPORT
Taxis are useless. Public transport (buses and trams) is grossly overcrowded and unsafe, although the metro is newly opened and slowly being extended.

SECURITY
Apart from pickpockets, foreigners rarely encounter criminals. Beggars are not a major problem in Calcutta, but tend to be found in shopping areas where they can be a nuisance.

GOA

Currency **Indian rupee**

A former Portuguese enclave on the west coast of India, increasingly popular with package tourists. There is an interesting mixture of both cultures, not least in the cuisine. Lots of Indian handicrafts and other gifts and souvenirs. Eating out can be incredibly cheap. Beer and local wine are readily available at roughly UK prices.

MADRAS

The main central shopping area is in Georgetown. Just to the south is the important shopping street of Anna Salai which includes a number of shopping malls. Worth visiting in Anna Salai are the Kashmir Government Arts Emporium, the Uttar Pradesh State Handloom Corporation, Kairali, Tanjore Art Gallery, Victoria Technical Institute, Kashmire Carpet Corporation, Poompuhar, Khadi Gramodyog Bhavan, Manjusha and Kaveri. The more serious collector might want to visit Heirloom in Anna Salai or Jamal's in Spencer's Plaza, but note that government listed antiques cannot be exported.

Dakshinachitra is a new village for handicrafts on the road to Mamallapuramm just before Muttukkadu. Each street represents an area of southern India and you can see craftsmen in their homes creating their wares. Here and in Madras itself, there are objects in bronze, copper, brass, wood or papier mâché as well as sculptures, jewellery, paintings with gold leaf, floor coverings and wall hangings.

The best saris come from Kanchipuram, 100 kms from Madras, and there are shops in Madras itself selling this high-quality merchandise, such as the Rada Silk Emporium on Sannadhi Street in Mylapore. Other shops selling a variety of saris include Roshanlal, Khadi Silks and Khadi Crafts on Anna Salai as well as Nalli House in T Nagar.

There are two English-language papers published in Madras – the *Hindu* and the Madras edition of the *Indian Express*. British newspapers arrive by airmail three to five days after publication. There are several good bookshops in Madras with an excellent choice of paperbacks.

EATING AND DRINKING
There are a number of good restaurants especially in the major hotels and there are several where it is possible to sample Southern Indian cuisine. In the hotels there are the Dakshin at the Welcomegroup Park Sheraton or the Raintree at the Connemara. For less expensive food try the Coconut Grove in Harrington Road or Kaaraikudi in Dr Radhakrishnan Saali.

TRANSPORT
Public transport is crowded and unsuitable for visitors. Taxis and auto-rickshaws are hazardous, but the easiest form of transport.

INDONESIA

JAKARTA

Language **Indonesian**
Currency **rupiah (Rp) of 100 sen. £1=3850,
Mar 1997**
Banks **0800–1400 Mon to Thur, 0800–1100
Fri, 0800–1300 Sat**
Credit cards **American Express, Visa, Mastercard**
Shops **0830–1600 Mon to Thur, 0830–1100 Fri,
0830–1200 Sat**
Bargaining **in markets and antique shops; discounts
in some shops**
Duty-free **yes, but expensive**
Tipping **10 per cent in hotels and restaurants if no
service charge; Rps500 a bag at the airport; not
necessary for taxi drivers, but small tip often given**

There is no recognisable single city centre in Jakarta. There
are the Old Town near the sea, Menteng further inland,
Kebayoran to the south and more modern suburbs such as
Kemang.

There are several shopping plazas. Ratu Plaza at Jalan
Jenderal Sudirman in Senayan tends to be expensive. Aldiron
Plaza in Blok M is more reasonable, with some fixed prices
and some bargaining. Melawai Plaza, also in Blok M, has
fixed prices. Duta Merlin shopping arcade at Jalan Gajah
Nada 3 – 5 in Pasar Baru is a very large complex with material
shops encircling it. Gajah Mada Plaza at Jalan Gajah Mada in
Kota is quite expensive with fixed prices. Blok M Plaza at
Jalan Panglima Polim Raya in Kebayoran Baru is up-market
and worth a visit. Plaza Indonesia at Jalan Thamrin behind
the Grand Hyatt has mainly expensive imported goods.
Ponkok Indah Mall in the south of the city includes Marks
and Spencer and Body Shop.

Blok M at Jalan Melawai V in Kebayoran Baru is the place
for copy watches, fake designer leather, factory over-runs and
hundreds of small shops. Pasar Glodak at Jalan Gajah Mada
in Kota is the Chinese market. Pasar Baru at Jalan Pasar Baru
is good for sports equipment, materials and crafts. Pasar
Cikini at Jalan Pengangsaan in Menteng has good gold jewellery shops above the fruit and vegetable market. Always bargain
and compare prices.

The Sarinah Department Store at Jalan Thamrin in Menteng is a good price guide for bargaining in the markets. Sogo at Plaza Indonesia is a large department store with an excellent supermarket. Seibu is next to Pasaraya and expensive.

When shopping for presents and souvenirs try first a visit to Pasaraya in Blok M. They have probably the best selection, with a whole floor for batik and the same for handicrafts, and are a good start for comparative shopping. If you have time, the streets then to visit are Jalan Surabaya in Menteng, Jalan Kemang Timur in Kemang or Jalan Ciputat Raya.

Among best buys are furniture and smaller items from wrought iron, rattan or teak, custom-made jewellery, batik, tailor-made clothing and shoes and handbags. Men might like a locally tailored batik shirt or a casual safari suit. For women there are plenty of batik sarongs.

Antiques are abundant. Most antique shops are concentrated in streets such as Jalan Ciputat Raya or Jalan Kemang Timur. Jalan Surabaya in Menteng is a flea market. A good time to go is Sunday afternoon. Madjapahit Arts and Curios in Jalan Melawai III behind the Pasaraya department store is recommended. Several shops sell Bangka tin in Jalan Palatehan and all give good discounts. Try Pigura Arts and Crafts at 41.

There is a good selection of jewellery on the top floor of Cikini Market and in Pasar Baru. Otherwise try Bulau Uras Indah at Jalan Puri Mutiara 1 in Cipete, Fandiasta at Jalan Kapten Mulyadi 93 in Barat, Indomas at Jalan Haji Samanhudi in Pasar Baru or Spiros at the Hotel Sari Pacific.

When buying rattan make sure that the items are sprayed for export and ask for a certificate. Try Kemang Rattan at Jalan Kemang 8. For woodcarvings go to the Woodcarving Shop at Jalan Tawakal Raya 11A, Grogol. Also try Toko Binatara at Jalan Wolter Monginsidi, Kebayoran Baru. For wrought-iron work ICAD at Jalan Fatmawati 80J is good.

Leather goods such as shoes, belts and bags can be made for you at The Snake Lady at Jalan Taman Hidayah 19 in Bendungan Hilir. Ben and Son at Jalan Kemang Timur 28B are good value. YP Creations also makes silk shoes and bags to order and is at Pulo Mas IIIB/4, Villa Sari Mas, Jakarta Timur.

Specialist dressmakers include The Pintuck Lady at Jalan Pejaten Raya No.17, Pasar Minggu or The Smocking Lady at Jalan Raden Saleh 52 in Cikini. There are many copy tailors in the covered market next to the Aldiron Plaza in Blok M.

For materials Batik Hajadi at Jalan Palmera Utara 46 in Palmera makes up tablecloths which are ideal presents.

Expensive, but maybe the best, is Iwan Tirta (PT Ramacraft) at Jalan Panarukan 25. Batik Berdikari at Jalan Mejid Al Anwar 7B in Kebayoran Lama is excellent with a factory on the premises. Ibu Bintang Nagara at Jalan Sekolah Kencana 26 in Pondok Indah has batik material. For quilts try Hanidas Collection Handicraft in Jalan Kemang. Yamarco at Jalan Sutan Syahrir 6 in Menteng caters for a more European taste in batik upholstery and lamps.

There are some fine lamps at The Lamp Lady at Jalan Utan Kayu 86A in Rawamangun. Flying Birds at Jalan Kemang Bangka 1 has an assortment of hand-sewn articles, etc. A one-stop shop for gifts if you are in a hurry is The Chic Mart at Jalan Kemang Raya 55 in Kemang.

There are limited numbers of magazines and newspapers available at the major hotels, but they are out of date and expensive. There are three English-language daily newspapers published locally – the *Indonesian Observer*, the *Indonesian Times* and the *Jakarta Post*.

EATING AND DRINKING

There is a great variety of reasonable places to eat in Jakarta. For local specialities try Mirasari at Jalan Kemang Utara 33 in Kebayoran Baru, but note that they do not serve alcohol. For a traditional rijsttafel go to Memories at Jalan Jend Sudirman 70 – 71 in Setiabudi or Oasis at Jalan Raden Saleh 47 in Cikini. Restaurants in the main hotels are good: wine is expensive, but in most you are able to take your own for a corkage charge of around £10.

TRANSPORT

Buses are fairly numerous and cheap, but always grossly over-crowded and uncomfortable if not dangerous. Taxis are available at most main hotels and at taxi ranks in the main shopping areas. There are also fairly reliable radio-taxi services. Taxi drivers' knowledge of Jakarta often leaves a lot to be desired. Charges are on a metered basis and are reasonably priced. Bajajs (motorised rickshaws) are available for short trips in towns, but not on major roads. Negotiate the fare in advance.

SECURITY

There has been an increase in petty crime directed against foreigners. Care should be taken against pickpockets and muggers, particularly against motorcyclists with a pillion passenger.

IRAN

TEHRAN

Language Farsi

Currency rial (10 rials=1 toman). £1=2355, Mar 1997 (official fixed rate, higher in the bazaar)

Traveller's cheques can be changed only into rials; take cash US dollars and change at banks or hotels

Credit cards Mastercard and Visa accepted by a few hotels, shops and banks; American cards not acceptable. Foreign currency must be declared on entry. Black market currency dealing risks arrest and imprisonment

Shops 0900–1300, 1600–2030 or later; Grand Bazaar 0900–1630

Refunds yes, with receipt

Bargaining yes, but fixed prices in Government Handicraft Shops

Duty-free little of interest except caviar; best quality Beluga is US$100 per kilo; medium quality at US$50 is good value

Tipping small tips at the airport, in restaurants or for boys who carry shopping are usual

Import/export restrictions foreign currency must be declared on entry; import of alcohol is forbidden; games such as chess and Monopoly and playing cards are regarded as gambling and not allowed; pre-recorded Western CDs and cassettes are banned. Antiquities, relics and ancient artefacts are prohibited exports; up to three square metres of carpet may be exported; the official limit for gold and silver is a million rials

Women are obliged to wear coats and headscarves at all times in public. Men should not wear shorts or T-shirts. You may therefore prefer to shop in the cool of the evening.

Most foreign women buy after arrival a *rupoush*, a sort of long, loose housecoat so as to comply with local dress rules. Many young Iranians wear jeans and trainers under their *rupoush*. Women will find that long coats are by no means all of gloomy black. There is a range of styles and colours and a light summer coat can be stylish and cost as little as £15.

Despite the crowds and the unbelievable traffic, shopping can be fun and colourful. Go down the main covered arteries of the Grand Bazaar and you will find whole passages of coppersmiths, cloth merchants, gold and silversmiths, carpet sellers and tailors. Shopkeepers are nearly always polite and friendly, but not many speak good English.

If you look hard enough you can find almost anything you want from designer clothes to smoked sturgeon, from 22–carat gold jewellery to fishing tackle. However, imported Western items are expensive, prices being based on an unofficial dollar exchange rate. Be sure whether a quoted price is in rials or in tomans. The latter are more commonly referred to and are worth 10 rials.

Iran is famous above all for its carpets. There is a great variety of designs, qualities and sizes. Generally speaking, the more knots the better. Take plenty of time to look around before deciding what you want and how much you are prepared to pay, what size you want, whether you want wool or silk or a mixture, old or new, geometric or floral design. There are plenty of dealers in the Bazaar and around Ferdowsi Square and they will usually quote you a dollar price. They will arrange the export of your carpets for you, but this is likely to take months rather than weeks and adds something like 25 per cent to the total cost. Dealers back home might be able to offer an equally good bargain at less trouble.

Recommended as souvenirs are carpets, kelims, prayer rugs, gold and silver jewellery, items of calligraphy or mother of pearl, marquetry including inlaid boxes, tea and coffee sets, local glass, photo frames, hubble-bubble pipes, copper, brass and candlesticks from glass or brass. Also available are mohair, cashmere, silk, items made from real camel hair such as toy camels and real Persian slippers. Look out for tablecloths (*kalamkari* work).

Try walking the main covered street of the Great Bazaar from the entrance on 15th Khordad Street. This is wonderful for gold, carpets, colour and atmosphere. Take a guide to ensure that you do not get lost. Manucheri Street is famous for antiques and is good for browsing: leather and luggage are also good. Karim Khan Zand Street is the centre for Iranian gold, mainly copies of Italian-style jewellery: prices are fixed by weight. The Friday Bazaar near the post office from about 1400 onwards is good for antiques and bric-à-brac.

Vali Asir Avenue has many clothing and other shops and is worth browsing in from Tajrish Square in the north down past the Park e Mellat (good handicraft shops opposite the park) and the Eskan Centre on the corner of Mirdamad Avenue (jewellery, glass and fashions) through Vanak Square (restaurants, fashions) as far as Vali Asr Square (materials and clothing). The Aban Market on Doktor Hasan Azodi Street and nearby Villa Street (also known as Nejatollahi Street) are the centre of the Armenian quarter. Around the corner from Villa Street is a good Government Handicraft Shop on three levels to give you an idea of prices you might pay elsewhere. There is also a row of handicraft shops in Talegani Avenue.

Foreign newspapers are not available. Some weekly magazines like *Time* and *Newsweek* can be found in some of the hotels. There are also three English-language newspapers which are government controlled, but carry some foreign agency reports.

EATING AND DRINKING

There are only a few moderate and inexpensive restaurants for those wishing to sample local cuisine. Restaurants are sometimes closed down when they become too popular. Recommended at the moment for local cuisine are Narenjestan in Attar Street and Khansalar in Alvand Street. Various kinds of kebabs are available at the Swiss Restaurant in Forsat Street, Nayab off Argentine Square and Alborz in Sohrevardi Street. The Ghaveh khaneh Sunnati (traditional Persian coffee house) just above the main railway station on Vali Asr Street offers *Ab Gusht* (traditional meat and bean stew).

Local sweets and pastries are very good, as is caviar. The best quality caviar is exported, however, and is almost unobtainable locally. The nut shops are good; taste before you buy. Iranian fruit is said to be some of the best in the world and has great flavour. There is a wide selection including some of the more exotic fruits. Locally produced cola and carbonated orange drinks are everywhere, imported varieties are available, but very expensive.

TRANSPORT

Taxis are cheap and readily available, but they tend to be old, uncomfortable and unreliable. Drivers are not particularly knowledgeable about Tehran. It is advisable to take a map and know roughly where you are going. Fares are very variable. Fix the price before setting off. Buses are plentiful, but not normally used by foreigners.

SECURITY

Personal security is not usually a problem and there are a few not very persistent beggars. Tourists are often objects of

curiosity, but are treated politely. There have been cases of
mugging but they are rare.

IRELAND

DUBLIN

Language **English, Irish**
Currency **punt (IR£) of 100 pence. £1=£1.024
    Mar 1997**
Banks **1100–1230, 1330–1500/1700 Mon to Fri
    UK cheque guarantee cards not recognised**
Credit cards **major cards accepted by most stores**
Cashpoints **yes, plentiful**
Shops **0930 to 1730 Mon to Fri**
Duty-free **at Dublin airport, limited in range of
    choice**
Tipping **customary, rates as in UK. Hotels normally,
    and restaurants often, show VAT on bills and add
    10 to 15 per cent service charge**

Dublin is a small capital city with two distinct centres divided
by the River Liffey and within easy walking distance of each
other. For shopping choice and value for money it is very similar to any town in the UK. In the past few years most of the
main British chain stores have opened branches. Prices are
generally higher than in the UK, although value is generally
better north of the river than in the Grafton Street area.
Grafton Street traditionally has been regarded as the Bond
Street of Dublin: it is now pedestrianised.

   In the centre the main shopping area is around Grafton
Street and Henry Street. The latter has a few market stalls for
a bit of atmosphere. There are a couple of department stores
in Grafton Street, Brown Thomas and Switzers, which provide
a good overview of what is available; you should be able to
buy most of your gifts there. The same goes for the shopping
centres such as the St Stephen's Green Centre in Grafton
Street, Doverscourt Town House Centre in Clarendon Street and
the Westbury Centre just around the corner. Some of the usual
UK multiples including Marks and Spencer and well-known
Irish variety stores such as Roches and Dunnes are to be
found. Dunnes is the nearest Irish equivalent to Marks and

Spencer. The more exclusive shops for women include Pia Bang. There are markets selling mostly second-hand bric-à-brac, craft items and books. There is also a large fruit and vegetable market in the centre of town.

There are plenty of touristy souvenirs featuring leprechauns, shamrock, anything green and Guinness labels, but there are many more worthwhile things. Avoid buying Waterford crystal in Dublin: try rather to visit the factory in Waterford itself. Look out also for Aran sweaters, tweeds, linens, lace, pottery and silver as well as consumables such as Irish whiskey, Guinness and cheeses. Smoked salmon is good, but do not buy it at Dublin Airport.

The three main Irish national daily newspapers are all in English. British newspapers can usually be obtained early in the morning. Books published in the UK are subject to a 20 per cent surcharge, but second-hand bookshops are plentiful. Easons and Fred Hanna are recommended.

EATING AND DRINKING

Restaurants are excellent, but expensive. Best value is lunch at as little as £10 a head. Beware the hefty surcharges to cover VAT and 15 per cent service charge. Although there is no real culinary tradition, there is excellent fish, including good salmon, but avoid the Dublin Bay prawns which most certainly will not come from there. There is good Irish dairy produce including cheeses. Recommended central restaurants include Frères Jacques in Dame Street and La Stampa in Danson Street.

The visitor must of course sample Guinness, which does not travel well, in the town in which it is produced. The whiskey too is a must and is distinct from the Scottish product. Try Jameson's, Paddy or Powers. Whiskey is an essential ingredient of your after-dinner Irish coffee.

Dublin, like London, has a pub culture. Although the pubs are not exactly the same as London's, and certainly not particularly smart, they are invariably packed and have their own distinctive atmosphere. Recommended central pubs include the Stag's Head in Dame Court, the Bailey in Duke Street, Kehoe's in Saint Anne Street and Toner's in Baggot Street.

TRANSPORT

Taxis are available, but are expensive. Dublin is well served by buses and trains.

SECURITY

Beware of petty street crime.

ISRAEL

Language Hebrew

Currency shekel of 100 agorot. £1=5.38, Mar 1997

Banks 0830–1230.The shekel is readily exchangeable and no black market exists

Traveller's cheques commission is high; bring some shekels and US dollars

Credit cards Visa is commonly accepted, Mastercard less so

Cashpoints widely available in Jerusalem and Tel Aviv; shekels can be withdrawn using UK cards; no withdrawal on the Sabbath

Shops 0830–1300, 1600–1900, Mon to Thur, 0830–1300 Fri, closed on Sats until sunset. Many shops close on Tue afternoons

Refunds tourists paying in foreign currency for goods worth over $50 at a business authorised by the Ministry of Tourism are entitled to at least a 5 per cent discount and the refund of 17 per cent VAT. Signs are posted in shops which offer this discount. Although VAT refunds are a complicated process, staff at the shops or at the Tourist offices can help with any queries

Sales genuine reductions, but the prices of some imported items are still above UK prices

Bargaining fixed prices in shops; bargaining expected in street markets

Duty-free at the airport; may still be more expensive than UK shop prices, although it is a good place to buy Dead Sea beauty products

Tipping not widespread

Export restrictions permits, available from the Antiques Authority in the Rockefeller Museum in Salahaddin Street in Jerusalem, are required for valuable antiques, defined as pre-1700

The cost of living can be high if one insists on imported goods. Good clothing, for example, can cost three times as much as in the UK. Some casual clothing, such as short-sleeved shirts, T-shirts and jeans, is reasonable.

Recommended buys include jewellery such as necklaces, silver, Roman glass and artefacts, Roman and old Jewish coins, antique pottery, diamonds, Palestinian jewellery, Palestinian craftwork such as inlaid boxes with mother of pearl, brassware, embroidered cushions, Hebron glassware and Gottex swimwear or Dead Sea beauty products, both made in Israel.

The *Jerusalem Post* is an English-language daily newpaper. There is a good bi-weekly current affairs magazine, the *Jerusalem Report*. Newspapers from England arrive generally the day after publication. They sell at three times the UK price. Books are much more expensive than in the UK. Some shops sell second-hand books, but these too are pricey.

Most hotels will offer meat as well as dairy foods. There are several restaurants where one can get a reasonable meal, but they offer limited variety and the cuisine tends to be uninspiring and/or expensive. There are only one or two places for a drink, and those that exist are expensive apart from the local beer and arak. Local wines vary in quality, but are drinkable as well as being relatively cheap. The best Israeli wine is from the Golan wineries. It is Californian in style and costs twice the price of its equivalent in the UK. Imported wines are not of the highest quality.

The favoured local fast-food snack is falafel in pitta bread, a deep-fried chick-pea ball topped up with salad, vegetables and houmous.

The Sabbath begins on Friday evening at sunset and ends at sunset on Saturday. It is strictly observed and there are no bus and train services from Friday evening to Saturday evening.

Security may prove problematic at times of tension between Jews and Arabs, particularly in the Walled City of Jerusalem and after Friday prayers.

JERUSALEM

Jerusalem is the seat of government of Israel. It is still politically and psychologically divided. Palestinian East Jerusalem, which includes the Old City, is administered together with Jewish West Jerusalem as one city by Israel.

Shopping in the Old City centres on David Street and the Street of the Chain. Outside the walls and to the west in the modern city centre, shopping is concentrated in King George V Street, Jaffa Street and neighbouring streets. Palestinian East Jerusalem lies to the north of the Old City. There the main streets are Salahef-Din and Sultan Suleiman both near Herod's Gate.

Marks and Spencer is among the shops in Israel's biggest mall, the Jerusalem Mall at Malha in the West of the city. In the south-west at Talpiot is the Canyon Israel Shopping

Centre. The Beit Hazranim Shopping Centre is in Yad Haharuzim Street and the Ben Yehuda Pedestrian Mall in the street of that name. The Bell Centre in the centre of town and the Cardo in the Old City are also worth a visit. Main hotels such as the King David all have their own shopping arcades.

Best buys include Palestinian craftwork such as olive wood carving, handmade pottery, inlaid boxes with mother of pearl, brassware, Judaica jewellery and embroidery.

No public services operate on the Sabbath, and no private shops open in the Jewish sector. Many Israeli shops open only on Friday morning and will not reopen before dusk on Saturday. The Muslim day of rest is Friday. English is widely-but not always well-spoken.

Tipping is not as prevalent in West Jerusalem as it is elsewhere in the Middle East but it is customary to tip the barber. Porters at the port of entry are tipped, but it is not necessary to give anything to a petrol-pump attendant. Those who give service expect some sort of tip, but you are not pestered in the street for baksheesh.

Sterling cheques can be cashed at authorised East Jerusalem money changers who may give a better rate for shekels, particularly at times of currency fluctuations.

EATING AND DRINKING

There are many restaurants in West Jerusalem for good food, but there are few bars. The principal East Jerusalem restaurants serving Palestinian food (much like Lebanese in style) are the Philadelphia and Al Zahra, both in Al Zahra Street.

TRANSPORT

Pavements are rough and some roads are unsurfaced or cobbled. Service (shared) taxis provide a good service within Israel and the West Bank, the main danger being the standard of driving. They run on the Sabbath. Bus services within Jerusalem and to surrounding towns are frequent and cheap. Discounted block tickets, 11 rides for the price of 10, are available from the driver on the bus.

TEL AVIV

Tel Aviv is a busy commercial metropolis contiguous with the ancient town of Jaffa, where there are some good restaurants. There are very few real bargains to be had. An exception is antique maps of the Holy Land where there is a great deal of choice, and prices are reasonable. A good source is Pollacks on King George V Street.

There are shopping centres at the Opera Tower at the junction of Allenby and Hayarkon Street and at the Dizengoff Centre in Dizengoff Street, which sell a wide variety of goods. Other shopping areas include the Nahalat Binyamin Mall near the Carmel Market and shopping arcades at the New Central Bus Terminal. There are numerous small shops and boutiques in the centre of town. Imported designer clothing can be bought in Kikar Hamedine. Leather goods and furs are to be found around Hayarkon-Yirmiyahu corner and in the heart of the business area. Diamonds and precious stones are to be found at the Diamond Exchange on the Tel Aviv-Ramat Gan border as well as in Netanya. Carmel Market, just off Allenby Street, is the largest open-air market. Some small clothing items including seconds Marks and Spencer products manufactured in Israel, can be bought there. Nearby Bezalel Market, near the corner of King George and Allenby Streets, is also worth a visit. The flea market is in Jaffa.

All major hotels have free brochures which include shopping guides, mostly for Israeli goods such as jewellery and diamonds or for art galleries where work by Israeli artists is on sale. There is a craft market at the Carmel Market on Tuesdays and Fridays. The old port in Jaffa has a number of workshops selling locally made jewellery and paintings. There is an artist's moshav (cooperative) at Ein Hod, off the Tel Aviv-Haifa motorway, which is well worth a visit.

The two best shops to buy English-language books are in branches of Steimatskys and Best Sellers.

EATING AND DRINKING

There are many restaurants in Tel Aviv and Jaffa reflecting the more than 100 countries from which the Israeli population has been drawn. These vary widely in style, price and degree of formality. For the best French-style cooking try the Golden Apple in Rothschild Boulevard, for Italian food Remi in Hayarkon Street. For more middle-of-the-road eating, Shaul's Inn at 11 Eliashiv Street for Oriental and Yemenite (Jewish) cuisine and the Yotvata in Town at 83 Herbert Samuel Promenade on Tel Aviv seafront for dairy food. Jaffa has many good seafood restaurants clustered in and around the old port, of which one of the best is Taboon.

TRANSPORT
There are good and cheap bus services, but these are usually crowded. Service taxis follow most of the bus routes and, at slightly more than the bus fare, are good value. Ordinary taxis are plentiful. They can be called from the hotels or stopped on the street.

SECURITY
It is recommended that you walk for some of the time in the city centre to allow you to browse in the shop windows. There will be no hassle from beggars and passers-by are always happy to give directions if you get lost. Tel Aviv is a friendly city and well used to helping visitors who do not speak Hebrew.

ITALY

Language **Italian**
Currency **lira. £1=2700, Mar 1997. There is no black market**
Banks **0830–1330 Mon to Fri**
Credit cards **widely accepted in larger hotels, restaurants and shops Visa preferred, then American Express**
Cashpoints **widely available**
Shops **0930–1300, 1600 to 1930 Mon to Sat. Most close Sun and until 1600 on Mon. Some close on Thur afternoon. In summer many do not reopen until 1700. In Aug many shops are closed for the whole month**
Refunds **not easy except in the bigger department stores like Rinascente or Coin**
Sales **Jan and Jul: genuine and recommended**
Bargaining **in larger shops *prezzi fissi* (fixed prices) are not open for discussion, but it is worth asking for discounts in smaller shops**
Duty-free **at the airport: toiletries and perfumery bought in town might be cheaper. VAT-free shopping for non-EU nationals is available in larger shops**

Tipping hotels and restaurants usually include a
service charge of 10 to 15 per cent in bills, but a
small tip in addition is normal. At railways and
airports there are fixed charges for baggage
handling, but a small tip in addition is normally
expected. Hotel porters should be given a
minimum of 5,000 and a maximum of 10,000 lire
Export restrictions the export of antiquities and
valuable artefacts is subject to the approval of the
Ministry of Education. Export certificates may be
slow in forthcoming. Keep all receipts, since tax
police may ask to see them

Italy occupies a foremost place in the world of fashion. Italian
men like to dress very informally whereas Italian women like
to display expensive fur coats, even in early April, in their
devotion to *bella figura* or keeping up appearances.

Designer shops abound and top-of-the-range fashions are
second to none. Medium-quality clothing is good, but more
expensive than in the UK. Check the finish on all clothing.
There is distinctly less choice for larger sizes. Shoe styling is
Italian, i.e. narrow. Mass-produced shoes are cheap, but are
generally of inferior quality and do not come in a range of fittings. Larger sizes can be difficult to find.

Shoes and leather goods in general are worth a look, as are
fashion items such as stylish suits and silk ties for men or silk
scarves for women. Those who appreciate good design will
like some of the glass, ceramics and jewellery which are widely
available. Otherwise food and drink items offer a multitude of
ideas for gifts and souvenirs.

Bars offering coffee and a stand-up snack are on almost
every street and are the cheapest places to eat, but beware of
sitting down outside: the bill could double. For sit-down
meals the trattoria or pizzeria is the next cheapest. A meal
consisting of a pizza or pasta followed by meat or fish, dessert
and coffee with house wine might cost around £25 per person
including cover charge. A good-humoured well-dressed crowd
is normally the sign of a good trattoria. Ristorantes are sometimes absurdly expensive and should be kept for a special
treat. However the traditional emphasis on differentiation in
price and quality between ristorante, trattoria and osteria is
now often meaningless and some places call themselves osterias
but charge the earth.

Pizzas are a must while in Italy . Those cooked in wood
ovens – *forno a legna* – are best. Also worth trying are *funghi
porcini* (mushrooms), *bresaola* (dried meat), *parmigiano*

(parmesan) and Italian sheep's milk cheeses, Italian wines and to finish *amaro, grappa* or *sambuca*.

Bars are a thoroughly Italian institution where you will find all sorts of coffee, ice-cream, alcoholic drinks, sandwiches and snacks. Italian wines and aperitifs are plentiful and cheap – French and German are harder to find and dearer. Italian beer is mainly of the light, lager type. Italians are the world's biggest drinkers of Scotch Malt Whiskey and there is always a good variety readily available and cheaper than in the UK.

ROME

Shopping in Rome can be confusing and tiring. It can also be fun. Stick to one small area at a time – distances can feel much further than they look on the map. Most things which can be bought in London can be bought in Rome too, at a price. Roman pavements and cobbled streets take a heavy toll on shoes and comfortable, durable footwear is essential.

The Ludovisi district around the Via Veneto is excellent for quality shopping, though prices are rather high. Window shop here and buy elsewhere. The historic centre (Centro Storico) of Rome – Via Sistina and Via Gregoriana, Piazza di Spagna, Via Condotti, Via Frattina and Via del Corso – is the area of the great fashion houses. Neighbouring streets abound with smart shops and boutiques which sell less expensive clothing and footwear, art objects and jewellery. In Via del Tritone, Via Nazionale and surrounding streets there are reasonably priced clothing shops of every kind. In the Via Margutta, Via Ripetta, Piazza del Popolo and Via Frattina areas, the little side-streets contain small shops, antique shops, art galleries, etc. Good quality antiques may also be found in Via dei Coronari and Via del Babuino. The Via Ottaviano and the Via Cola di Rienzo district, not far from the Vatican, are where Romans shop.

Another good shopping area is between Via Salaria and Via Nomentana, especially the Rinascente department store on Piazza Fiume. In the Via della Croce are food shops selling imported specialities from all over the world. Also good is Castroni at Via Cola di Rienzo 196. Just out of town are two American-style shopping malls. La Romanina is just off Exit 20 from the Grand Raccoardo Annulare. Cinecitta Due is at Viale Palmiro Togliatti 2. Stores open from 1000 to 2000.

Among quality department stores are La Rinascente in Via del Corso and in Piazza Fiume. Coin on Via Libia or in Piazzale Appio near San Giovanni and elsewhere is Rome's equivalent to British Home Stores. Upim and Standa have branches all over Rome, economical and convenient, equivalent to Littlewoods or C&A.

The most picturesque market is that of Porta Portese with all kinds of bric-à-brac and clothing. The market takes place every Sunday morning in Piazza Porta Portese. For old prints there is the market at Piazza Fontanella Borghese every morning of the week except Sunday. Another market worth visiting is in Via Sannio near San Giovanni where stalls sell shoes and clothing, old and new. Food markets include those at Piazza Vittorio Emanuele, Piazza Alessandria and the Campo dei Fiori. At the beginning of December there is a Christmas market at Fiera di Roma on Via Cristoforo Colombo followed from the middle of the month by a children's market on Piazza Navona.

Local specialities worth taking home include shoes, designer shoes from Via Condotti or much cheaper shoes from market stalls and shops around the Trevi fountain. Silk ties are available everywhere, even on street stalls, but if you want to spend real money, Ferragamo in Via Condotti or Cravatta at Piazza San Lorenzo are for you. Venetian glassware is at Modigliano's in Via Condotti. T-shirts with good designs are available cheaply from stalls in Piazza Navona and everywhere tourists go. Romans wear heavy, elaborate but wonderful costume jewellery which is available in all the shopping areas already mentioned. Interesting masks are in the Via Sistina. Leather goods on street stalls are worth looking at, as are the ceramics in the basement of Rinascente. Other possible gifts include salamis, cheeses, wines, *amaro* and *grappa*.

British newspapers and some weeklies can be purchased in Rome on the afternoon of the day of issue. Sunday newspapers can be purchased on the Sunday morning or the day after. Prices from kiosks are four to five times higher than in the UK. The *International Herald Tribune* is published in Rome every day except Monday. English language books are available, but are much more expensive than in the UK. The best shop to try is the Lion Bookshop at Via del Babuino 181.

EATING AND DRINKING

Roman food and wine are renowned. There are innumerable eating places to suit all pockets. Some of the more moderately priced places offering local cuisine in the historic centre are Trattoria Vito in Via delle Colonelle, Monserrato in Via di Monserrato, Costanza in Piazza del Paradiso, Pierluigi in Piazza di Ricci, Da Mario in Via della Vite and Tosca in Largo dei Chiavari.

Otherwise try Trattoria la Gensola in Piazza della Gensola

in Trastevere, Il Giardino in Via Zuccheli in the Via Veneto area or Orazio in Via di Porta Latina in San Giovanni; in the Porta Pia area are either Taverna Flavia in Via Flavia, Coriolano in Via Ancona or Da Vincenzo in Via Castelfidardo.

TRANSPORT

Public transport is cheap and reasonably efficient, although often overcrowded during the rush hours, when pickpockets are at their busiest. Rome has a good network of bus and tram routes as well as an underground system. There is a flat-rate fare which entitles you to use the bus and metro for unlimited travel for 75 minutes. Tickets are available at tobacco kiosks and news stands and must be validated before starting your journey. Daily and weekly passes can also be purchased. There are several good radio-taxi services. Only use official taxis and ensure the meter is working. There are extra charges daily after 2200, on Sunday and for parcels or luggage. Taxis cannot normally be hailed. Although the fare includes service, an extra 10 per cent tip is always welcome.

SECURITY

Tourists are safe in Rome, but their belongings are not. Pickpockets and bag snatchers are always active, especially during the tourist season. Do not carry valuables with you in the street or on public transport. If you do need to carry a bag keep a firm grip on it. Watch out for mopeds and gypsies, especially gypsy children. Beggars are not aggressive and do not hassle.

Otherwise it is perfectly safe to walk to shopping areas from a central hotel.

FLORENCE

Florence is one of Italy's more expensive cities. The main shopping area is between the Piazza del Duomo and the river, with the hub along the Via Roma, Via dei Calzaiuoli and Via Por Santa Maria which lead to the Ponte Vecchio. Several top-level designers are represented along the Via Tornabuoni. For those looking for more reasonably priced clothing, the major department stores of Coin, Rinascente, Upim and Standa have branches in the city. For enthusiasts there is a flea market on the Piazza dei Ciompi.

Good places for crafts and souvenirs are the Loggia di Mercato Nuovo on the Piazza del Porcellino or the Loggia degli Uffizi in the Piazzale degli Uffizi. Leather goods including shoes can be a good buy. The Ponte Vecchio in particular is famous for its goldsmiths, silversmiths and jewellers. Worth looking for in the boutiques are quality lace and knitwear, silks and brocades or lingerie. There are plenty of antique shops for enthusiasts who can afford them and the area around the Piazza Santa Croce is good for books. More reasonable gifts or souvenirs such as wines, hams and other edibles are to be found in the nearest supermarket.

British newspapers and periodicals are on sale on news stands from about 1800 on the day of issue at prices well above those in the UK.

EATING AND DRINKING
Good-value eating places are to be found around the Central Market.

TRANSPORT
Public transport is generally reliable. Bus tickets are purchased at e.g., a tobacconist before travel and are validated in a machine on board. Taxi services are good, but there are few public ranks. It is usual to call taxis by telephone.

SECURITY
The risks are lower than in other parts of Italy, but precautions have to be taken against all forms of theft including bag snatching.

GENOA

The historic centre around the Via XX Settembre is easily covered on foot. There are one or two well-known stores including Standa, Coin, Upim or Rinascente, as well as a large indoor market selling fresh food.

Most British newspapers can generally be bought from the major news stands the day after publication. A few of the larger bookshops stock a selection of English-language books, but their rate of mark-up is high.

Personal security measures should be taken, particularly in the area of the port.

MILAN

The cost of living is the highest in Italy and higher than London. Milan is great for window shopping in the extremely expensive Duomo and Via Vittorio Emanuele or the high-fashion Via Montenapoleone and Via della Spiga where shops like Gucci are to be found. The Brera area is charming, with lovely, but again expensive, shops. The Corso Buenos Aires is a general shopping street equivalent perhaps to Oxford Street.

All the fashion houses are to be found in Milan, including Dolce and Gabbana. Salvatore Ferragamo in Via Montenapoleone 3 and 30 is a must in January and July during sale times. There are also outlets which specialise in selling the previous season's items at great discounts, such as Il Salvagente at Via Fratelli Bronzetti 16. 20129 is supposed to be the largest bargain basement in Milan and sells all the big Italian designer labels at a discount. There is a nameless shop in Via Vittorio Emanuele, opposite the Max Mara shop, which sells the latter's previous season's stock at a discount. Other fashion factory outlets are Frosio at Via Milano 3, Cit Spa at Via Matteucci 19 and Mila Schon Spaccio at Via Guido Rosso 1.

There is no Marks and Spencer or Mothercare in Milan (for the latter you have to go to Switzerland), but Habitat has opened round the corner from the Duomo, and Laura Ashley is to be found (hugely expensive) at Via Brera 4.

When looking for presents in a hurry you could do worse than shop for consumables at Motta in the Piazza Duomo. Tomato and ink spaghetti can be an exotic offering and funghi porcini and fresh parmesan go down well. Lemoncino, a delicious southern Italian alcoholic lemon drink is also to be found there. Cheaper versions can be found in supermarkets like Esselunga and Pam, which are located all over Milan.

Pasticcini are the tiny cakes eaten with coffee after a meal instead of chocolates. For a cheaper range try Esselunga at the top of Viale Papiniano near the market.

Fiorucci at Via Vittorio Emmanuele 4 in the Duomo area has a good selection of presents from Italian sunglasses to the latest Italian design kettles and children's clothing – not cheap, but nice. If you take your passport with you to La Rinascente, the famous department store in Piazza Duomo, you can get a 10 per cent discount on toiletries and perfumes, though duty-free may still be cheaper.

What is fun, and can be rewarding, is to go to the many markets in Milan. It is said that you can see very sophisticated Milanese ladies bargaining for designer T-shirts at the Papiniano

Market on Tuesdays and Saturdays. There are many markets for clothing of all sorts such as Via Benedetto Marcello on Tuesday and Saturday, Via Moretto da Brescia on Monday, Piazzale Martini on Wednesday, Via Pietro Calvi on Thursday and Largo Quinto Alpini on Friday. Go in the morning. The Naviglio area (*naviglio* means canals) is always nice for a stroll, but on the last Sunday of every month there is also a popular antiques market there.

Flowers are worth buying from one of the many florist kiosks. Prices are fairly high, for example, expect to pay 12,000 lire, about £5, for five lilies and some greenery. If you are invited out to dinner in Milan, flowers are considered a nice present, but do not take chrysanthemums, which are associated with cemeteries. Flowers given in odd numbers are thought to bring luck.

Most of the quality British newspapers are available on the afternoon of publication from one of the many street kiosks. The *Independent* will cost 4,300 lire. There is no local English-language newspaper, though the *Informer* describes itself as 'the only monthly guide in English to surviving and thriving in Italy'. Choice of magazines is more limited. There are plenty of outlets selling books in English such as the English Bookshop at Via Mascherone 12 near the Conciliazione stop on the metro, or the American Bookshop at Via Camperio 16, close to the Cairoli stop . There is a wide choice, on average about one-third more expensive than in the UK.

TRANSPORT

The metro is clean and efficient and the bus and tram systems work well. There is a flat rate of 1,500 lire for each journey up to 75 minutes. A carnet of 10 tickets costs 14,000 lire. Tickets are purchased from kiosks in the street. Taxis are available at ranks or can be telephoned for; they are fairly expensive.

SECURITY

Watch out for your handbag and wallet, particularly in the Duomo area, at the castle and in the metro, and beware of child hustlers. The Central Station also attracts skilled thieves.

NAPLES

The hub of Naples is the Corso Umberto 1 running from the Central Station on the Piazza Garibaldi to the historic centre, on and around the Via Benedetto Croce.

EATING AND DRINKING
Restaurants are plentiful and eating out is popular provided one likes Italian food. Standards vary and Neapolitans are not cosmopolitan as regards food. Average costs at a typical restaurant are reasonable by UK standards, though top-class restaurants are expensive. Naples is synonymous with pizza. Try Trianon da Ciro at Via Pietro Colletta 46.

TRANSPORT
There is a reasonably good bus and tram service supplemented by a cross-city underground railway line. Although often crowded, these are relatively inexpensive. Taxis are plentiful and may be summoned by telephone. Ensure that the meter is activated before starting the journey.

SECURITY
Petty street crime is prevalent.

IVORY COAST

ABIDJAN

Language **French**
Currency **CFA franc. £1=945, Mar 1997**
Cashpoints **Citibank takes Visa**
Shops **0800/0830–1200/1230, 1500/1530–1900/1930 Mon to Sat. Some supermarkets and small stores in the centre of town and markets open on Sun. Many shops and restaurants are closed in Jul and Aug**
Tipping **10 per cent is usual in most retaurants and hotels; even where service is included staff look for a small tip. Porters who carry shopping to cars expect a small tip; those in luxury hotels expect generous ones. Taxi drivers expect the meter charge to be rounded up**

Abidjan is widely regarded as the most sophisticated capital in West Africa and it is a good place for discovering arts and crafts which make ideal gifts and souvenirs. It is also famous for coffee, cocoa and reggae. Supermarket prices are in general about double those in the UK, and most food is imported from France. Most clothes are also imported from France and are expensive.

The majority of visitors will see only up-market areas such as Le Plateau and Cocody, but the Treichville Market is one of the largest in West Africa, with a huge selection of crafts and other wares. There are also the Plateau Marché in the Boulevard de la République and the Senegalese Marché across from the Hotel du Parc. The fish market is at the Port de Pêches, off Boulevard Marseilles.

There is a market on the road to Grand Bassam with local crafts and handiwork. At the Bureau of Tourism in Grand Bassam itself you can watch local artisans creating their bronzes, batiks and other wares. The Fraternité des Handicappés in the Rue de la République in Plateau is good for crafts. Also in Plateau, shops for gifts and souvenirs include L'Art et la Table and Marco Polo in the Rue Gorgas, Fifth Avenue in Rue du Commerce, Autrement in Imm Borg or MB Boutique in Avenue Chardy. Also try La Rose d'Ivoire in the Hotel Ivoire or Galeria Akag next to the Novotel. The Hotel Ivoire is also good for gold and silver as are the jewellers along the Boulevard Delafosse in Treichville.

Particularly recommended for gifts and souvenirs are traditional woodcarvings including masks.

Jeans and cords are made locally and shoes, especially flip-flops, can be bought. In the markets there is a variety of tie-dyed and other T-shirts, sometimes with matching skirts for women and also the caftan-style local dress known as the bou-bou. These are not expensive, though the quality of the sewing can vary.

Some British newspapers can be bought. Books in English, usually paperbacks, are few and far between but only a little more expensive than in the UK. The Librairie du Carrefour in Cocody has a stock of English paperbacks.

Eating and Drinking

Eating out is expensive. Most of the hotels have reasonable restaurants. Other recommendations are Le Lagon Bleu on the lagoon on Boulevard Lagunaire at the end of Avenue Chardy, the Regent on Avenue Delafosse, the Restaurant de Pêcheurs at the fish market, Le Wafou Village Hotel on Boulevard de Marseille at Km 7, Chez Babouya in Rue 7 in Treichville and La Bonne Fourchette behind Cocody Market. Local fish, avocados and fruit are particularly good.

TRANSPORT
The bus network is not generally used by tourists. Taxis are plentiful and reasonable in price provided the journey is properly metered. Confirm the fare before starting the journey.

SECURITY
The markets are always crowded, so take the minimum amount of money and leave all valuables behind. Street crime including mugging is not unknown.

JAMAICA

KINGSTON

Language **English**
Currency **Jamaican dollar (J$) of 100 cents. £1=54.46, Mar 1997**
Banks **0900–1400 Mon to Thur, 0900–1200, 1430–1700 Fri**
Shops **0900–1600 Mon, Tue and Thur to Sat; 0900–1200 Wed**
Tipping **most hotels and restaurants apply a 12-15 per cent service charge; additional tipping is not necessary**

There is plenty to buy in Kingston. It is just a matter of finding it in out-of-the-way places and being prepared to pay the prices. Boutiques carry large stocks of locally made clothes which are relatively inexpensive, although quality can be variable. There are a number of shopping plazas in the Constant Spring Road area. In total contrast Kingston also has a considerable number of shops located in private homes such as Wanderer at 3 Queensway for gifts and jewellery or Signatures in Dilcoosha Avenue for clothing, china, crystal and jewellery. Mijan on Barbican Road has a good range of locally designed clothing and accessories in natural fabrics. Angela's on Merrick Avenue is worth a look for gifts and souvenirs.

Luxury goods for the tourist trade are readily available. Those looking for something more ethnic in the way of gifts and souvenirs have a difficult time. The Craft Cottage in the Village Plaza on Constant Spring Road has a range of locally produced crafts such as wooden items, ceramics, leather goods, basketware, paintings, coffee and spices. The Magic Kitchen at the same location is also worth a look. Patoo in the Manor Park Plaza is more up-market. Countryside in the Manor Centre on Constant Spring Road is good for cheap Blue Mountain coffee. Do not forget reggae records or rum.

The two main bookstores have a fairly good selection of paperback and hardback books which are reasonably priced although more expensive than in the UK.

EATING AND DRINKING

The choice of places for eating out is limited. Devon House has four restaurants of which the Grog Shoppe offers reasonably priced, basic local cuisine while the Coffee Terrace does good light lunches. The Devonshire is good, but expensive: visit the new Thai restaurant. Gloria's Rendezvous in Port Royal has excellent seafood. Ivor's is high above Kingston with spectacular views. The Blue Mountains Inn is expensive, but has a magical setting.

Patties are very popular as a snack or lunch, the equivalent of Cornish pasties. There are many varieties of Jamaica rum and various rum-based liqueurs which are very reasonably priced. Red Stripe beer is famous and very popular. Only slightly more expensive is locally made Guinness, Mackeson and Heineken. A number of known brands of cigarettes and tobacco are made locally, as are excellent cigars.

TRANSPORT

Bus services are definitely not recommended. Taxis can be summoned by telephone and are plentiful, but also expensive and not particularly reliable mechanically or otherwise.

SECURITY

Robbery and violent crime are a problem, particularly in Kingston. It is not advisable to visit the poorer areas of town unless your visit is essential; you should certainly not go there after dark.

JAPAN

Language **Japanese**
Currency **yen (Y) of 100 sen. £1=197, Mar 1997**
Banks **0900–1500 Mon to Fri, 0900–1200 Sat**
Credit cards **Visa, Access (Mastercard), American Express, Diners Club most commonly accepted, but cash expected in e.g. Japanese-style hotels**
Shops **0900/1000–1830/1900; department stores 1000–1800, Mon to Fri, 1000–1830 Sat. Many shops open seven days a week, those that close once a week do so mid-week**
Sales **seasonal, in all shops, good for clothing and sports equipment**
Tipping **offering a tip can be considered insulting. There is usually a service charge of at least 10 per cent in hotels and restaurants and a 5 per cent tax on meals or drinks costing Y5,000 or over per head**

Prices in Japan as well as being very high, tend to be very uniform, but careful shopping can produce bargains even by UK standards.

If you are over a women's size 12 or a man of more than average stature you may have difficulty in finding clothing which fits.

Almost everything is of very high quality. Shop staff all have impeccable manners and are very attentive to the customer. Your purchase will always be beautifully presented and carefully gift-wrapped. Even buying everyday items in the local convenience stores is a pleasant experience. Large department stores offer a huge range of products, very similar to the department stores in the West, while thousands of small, family-owned shops sell everything from top-of-the-range handmade silk kimonos downwards.

For gifts and souvenirs you could purchase relatively inexpensive *yukaku* (a variety of typical Japanese souvenirs) or very expensive antiques. There is a wide range of other products, including ceramics, old paintings and musical instruments, swords, lacquerwork and pearls. Further ideas would include ikebana, chopsticks and holders, washi paper products, woodblock prints, kokeshi dolls, umbrellas, traditional wooden toys, kimonos and obi, fans and screens - or the very latest in electronics. However prices will probably be lower in

Hong Kong or Singapore, and even so called tax-free shopping might not always offer best value.

There are four morning and one evening newspaper published locally in English. The leading newspaper is the *Japan Times*, but it has a very early deadline. The others are the *Mainichi Daily News*, *Daily Yomiuri* and *Asahi Evening News*. The *Financial Times* is printed in Tokyo. English and American books are available in hotel bookstores and in specialised shops. The selection is reasonable, but prices can be high.

The Japanese eat out probably more than any other people. There are tens of thousands of restaurants serving everything from a bowl of noodles at Y500 to vastly expensive meals in geisha houses. A simple full meal with drinks runs the whole range of costs, but at a reasonable Japanese-style restaurant can be as little as Y4,000. Fixed menus at lunchtime can be very good value for money. A good Japanese meal in the right surroundings costs twice as much as a European meal. Restaurants will each specialise in a particular cuisine such as *sukiyaki* or *sushi*. Most people acquire a taste for at least some Japanese dishes such as *tempura* (fried fish and vegetables) and *sukiyaki* (thinly sliced beef cooked in a special stock). Good lager beer such as the famous Kirin or Sapporo is made in Japan, and local wine is improving in quality. Saki is an acquired taste, but should be tried. There are Japanese-made spirits, and soft drinks of all brands are available. Japanese Whiskey is like Scotch in flavour but Scotch is now widely available.

TOKYO

Shopping seems to be a national sport in Japan and Tokyo is a wonderful place to window shop. It is however an extremely expensive city – perhaps the most expensive in the world.

Large department stores are clustered around the main railway stations and the famous Ginza shopping area. This is home to most of Tokyo's prestigious shops and definitely the place to see and be seen, with fashionable boutiques as well as department stores.

An interesting way to shop in Tokyo is to visit the district that specialises in a particular product such as paper. These areas tend to be much better value than the department stores and larger commercial centres and have far more character. Asakusa is full of little shops selling paper and anything to do with paper. Washi (highly decorative paper used mainly for crafts) is probably cheaper here than anywhere else in Tokyo.

Asakusabashi has large supplies of washi, but also sells stationery, craft items, seasonal decorations and cheap toys. Asakusa Cannon is crammed full of souvenir shops aimed directly at Western tourists. Kappabashi is a fun place to visit, the wholesale area for kitchen and restaurant supplies including jelly moulds in the shape of Mount Fuji. Harajuku is a teeny-bopper's paradise with its high-fashion boutiques for teenagers, the place to hang out if you are under 20 and look about 14. Ueno is the area to shop if you want to soak up the atmosphere of everyday Tokyo. Home of the panda bear (Ueno Zoo), the area is full of discount shops where you can buy most things including clothes, cosmetics, toys and all types of food. Akihabara is the centre for electronic and electrical equipment where some good bargains are available. Aoyama is the fashion centre of Tokyo with most international designers represented in some very high class boutiques. You can pick up a Gucci handbag, an Issey Miyake creation and a Rolex watch without wearing out the soles of your Charles Jourdan shoes. Kanda is the place for books. It also specialises in sports equipment and is a good place to shop if you are a martial arts enthusiast. Several more areas are worth visiting if you really want to shop till you drop. Shinjuku and Shibuya are highly commercialised general shopping areas offering little in the way of traditional Japanese atmosphere.

However, if you do want to see the Japanese department stores Takashimaya in Ginza district is superb, the food hall is especially mind-blowing. (Mitsukoshi and Matsuzakaya are also wonderful stores.)

For the tourist who wants to take back a few genuine Japanese souvenirs the Oriental Bazaar is unbeatable. Situated half-way down Tokyo's equivalent of the Champs Elysées, Omote-Sando Dori, it cannot be missed with its eye-catching façade typical of an old Japanese building.

EATING AND DRINKING

IMA-ASA in Shinbashi is an old-established restaurant. Three restaurants in Akasaka also serving Japanese food are Minami, Restaurant Suntory and Kushinobo. In Rippongi are Fukuzushi and Kisso.

TRANSPORT

Tokyo has extensive and efficient underground and surface railway systems. Fares are reasonable, starting at Y140 on the subways and less by surface routes. Out of rush hours the systems are still quite crowded, but tolerable. There is an extensive bus network, cheap, but crowded and prone to traffic delays.

Taxis are numerous, but not cheap, the minimum fare being Y600.

OSAKA

A bustling and somewhat unattractively urban town. Some shops and restaurants were destroyed in the earthquake of January 1995 and are still in the process of being replaced.

Many visitors will get to know only Kita-ku in the north and Minami-ku in the south of town. In Kita-ku the Umeda Chika Centre between Osaka and Umeda stations is an underground shopping centre which gives an overview of what is available. Minami-ku, south of Shinsaibashi underground station comes alive in the evenings. Amerika-Mura is an area which has many fashionable shops and eating places. Another good place for eating is Dotomburi Street.

The underground railway system is much less extensive than in Tokyo.

JORDAN

AMMAN

Language **Arabic**
Currency **Jordanian dinar (JD) of 1,000 fils.
£1=1.13 Mar 1997 Prices may be quoted in
piastres or girsh**
Banks **0830–1430 Sat to Thur**
Shops **0800/0900–1900, Sat to Thur; most shops
close Fri. Some close for lunch between 1300 and
1600**
Duty-free **Queen Alia Airport has a limited duty-free
shop usually open only during normal shop hours**
Tipping **10 per cent for hairdressers and waiters;
bag-packers, petrol-pump attendants and taxi
drivers a few hundred fils**

Jordan imports much of its food and almost all manufactured goods. As a consequence the cost of living is high.

For gifts and souvenirs there are brass pots and Bedouin jewellery and rugs. Most are expensive. More modern gold and silver jewellery can be found in the gold souk in the centre of town. Dead Sea mud products are worth a look.

The Noor Foundation has various workshops and sales of local crafts including clothing, cushions, small embroidered items, ironwork and ceramics. Bani Hamida House sells rugs which are handmade by the Bani Hamida village women. Next door is River Jordan Design which sells bedspreads, tablecloths and small gift items such as Bedouin dolls. Do not expect any of these outlets to be cheap. Silsal is a ceramics shop off Zarhan Street where prices are quite reasonable. The Hebron Glass Shop is off the Dead Sea road through Naur. Try Leila Jirez on Jebel Hussein for Palestinian needlework, the Jordan Craft Development Centre on Second Circle or the Oriental Souvenir Shop at Third Circle–Prince Mohammed Street. Half-way down King Faisal Street is the Mango Market with small shops selling silk flowers and materials. A little further down on the same side is Kaftan Corner, an arcade of caftans. For sheepskin and leather, try the Leather Shop, opposite the Holiday Inn.

Sweifeih is a new shopping area which has become the "in" place to open a new shop. Jebel Hussein at Maxim Circle and Third Circle-Prince Mohammed Street is still worth trying, but styles are not so Western. Shoes are expensive in the smarter shops, but good value can be found at Red Shoe in Rainbow Street in their twice-yearly sales.

British newspapers and periodicals are available in most hotel shops, larger supermarkets and some bookshops or newsagents. The *Sunday Times* can cost up to JD4.5. English-language books are expensive, but a large selection is available in various shops in Sweifeih and down Gardens Street near Safeway. There is one English-language daily, the *Jordan Times*, and one weekly, the *Star*, published in Amman.

EATING AND DRINKING
There is a wide range of restaurants and hotels. Taxes totalling 20 per cent are added to all food and drink bills. For Lebanese and local food try Abu Ahmed on Third Circle and in Green Valley (near the Amra). For Italian food there are Leonardo's at Shmeisani or Romeros off Third Circle. For cakes and patisserie Café Mocha on Abdoun Street or the Marriott Hotel coffee shop are recommended.

TRANSPORT
Most tourist hotels are in Western Amman and if you wish to shop in the centre of town you will need a taxi, by far the best form of public transport. Taxis are readily available and cheap

in all the main towns. In Amman tourists tend to use the yellow
regular taxis which have meters, which do not always work. The
average fare from western Amman to the city centre will be
about JD1,500. White service taxis operate on fixed routes
and on a sharing basis.

SECURITY

Amman is relatively free of crime against tourists although
there are beggars who can be persistent, trying to sell you
small items you do not need.

KAZAKHSTAN

ALMATY

Language **Russian**
Currency **tenge. £1=120.58 Mar 1997**
Credit cards **accepted in some shops**

The National Museum is one of a number of good places to
purchase traditional Kazakh carpets, which are of good quality
and reasonably priced. Good fur hats of the Russian variety
(*shapki*) can also be purchased.

Those locals who can afford it use the local market, the
Green Bazaar, which is open six days a week, closed on
Monday. Prices are high by local standards, but are not fixed
and bargaining is the order of the day. There are a number of
shops carrying imported goods, these can be expensive and
supplies are uncertain.

EATING AND DRINKING

Eating out can be a disappointing experience, though there are
some establishments in town where one can get a reasonable
meal.

TRANSPORT

In winter, when it is not actually snowing, the pavements are usually icy and dangerous. Public transport such as it is is inefficient,
does not run to a timetable and is dangerous because of overcrowding. It is not recommended. There are few decent taxis
in town.

SECURITY
As in all of the former Soviet Republics there is a growing incidence of violent crime in Almaty including muggings, burglary, car-theft and car-hijacking.

KENYA

NAIROBI

Language **Swahili, English**
Currency **Kenya shilling (Ksh) of 100 cents. £1=88, Mar 1997**
Banks **0900–1500 Mon to Fri, 0900–1100 on the first and last Sat of the month**
Traveller's cheques **banks give slightly better rates of exchange than hotels; visitors are strongly advised to avoid street money-dealers**
Credit cards **American Express, Visa, Mastercard and other major cards widely accepted through out Kenya**
Shops **0830–1730 Mon to Sat. The City Market opens 0730–1800 Mon to Fri, 0730–1600 Sat and 0800–1300 Sun**
Bargaining **yes, especially in markets and curio shops**
Tipping **there is no general scale of tipping; in restaurants with no service charge 5 to 10 per cent should be sufficient**

A walk along Standard, Kaunda and Mama Ngina Streets and Kenyatta Avenue will expose you to arts and crafts from all over the African continent. Between Kigali and Tubman roads there are numerous shops and kiosks selling curios and jewellery. On Muindi Mbingu Street is the City Market, as well as clothing and fabric shops. Kenya grows beautiful flowers and they are available at pavement stalls both in the city and at suburban shopping centres.

Souvenirs of all kinds are widely available in shops, markets and from street traders offering the usual "elephant hair" or copper bracelets, Masai stools or spears. All the tourist hotels have good quality, but expensive shops for crafts and souvenirs. Some recommended buys include *kikapus* (large woven shopping bags); *kangas* (lengths of cloth with bright designs, ideal as beach wraps); safari clothing; best quality Makonde statues in ebony (they come from Tanzania); all sorts of other carvings (soapstone has to be handled with care) and semi-precious stones such as those used in the solitaire sets from Rockhound at 256 Collins Road in Karen.

African Heritage on Kenyatta Avenue claims to have Africa's largest selection of handicrafts and jewellery. For gem-stones and semi-precious stones and woodcarvings try Treasure Trove in Kaunda Street, Batiks and Jewellery in the Inter-Continental and M.T. Parekhi in Muindi Mbingu Street. For women's clothing try Go-between or Tinga Tinga at the Ya Ya Centre or Laid Bare at the ABC Centre. Colpro in Kimathi Street has a wide range of safari clothing. Men's informal safari suits can be bought from tailors or ready-made at about the same price as in the UK. Men's desert boots or brogues from Bata (there is a branch in the Hilton Hotel) are reasonable and of fair quality. Benetton has opened in the Esso Plaza with prices comparable to those in the UK. English is the language of official business and English speakers will be found here, and even in the remoter parts of the country.

British newspapers are available on the Nairobi news stands within a day or two of publication, but the price is high. The main local English-language newspapers are the *Nation*, the *Standard* and the *Kenya Times* (owned by the KANU political party) and their Sunday editions. Some very good bookshops now stock new paperbacks at around UK prices. There is a good selection of books on Kenya, for example, at the Nation Bookshop next door to the New Stanley Hotel. The Kenya Museum has many informative books and some are cheaper than in the UK, depending on the exchange rate.

EATING AND DRINKING

Good food abounds in Nairobi. In the city itself there are plenty of restaurants of all kinds of cuisine at reasonable prices. The standard is generally high. The local beer (Tusker or White Cap) is good. Fruit of high quality is in abundance. For a traditional English meal at a low price in colonial sur-roundings get a member to take you to the Muthaiga Club. The main hotels have various restaurants including pool-side cafés at the Hilton and Serena. For a lunchtime snack take in the atmosphere of the Delamere Terrace of the Norfolk Hotel or try the New Stanley. Meat-eaters will love the Carnivore on Langata Road, between Wilson Airport and the Nairobi National Park. Taking the overnight train to Mombasa ($40 first class) gives access to the Tamarind Restaurant, once described by the London *Financial Times* as the best in the third world.

TRANSPORT
Buses and minibuses (*matatus*) are not a realistic proposition for the traveller, but the centre of Nairobi is small enough to cover on foot. There will be hassle from money changers, street traders and beggars, but they are generally friendly. Look for Kenatco taxis or London Black Taxis. Agree a price for your journey before entering the car.

SECURITY
Do not wear jewellery, including earrings, when shopping, especially in the city centre, and do not walk around after dark. Mugging and other violent crime is not unknown.

KOREA REPUBLIC OF (SOUTH)

SEOUL

Language **Korean**
Currency **Korean won (W) of 100 jeon. £1=1400, Mar 1997**
Banks **0930–1630 Mon to Fri, 0930–1330 Sat. There are limitations on trading in US dollars or won and black markets exist in Namdaemun and Itaewon-dong**
Credit cards **major cards accepted in principal hotels and restaurants and a growing number of shops; many establishments only accept Korean-issued cards, some merchants add a 4-5 per cent surcharge**
Cashpoints **accept only locally issued cards; visitors obtain cash advances at bank counters only**
Shops **department stores open from 1030–1930, each one closes on a different day. In Itaewon shops open mostly around 0930 and close about 1930. Namdaemun market opens at 12 midnight and closes at 1700. Dongdaemun market opens from 0800 till 1830. Both are closed on Sun**
Refunds **not usually given, but goods can normally be exchanged within two weeks of purchase if you**

**retain the receipt and the goods are in good
condition**
Bargaining **in department stores and hotel shops
prices are fixed in other places ask for a discount**
Duty-free **on the ninth floor of the Lotte
department store and at the Donghwa duty-free
shop in Taepyung-ro, near the Koreana Hotel**
Tipping **not customary, but you may not receive
loose change. 10 per cent is appreciated for special
services. Hotels and restaurants add a 10 per cent
service charge, so tipping is not expected**

Shopping in Seoul can be fun, so long as you think of trying
to reduce prices as a game. The best thing is to look around
many shops before you decide to buy and always ask for a better price. This is not always easy since most small shopkeepers,
like the majority of traditional Koreans, including taxi drivers,
do not understand English or at most a few words only. When
buying clothes make sure that they are made to fit the Western
shape. Be prepared in Itaewon for young people trying to
attract customers in from the street. If you do not want to go
in, just refuse politely.

The main shopping areas are Insadong in the centre of the
city north of the Han river and near the City Hall (there is a
concentration of shops around the triangle formed by
Insadonggil, Taehwan-gil and Ujonggugno) and Itaewon, particularly along Itae'wonne and Panp'oro. Virtually all vendors
in Itaewon speak English.

There are several underground arcades such as those at
Sogong, Myong dong and Namdaemun. There are also many
department stores including Lotte, Midopa and Shinsegye in
Insadong and Hyundai and Galleria in Apkujongno south of
the river. The two main market areas are at Dongdaemun
(Eastgate) and Namdaemun (Southgate).

World-famous international designer goods such as
DKNY, Dior and Ricci are sold in the major department stores
and Hyundai stocks Aquascutum, Daks and Jaeger. Sisters in
Haewon-Dong has interesting handbags. Around the corner in
Itaewon Market Na-Sung at number 53 has designer items,
but it is local and more specialised merchandise which will
attract most visitors.

In Insadong *celadon* (pottery), calligraphy scrolls, traditional
paintings, masks, fans, rice paper, writing brushes and other
antiques are available. In Itaewon you will find ginseng,
Korean chests, leather and silk goods, clothing, *celadon* and
paintings. In Namdaemun Market there are *celadon*, paintings,

ginseng, flowers, fish and market produce. The Seoul Antique
Market in Changan-dong near the Sheraton Walker Hill Hotel
has several buildings full of of antique shops which sell
Korean chests, paintings and crafts.

Many visitors cannot leave Korea without a Korean chest.
These come in varying sizes and designs and can be either true
antiques or good reproductions. Prices vary. Ginseng is
famous and quite portable as a gift or souvenir. Handicrafts,
jewellery and leather goods such as handbags can be had at
reasonable, if not cheap, prices. Locally manufactured leather
shoes, either off the shelf or made to measure, or sports shoes
can be good value. Silk scarves or ties and sports jackets are
also worth looking at. All these items are widely available in
the locations already mentioned. Specialist shops include the
Korean Folk Handicraft Centres in Socho-ku on the first and
second floors of a four-storey granite building near the New
Core department store, not far from the Express Bus
Terminal, and also opposite Namdaemun Gate.

The Kyobo bookshop in Taepyoungro, across the road and
one block up from the Koreana Hotel, has the best selection
of English-language books. The best places to buy newspapers
are the shops of the five-star hotels such as the Westin Chosun
and the Grand Hyatt. Two daily English-language newspapers,
the *Korea Herald* and the *Korea Times*, are published locally.
Otherwise books and newspapers tend to be expensive.

EATING AND DRINKING

There are innumerable restaurants serving Korean food. This
is generally highly spiced and can be an acquired taste.
Standards vary, as do the prices. Korean food is generally the
least expensive. Since menus are not often in English, it is useful
to know the names of some of your favourites. Try *bulgogi*
(marinated beef), *samgyetang* (ginseng chicken), *bibimbap*
(vegetables and rice) and local drinks such as *soju*, *jeongjong*
or *makkully*. Most hotels have a Korean restaurant, or try the
tenth and eleventh floors of the Lotte department store.
Korean restaurants in Itaewon include the Hamilton Garden
in the Hamilton Hotel or the nearby Itaewon Garden or Silla
Galbi (in the Chunghwa apartment supermarket building),
both in Itaewon-dong. Locally brewed Budweiser and other
lager-type beers are available. Teas such as *sanghwa-cha*, ginger
or lime tea are very interesting to try – perhaps in one of the
traditional tea-rooms in Insadong. It is not recommended,
however, to eat in the street markets.

TRANSPORT

If you are in the city centre you can walk to most of the major shopping areas and the major hotels also provide free shuttle buses to Itaewon throughout the day. There is an extensive bus and underground system within Seoul. This is clean and cheap and usually crowded. The underground is perhaps easier to use, since it is relatively simple to alight at the correct stations which are numbered as well as named. Both systems run from early morning until around midnight.

Taxis are relatively cheap and numerous, but are not always easy to obtain. Most taxis used to be service taxis, but recently de luxe (yellow top) taxis have been introduced. When using a taxi take a map and preferably have your destination written in Hangul script.

SECURITY

Seoul is still a relatively safe city, though reasonable precautions should be taken especially after dark.

KUWAIT

KUWAIT CITY

Language **Arabic**
Currency **Kuwaiti dinar (KD) of 1,000 fils.**
   £1=0.49, Mar 1997
Banks **0800–1200 Sat to Thur (0830–1230 in**
   Ramadan)
Shops **0800–1200/1250, 1530–1600/2030 Sat to**
   Thur (0830/0900–1230, 1930–0130/2000 in
   Ramadan)
Tipping: **10 to 15 per cent service charge is generally**
   added to hotel and restaurant bills. Small tips
   expected by porters at hotels and by barbers.
   There is a flat rate at the airport. Taxi drivers are
   not tipped

Generally speaking the shopping facilities are excellent. New shopping arcades have sprung up all over town among the older shops and the souks. The only inconvenience is that shops of one kind tend to be grouped together, forming, for example, the shoe souk or the plant souk so that you may have to visit several areas to get everything you want. Casual cotton clothing from India and Taiwan is available in the souks, but can be on the gaudy side. There are a lot of pirated pop-cassettes and videos, but remember it is illegal to import these into the UK and other Western countries.

The Sultan Centre is popular (four branches, and more planned). Its range compares with a large quality supermarket such as Sainsbury or Tesco, but it also carries items such as sports equipment, electrical goods and luggage. Familiar names to be found among the shops include Next, British Home Stores, Benetton, Body Shop, Ouiset, Mothercare and Dash, but prices are higher than in the UK and ranges are limited. The souk, extensively damaged during the Iraqi occupation, is less interesting than in some other Gulf states, but some handicrafts can still be found.

British newspapers are on sale in hotels and bookshops on the day after issue, but cost up to four times the UK price. Two English-language daily newspapers are published in Kuwait. Magazines can be four times the UK price. There are a few bookshops stocking new English language books and magazines, but the range is still fairly small and they are much more expensive than in the UK.

EATING AND DRINKING

Dinner at a luxury hotel will be reliable, but expensive. There is a growing number of cheaper restaurants and one particularly popular local Indian restaurant is the Moghul Mahal. Alcohol is universally unavailable.

TRANSPORT

There is a public bus service, but it is not much used by Europeans. Taxi drivers are not always ready to stop, usually do not know the way and rarely speak English. Agree the fare beforehand. There is no need to tip taxi drivers, who are inclined to overcharge.

LAOS

VIENTIANE

Language **Lao**
Currency **kip (K). £1=1425, Dec 1995**
Traveller's cheques **take cash US dollars**
Credit cards **only in hotels, some restaurants and shops, with 3 per cent charge**
Shops **0900–2100**
Refunds **difficult**
Bargaining **expected**
Duty-free **at the airport and Friendship Bridge, but unlikely to offer substantial savings**
Tipping **not for taxi drivers**

Top recommendations for gifts and souvenirs are silverware, coffee beans, silk or cotton local clothing and handicrafts such as woodcarvings and rattan. The local Lao Lao rice whisky might also be worth sampling. The centre of all shopping is the Morning Market.

The local weekly *Vientiane Times* is the only English- language newspaper available. The Raintree Bookshop has an average range of English-language books.

TRANSPORT
The central shopping area is within walking distance of most hotels. Public transport and taxis are, however, available.

SECURITY
Security presents no problems and there will be minimal hassle with beggars.

Latvia

Riga

Language **Latvian**
Currency **lat of 100 santimes. £1=0.93, Mar 1997**
The currency is freely convertible (but not easily outside the Baltic States). There are no local restrictions on import and export
Banks **0900–1700 Mon to Fri**
Traveller's cheques **take dollars in cash; defaced notes or those issued pre-1990 will be refused. The many exchange bureaux in central Riga offer better rates than hotels for cash**
Credit cards **can be used in hotels and the more up-market shops and restaurants**
Cashpoints **six, for EC and Mastercards, including the airport and Metropole Hotel**
Shops **0900–1900 Mon to Fri, many close earlier on Sat, some open on Sun**
Sales **yes, but unlikely to offer attractive bargains**
Duty-free **at the airport; particular brands cannot be guaranteed, but prices are a little lower than in town**
Tipping **becoming more usual in hotels and restaurants. No fixed rates, but a few santimes in a taxi and up to a lat (depending on the total bill) in a restaurant should suffice**
Export restrictions **permission needed to export art and antique items; reputable dealers will arrange this; retain the receipt**

Following independence, Latvia is undergoing a continuous face-lift. New shops and restaurants are opening daily and local supply of foodstuffs and other goods has improved considerably. The majority of shops are specialist: department stores or supermarkets as we know them do not exist.

The cost of living is catching up with that in the UK. Some restaurants and imported drinks are expensive. Clothing and shoe shops are fairly basic and quality is poor though improving. In winter the snow quickly turns to ice or slush which makes walking difficult, expecially in the Old Town's cobbled streets. Moon boots or water-resistant walking boots with a good gripping sole are useful. Fur coats are worn a lot in Riga and fur hats are easily bought. Padded down coats are on sale in winter, outside the central market for example.

The main shops are located in Brivibas, Terbatas, K. Barona and Caka – basically within the grid from Elizabetes northward to Bruninieku. The Old Town (south to the river from the boundary of Brivibas to the west, Aspazijas to the north and 13 Janvara to the east) has some small boutiques and souvenir and craft shops. The equivalent of the Soviet GUM department store is Universalveikals Centre, located in Valnuiela just around the corner from the Hotel Riga. The main market, Centralais Tirgus, is close to the bus and train stations and is an interesting cultural experience. The smaller market, Vidzemes Tirgus, on Brivibas at the junction with Matisa iela, is less stressful.

Although familiar names such as Benetton, Bally, Cardin and Dior, Rocher and Lapidus are now to be found, most visitors will be more interested in other things. For traditional handicrafts go to Dailrade at Valnu 28, Tirgonu 10 or Terbatas 30. For amber try A & E at Jauniela 17, for handmade leather goods Tine at Valnu 2. Red and black caviar is obtainable in the fish section of the central market. Russian traditional gifts are obtainable at the street market on Filharmonijas Square a couple of blocks south from the Hotel de Rome and Soviet memorabilia from almost any antique shop. Latvian traditional linens can be found in most souvenir shops.

British newspapers and magazines are most likely to be found in hotel shops and cost around 2 lats. The *Baltic Times* is a lively local weekly at a quarter of the cost. Books produced locally are very good value, imported ones less so. The biggest foreign-language bookstore is Jana Rozes (Elizabetes 85a, Barona 5, Brivibas 90, Dzirnavu 57).

EATING AND DRINKING
There is an increasing number of restaurants. Many Latvian establishments serve a similar menu to each other, tending to be simple and greasy, but the atmosphere makes up for that. Grey peas in bacon fat are recommended only for the intrepid. Pancakes with caviar and the local dark rye bread are good. Alcoholic beverages are readily available. The local beer tends to be brown, heavy and quite strong. Prices, especially of wine, tend to be high. Specialities are Riga champagne and Rigas balzams, a kind of bitter sold in a pottery bottle.

TRANSPORT
The tourist hotels are all within easy walking distance of the main shops. Public transport consists of trams, trolley-buses

and diesel buses. They are fairly cheap, but crowded in the rush hours and not regularly used by visitors. Taxis are licensed, but may not carry meters or display tariffs, in which case establish the fare before starting the journey.

Lebanon

Beirut

Language **Arabic**
Currency **Lebanese pound (L£) of 100 piastres.**
 £1=2467, Mar 1997
Banks **almost any known currency can be**
 exchanged freely. Although prices in shops are in
 Lebanese pounds they can be paid in US dollars
Credit cards **accepted in large shops and**
 restaurants, but not in smaller establishments
Shops **0700–1900 Mon to Sat for supermarkets;**
 some open for a half day on Sun. Smaller shops
 may open early and close as late as 2200
Duty-free **at the airport; cigarettes and alcohol are**
 not much cheaper than in town
Tipping **service charge of anything up to 25 per cent**
 is included in hotel and restaurant bills; waiters
 also expect you to round up the bill. Tipping is not
 usual for taxi drivers

The days of Beirut as the Paris of the Middle East are no more, although valiant efforts are being made towards normalisation. The exodus due to civil war has resulted in a lower standard of living for many. In the past few years there has been a trend for many businesses operated by Christians to transfer to the former Christian enclave north of the city.

Much of the area around the Green Line which used to divide the Muslim and Christian areas is being redeveloped to build a new city centre. There is one main department store on the main Tripoli Autostrade and several sizeable shops and shopping malls, but Beirut is still full of small shops specialising in one product. Competition is fierce and bargains can be found. The Lebanese are on the whole very fashion-conscious. They follow the latest styles from Rome and Paris, whose clothing is imported – or copied. Most educated Lebanese speak English. In the more popular markets only Arabic may be spoken, but it is always possible to negotiate using hand gestures.

In central Beirut the main shopping areas are Hamra Street and Verdun Plaza in West Beirut and Ashrafieh in East Beirut. Many hotels with shopping centres near by are located further north along the coast in areas like Jounieh and Maameltein. Kaslik is an up-market area of Jounieh where many expensive clothing and jewellery shops are to be found. The ABC department store is situated on the main autostrada in Dbayeh, to the north of Beirut.

There are not many traditional crafts made in Lebanon. The best are sold at the Artisanat du Liban, and include bags, gowns, slippers, blue glass, copper, silverware and inlaid items such as backgammon boards and jewellery boxes. There are many hubble-bubble pipes with mild fruit tobaccos.

There are many bookshops. Some have English-language books, but there is not a wide choice and they are expensive. There is a reasonably good bookshop called Librairie International on the ground floor of the Gefinor Centre in central Beirut.

EATING AND DRINKING

Food is the Lebanese passion. Local food is very varied and especially good for vegetarians. Lunches can take hours and are eaten with Lebanese arak, similar to ouzo in Greece or Pernod in France. There are numerous restaurants, often quite expensive, offering Lebanese and other cuisine. Some may be closed on Monday. Lebanon produces excellent wines and most locals drink it in preference to the imported product.

Pistachios, handmade chocolates, wine and arak make acceptable small gifts. Cigarettes are very cheap compared with prices in the UK and alcohol costs about two-thirds of the UK prices.

TRANSPORT

There is little in the way of public transport. Taxis are usually service taxis, travelling fixed routes.

SECURITY

Life in Beirut is returning to normal with the odd hiccup now and again. Shopping is safe, but pickpockets can operate in crowded places.

LESOTHO

MASERU

Language **Sesotho, English**
Currency **loti (plural malote) (M) of 100 lisente,
linked to the South African rand. £1=5.5,
Sep 1994**
Credit cards **major cards accepted in restaurants,
etc., but not petrol stations. The most widely used
are Barclaycard and Visa; Mastercard is
acceptable; American Express has been known to
cause difficulties**
Tipping **service charges are not included in
restaurant and hotel bills: a tip is usually expected**

Lesotho is one of the world's poorest countries and
Bloemfontein is only one and a half hours away. Practically
every item on sale is imported from South Africa. Lesotho is a
member of the Southern African Customs Union, so there are
no extra customs formalities or exchange controls. Available
local clothing tends to be cheap and cheerful.

There is a bookshop in Maseru, one of a South African
chain, which stocks a limited and expensive range of books.

EATING AND DRINKING
Eating out costs less than in the UK, but the quality is variable
and the choice of restaurants is not extensive. Alcohol is readily
available. The beer is of the lager variety. The wines are South
African. The main bar in Maseru, frequented by both expatriates and locals, is in the Maseru Club which also offers snack
food and bar lunches.

TRANSPORT
There is no public transport suitable for visitors.

SECURITY
Crime, sometimes violent as in so many places today, is a concern. Sensible precautions are necessary.

Liberia

Monrovia

Language **English**
Currency **Liberian dollar L$ of 100 cents, officially at
par with the US dollar. £1=1.55, Mar 1997.
There is a black market**
Banks **0900–1300 Mon to Thur, 0900–1500 Fri**
Tipping **a few dollars is customary in restaurants
Hotels usually add 10 per cent to the bill. Small
tips are given for all minor services, but not to taxi
drivers**

The Foreign Office advises British nationals against visiting
Liberia. Conditions have been highly volatile and security has
been a major concern.

Most shops are in the Pan African Plaza opposite the
University or in the centre around the Broad Street, Benson
Street, Center Street or Randall Street areas. Waterside
Market is also extremely active.

Worthwhile gifts and souvenirs include masks and woodcarvings, soapstone, basketware and batik. Benson Street in
particular is good for clothing. Safari suits are widely worn
and can be made locally at a reasonable price. There is also a
good selection of tie-dye dresses available cheaply. The finish
is not very professional, but they are a popular buy.

There used to be plenty of American magazines available
but very few British magazines or books in English.

Eating and Drinking
There is a variety of restaurants and bars in Monrovia,
although none is of a high standard. Alcohol is expensive.
Under present conditions it is best to keep to such of the main
hotels as remain open.

Transport
Visitors do not normally use local buses, but taxis are numerous
and much used by expatriates. It is usual to share a taxi with
other passengers, although it is possible to book a taxi for
oneself.

LIBYA

TRIPOLI

Language **Arabic**
Currency **Libyan dinar (LD) of 1,000 dirhams**
  £1=0.54, May 1996
Banks **0800/0830–1200/1230 Sun to Tue, Thur;**
  0800–1200, 1600–1700 Wed and Sat
Traveller's cheques **take US dollars in large and small**
  denominations
Tipping **10 per cent is standard**

UN sanctions imposed since April 1992 include a ban on flights to and from Libya. Huge import levies put up the price of imported goods and reduce the range available in the shops. There are still penalties for the possession of alcohol.

Most worthwhile areas are easily covered on foot. Main shopping is in the area around the Green Square next to the castle. Suq Al-Mushir is popular with tourists. Sharah Awal September and Sharah Mohammed Magarief are worth a look, as are, to a lesser extent, Sharah Mizran and Sharah Amr-Ibn Al-As. Recently many shops have opened in the area where most expatriates live. One has Tesco as its main supplier, but the prices bear no comparison with those in the UK.

There are some crafts such as leatherware and woven goods which are worth considering. Good jeans and T-shirts are available at reasonable prices. Stamps make colourful and easily portable gifts and souvenirs.

English-language books can virtually not be found.

EATING AND DRINKING
Apart from dining rooms in the major hotels such as the Mehari and the Grand, there are few restaurants in Tripoli worthy of the name and the absence of alcohol helps to make eating out a less than lively occasion.

TRANSPORT
The public bus service is not suitable for Europeans. Taxis are only easily available in the city centre and are expensive.

SECURITY
Security generally is good.

LITHUANIA

VILNIUS

Language **Lithuanian**
Currency **litas (Lt) (plural litai). £1=6.40, Mar 1997**
Banks **the litas is freely convertible; US dollars can be used for cash transactions**
Credit cards **many hotels and restaurants accept major cards including Visa and American Express**
Tipping **increasingly widespread; waiters will some times expect you to leave a huge Western tip. A few litai is enough**
Export restrictions **the only major restrictions are on national artwork treasures, including icons. Before exporting pieces of art over 40 years old, the Ministry of Culture at Snipisku 3 must be consulted. Special permits and 200 per cent duty may be demanded**

There has been tremendous growth in the retail sector in the past year with new supermarkets, restaurants, cafés, hotels and a variety of new shops which are brighter and the assistants a little friendlier than in the old ones. Someone normally speaks English or German. The main central shopping area is along Gedimino Prospektas and streets running off it. Interesting antique, craft and art shops are located in the Old Town.

Goods of interest to the visitor include not only clothing such as fur coats (for those who wear them, and the locals do), but also books, handicrafts, jewellery, linen, glass and pottery as well as antiques and religious icons.

Specific recommendations include furs from Nijole at Savacious 8 or Gedemino 3a, Lithuanian vodka and caviar, available at most supermarkets, amber jewellery or stones from Sage at Ausros Vartu 15 or Amber at Ausros Vartu 9, locally made linens and woven goods such as mats, bookmarks and sashes from Vitrazas at Gedimino 17 or the Folk Art Shop at Zydu 2 and wooden spoons and carvings such as walking sticks from the handicraft market on Pilies in the centre of the Old Town which is good for many things including also pottery and ceramic bells or wind-chimes.

The nearest equivalent to department stores are Vilniaus Centrine Universaline Parduotive at Ukmerges 16 or Valstybine Universaline Perduotive at Gediminopr 18, both closed on Sunday and not particularly recommended.

Designer boutiques at present include Burda, Levi, Benetton and Adidas. Juozas Statkevicious at Ausros Vartu 3 is a local designer of women's fashions. The Stikliais boutique at Gaono 5 is expensive and up-market. For local fashions try also Salonas 7 at Paumenkalnio 40. Vilga at Bazilijon 3 is a factory outlet for leather bags. For handmade knitwear and sweaters go to Otrik in Dominikon.

More and more antique shops are opening around town offering mainly icons, coins, stamps, old books, jewellery, silverware and Soviet memorabilia. Try the following in the Stikli/Dominikon area of the Old Town – Antikvarini daikt komisas, Solda or Tautodaile ir Antivarietas. Also worth visiting are Versme at Didzioje 27 and Senamiescio Antikvariata at Daukanto Square 2/5. For local paintings, ceramics and sculptures try Vartai at Vilniaus 39 or Arka at Ausros Vartu 7. For postage stamps and coins go to Filatelja at Arkli 22.

The farmers' market at Kalvaarij 61 is at its best on Saturday and Sunday mornings in summer. Beware pickpockets. The Garlinai flea market is just outside town just off the Vilnius to Kaunas highway.

Foreign newspapers are difficult to find, although some, days old, are to be found at the Penki Kontinental Bookstore and the Hotel Draugyste. The *International Herald Tribune* costs 9 litai. There are also the local English-language *Baltic Times* and *Lithuanian Weekly* (actually bi-weekly). For books try Littera at Sv Jono 12, Rutos Knygos at Daukanto Square 2 – 13 or Foreign Books at Trak 5a.

EATING AND DRINKING

There are many good restaurants in Lithuania and more and more private restaurants and cafés are emerging serving reasonable food at reasonable prices. Stikliai at Gaono 7 serves local delicacies such as *blinai* (mini-pancakes with caviar). Other local delicacies are *cepelinai* or Zeppelins (potato dumplings with minced meat filling) and *kugelis po dangciu* (potato pudding). Other restaurants worth trying are Turistas at Ukmergès14, Marceliukes Kletis at Tuskulenu 35and Ritos Smukle at Iki Commercial Centre, Zirmunu 68. Lithuanians have an affinity for sweets, so there is quite a variety of local chocolates and tortes. Locally produced beer, vodka and sparkling wine are of good quality, although the vodka is not for the faint-hearted. Mead is a honey-based brandy whose alcohol content may be as high as 50 per cent. Western cigarettes are cheap.

TRANSPORT
There are good local transport services – convenient, efficient and fairly clean, but also tending to be extremely crowded. Watch your personal possessions. Taxis are readily available and cheap. There are now many companies offering a variety of different vehicles including some Mercedes and larger VW models. Your hotel should be able to recommend a reputable firm.

LUXEMBOURG

Language **French**
Currency **Luxembourg franc (LF) of 100 centimes. £1=54, Mar 1997. Belgian currency is legal tender in Luxembourg, but not vice-versa, although the banks are required to exchange at par**
Banks **0900–1200, 1330–1630 Mon to Fri**
Traveller's cheques **Eurocheque widely used**
Credit cards **Visa, Access, Diners Club, Eurocard and other cards are accepted in larger establishments**
Shops **0930–1800 Mon to Sat. Many shops do not open Mon morning and lunchtime closing is common**
Tipping **service charge varying from 10-20 per cent is added to the bill in all hotels and restaurants; no further tip is expected, although a small additional amount may be given for personal services. Taxi drivers expect about 15 per cent of the fare**

Luxembourgers spend a lot of effort and money on their appearance. The country is the size and population of Dorset, so although citizens enjoy one of the highest standards of living in the EU, there is not the range of shopping to be found in bigger European capitals, many of which are sufficiently near by to make a trip for any serious shopping perfectly feasible.

There are a few good dress shops, which tend to be extremely expensive. Prices are considerably higher than in the UK for almost everything except alcohol.

British newspapers and some magazines are available, the former usually on the afternoon of the day of publication. There is a weekly English-language newspaper which has a very limited coverage of events in Luxembourg. Chapter One sells English-language books as do Magasin Anglais and Librairie Ernster. There is a good selection, at prices about 25 per cent higher than in the UK.

EATING AND DRINKING

Luxembourgers enjoy good food with generous helpings and make good use of the many restaurants in the city and in the countryside. Meals are nevertheless expensive. A recommendation at relatively reasonable price is EMS in the Place de la Gare.

TRANSPORT

Public transport throughout the Grand Duchy is efficient and frequent. Taxis do not cruise on the streets; there are three or four taxi ranks in the middle of the city.

MACAO

Language Cantonese, Portuguese
Currency pataca (M$) of 100 avos. £1=12.80, Mar 1997. Hong Kong dollars accepted one to one, to the disadvantage of the visitor
Tipping 10 per cent service charge is standard in hotels and restaurants, but a small additional tip is appreciated

Macao is Portugal's only remaining colony, situated almost next door to Hong Kong. There is an interesting mix of Chinese and Portuguese cultures, reflected in the cuisine. Gambling is a major industry and the main attraction for visitors. English is quite widely spoken and bargaining is widespread in the street markets.

Apart from the markets there is a branch of Yaohan, the Japanese department store, to give an idea of what is available. There are some interesting shops at the bottom of the steps of St Paul's church, for example, for good cheap porcelain or quality T-shirts. Best is the stamp shop. Send a postcard home with stamps of snakes, fishes or buildings - the selection is wide. For $20 you can create the most colourful envelope you'll ever send.

English-language reading material, apart from the Hong Kong press, is in short supply.

EATING AND DRINKING
Seafood and fish are good. Alcohol and tobacco are cheap.

SECURITY
Personal security should present no great problem.

MADAGASCAR

ANTANANARIVO

Language **Malagasy**
Currency **franc malgache (FMG) of 100 centimes.**
  £1=6650, Nov 1996
Tipping **where there is no 10 per cent service**
  charge, tips may be the only source of income for
  the waiters

Imported goods, mainly from South Africa and France, are now on the shelves, although they are more expensive than in the UK and the choice is limited. Local wares include clothing, artefacts in wood, shell, horn, leather or raffia and an excellent range of polished semi-precious stones. The main supermarkets are well stocked with liquor, but it is expensive. There is a local Bata factory producing good value shoes. With a bit of searching you should find something worthwhile.

All local books are in French, and very little is available in English.

EATING AND DRINKING
The cost of meals tends to be comparatively cheap, while that of imported drink is high. There is a wide variety of fruit both tropical and temperate available in season. Madagascar exports a quantity of beef to the EU. Rabbits are available as well as ducks and guinea fowl. Local pâté de foie gras is outstanding. Shrimps are exported to the UK and a full range of

shellfish is available. There is local production of coffee and tea. Local chocolate (Robert's) is extremely good. There is a small local wine industry producing cheap and adequate wines. There is local production of soft drinks, but fruit is so cheap that freshly squeezed juices are best.

TRANSPORT

It is usual to agree taxi fares in advance of hiring and it is not customary to tip. By British standards fares are low, but so, often, is the quality of the vehicle. There are plenty of buses, but these are overcrowded and unsafe. Cars can be hired with a driver. In some towns rickshaws remain an acceptable means of transport.

SECURITY

It is wise to remove all jewellery when visiting the main markets and to take special care if carrying a bag or wallet in the street or in the markets. Poverty is depressing and beggars are a nuisance. In town you are pestered for money and there is the threat of mugging.

MADEIRA

FUNCHAL

The Portuguese language and currency are both in use. Off the north-west coast of Africa, the island is a long-standing favourite with tourists. It is famous for its plants and flowers as well as for traditional items such as embroidery, tapestry and wickerwork.

The Old Town is very atmospheric for shopping and there is a department store (Camachos) near the cathedral.

Both food and drink are cheaper than in the UK.

MALAWI

LILONGWE/BLANTYRE

Language **English, Chichewa**
Currency **kwacha (K) of 100 tambala. £1=24.38,
   Mar 1997**
Credit cards **accepted by some restaurants and most
   hotels**

The British connection has left a strong mark. Imported goods
cost up to three times the UK price. Imported finished goods
are also limited in range and items disappear from the shops
from time to time.

Lilongwe is the capital, but is more like a provincial town
compared with Blantyre, which remains the leading commercial
centre. In contrast to Lilongwe's wide open spaces, Blantyre is
relatively built up and has an air of city bustle about it. There
is a wider range of shops and goods than in Lilongwe.

New Lilongwe or the Capital City Area was built some five
miles from the Old Town, which has a large shopping area,
housing most of the small Asian businesses where almost anything is to be found. Jogees is good for spices and Indian
foods, The Macoha Tie and Dye Centre along the Blantyre
Road stocks materials and ready-made clothing. The Old
Town Market not only sells food, but has a large area for
hardware. The clothing area is known locally as the bend-over
boutique. The market is also good for items such as baskets
and clay pots. Traditional Malawian wooden handicrafts are
available at the small market just outside the Old Town. You
should always bargain in the markets.

In Capital City there are some places worth a look in Chief
M'mbelwa House such as the Wild Side gift shop, although
most items come actually from Zimbabwe. In Centre Arcade
House a short walk away is the Cat's Whiskers for arts and
crafts and the Gallerie Africaine art gallery. The Capital City
Market, also known as the German Market, is a short drive
away from the Capital City Area and has prices somewhat
higher than the main market in the Old Town.

Some British newspapers, magazines and books are available,
but tend to be expensive. Local English-language newspapers
give a limited coverage of international affairs. The South
African edition of *International Express* newspaper and
Weekly Times incorporating the *Guardian* are available. For

books try the Times Bookshop in Old Town and the Central Bookshop in Capital City.

EATING AND DRINKING

Lilongwe has only a few restaurants. Standards are reasonable, but service is haphazard. Most tastes are catered for – Chinese (the Golden Dragon), two Indian (Hut's and Modi's), two Korean (Koreana and the Korean Garden), while the Capital and Lilongwe Hotels have continental restaurants (the Greenery and the Maligunde respectively). Blantyre fares a little better with probably the best restaurant in the country at the Blantyre Sports Club.

Soft drinks, locally brewed Carlsberg beer, wine and spirits are generally available. A good range of cigarettes and small cigars is available. There is an excellent supply of fresh and cheap fruit.

TRANSPORT

For all practical purposes public transport is non-existent. Minibuses are always overloaded and therefore not very safe. Taxis are few and unreliable.

SECURITY

Visitors should exercise reasonable care and be on the alert for muggers, bag snatchers and confidence tricksters.

MALAYSIA

KUALA LUMPUR

Language Malay; in Sarawak, also English
Currency Malaysian dollar or ringgit (M$) of 100 sen. £1=3.97, Mar 1997
Banks 1000–1500 Mon to Fri, 1930–1130 Sat
Credit cards all bigger hotels, restaurants and shops take most major credit cards
Shops 0830–1830 Mon to Sat
Bargaining worth trying, especially at market stalls
Tipping not widespread, but becoming more common in hotels and restaurants. 10 per cent service charge added to bills as well as 5 per cent goverment tax

Clothing can be bought at reasonable prices either made to measure or off the peg. Batik is the locally produced colourful cotton material which is made up into long-sleeved shirts for evening wear. Safari suits are also popular. Larger sizes may be hard to find. Shoes can be made to measure. The Central Market on Jalan Hang Kasturi is now a busy food and shopping centre and well worth a visit, but beware of pickpockets.

The main shopping, commercial and hotel area is between Jalan Ampang, Jalan Tun Razak, Jalan Sultan Ismail and Jalan Tuanku Abdul Rahman. The latter, also known as the Batu Road, is a good place to start window shopping and to look for souvenirs. Mun Loong at 113 is a large department store, to give an initial overview. The Globe Silk Store at 185 is modestly priced. Peiping Lace is at 217; Selangar Pewter is at 213.

Jalan Sultan Ismail includes not only KL Plaza, but also Bukit Buitang Plaza and Sunyai Wang Plaza. There are other shopping centres in the area such as City Square, Plaza Yair Chiaren, Plaza Ampong Park as well as Kompleks Campbell and Kompleks Pertaina on Jalan Dang Wang.

Chinatown enjoys a lively atmosphere and is to the south of the Central Market in an area bounded by Jalan Sultan, Jalan Tun H.S.Lee and Jalan Petaling. There are many interesting shops in Petaling Street, particularly for china and glass. There are batik stalls on the Jalan Masjid India side of the Batu Road. All the big hotels have boutiques where you will pay more, but where it may be easier to find exactly what you want. The most up-market outlet is the Kutang Crafts Shop in the Equatorial Hotel. Their factory on the road to Sungei Buloh is well worth a visit, but for top value visit the batik shops at the front of the Batur caves.

There is a good shop selling oriental carpets on the first floor at Yow Chuan Plaza which is especially good for nomadic carpets. For pewter try Selangor Pewter in Baku Road, where there are several rattan shops. For made-to-measure shoes go to Shanghai Shoe Store in Jalan Bandar. For woodwork Kok Art and Craft at 204 Jalan Negara Dua, Taman Melawati has an extensive range which includes antique furniture. Peiping Lace on the Batu Road is recommended for traditional Chinese woodwork. Bukit next to Tunku Honey Foodland or My Fair Lady in Jalan Imbi will pack orchids to take to the UK by air.

Handicrafts may also be obtained from the Bukit Nanas Convent, the Cheshire Home, Leprosarium, Prison Shop or Tourist Shop in Jalan Ampang. The Karyaneka Handicraft Centre in Jalan Raja Chulan and the nearby Handicraft

Museum feature all the traditional arts and crafts such as pewter and batik for sale.

There are five local English-language newspapers, of which the most widely read are the *New Straits Times*, the *Malay Mail* and the *Star*. There are many excellent bookshops with a wide range of literature with prices roughly on a par with UK prices. Magazines appear late and cost about one and a half times the UK price.

EATING AND DRINKING

Eating out is exciting because of the wide variety of local cuisines mirroring the population mix. Restaurants abound and prices range from very cheap foodstalls to very plush restaurants. The Neptune Restaurant at Jalan Imbi features barbecued crab. For local cuisine try Rasa Utara and Satay Anikaare in Bukit Buitang Plaza, Seri Malaysia or the Yazmin in Jalan Kia Peng or the Nelayan Floating Restaurant in Titiwangsa Lake Gardens.

TRANSPORT

Public transport is plentiful, but precarious. Taxis are abundant and cheap and are probably the main form of local transport used by expatriates. Beware of taxis that do not use meters, especially around the hotel area of town. Insist that the meter is switched on before you set off.

SECURITY

Beware of bag snatchers. Jewellery is also at risk.

MALDIVES

MALE

Language **Divehi**
Currency **rufiya (Rf) of 100 larees. £1=19.60.**
   US dollars widely accepted

South-west of Sri Lanka, the Maldives is an expensive and increasingly popular resort with package tourists. English is widely spoken.

Malé is a small town and usually only a transit point for tourists on their way to the resorts. Sarongs and wovenware are popular, but the use of turtleshell in crafts is now forbidden by international convention.

Fish and seafood are good and recommended.

MALI

BAMAKO

Language **French**
Currency **CFA franc. £1=945, Mar 1997**

The centre of Bamako is on and around the Boulevard du Peuple. There is an artisans shop next to the Grand Mosque. Apart from the usual tie-dye, rugs and crafts such as leatherware and woodcarvings, both gold and silver jewellery are popular, but beware of controls on the export of artefacts.

MALTA

VALETTA

Language **Maltese**
Currency **Maltese pound or lira of 100 cents.
£1=0.62, Mar 1997**
Shops **0900 to 1300, 1600 to 1900**
Tipping **10 per cent is standard**

The major shopping centres are in Valletta and Sliema and the main public market is in Valletta. Import restrictions have eased in recent years, so that a greater range of goods is available. Marks and Spencer have shops in Valetta and Sliema, but at double UK prices and with limited stock. Body Shop has a shop in Sliema. Good ready-made clothing is available, but at a price. Jeans of all types are produced locally for the major brands. Neither tailoring nor English cloth is as expensive as it is in the UK.

Malta is renowned for its craft handiwork such as lace and silver filigree as well as leather, pottery and handknits. Glass too can be a worthwhile buy. A good place for looking at these and other artefacts is the Malta Craft Centre in St John's Square in Valetta.

There are one daily and two Sunday English-language newspapers (*the Times*, the *Sunday Times* and the *Independent*). Newspapers from the UK are on sale the same day on Sundays and the day following publication on weekdays. Most newsagents stock a full range of British magazines within a few days of publication, but the cost is about twice that in the UK. A wide selection of hardback and paperback books is offered in several good bookshops.

EATING AND DRINKING

The tourist industry has encouraged growth in the number of hotels and restaurants. The quality of food and service varies. Prices at the upper end of the market are comparable to those in the UK. In late summer there are supplies of delicious locally caught fish – lampuki, dentici and grouper. Swordfish is popular and can be bought from the fishermen at the bays around the north of the island. There is an excellent fish market at Marsaxlokk early on a Sunday morning. The strawberry season is long and the produce is good.

Local beers and minerals are good and cheaper than in the UK. Local wine is cheap and generally drinkable. Tobacco and cigarettes are cheaper than in the UK, but becoming more expensive in line with government health initiatives.

TRANSPORT

Bus services are frequent if erratic. Fares are low. Taxis are not always readily available and it is not possible to hail a passing taxi in the street. Charges are relatively high, but metered. Taxi meters are required by law and heavy penalties are imposed on drivers who try to avoid using them. It is advisable, however, to make sure that the meter is working at the outset of any journey. Taxis are identified by red number plates.

MARTINIQUE

PORT-DE-FRANCE

Martinique is very French and very expensive, with good food.

There are lots of imported goods in the shops around the Rue Victor Hugo, but there are also markets for T-shirts or the usual range of crafts such as leatherware or seashell jewellery. Local rum is good; the best is superb.

MAURITIUS

PORT LOUIS

Language **English, French Creole**
Currency **Mauritius rupee (R) of 100 cents.**
   £1=33, Mar 1997
Banks **0930–1430 Mon to Fri, 0930–1130 Sat**
Shops **from 0930 onwards. Half-day closing on Thur**
   in Curepipe and on Sat in Port Louis
Refunds **very difficult**
Bargaining **yes, except where prices are clearly**
   marked; expected in markets
Duty-free **several jewellery shops on the island and**
   plans to open a number of general duty-free
   shops
Tipping **generally 10 per cent; not expected by taxi**
   drivers

As the economy has improved, the range of goods available locally has expanded greatly, but the prices of imported goods have to take into account freight charges, tax and high mark-ups.

Local specialities include a wide range of linens and textiles, including cashmere, and gold. Handicrafts include hand embroideries as well as woodcarvings of ships or dodos. Sweaters and pullovers can be bought at attractive prices.

The markets in Port Louis, Quatre Bornes, Curepipe, Vacoas and Rose Hill are colourful, with the lowest prices often found in Port Louis. The market in Queen Street is worth a visit and is good for spices, souvenirs, leather goods and herbs for every ailment.

There are shopping centres at Galleries Evershine Shopping Centre in Rosehill and at Orchard Arcade in Quatre Bornes, as well as the Fon Sing Building in Edith Cavell Street or Happy World Shopping Centre, both in Port Louis. Also in Port Louis the Super Centre in Dumas Street stocks South African Woolworths wear. There is a Woolworths store selling some Marks and Spencer items at the Phoenix Centre. Corderie Street, Port Louis, is full of small shops selling materials of every conceivable type and other merchandise. It is great fun to wander along.

Better quality shops worth looking at include India Handloom in Sir Willian Newton Street, Port Louis, for pure silks and cottons. Ghanty et Fils in Salaffa Arcade, Curepipe has a good selection of silks including raw silks. Cassam Sulliman in Corderie Street, Port Louis often has something a bit unusual. The Floreal Knitwear Factory Shop is in Floreal Road, Floreal.

For gifts and souvenirs there are several possibilities. Spès charity shops are in Labourdonnais Street, Quatre Bornes, with branches in Curepipe and Impasse St Thérèse. They have a wide range of handicrafts including weaving, pottery, basketwork, toys and linens. The Women's Self Help Organisation is in Royal Road, Curepipe, the Trou aux Biches Hotel and the Meridian at Le Morne. They have locally embroidered tablecloths, blouses and baby clothes, as well as articles embroidered to order. Wooden toys can be bought at the Save the Children workshop next to the Vacoas Market. There is very little problem in shopping in English, but prices in the market tend to be higher for non-Creole speakers.

Most newspapers are in French, but British newspapers are eventually available. There are also various magazines, but watch out for the dates – some are rather elderly.

EATING AND DRINKING

The local mix of French, English, Asian and Chinese is reflected in the cuisine. Seafood and Creole cuisine are particularly recommended, although a lot of the best fish is exported to Reunion. Local venison is obtainable during the hunting season. Local chicken, guinea fowl, turkey and duck are all good.

The best restaurants tend to be very expensive. Restaurants in Port Louis are generally not open in the evenings or at weekends. The north and west coasts are well served by good restaurants, particularly in the Grand Baie area.

Wine sold in restaurants and hotel restaurants in particular is expensive. A tax of 10 per cent on bills adds considerably to the cost of eating out.

Locally manufactured gin (Gilbeys) and rum (Green Island) are good and inexpensive. Local beer is good and inexpensive as are locally produced soft drinks. There is a wide range of relatively inexpensive locally bottled whiskies on the market, but those imported in the bottle are expensive. French and South African wines are increasingly available.

TRANSPORT

There are few pavements, even in town, and pedestrians have to walk on the roads. Shopping centres are well spread out, so transport will be needed in exploring. There are cheap and frequent bus services, recommended for the young and adventurous only. In taxis discuss the fare first because absurdly high rates are asked of tourists. Rates are advertised inside taxis. Double them, as you are expected to cover the return to base.

SECURITY

Personal security worries are fewer than in the UK and the visitor will experience little hassle.

MEXICO

MEXICO CITY

Language **Spanish**
Currency **peso. £1=12.76, Mar 1997**
Banks **0900–1330 Mon to Fri**
Credit cards most cards, except American Express, widely accepted. Some small businesses charge an extra 5 to 10 per cent
Shops **1000–1900 Mon, Tue, Thur, Fri, 1100–1200 Wed, Sat**
Tipping **10-15 per cent expected almost everywhere, except in taxis**
Export restrictions **the export of genuine pre-Columbian artefacts is prohibited**

Shopping in Mexico City begins at the Zona Rosa with its mixture of shops and markets with a good choice of restaurants. This lies between the Paseo de la Reforma, Avenue Chapultepec, Lieja and Insurgentes Centro. Presidente Masarik is a whole street of designer shops with a very good selection of restaurants.

Mexico prides itself on its silver, weaving, woodcarving, rugs and carpets and other ethnic craft items. The Museum of Popular Arts stocks handicrafts from all over the country. Also try the San Juan Market of the Mercado de Londres in the Zona Rosa. There are many other markets which sell a range of goods. La Ciudadela Market is located on Balderas near the metro station of that name. San Juan Market is on Ayuntamiento, Metro Juarez. Merced Market is directly outside the metro station of that name. La Lagunilla is on Comonfort, metro Allende. Sonora Market is on Fray Servando Teresa de Meir Street, metro Merced. Jamaica Market is near La Vige, metro Jamaica. Other markets worth trying are the Saturday Market in San Angel and the Sunday art market near the junction of Insurgentes and Reforma.

Outside Mexico City itself the market at Toluca is good for woven serapes, shoes, leather jackets and handbags. (Leather goods in general are an excellent buy in Mexico.) It can be crowded at weekends. Cash sales only and not much bargaining, but reasonable prices.

Mexico is a leading producer of silver. At the silver market in the Zona Rosa you will find the best silver at the most competitive prices. Cruet sets and napkin rings are very nice.

Be prepared for lots of hassle, but stand your ground and bargain and you will eventually get the best price around. When bargaining, drop the price by at least half initially and work up to whatever you think the article is worth. Usually this will be something like 60-70 per cent of the asking price, but if you really want an object, be sure to get it because you will never see the same thing again.

Apart from the silver, there are many different kinds of ceramics around, all at very reasonable prices. Wooden carved trunks are also a very good buy, as they are all hand-carved and come in various colours and sizes. Glassware is another good buy, although it may take time and patience to pick six things of the same pattern, unless you have them all made to order at one of the glass factories. Local jewellery is worth considering. Wall hangings can be as colourful as you wish them to be, pastels or primary colours, there are choices in all colours.

American newspapers and magazines are on sale and

British newapapers are more readily available since the reintroduction of the direct BA flight. There are some shops selling English-language books, more American than British, which are expensive.

EATING AND DRINKING
When eating out, there is everything from the traditional Mexican eating place to restaurants of international standard. Prices on the whole are cheaper than in the UK. Eating at roadside stalls can be asking for trouble and should be avoided. Locally produced spirits such as tequila, gin, vodka, rum, cheap brandy and some liqueurs, such as Kahlua, are available at very cheap prices. Reasonably priced local table wines are also available. Local lager-type beers such as Dos Equis, Corona and Sol are of good quality. Darker beers are also readily available. Most US brands of cigarettes are cheap and some British brands are manufactured locally.

TRANSPORT
The cheapest form of transport is by bus and metro and all forms of public transport are adequate to good if reasonable care of belongings is taken. It is not advisable to use them during rush hour, when they get very crowded and women may be subjected to unwanted attention. Avoid private taxis parked outside the main hotels. Keep rather to the radio-controlled Sitio taxis, particularly recommended for single females after 1700 or so. They have an S preceding their number. Legal taxis have an L.

SECURITY
The threat of crimes against the person is higher than in London. Sensible precautions should be taken.

MONACO

Language **French**
Currency **French franc**
Banks **900-1200, 1400-16.30 Mon to Fri**
Credit cards **All major cards accepted**
Cashpoints **Yes, plentiful**
Shops **900-1300, 1500-1900 Mon to Sat**
Tipping **Expected in restaurants**

Finding good value in a place like Monaco is as likely as breaking the bank at one of the local casinos. Many of the top names in fashion, jewellery, and art have an outlet in one of the little shopping centres that cluster around the Hotel de Paris and the Casino de Monte Carlo. They are there to profit from the comings and goings of the rich and famous, and one should really at least be the former to do any serious shopping here. There are many better and cheaper places to spend one's money, and the less rarified atmosphere of another, less prestigious city somewhere further along the coast is probably worth waiting for.

EATING AND DRINKING
Excellent restaurants serve both Italian and French cuisine all over Monaco, but there are few that are particularly good value for money. The Café de Paris opposite the Casino offers solid French fare that is slightly over-expensive, but the views of the main square and an ample terrace for sunny days help to offset the painful prices. Just behind the Café de Paris complex as you walk away from the Casino is a bi-level shopping arcade where there is a choice of several slightly more reasonably-priced restaurants. If price is no object, try the Michelin starred Louis XV restaurant in the Hotel de Paris.

TRANSPORT
Monaco is certainly small enough to walk around, but the steep hills on which the city is built tend to dampen the wanderlust of even the healthiest of visitors. Buses are available and serve many parts of the town; look for the destination on the front of the bus. Taxis are expensive, but a nice option if you can find one.

SECURITY
Monaco is generally very safe, but as a magnet for the world's high rollers it also attracts a criminal element hoping to profit from the relaxed atmosphere and easy money. The usual precautions apply.

MONGOLIA

ULAN BATOR

Language **Mongol**
Currency **tugrik (T) of 100 mongs. £1=785, Nov 1996**
Banks **the banking system is undeveloped, but changing dollars into tugriks is easy; dollars are accepted almost everywhere**
Credit cards **becoming accepted**
Shops **1000–1800, closing at 1600 on Sat**
Refunds **an interpreter would be needed to even attempt one**
Bargaining **yes, for antiques, art and jewellery in the markets, even where prices are fixed**
Duty-free **the new airport terminal has very good duty-free shopping. Perfume prices are in dollars what they are in pounds at UK airports**
Tipping **becoming common: no fixed amount**
Export restrictions **certificate from the Ministry of Culture needed for all antiques**

What is available in Ulan Bator today will probably not be available tomorrow. Quite a lot of what is in the markets and shops is past its sell-by date or about to be. There are, however, many things which will interest the tourist. These include cashmere articles, pure wool carpets both handmade and machine-made, leather goods, paintings, woodcarvings, ethnic dolls, silver bowls, silver and coral jewellery, various antique items such as snuff bottles and silver pipes. Camel-hair cardigans and leather or suede coats might be worth a look. Fur hats with ear-flaps, when available, are relatively cheap, and good lined mittens can be bought.

Most shopping is done in the main hotels, the State Department Store (known locally as Harrods), a few small shops selling imported goods or one of the markets. Dollar shops and museum shops also stock some recommended best buys. When buying cashmere or carpets it is often better to look at the range at one of the factory shops, such as Gobi or Buyan for cashmere. Your tour operator or hotel should be able to advise you on this. The Sunday and Wednesday Market also carries a range of items, but petty crime is common there.

There are no shops selling English-language books and

newspapers, but there are two locally produced weeklies, the *Mongol Messenger* and the *UB Post*.

EATING AND DRINKING

There is a lack of restaurants and the local cuisine is not for the gastronome. There is a good Japanese restaurant and a recently opened Korean restaurant in the Children's Park for which it is advisable to book. There is also a Russian restaurant for which it is essential to book. The local vodka, *arkhi*, is worth trying and there is also *kumis*, a fermented mare's milk for which many foreigners acquire a taste.

TRANSPORT

Buses are overcrowded and not recommended. A regular taxi will cost 130 tugriks per kilometre, but a passing car will also stop for you and charge the same fare.

SECURITY

Petty crime is increasing and care is needed over personal security. Begging is becoming more of a problem.

MONTSERRAT

PLYMOUTH

Currency **East Caribbean dollar, fixed to the US dollar at US$1=2.7**
Banks **0800–1200 Mon to Thur, 0800–1200, 1500–1700 Fri**
Tipping **10 per cent service charge usually included in hotel and restaurant bills**

There is volcanic activity in the southern part of the island and Plymouth has been evacuated since April 1996.

Most basic items are imported from the USA or neighbouring islands. Shops are generally rather functional and characterless, with a limited range of stock associated with a small resident community which tends to travel for its quality shopping. The only local newspapers are the *Montserrat Reporter* and *Montserrat Times*, which appear on Friday. A selection of US newspapers and magazines is available, but they are expensive.

EATING AND DRINKING

Restaurants in the hotels provide wholesome meals which tend to be expensive by UK standards. The Bilhan Valley Restaurant, 15 minutes from town, is a little more up-market. Just outside town both Niggy's and Ziggy's are good. In town itself there are the Ocean Terrace or the Oasis and for lunch, Moles Bar.

MOROCCO

Language **Arabic, French**
Currency **dirham (DH) of 100 centimes.**
   £1=15, Mar 1997
Banks **0815–1130, 1415–1630 Mon to Fri in**
   winter, 0815–1130, 1500–1700 Mon to Fri in
   summer
Credit cards **Visa and Access accepted by many**
   hotels and restaurants, and by some shops dealing
   in high-value handicraft items like carpets.
   American Express and Diners, can also be used
Cashpoints **some**
Shops **0900–1200, closed for lunch until 1500.**
   Closing times vary according to season
Bargaining **expected in souks**
Tipping **service charge not normally added to bills**
   in hotels, restaurants, etc.; a tip of 10 per cent is
   much appreciated. DH 5-10 is enough for
   porters

Carpets are graded by a state agency and are a best buy, although Moroccan carpets are not among the first rank internationally. Otherwise there are items such as leather, copper, brass and silver or cassettes of local music. Sizing is basically French, but inconsistent.

Unusually for a Muslim country, the working week remains Monday to Friday with Saturday and Sunday as the weekend. As in other Muslim countries, Ramadan is not a good period for doing business.

Resist any heavy sales pressure from guides and others to buy unwanted carpets or other goods. Always bargain in the souks. The price you pay is determined by how much you want the article. Do not begin to bargain unless you are sure that you want the article and be willing to walk away if you think that the price is not fair. Store owners expect often to get anything from 25 to 50 per cent less than the asking price. French can be used for most shopping and bargaining.

Local cuisine is not exceptional, but there are one or two reasonable restaurants. Local beer (including Heineken made under licence) is always available and has a good flavour, although it is not very strong. Soft drinks include Coca Cola, even when boycotted in most of the rest of the Arab world. Local fresh coffee is very good and cheaper than in the UK. Local wines are widely available, although their merits are hotly debated.

The ubiquitous guides who push themselves forward, particularly in the historic cities like Fes and Marrakech, can be a real nuisance. Women unaccompanied by a man are particularly liable to harassment.

CASABLANCA

Casablanca is a large modern city with busy shopping streets. It is the commercial capital of Morocco, with a wide range of shops and restaurants. Good quality casual clothing, including Benetton, is available at prices less than in the UK. Nevertheless, British Airways apparently find it worthwhile to offer shopping trips to Gibraltar.

The largest market is the Marché Central on Boulevard Mohammed V, one of the main shopping streets, open from 0800 to 1300 daily. Other good shopping areas include districts such as the Maarif and the areas near the Hotel Idou Anfa and Lyceé Lyautey. The Galerie Benomar and Benomar Centre are shopping centres both located in the Maarif. Centre 2000 is near Casablanca Port Railway Station and Galerie Galilee in the Rue Galilee. The only real department store is Alpha 55 in Avenue Mers-Sultan.

The Habbous (New Medina) is a souk offering a wide assortment of handicrafts including leather products, rugs, kaftans and brassware. Most rugs are graded by a government agency before sale.

Aux Arts Islamiques in Passage Tazi, 6 Avenue Hassan II specialises in traditional Moroccan jewellery and silver items. Coopartim behind the Hyatt Regency Hotel and Ensemble Artisanal at 195 Boulevard Bordeaux are state-run co-operatives with fair prices and quality.

British newspapers and some magazines are available at the main bookstalls, although Rabat is a better place to look for them. The American Bookstore is at 1 Place de la Fraternité.

EATING AND DRINKING

At the top end of the market there is some excellent French food, especially fish. For fish try Le Dauphin at 75 Boulevard Houphouet Boigny or Restaurant du Port de Peche. For Moroccan food try al Mounia at 95 Rue Prince Moulay Abdallah or Le Tajine in Centre 2000.

TRANSPORT

Bus services are not convenient and are often very overcrowded, particularly at peak times. A local taxi (which is normally red) will not always take you where you want to go and drivers may pick up other passengers going in the same direction. A "grand taxi", usually a Mercedes, is necesary to get to the airport. Always negotiate a taxi fare in advance. Meters invariably do not work.

RABAT

It is cheaper and often more pleasant and more efficient to buy in Ceuta, Spain or Gibraltar.

Casual cotton clothing is available in the Medina, of acceptable quality for summer wear. Leather goods are of reasonable price and quality and can be made to order. Other best buys include carpets, silver, marquetry, brass and copperware. Local music on cassette is a popular cheap buy.

The full range of British newspapers is normally on sale the day after publication. So is *The Economist*. The few English-language books available are expensive.

EATING AND DRINKING

There is a fair range of restaurants with prices reasonable by UK standards. The cuisine is generally competent without being particularly exciting. Couscous and kebabs are staples. There is a dearth of really good restaurants.

TRANSPORT

Buses are reasonable in an emergency. Taxis are likely to be service taxis covering a fixed route.

SECURITY

As in many countries, there is a certain amount of street crime.

Mozambique

Maputo

Language **Portuguese**
Currency **metical (MT) of 100 centavos**
£1=17300, Sep 1996
Traveller's cheques **accepted by arrangement in major hotels. US dollar and South African Rand accepted in hotels and many major outlets. It is illegal to change money anywhere other than authorised places. There is a black market, but there are forged notes in circulation and these facilities are usually available only in unsafe areas**
Credit cards **only in major hotels by arrangement**
Tipping **10 per cent expected in restaurants**
Export restrictions **meticals may not be exported**

Prices change frequently and swiftly. Although Mozambique is the poorest country in Africa, most transactions are based on the US dollar and virtually all goods including fresh fruit are imported from South Africa. Many locals prefer to leave their serious shopping for their next visit to South Africa or perhaps Swaziland. Some knowledge of Portuguese is essential.

None of the major store chains, either European or South African, has opened here. Payment is now made in meticals, but some shops will still accept US dollars and rands. Shopping areas are spread out throughout the city. The Central Market on Avenida 25 Septembro is a typical African public market whose original entrance was designed by Eiffel (the man who designed the tower in Paris). Handicrafts, cashew nuts of various flavours and hues and petty criminals abound. The fish market on the Avenida Marginal comes alive at 1500 daily. Most top-quality stuff is now exported, prices are high and the scales are very much on the side of the seller, but it is fascinating to wander and admire the range of shellfish on sale.

Handicrafts range from baskets to carvings in a variety of media, all readily available from markets, street hawkers or galleries. Makonde carvers from the north make some intriguing works. Batiks are popular and a favourite tourist pastime is to flip through a pile of handmade batiks carried by a street hawker. Goods made from ivory abound, but while it is legal to purchase them here it is illegal to import them into most other countries. On Saturdays an open-air craft market is usually held on the street at Praca de 25 Junho near the Fortaleza. This is well worth a visit and there is everything from elaborate carved chests in sandalwood to ceramics and carvings and walking sticks made from ebony. You must bargain: offer half what the seller wants and then edge up to an agreed price.

European weekly newspapers and periodicals are available at hotel outlets, but they are expensive. The *Mail* or *Guardian* will cost about US$3.50. South African newspapers are also available.

EATING AND DRINKING

Restaurants open and close with regularity, but the following are some of the longer established eating houses which are popular. Costs are per head exclusive of drinks. Piri Piri is a pavement café with chicken and prawn dishes averaging US$ 4-5. The Polana Hotel offers a buffet at US$18 or à la carte at US$25. Pequim offers affordable seafood or meat dishes at between US$5 and US$10. El Greco serves pizzas and Italian food at between US$4 and US$10.

TRANSPORT

There is no public transport system at present. Locals travel by *chapas* which are for the most part unsafe and therefore to be avoided. A limited number of taxis is available outside the main hotels. Fares must be agreed with the driver in advance.

SECURITY

Crime has increased dramatically and usually involves the use of some sort of weapon. Take care during the day and only walk out at night in an organised party. Never flash large sums of money or wear expensive jewellery.

MYANMAR

(SEE BURMA)

NAMIBIA

WINDHOEK

Language **Afrikaans, German, English**
Currency **Namibian dollar (NJ$) of 100 cents.**
  £1=7.05, Mar 1997
Credit cards **widely accepted within**
  Windhoek, but less so outside
Cashpoints **plenty within the city**
Shops **0800–1700 with an hour's break for lunch.**
Refunds **usually possible if a receipt is produced**
Duty-free **facilities at the airport are minimal. Buy in**
  Windhoek before departure
Tipping **10 per cent to bills in better restaurants**
  before General Sales Tax at 11 per cent is added.
  Small tips for service at garages, hairdressers and
  bars are appreciated

The shops are well stocked and practically everything is available. Most imported goods are dearer than in the UK, but local produce and imports from South Africa are reasonably priced. All shopping can be done in English.

The axis on which Windhoek revolves is Independence Avenue. There are arcades just off it which retail a variety of merchandise and are well worth exploring. Particularly worth a look are the Gustav Voigts Centre, Levinson Arcade and Post Street Mall with its daily market selling typical African crafts.

Other than Post Street Mall, there is a small souvenir shop on Independence Avenue called Bushman Art and the Namibian Crafts Centre is at 40 Tal Street. You will find good quality handmade wooden carvings of animals, small carved items of furniture, basketware, jewellery, fabric paintings and leather goods.

Model, a local supermarket, supplies South African Woolworths clothing and underwear, of similar quality to Marks and Spencer. There is a branch at the Wernhill Park shopping mall on the east side of Mandume Ndemufavo Avenue.

There is a local English-language press and South African newspapers are widely available. British and German newspapers are also obtainable. The choice of books is large and prices are not too outrageous. CNA is the equivalent of W.H.Smith.

EATING AND DRINKING

There are many restaurants and steakhouses, all reasonably priced. It is worth trying the Gourmet Inn (195 Jan Jonker Road), the Homestead (53 Feld Street), Saddles (Maerua Park), Kaiserkrone (Post Street Mall), Gathemann (Independence Avenue) and the Furstenhof Hotel on Bulow Street. Game is very popular and well worth investigating. Fish and seafood at the coastal resorts are excellent and a welcome change from the usual meat fare in Windhoek. South African wines are good and reasonably priced, as is the beer. Both are readily available in any bottle store.

TRANSPORT

Windhoek is a small town, and tourist hotels are very central and close to the shopping areas. There is very little public transport. Taxis are sometimes available at the bus stop in Independence Avenue, but they do not cruise. They tend to ply the same routes as buses.

SECURITY

Theft is increasing. Take sensible precautions. Care must be taken when using taxis to and from nightclubs in the townships or when parking a car there.

NEPAL

KATHMANDU

Language **Nepali**
Currency **Nepalese rupee (R) of 100 paisa.**
   £1=96.10, Jan 1997
Tipping **10 rupees is the minimum tip for a minor service and in small restaurants; leave 10 per cent for good service in larger ones. Larger tips should be given to travel and trekking guides. Tipping taxi drivers is optional**

Kathmandu can be a confusing place to find one's way around. Locations generally refer to areas, and individual streets often have no name. Shopping fluctuates rather unpredictably, since most goods are imported, but availability and shopping generally are getting better.

Nepal has some interesting traditional crafts and there are several shops selling these. There are woodcarvings as well as many brass and other metal ornaments. Quality and sophistication vary and so do the prices. As well as local crafts, Tibetan ones are available from refugees. These include rugs and carpets, jackets, bags and other goods. Indian handicrafts are also available.

Several shops sell sports shoes and equipment and ready-made clothing from India or Hong Kong, but quality is variable and availability limited, particularly in larger sizes. A good variety of material is available cheaply and tailors can make up.

It is possible to get by with English in the shops.

There are several bookshops in town which stock English language books. New novels frequently appear in paperback much earlier than in the UK.

EATING AND DRINKING

There are lots of restaurants in Kathmandu ranging from inexpensive but adequate to five-star hotels. All restaurants, apart from those in the hotels, tend to close by 2200. A reasonable selection of beer, soft drinks and mixers is available.

TRANSPORT

The buses are not usually used by foreigners. There are taxis, three-wheel tempos (buggies) and cycle rickshaws which are not expensive and are usually available in most areas of Kathmandu, but are very dificult to find after dark. After dusk you have often to negotiate a price with a taxi. Make sure that the meter is turned on. A surcharge above the amount shown has to be paid because of inflation and fuel costs, but this charge has been incorporated in the new taxis.

NETHERLANDS

Language **Dutch**

Currency **guilder (Dfl)of 100 cents. £1=3.05, Mar 1997**

Banks **0900–1600 Mon to Fri. There are no exchange restrictions**

Credit cards **accepted in a wide range of shops and restaurants, but many transactions continue to be made in cash**

Shops **0900–1800 Tue to Fri, 0900–1700 Sat. On Mon most shops do not open until 1300, dept stores at 1100. Late night shopping on Thur is until 2100. Shops are allowed to stay open on occasional Suns throughout the year**

Refunds **yes, within seven days**

Duty-free **at Schipol airport, open 24 hours: cigarettes and spirits are cheaper at the airport; cigars, perfume and wine are cheaper in town**

Tipping **most restaurants and hotels include a 15 per cent service charge in their bills. Taxi drivers sometimes add 15 per cent to the fare. Cloakroom attendants expect a tip of at least 25 to 50 cents**

Export restrictions **export certificates from the Dept of Antiquities needed for antiques**

The level of prices for consumer goods is generally higher than in the UK. Bargains are few and far between and price -cutting less prevalent than in the UK or USA. Almost everyone can speak English in the shops.

The best place to go for the real hand-painted Delftware as well as other souvenirs is Delft itself, a beautiful old town well worth a visit. It is only about nine kilometres from The Hague by tram, bus or train. Other recommended gifts or souvenirs are candles and unusual candle-holders, glassware, vases, tobacco and cigars, or even tourist staples such as clogs, windmills, dolls, and, of course, flower bulbs. Glass and crystal, pewter or silver might be worth a look. Always popular are the consumables – cheeses and chocolate, liqueurs, Jenever gin or even Advocaat.

Most British newspapers and periodicals are usually available at newsagents, hotels and kiosks on the same day as they appear in the UK. They cost at least twice as much as in the UK.

There are restaurants in all price and quality ranges and of most international types. Lunch with wine in a good restaurant costs about Df170-120 a head. Dinner costs rather more.

Indonesian *rijstafel* is extremely popular. Dutch cuisine includes herring and eel, while the local fastfood is chips with mayonnaise. Look out for *panjnekoeken* (pancakes), *proffetjes* (tiny pancakes), *haring* (herring), *erwentensoep* (pea soup), *hutspot* (mashed potato with carrot and onion), *kroketten* (croquettes), *bitterballen* (meatballs) and *uitsmijters* (ham or cheese with fried eggs on bread). Other Dutch treats are *drop* (liquorice either sweet or salted - an acquired taste), *stroopwafels* (syrup waffles) and in winter *olieballen* (large round doughnuts) and *warme chocolade* (hot chocolate with whipped cream).

AMSTERDAM

Amsterdam is the capital and largest city of the Netherlands. Despite the political ferment and the febrile attractions of the red-light district, the solid core of Amsterdam remains much as it was.

Leading south from Dam, the main square, are the main shopping streets of Kalverstraat and Leidsestraat. The local Harrods, or De Bijenkorf, is on the square itself, as are other department stores such as Peek and Cloppenburg and C&A.

More up-market shopping streets are to be found further south still in the museum quarter around P.C.Hoogstraat, van Baerlestraat and Spiegelgracht. This is also the area for antiques, for example in the Nieuwe Spiegelstraat or Kerstraat.

There are lots of interesting small shops to be seen on your tour of the canal circle in Herengracht, Keizersgracht and Prinsengracht.

The Albert Cuyp Market in the street of that name is immense, popular and open daily with its range of produce and many other goods. The famous floating flower market is at the top of the Leidsestraat. Not cheap, but many cannot resist buying.

Perhaps the best buy is real Delft china, not one of the derivatives, which will not be cheap anyway. Be sure to go to De Porceleyne Fles next to the Muntplein which is where Kalverstraat joins Leidsestraat. Diamonds are synonymous with Amsterdam, but you should know what you are doing to buy with confidence.

EATING AND DRINKING

A special place to eat is Swarte Schaep at Korte Leidsedwarsstraat 24. For local cuisine try Hotel die Port van Cleve. For rijstafel Orient at Van Badestraat 21. Lucius at Spuistraat 247 specialises in fish.

TRANSPORT

City transport is efficient and includes metro, bus and tram. Buy a 10-journey *strippenkaart* or a day-ticket from the tram driver. Taxis cannot be hailed on the street, but the metered charge includes service. Bicycles are popular and can be hired at the Centraal Station.

THE HAGUE

The Hague is the seat of government and has a slower pace of life than Amsterdam. Scheveningen, a few kilometres away on the coast, is much livelier. Shopping in the centre of The Hague is concentrated around Grote Markt Straat, Spui Straat and Hoogstraat down to the Palais Noordeinde. The two largest department stores are Vroom and Dreesmann and De Bijenkorf, both in Grote Markt Straat. Marks and Spencer have opened in the Spuistraat and include a food hall. Other familiar names include C&A, Body Shop, Miss Selfridge and Etam.

Between Spui Straat and Gravenstraat is "The Passage", an enclosed arcade with souvenir shops and cafés. Up-market and designer clothes shops can be found in Hoogstraat. Behind C&A is Chinatown with restaurants, shops and a covered market. The main general market is away from the centre at Herman Costerstraat: it opens on Monday, Wednesday, Friday and Saturday. There is an antique and book market at Lange Voorhout from May to September on Thursday and Sunday. In Denneweg, off the Lange Voorhout, you will find some antique shops interspersed with eating places. The Leidschenhage shopping area on the outskirts of The Hague is pedestrianised and includes branches of most of the large department stores.

There are expensive china and glassware shops in Hoogstraat, Blokker in Spuistraat and the department stores are a little more down-market. The Passage and Denneweg are also good for souvenir shopping.

Shops at Scheveningen are open from 1000 until 2200 every day of the week from March to October.

Newsagents can be found in Noordeinde, Venestraat and in

the basement of Vroom & Dreesmann. A large selection of English books is available at the American Bookstore in Lange Poten.

EATING AND DRINKING

It is unwise to count upon obtaining a meal after about 2100 at most restaurants in the centre of The Hague. A recommended Indonesian restaurant is Garoeda at Kneuterdijk. Restaurants in Schevinengen stay open later. At the harbour are several good restaurants including an excellent, but expensive, fish restaurant, Ducdalf at Dr Lelykade 5. A very nice coffee and tea shop is t'Goude Hooft at the corner of Hoogstraat and Groen Markt. The Hotel des Indes serves afternoon tea or morning coffee in beautiful surroundings.

TRANSPORT

There is an excellent public transport network. Tickets for buses and trams are obtainable at railway stations or at any shop displaying the HTM sign. It is cheaper to purchase multi-tickets (*strippenkaarten*) in advance, although on the bus or tram you can also pay the driver. One strip must be stamped for each zone travelled. Taxis do not pick up fares in the street. You must wait at a clearly marked taxi rank. Taxis are numerous, but expensive.

NEW CALEDONIA: GRANDE TERRE

NOUMEA

New Caledonia is featured in up-market travel brochures such as the Club Med. It is very French, very fashionable and very expensive. Even the food is not a particularly good bargain here, as it usually is where French influence is considerable.

There are some expensive shops in the town centre around the Rue de l'Alma. The favourite traditional souvenirs with tourists include war clubs.

NEW ZEALAND

Language **English**
Currency **New Zealand dollar (NZ$). £1=2.29,**
  Mar 1997
Banks **0930–1630**
Cashpoints **yes**
Shops **0900–1700 Mon to Fri, closed Sat afternoon;**
  late night shopping once during the week
Tipping **no: the governmment indicate publicly that**
  they prefer visitors not to tip. In expensive hotels
  the waiters may try to secure tips from overseas
  visitors who are not aware of the local form. Offer
  a tip for exceptional service, but it may be refused
Import/export restrictions **the agricultural industry**
  is protected as fully as possible from the
  introduction of harmful diseases. Wickerwork and
  crafts, particularly from the third world, are
  subject to inspection and may be confiscated

The range of shopping available can be limited, as is only to
be expected in a country of only three and a half million
inhabitants. Shopping facilities are unexciting, but sufficient
for normal needs. With the exception of food supermarkets,
there is virtually no price cutting competition in the shops.
Retail price maintenance is the norm rather than the exception.
There are frequent sales, but they do not generally offer as
large cuts in prices as in the UK.

There is no equivalent to Marks and Spencer or John
Lewis, either in range or quality. Department stores and chain
store boutiques do, however, offer a variety of reasonably
priced "young" fashion. Hand-knitted sweaters can be expensive, but are good and perhaps the nearest thing to a genuinely
local craft gift or souvenir. Also good, but not cheap are
Swann-Dri jackets, the local equivalent of the British Barbour.
Shell jewellery is another speciality. Look out for traditional
Maori crafts, including carvings in bone, wood or jade.

A good proportion of cheaper restaurants have a licence
which allows diners to bring their own wine (BYO). Pubs are
getting better at serving food reasonable in both price and
quality. Cuisine tends to be fairly straightforward, with a traditional British influence. The fish is excellent, but will be
unfamiliar to the visitor from the northern hemisphere.
Varieties include terakihi, orange roughy and groper, hoki and
red and blue cod which are not like the Atlantic variety.

Seafood such as oysters and mussels are also good, as is the lamb and dairy produce. New Zealand wines are a bit cheaper than they are in the UK, and have an increasing international reputation for quality. Steinlager is the world famous local brew, but there are many other brands.

Petty street crime is increasing.

AUCKLAND

Auckland is a sprawling city which covers a very large area. This has led to pockets of shopping centres which over the last few years are changing into shopping malls, although on a smaller scale than in the UK.

The main central area of Auckland City has a reasonable cross-section of shops, similar to a decent regional shopping centre in the UK. The only surviving department store is Smith and Caughey in Queen Street, which is also the main shopping precinct. The Atrium is a recent development comprising a number of shops on four levels.

There is a fair mix of retail outlets in Auckland City with all the major chains being represented. There are Hallenstein's for men and Katie's for women's clothing; Stevens for household goods and Farmer's, a traditional department store.

Parnell and Newmarket are two suburbs whose growth is leading them to merge with each other. Parnell is one of the more prestigious parts of Auckland with a good blend of antique-cum-interior-design stores with restaurants, coffee bars and brasseries, florist and wine shops, but with a dearth of practical everyday outlets such as ironmongers. There are also many good restaurants. Newmarket is similar in pattern, but with a better mix of traders and in terms of size would almost equal central Auckland. Leven's, a nationwide store, has one of its largest branches here and the 277 Centre has a mix of specialist shops, brasseries, boutiques, etc. The two combined provide better shopping than in Queen Street.

On the other side of town Ponsonby and Herne Bay are also growing together and may come one day to rival Parnell and Newmarket.

The majority of British Sunday newspapers are flown to Auckland direct and are available on the Wednesday following publication, at a cost of about £4. There are a number of local weekly magazines and there is a thriving trade press operating from Auckland. There are many well-stocked bookshops and although prices are higher than in the UK, frequent sales produce some notable bargains.

EATING AND DRINKING

Most shops are shoulder to shoulder with restaurants and coffee bars, most of which are very good.

On average the standard of restaurants is quite high with affordable prices when compared to UK town prices. A restaurant in Ponsonby offered a special Christmas menu with five courses, each accompanied by a different wine. The first course came with a 1985 champagne. The fixed price was about $90 or £40.

TRANSPORT

Auckland has a bus service. Taxis are plentiful, but cannot be flagged down in the street.

WELLINGTON

The main shopping area is centred on Lambton Quay, with the railway station at its north end and neighbouring streets. A good place for arts and crafts is Wakefield Market at the corner of Taranaki Street and Jervois Quay.

For clothing go to Kirks. There is also a Country Road, Hallenstines (similar to Gap) and K Mart as well as a number of local chains and boutiques. European and American clothes are relatively expensive.

Local newspapers such as the *Dominion* carry both local and international news. Some British daily and weekly newspapers and many British weekly and monthly magazines are on sale. British and American magazines are normally two or three months out of date. There is a good selection of both British and American paperback and hardback books. Books are more expensive than in the UK, but not prohibitive. Bennett's Government Bookshop at the corner of Lambton Quay and Benson Street has a range of books about New Zealand.

EATING AND DRINKING

There are many restaurants with a wide range of cuisine. Quality and price vary enormously. Courtenay Place and Cuba Street are good for more up-market places.

TRANSPORT

City transport is generally well maintained and fares are moderate. There are buses, trolley-buses and suburban electric trains as well as a cable-car (tram) from Lambton Quay. Taxis are plentiful, but you can only get one by telephoning or queue-

ing for one at an authorised stand, as opposed to flagging one
down in the street.

NICARAGUA

MANAGUA

Language **Spanish**
Currency **córdoba (C\$) of 100 centavos. £1=14.57,
    Mar 1997**
Traveller's cheques **do not bring sterling or sterling
    denominated traveller's cheques: cash US dollars
    are popular: hotels and some other outlets price in
    dollars and convert to local currency. Avoid street
    traders who may offer marginally better rates, but
    try to cheat you**
Credit cards **widely accepted**
Cashpoints **some**
Shops **hours variable, but most shops open
    1000–1700/1800 Mon to Sat. Some close for lunch,
    but this is becoming less common, as is closing on
    Sat afternoon**
Bargaining **not customary; market traders may
    offer a small discount to secure a sale**
Duty-free **at the airport, but uninteresting.
    Nicaraguan rum is probably the best buy**
Tipping **10 per cent is expected for the usuals
    services; restaurant bills sometimes include 10 per
    cent tax and service charges. Most people leave
    the small change as an additional tip**

Managua is one of the world's more confusing cities. Even
with a car and driver, a visitor will find it hard to orientate.
There are few street names or house numbers. In addition, the
city centre has never been rebuilt following the 1972 earthquake,
although some of the devastated area is now repopulated by the
very poor in their makeshift homes. The latest street names may
vary both from those on available maps and those in general
usage. Try to ensure you know where you are going before you
set out.

Wealthy Nicaraguans still do much of their shopping in
Miami. Local shopping is sufficient for most basic needs, but

imported goods other than staples carry luxury tax as well as VAT. Only a few handicrafts can be regarded as bargains.

There are several large shopping complexes such as the Centro Commercial across from the Roberto Huembes Market or the Metrocentro by the Ruben Darrio roundabout close to the new cathedral. There is a shop in the Metrocentro called Pewter which is worth a look for souvenirs. The La Galeria department store is also quite close to the new cathedral.

The Huembes, or central market, has a large craft section. There is also a good craft market on the first Saturday of each month at the Centro Cultural Managua, based on the ruins of the pre-earthquake Gran Hotel and close to the old cathedral. Best buys include hammocks, but the coloured ones use synthetic thread which can fade with time. Look out for black coral jewellery, sometimes with a few malachite beads, but beware of buying items made from turtleshell or lizard skins. Pottery and primitive paintings are well worth a look. The work of painters from the Solentiname Islands in Lake Nicaragua is particularly highly prized. Other popular souvenirs are cowboy boots or hats as worn by real cowboys in the countryside.

Masaya is an excellent place for buying handicrafts to take home as gifts or souvenirs. It lies just 26 kilometres south of Managua and is the craft capital of Nicaragua. The central market attracts traders from all over the country. Masaya is well known for its embroidery, and Marisol, opposite the old railway station, is worth a visit for clothing and linens. Hammocks are the other big buy. A little further to the south is the pottery village of San Juan del Oriente, where goods on offer vary from cheap folk-style to the most refined.

The *New York Times*, *Miami Herald*, *Time*, *Newsweek* and *The Economist* are readily available, but are expensive.

EATING AND DRINKING

Nicaragua exports beef, seafood and coffee as well as some fruit and vegetables, so there is good food to be eaten here. The local cuisine can become a little boring, as it is beans, rice and tortillas with everything, but there are some nice places. Los Ranchos in front of the Ministry of Foreign Affairs is the top business restaurant. El Eskimo next door is also popular for lunches. Other recommendations include La Marseillaise on the Calle Principal de Los Robles, El Meson Español in Bolonia, San Juan de la Selva or Las Lugoon, the Carretera a Masaya, Pasta Fresca, two blocks south of the Intercontinental and Pollo Supremo, with branches all over Managua. Wine of any sort of quality is expensive in restaurants, although Spanish table wine can be bought in a supermarket for a couple of pounds or so. Local beer and rum are worth trying.

TRANSPORT
Public buses are rarely used by visitors, since they are hot, crammed with people and popular with pickpockets. Red taxis are reliable, but expensive, especially if taken from a hotel. Regular taxis are less expensive and less reliable. Fares should be negotiated before starting a journey.

SECURITY
Crime is on the increase. Street crime is prevalent and sensible security precautions are necessary. Take particular care at night and avoid certain areas.

NIGER

NIAMEY

Language **French**
Currency **franc CFA West African. £1=826, Mar 1997**
Traveller's cheques **franc denominated and cash. French francs are recommended**
Credit cards **only in up-market hotels and restaurants**
Shops **0800–1250, 1500–1830**
Import/export restrictions **no restrictions on the import of foreign currency**

The Grand Marché on the Boulevard de la Liberté is the focal point for shopping. You will find all that is available there and in the surrounding streets such as the Rue de Gaweye. The Musée Nationale has a shop where you can buy gifts and souvenirs. Prices are fixed and high, but range and quality are good.

Look out particularly for the Tuareg or Hausa influence in handicrafts. Recommended are silver desert crosses, necklaces and other jewellery, colourful wall hangings, calabashes and leatherwork.

Most newspapers, magazines and books available are in French, and relatively few are in English.

EATING AND DRINKING

The French influence is marked in the cuisine. By and large keep to the main hotels such as the Terminus or the Gaweye.

TRANSPORT

Taxis are usually service taxis covering fixed routes and shared.

SECURITY

Petty street crime and begging can present problems. Do not walk around town at night.

NIGERIA

Language **English**
Currency **naira (N) of 100 kobo. £1=127.18, Mar 1997**
Banks **0800–1500 Mon, 0800–1300 Tue to Fri.**
  There is a flourishing currency black market, but dealing is illegal, and the difference in rate compared with most hotels or exchange bureaus is not great
Credit cards **only accepted in international hotels**
Tipping **"dash", from the Portuguese word for "to give", is a common form of compensation in money, goods or favours. It is normally paid before the service is given**
Import/export restrictions **the import and export of naira is rigidly controlled; stringent controls are imposed by the National Museum in Lagos on the export of antiques**

Imported goods are very expensive. Many local products are quite reasonably priced, but some are of inferior quality. Prices are variable and negotiable.

Hawkers and street traders sell "copy" watches and there are plenty of pirated video tapes. Casual wear such as copies of Chanel T-shirts, usually made in Thailand, can be bought in the local markets. There are no shops where one would buy European clothes off the peg, but caftans made in local batiks are plentiful.

Like most countries in Western Africa, Nigeria has a long and proud cultural tradition. This is often reflected in the arts and crafts available as gifts and souvenirs. Recommended buys include bronzework, leather, woodcarvings, calabashes, traditional musical instruments, batiks and other textiles. Also cassettes of Nigerian music.

Nigeria has long been a major market for beer and Guinness has been brewed locally for years. This and other local brands are good, if sometimes a little on the strong side.

ABUJA

Abuja, the new capital, remains somewhat cold and soulless, with all the advantages and disadvantages typical of a brand-new city. Among the disadvantages is limited shopping, certainly more so than in Lagos, but things are changing. A new super-store has been opened although the range of goods is not remotely as wide as in a British supermarket. There remain still relatively few shops, as opposed to market stalls, and availability is rather limited. Some people prefer to do a lot of their shopping in Kaduna or in Lagos.

British and other Western newspapers are sometimes available in hotels two or three days after publication. There are shops which stock some books, but there is very little choice.

EATING AND DRINKING
There is an Indian/Chinese restaurant and others are planned. The Hilton and Sheraton are reasonable.

TRANSPORT
Public transport has yet to be developed properly. Taxis already operate, although the roadworthiness of some is questionable. Most taxis are service taxis. Motorcycle taxis are becoming popular.

LAGOS

Lagos Island is still the main commercial centre and Broad Street is the shopping hub. Just before you get to Carter Bridge are the markets of Ebute Ero and Isale Eko. Jankara Market lies about a quarter of a mile north of Broad Street.

Owing to security problems on Lagos Island, much shopping is now done on Ikoyi and Victoria islands. In Ikoyi there are shops and eating places in Avolano Road; the Falamo Centre is a major feature. A good place for buying gifts and souvenirs or just window shopping is the Onikan National Museum on Avolano Road. Most hotels have their own shops.

There are also several markets for local arts and crafts. Materials are often seconds.

British newspapers are usually available in hotels or at the airport on the day after publication. There is a limited supply of books in the hotels and at bookshops in Broad Street and the Falamo Centre.

EATING AND DRINKING

There is a reasonable selection of restaurants with a variety of cuisines, easily found in the main thoroughfares such as Broad Street and Avolano Road. Try also the Bristol Hotel in Martin Street, just off Broad Street. The restaurant at the National Museum is a good place to sample local specialities and palm wine.

TRANSPORT

Public transport is extremely poor and to be avoided if at all possible. Buses are overcrowded and unsafe. Taxis are unreliable and recklessly driven, subject to the whims of often chaotic traffic conditions. Hassle with drivers is common. Establish the fare first.

SECURITY

Security is a problem. Be alert and do not be ostentatious. It is unsafe to walk around Lagos at night.

NORWAY

OSLO

Language **Norwegian**
Currency **krone (Nkr) of 100 ore. £1=10.95, Mar 1997**
Banks **0815–1545 Mon to Wed and Fri, 0815–1800 Thur**
Credit cards **accepted in shops and hotels**
Shops **0830–1700 Mon to Fri, 0830–1400 Sat**
Sales **yes, and special offers; bargains can be obtained**
Duty-free **VAT-free shopping available in larger shops**

Karl Johans Gate marks the centre of Oslo and it is good for shopping and eating places as well as for general atmosphere. Most items, including clothing, are about 50 to 100 per cent more expensive than in the UK. Many Norwegians shop for clothes and other goods abroad, expecially in the UK. Weatherproof footwear is better purchased in Norway, as it is usually of a high standard and specifically designed for Norwegian conditions. Ski clothing is a good buy, particularly at sale time. Norwegian waterproof clothing for children is extremely good, as are winter boots. Norwegians are very home-conscious and there are many lovely shops offering a plentiful supply of household goods.

Other things worth looking at – although none will be cheap – are reindeer-skin items, knitwear, woodwork as well as brass, pewter and enamel.

Some knowledge of Norwegian is useful when shopping although many Norwegians speak English well.

British newspapers are readily available, usually in the late afternoon on the day of issue. A good selection of hardback and paperback books in English is available, but they can be double the UK price.

EATING AND DRINKING

The number and range of restaurants is growing slowly. Most tastes are catered for, but people used to larger cities will still find the choice narrow. Meals are expensive, especially when taken with wine. Drinks are also expensive in the bars, particularly spirits, which few people drink when out. Locally produced lager and soft drinks are good and can be obtained relatively cheaply.

TRANSPORT

Public transport consists of buses, trams, a suburban railway system similar to the London Underground, but above ground except in the centre of Oslo, and regular ferries. The system is good and runs to timetables. A *flexikort* is valid for 10 journeys.

Rather than hail a taxi on the street, it is usual to go to or to telephone a taxi rank. Taxis can be difficult to obtain, but can be booked in advance.

OMAN

MUSCAT

Language **Arabic**
Currency **Omani rial (OR) of 1,000 baisas, pegged to the US dollar. £1=0.63, Mar 1997. There are no restrictions on remittances to and from Britain**
Banks **0800–1200 Sat to Wed, 0800–1130 Thur**
Credit cards **accepted by major hotels**
Shops **0900–1300, 1600–1900 Sat to Thur, closed on Fri**
Tipping **service charge added to bills in restaurants, but an additional tip always appreciated**

The overall cost of living is higher than in the UK and it is very rare to find goods in short supply. British Home Stores, Mothercare and J.C.Penney have local stores recently opened. There is also a Benetton and lots of shops with fake Levis from Bangkok at reasonable prices as well as fake designer T-shirts and other items. Liquor licences are needed to buy liquor. English is very widely spoken as a second language.

The main shopping areas are to be found at Qurum, Medinat Al-Sultan Qaboos and Ruwi. Muttrah is the port and the main souk is there, with a small entrance on the Corniche. Many silver and gold items are to be found in the souk. The fish souk is at Mina Qaboos Harbour and there are many different local specialities from the sea which can be sampled in restaurants.

The MSQ Centre is a shopping complex at Medinat Al-Sultan Qaboos with a wide range of shops, including a Family Bookshop and a Body Shop. There are several shopping complexes at Qurum with a variety of small shops. The Sabco Centre includes stores selling jewellery, gold, gifts and handicrafts, carpets and bamboo. The Al Wadi Centre, Alasfoor Plaza, Al-Araimi Centre, Al-Harthy Centre, Qurum Commercial Centre, Capital Commercial Centre and Al-Khamis Centre all sell similar goods.

Also at Qurum is British Home Stores (also stocking Mothercare) with prices about 25 per cent above those in the UK. J.C.Penney is in the Al-Araimi Centre. Prisunic is in the Capital Commercial Centre with many imported expensive French items. Benetton is also to be found there. The shopping area in Ruwi is near the Sheraton. There are lots of small shops strung out along Ruwi High (Souk) Street and in the immediate neighbourhood selling a range of goods including gold and jewellery, fabrics and food.

The Shati Al-Qurum Centre includes the Oman Heritage Centre which carries a range of ethnic items, fabrics, weaving, pottery and copper. The Ministry of National Heritage and Culture has shops in most hotels and shopping centres selling similar items and rugs, chests and coffee pots. More up-market items, including antiques and silver, are to be found at Antique World in the Al-Harthy Centre. For gold and silver and other jewellery try Al-Felaij in the Sabci Centre, MAS in Alasfoor Plaza or Ruwi Jewellers in Al-Kamis Plaza.

The main bookshop is the Family Bookshop which has branches throughout Muscat and carries a good selection of books, though they tend to be expensive.

EATING AND DRINKING

Hotel restaurants provide a wide range of European and other food and there is a good variety of other restaurants in the Capital Area. For local cuisine try Ali Baba in Ruwi High Street, Candles in Al-Burj off Al-Noor Street or Mijana in the MSQ Centre.

TRANSPORT

There is a bus system run by Oman National Transport. Buses are not used by Europeans. Taxis, the usual form of transport for Europeans, are readily available. Women may use them without concern in the daytime. There is no telephone service to call taxis, but you may be able to hail them from the street in town or at hotels. There are no meters in taxis. Fares are usually negotiated in advance. They are usually more expensive from hotels.

PAKISTAN

Language **Urdu, English**
Currency **Pakistan rupee(R) of 100 paisa.
£1=64.12, Mar 1997. The rupee now floats
against a range of currencies**
Banks **0900–1300 Sat to Wed, 0900–1100 Thur.
Officially authorised money-changers are
permitted and offer a better rate than the official
bank one. There is a high risk of forged currency
and other unscrupulous dealings on the black
market**

Credit cards accepted in major hotels and larger
  shops
Cashpoints some
Shops variable, generally 1030–2000, some close for
  lunch
Refunds retailers will replace goods rather than
  refund
Sales only in a few up-market outlets
Bargaining yes, for most commodities, but not for
  groceries
Tipping a small tip is normal in hotels and
  restaurants, where service of 10 per cent has been
  added. Requests for baksheesh from beggars and
  small boys are frequent. Pay Rs5–10 for a couple
  of bags to boys who offer to carry shopping
Import/export restrictions items such as computers
  should be declared on entry to avoid possible
  problems

A wide variety of imported products can be found in the general stores, but prices tend to be high. English is widely spoken in
the main cities and most of the better shops will usually have
someone who speaks English on their staff.

Local labour being cheap, handicrafts are reasonable in
price. Recommended buys are jewellery, silver, onyx, carved
woodwork and dhurries. There are also lovely copper and
brass objects, and great varieties of rugs and wall hangings.
Good leather items such as spectacle cases, wallets, handbags,
briefcases, suitcases, etc. are also reasonable in price, but do
carefully inspect the fittings and finish.

Those keen on embroidery will find local thread easily
available and much cheaper than in the UK. Towelling dressing
gowns are very good value, as are towels and bed-linen. Men's
tailoring is much cheaper than in the UK. Many men get suits
and shirts made. Men's suitings are good value, although
other materials are not always to Western taste. Pirated video
and pop tapes and CDs are available at less than the UK price
but beware of trying to import these back to Europe.
Spectacles are also cheaper. Some sporting goods are cheap,
but not trainers and other sports shoes.

The quality of food and standards of hygiene in restaurants
is very variable. Some of the most reliable restaurants are to
be found in the big hotels, which often offer a range of
cuisines. The largest hotels have liquor licences for foreigners
who are resident with them, but they are unable to serve alcohol
in any of the public rooms including restaurants, and their

stock is limited and very expensive. A wide range of exotic fruits is available and they make good juices.

Requests for baksheesh from beggars and small boys are frequent.

ISLAMABAD/RAWALPINDI

Islamabad has the advantages and disadvantages to be expected of any new city. Each sector of the city has a shopping centre and there is no main shopping area. Each shopping centre or bazaar has a mixture of shops and you can buy most things in most bazaars, but each bazaar has its specialities. Rawalpindi is only 12 miles from Islamabad. The goods on sale in the bazaars there are on the whole cheaper and more varied than in Islamabad, but the traffic is much heavier and it is more difficult to find your way around. You can buy most things in Islamabad or Rawalpindi if you know where to look, except items forbidden to Muslims such as alcohol and pork products. The markets can be dirty and dusty, but many newer shops are well maintained. New shops such as Benetton and Hang Ten are opening and old shops are changing all the time. Shops tend to be small and many are open-fronted. You will often find several stores in a row selling the same items and many general stores selling a mixture of goods. There are no department stores in the UK sense, although some shops describe themselves as such.

British newspapers and magazines are available one or two days late, but at up to three times the UK price. Sunday papers are available on Tuesdays. There is a wide selection of books for all ages and some paperbacks are cheaper than in the UK.

TRANSPORT
Public transport is cheap in Islamabad and Rawalpindi, but crowded. Taxis are a better option, but not recommended. They are cheap, although the fare should be negotiated before getting in.

KARACHI

For atmospheric shopping the larger local markets are recommended. The Empress Market in Saddar is essentially a produce market. The Bohri Bazaar near by is a maze of small shops crammed into claustrophobic streets with an amazing range of pots and pans, materials and almost everything else you can think of. The Zainab Market in Abdullah Haroon Road specialises in arts and crafts. Hard bargaining is necessary, expecially for the more expensive craft items. Some of the more popular handicraft and artisan items include leatherwork, lampshades, silverwork, 22-carat gold, woodcarving, woodwork with inlaid brass, Kashmiri shawls, embroidery, silk paintings, onyx, brass, copperwork, carpets and wall hangings. Check an item carefully before finally buying, particularly onyx for possible cracks.

The Sheraton Hotel Arcade has some good, but not cheap, shops for items such as jewellery, silver and gold. Pakistan-made oriental-type carpets are available from shops all over Karachi. Afghan Carpet on Khaliq-Uz-Zaman Road near the Submarine Roundabout has an impressive range of carpets and other goods such as onyx and leather in its adjacent handicraft shop. Dhurries are readily available from bazaars and handicraft shops. Galleria Gultex in the Marriott Hotel is more up-market, but also carries good-value linen goods. There is a new shop opposite the Copper Kettle on Mall Square which also sells a good selection of linens and even exports to the UK. Jafferjee's at Mehran Heights has good leather accessories. Solo in the Shaheen Centre at Clifton sells indigenous crafts including hand-block printed cloth and some interesting handmade jewellery. There are many boutiques off Zamzama Boulevard selling clothing more Eastern than Western in style, but interesting. The shops around the Agha roundabout are also worth browsing in.

There is a duty-free shop at the airport and one in the town with no alcohol, inconsistent availability and variable savings.

English-language newspapers both local and British (one day late) are on sale at all the leading hotels and at supermarkets. The Asian versions of *Newsweek*, *Time* and *The Economist* are cheap and readily available, as are some women's magazines. A limited range of best-seller paperbacks can be found in hotel bookshops.

TRANSPORT

Hotels in the town centre are not recommended, and the main tourist hotels are not within walking distance of the main shopping areas. Buses are badly maintained, overcrowded and not recommended. Taxis can be ordered by phone from most of the major hotels. Establish the fare first, since meters are often out of use. It is best to have some idea of how to get to the required address. There are also scooter-taxis (rickshaws) and the horse-drawn Victorias, much loved by tourists. Again costs are immensely variable.

SECURITY
The main shopping areas and markets are usually safe, but there are areas where a woman should not venture alone. Some hassle with beggars is to be expected.

PANAMA

PANAMA CITY

Language **Spanish**
Currency **balboa, of 100 centisimos; at par with the US dollar. £1=1.56, Oct 1996**
Traveller's cheques **dollar denominated. Notes in circulation are US dollars; both US and locally minted Panamanian coinage are legal tender**
Duty-free **at the airport is expensive, in many cases comparable goods can be found in town at lower prices**
Tipping **10 per cent in hotels and restaurants; taxi drivers do not expect tips**

Panama City is a mixture of old and modern. The centre has department stores and scattered shopping centres, while the suburbs are considerably less affluent. Panama boasts the longest shopping street in the world. It starts at Avenida Central – the cheap end – and becomes Via Espana – the more expensive end of the street.

A great deal is imported from the US, and most things are to be found. The cost of quality clothing is high, though cheap bargains can be found for informal wear. The local *guayabera* (a short-or long-sleeved dress shirt worn outside trousers) is popular for both formal and non-formal occasions and makes a useful gift or souvenir. There is a large selection of footwear, although the UK offers better value for money.

English is widely spoken and understood as a result of years of influence from the US and the Caribbean. The only British newspaper available is the *Financial Times*. The satellite edition of the *Miami Herald* is distributed by one of the local newspapers. Books in English, usually American bestsellers, are available, but at a cost.

EATING AND DRINKING
Food is mainly US-style. A wide range of eating places is available, but wine is expensive. Cigarettes are cheaper than in the UK.

TRANSPORT
Buses in the town are cheap, but generally very old, noisy and crowded. The taxi service is adequate and cheap but the drivers' knowledge of the city is not always extensive. There are large tourist taxis which operate from all the main tourist hotels but they are much more expensive.

SECURITY
Exercise extreme caution. Muggings occur even during daylight and there are occasional hold-ups in restaurants.

PAPUA NEW GUINEA

PORT MORESBY

Language **English**
Currency **kina (K) of 100 toea. £1=2.23, Mar 1997**
Tipping **uncommon and discouraged**

The cost of living is generally very high compared with that in the UK. Many goods are imported from Australia, New Zealand, Germany, the UK and Hong Kong, and are fairly expensive. Port Moresby's two main department stores and a number of small dress shops sell mostly Australian-and Asian-made clothing. Quality is variable, prices high and choice limited.

There are three local English-language newspapers – daily there are the *Post Courier* and the *Nation*, while *the Times* appears weekly. Newsagents sell mainly Australian press and some American periodicals. *The Economist* is on sale. There is a fairly wide range of books, but they are very expensive.

EATING AND DRINKING
The four main hotels have reasonably good restaurants. Wines and beers are expensive.

TRANSPORT
Public transport is erratic and not used by expatriates. Taxis

are not reliable and the drivers are not acquainted with residential areas.

SECURITY
There is an ever-present threat of criminal activity.

PARAGUAY

ASUNCION

Language **Spanish**
Currency **guarani (G) of 100 centimos. £1=3430, Mar 1997**
Shops **most open early, close at noon for the siesta, reopening again around 1530**
Tipping **taxi drivers expect a reasonable tip; 10 to 15 per cent is customary in restaurants, hotels and hairdressers**

Imported goods are expensive, but there is a fairly wide range of crafts which are ideal as gifts. Sandals and light shoes can be made to measure, although they tend to wear out quite quickly. Flat-heeled shoes or walking shoes with good soles are essential for protection against Asunción's cobbled and gravelled streets and roads.

Books is a shop selling English-language books, usually imported from the USA and at high prices. Very few magazines are available, apart from *Time* and *Newsweek*.

EATING AND DRINKING
There are many restaurants, generally of acceptable standard. There is good river fish although little variety; the most popular are surubbi, dorado and pacu. Local fruit is plentiful and cheap in season. There is a wide range of alcohol at prices much lower than in the UK. Good locally made beer and soft drinks are available. The local wine is not recommended.

TRANSPORT
Trams are very slow and subject to breakdowns, but they are a unique way of seeing the city. They do not run at lunchtime or after 1900 and Sundays. Buses are frequent, overcrowded, uncomfortable and prone to accidents. The taxi service is adequate and

relatively cheap. Use taxis with meters rather than those with-out.

PERU

LIMA

Language **Spanish, Quechua**
Currency **sol of 100 cents. £1=4.2, Mar 1997**
Banks **0830–1130 Mon to Fri, Jan to Mar, 0845–1245
Apr to Dec. US dollars are accepted everywhere**
Credit cards **accepted in some shops, particularly in
tourist areas**
Shops **1000–1300, 1700–2100**
Duty-free **at the airport, not a wide selection of
goods**
Bargaining **common in the markets**
Tipping **generally 10 per cent; some restaurants will
already have added that to the bill**

Shopping is developing fast and several new centres are under construction. The centre of town (Chinatown) has plenty of shops, but most visitors will find themselves staying and shopping in more up-market areas. Miraflores and San Isidro are still best for quality shopping. In Miraflores there are shopping arcades off Avenida Larco and Avenida La Paz such as El Alamo and El Suche which are worth exploring and San Isidro has the Centro Commercial San Isidro at Paseo de la Republica 3440 and the Centro Commercial Camino Real on the avenue of that name. A large enclosed mall is the Centro Commercial Caminos del Inca at Avenida Angamos/Avenida del Inca in Chacarilla.

The shops are very well stocked and prices are generally competitive. Clothing is expensive and not hard-wearing, although tailoring is relatively inexpensive and locally purchased cottons and materials are reasonable. For everyday clothing try the large stores such as Santa Isabel or Saga. Handbags and other leather goods are attractive; Alda has branches in various shopping centres.

The Indian market on Avenida Marina has an excellent selection of Peruvian crafts – pottery, silverware, paintings, woodcarving, alpaca jumpers, rugs, blankets, etc. at good prices, but you should check the merchandise before you buy. There is a similar market at Petit Thouars in Miraflores.

Specialist outlets for alpaca, perhaps the best buy of all, include Las Manos Peruanos at La Paz 646, Miraflores, La Gringa at La Paz 552, Miraflores, Royal Alpaca at La Paz 646, store 5-14-15, Miraflores, Alpaca II at Larco 859, Miraflores, Mon Repos at Ramiro Priale and Lanificio at Avenida Alberto del Campo 285, San Isidro.

Specialist outlets for silver jewellery and similar wares include Torres Della Pina on level A in the Caminos del Inca. It has a factory outlet, open mornings only, at 264 Chacas, Breñao. This is cheaper, but in a somewhat dubious area. Other outlets for crafts are the government-run Artesianas del Peru at Jorge Basadre 610 in San Isidro, Artes Manual Blas at Ocharan 183 in Miraflores, Artesania Kuntur Huasi at Ocharan 183 in Miraflores and Warike at Commandante Espinar in Miraflores.

Little English is spoken and a knowledge of Spanish is useful.

English-language books and magazines, when they are available, are expensive. Try ABC Bookstores at Edificio El Pacifico in the Avenida Diagonal or Epoca at Comandante Espinar, both in Miraflores.

EATING AND DRINKING

There are lots of different restaurants where good meals can be had at varying prices. Fish restaurants are plentiful and often good. Local cuisine is worth trying. Barbecued guinea-pig tastes a bit like rabbit. Top of the local range are Las Brujas de Cachiche at Bolognesi 460 in Miraflores and José Antonio at Moneagudo 200b in San Isidro. Chinatown has lots of ethnic restaurants. Pizza Alley is off the Avenida Diagonal. Pisco sour, a local drink with a base of grape brandy, is inexpensive and very popular: it can be bought in fancy bottles in the markets. Local beer is good and cheap. Most kinds of soft drinks and mixers are available. Fresh fruit drinks are inexpensive. Peruvian wines are plentiful, but only one or two brands are any good. They are not much cheaper than Chilean or Californian wines.

TRANSPORT

Buses are not used by visitors. Taxis are usually available and fairly cheap, although you should agree a price before getting in.

SECURITY

Be vigilant when shopping, especially in markets. Muggings

and street crime are common.

PHILIPPINES

MANILA

Language **Filipino**
Currency **Philippine peso (P) of 100 centavos.
£1=42.11, Mar 1997. The currency is freely
convertible**
Banks **0900–1600 Mon to Fri**
Traveller's cheques **dollar denominated; bring dollars
in cash**
Credit cards **accepted in some outlets, some charge
5 per cent**
Shops **1000–2100, every day except Christmas Day.
Rustan's department store opens its general shop
at 1100, its foodhall at 0900**
Refunds **difficult; even for defective merchandise**
Sales **before Christmas, but few genuine bargains**
Duty-free **stores in town and at the airport; marginally
cheaper for some items**
Bargaining **possible in the markets and at souvenir
stalls. Prices in the stores are fixed**
Tipping **expected for all services. Most hotels and
restaurants add 10 per cent service charge to the
bill, but waiters still expect a tip; leave any coins
in the change plus 10 or 20 pesos. Taxi drivers
expect 10 per cent**

Many people in Manila prefer to shop in Hong Kong,
Singapore or Bangkok, but with the gradual improvement in
the economy, shopping is getting better. The city is fast moving
into the system of expansive shopping malls. All are
air-conditioned which tends to attract large crowds escap-
ing the heat and humidity outside. You should be able to get
most things you need, but you may have to hunt for them.
What you see is what you get, and get it now for tomorrow it
may be gone.

Foreign brands are relatively expensive and may be in short
supply. The quality and finish of locally made goods is often poor.
Although local stores stock a huge range of ready-made clothing,

the larger European will be frustrated in finding a decent fit. Filipino feet also tend to be short and narrow. Design, style and material of clothing are all Asian orientated, although Marks and Spencer have several boutiques, mainly catering for smaller sizes.

The commercial centre of Manila is known as Makati. The shopping area is now one very large mall named Quad. It has four distinct arms which join at the centre. The two shopping floors offer a vast range of goods and services. Marks and Spencer and Body Shop are represented. The third floor includes a Street Life, based on the American system of eat a little from everywhere and pay on leaving. Landmark, a department store, is next door. Rustan's, another department store, is more up-market, but further away. To the north of Makati is Pasig, which has a similar shopping system to Quad known as Megamall. This includes J.C.Penney as well as Marks and Spencer. The arcade at the Shangrila-Edsa Plaza Hotel includes Pringle and a Clarks shoe shop.

The *barong* is the Filipino embroidered shirt worn open-necked over a T-shirt and hanging outside the trousers; you can choose between the short-sleeved polo *barong* or the more formal, long-sleeved *barong tagalog*. The material is made from a banana-leaf fabric. The finer the material, the more expensive the shirt. All are to be seen in almost any quality clothing shop. Other banana-leaf items worth looking out for are table linens and handkerchiefs. One of the best buys is embroidered table linen, although good quality cloth is not always easy to obtain. Silk is more expensive than in Hong Kong or Thailand.

Local crafts are abundant and include shell crafts, wood carving, coral boxes and delicate filigree silverwork. The main outlets are Tesoro's and Balikbayan Handicrafts, both of which are on Pasay Road in Makati. Carved wood should be treated before you take it home. Pearls are another popular item. Basketware is widely available. Silverwork is also to be had at the St Louis nuns' silverworks for those who are making the 150 mile trip to Baguio: it is good value, and if they do not have what you want, they will make it.

Nayong Filipino is only a few hundred yards from Manila Airport. It consists of a number of islets representing the arch-ipelago of the Philippines. Souvenirs are available at prices often cheaper than similar goods in the shops of Manila.

The Times costs about £1. A wide range of American mag-azines is found at Buffins, which has a branch in every mall. There are local newspapers in English. National Bookstore outlets stock a large supply of paperbacks, mainly from the US. They are no more expensive than in the UK.

Eating and Drinking

Manila is full of restaurants of the most diverse cuisines and prices. A meal at the La Scala would cost about £40 per head with wine, while you enjoy the waiters and waitresses singing extracts from popular classics. La Soufflé, a typical and popular wine bar right in the heart of Makati, would cost perhaps £20 per head without wine. The New Orleans Steak House would cost about £10 per head without wine. Wine is expensive in restaurants, say £25 per bottle.

Local fresh fish such as lapu lapu, tanguine, red snapper, blue marlin, bangus, swordfish and tuna are plentiful and good. Spicy crabs must be tried. There are many local vegetables and fruits which the adventurous will wish to try such as Chinese cabbage or star apple. Dog meat is not recommended, even though it is often served at homecoming celebrations. *Lechon*, or suckling pig, is excellent, as are tropical fruits. Many people take home boxes of mangoes or dried slices of mango or pineapple.

Kalamansi juice and soda is a refreshing drink. Choice and quality of wines and spirits are still fairly limited, although good Australian wines now abound and other countries are beginning to export to the Philippines. Locally made rum and Gilbey's gin, produced under licence, are good and cheap. Local beer of the lager variety is plentiful and good, as are local cigars.

Transport

Buses (some air-conditioned) and converted jeeps (jeepneys) provide a frequent and cheap, if basic, means of transport in Manila. Taxis engaged outside a reputable hotel are usually metered and generally clean. Some drivers may refuse to take you on short journeys or try to charge more than the metered fare.

Security

Sensible precautions are necessary, although there is a considerable security presence around all major malls and stores. There is an ever-present risk of robbery, and the number of tourists involved in druggings or other con tricks is high. Beggars are widespread.

POLAND

WARSAW

Language **Polish**
Currency **zloty. £1=4.93, Mar 1997**
Credit cards **accepted at most major hotels, some restaurants and in some larger shops**
Shops **0700–1800 for food shops, 1100–1900 for others**
Refunds **difficult**
Export restrictions **the authorities are very strict about the export of works of art, especially paintings and books published before 1945**

The main shopping areas in the centre of Warsaw are ul Chmielna and Nowy Swiat (which is good for window shopping and Blikle's café); the Old Town area, especially the Old Town Square, ul Swietojanska and ul Nowomiejska; Marszalkowska and Jerozolimski, which are both good for general shopping. Ul Mokotowska and nearby streets have some interesting boutiques. There are at present no UK retailers represented in Warsaw. Many of the shops and markets popular with visitors are scattered all over town, so transport will be necessary.

There are good general markets such as Polna near Pl Politechniki and Sadyba at the corner of Powsinski and Komorska which sell fresh produce and a wide range of other goods. Specialist markets include the flower market (open until 0900) at the corner of Krakowska and Bakalarska, Kolo for antiques, open on Sunday at Njawlska, Stadium, the Russian market, at Rondon Waszyngtona and the silk flower market and accessories at the corner of Krakowska and Podborska.

Local specialities include amber and silver jewellery, Krosno glass, crystal, Boleslawiec pottery, woodcarvings, sheepskin rugs, slippers and hats, hand embroidered items such as place mats and napkins and a large variety of vodkas. All these are much cheaper than similar items in the UK. Although prices are rising, it is still possible to buy many of them for less than the equivalent of £10 sterling. Sheepskin rugs and hand-embroidered table-covers cost more than £10, but are only about a quarter of the UK price. Last but not least, the best *paczek* (doughnuts) ever, especially those from Blikle's. Polish doughnuts are very light and in the Blikle example are covered in a thin glacé icing, sprinkled with chopped orange peel and filled with rose-petal jam.

There are many places to go for local arts and crafts. Arex at ul Chopina 5B is a treasure house of painted wood carvings such as storage chests or dolls in national costume. Ceramica Artystycana at ul Modzelewskiego 79 is a small shop crammed with goods. The Jewellery Shop at the Marriott has a breathtaking selection of amber and silver jewellery. MP Gallery at Old Town Square 9/11 stocks artistic handmade silver, gold, amber, crystal and glass. Kwiaty-Upominski is less expensive than the Marriott or MP. Jedwabie at ul Jerozolimskie 42 sells hand-painted silk items. Away from the centre of town there are other outlets. Dual at ul Kruczkowskiego 8a is worth a visit for its extensive range. Silver Point is at ul Maja 10 and sells, obviously, silver, but also amber. Szuflada at ul Kaweczynska 4 sells amazing pottery designs at reasonable prices. JAP at ul Mazowiecka 7 has leather, furs and porcelain.

Most things are now readily available and new shops open up daily. Poland is a good place to stock up on glassware: there is beautiful glass and crystal to suit most tastes from cut glass from Silesia to very simple modern lead crystal from Krosno. Stocks in the the shops can be limited and unpredictable. Cepelia at Plac Konstytutji 2 and 5 has a wide selection of glass and other goods. Lucja at ul Nowomiejska 1/3 will engrave Krosno glass and crystal if you wish. The Polna Market caters for foreigners with prices close to Western ones.

Ice skates are particularly cheap in Poland. The Ski Market on Czerniowiecka Street is a good source of ski clothing for both adults and children. It is open during the winter on Sunday mornings. Fur hats with ear-flaps can be bought locally. Warm wool coats can be made to measure at reasonable prices. Boots and gloves can also be acquired locally. CDs are fairly cheap, but quality and durability is not always up to Western standards.

British newspapers, magazines and paperbacks are available in the larger hotels, but they can be quite expensive. There are some books and publications in English, mostly guides to Poland or some beautiful Russian art books which are inexpensive. Specialist bookshops selling English-language books and newspapers include Co-Liber at pl Bankowy 4, Bookland at al Jerozolimskie 61, the American Bookstore at ul Krakowskie Przedmiescie 45 and Empik at ul Marszalkowska 116/122. Prices are comparable with those in the UK, and cheaper in some cases.

EATING AND DRINKING
Traditional Polish cuisine is heavy and plentiful, although some establishments aim for tourists' preferences. The Old Town is a good place to start. Bazyliszek is at Old Town Square 3/9. Fukier is at 27, Gessler at 21 and U Barssa at 14. Near by are Kmicic at ul Piwna 27 and Honoratka at ul Miodowa 14. Wilanow is at ul Wiertnicza 27. Poland is famous for its smoked meats, hams, sausages, etc. which are delicious and widely available. Good quality caviar is available but is now extremely expensive.

TRANSPORT
Bus and tram services are good and cheap and there are many taxis.

SECURITY
There are rising levels of street crime.

FRENCH POLYNESIA: TAHITI

PAPEETE

Tahiti is very much Club Med territory and far from paradise. Apart from the tourism, pearls are the main foreign exchange earner, but they are not cheap. The traditional *pareu* is worn by both men and women. Handmade quilts are wonderful, but rightly expensive. Local carvings and mother of pearl work are worth a look.

In the food line, the traditional Tahitan buffet must be tried.

PORTUGAL

LISBON

Language **Portuguese**
Currency **escudo (Esc) of 100 centavos.**
  £1=273, Mar 1997
Banks **0830–1200, 1300–1430 Mon to Fri**
Shops **1000–1300, 1500–1900 Mon to Fri, 1000–1300**
  Sat
Tipping **service and taxes are included in all hotel**
  and restaurant bills, but in restaurants a small tip
  is usual. A cinema usherette also expects a tip

Lisbon is built on seven hills and can be tiring to walk around. Parking and walking in the narrow streets can be difficult. Pavements and roads in Lisbon are cobbled and hard to walk on unless wearing comfortable shoes.

The centre of the town – the Baixa – contains the main shopping area and restaurants. There is the Feira da Ladra on Tuesdays and Saturdays, mainly a flea market and clothes. There are large and colourful food and household markets a short ride out of Lisbon at Carcavelos on Thursday and Cascais on Wednesday.

In Lisbon there is a branch of Mothercare and three small Marks and Spencer outlets with prices higher than in the UK. Body Shop charges UK prices.

The overall cost of living now compares with that in much of the rest of Europe, but there are still some items cheaper than in the UK – public transport and taxis, wines, modest meals out, seasonal fruit and vegetables.

Portugal is renowned for its leatherwork and a wide range of shoes is available for all the family. Prices are favourable although quality can vary. Shoes tend to be narrow and larger sizes may be difficult to find. Women will find plenty of sandals and good summer shoes.

There is a wide range of clothing in the shops at prices higher than in the UK, quality for quality. Premium prices are charged for imported luxury clothing. Short and petite women will enjoy shopping for clothing in Portugal, where women are very fashion-conscious.

Certain items can disappear from the shops, particularly during August and September, when factories are likely to close.

Best buys include tiles with Moorish influence and fado recordings of Amalia Rodriguez. Also worthwhile might be jewellery in gold or silver and items such as leather, textiles, pottery and basketware.

British newspapers are widely available. All books in English are considerably more expensive than in the UK.

EATING AND DRINKING
Both food and wine are cheap and good. Portugal is full of restaurants from the simple to the five-star. The Portuguese eat out a lot, and it is still possible to enjoy a pleasant meal in a restaurant mid-week and not break the bank. Most restaurants cater for families. The food is mainly traditional Portuguese. Seafood and fish are particularly good.

Portuguese wine is excellent. Port is a must, including the white. Beer is also good. Soft and fruit drinks tend to be sweeter than British taste.

TRANSPORT
There is a good, but limited, underground system in Central Lisbon. Trams and buses provide a good and cheap means of transport, although they are very crowded during the rush hours. Taxis are fairly cheap, widely available and much used.

SECURITY
Beware of pickpockets and petty street crime.

PUERTO RICO

SAN JUAN

Apart from the modern malls, there is still plenty of traditional shopping in the old walled city. Crafts available include all the usual favourites such as basketware, ceramics, lace and woodcarvings.

Food, such as stews and citrus fruits, is good. Local coffee, rum and cigars are all recommended.

QATAR

DOHA

Language **Arabic**
Currency **Qutar riyal (QR) of 100 dirhams. Linked to
the US dollar. £1= 5.93, Mar 1997.
No foreign exchange restrictions**

Three modern air-conditioned supermarket-cum-department
stores called the Centre, Salam Plaza and Salam Studio have
revolutionised shopping in Doha. Many items are no more
expensive than in the UK and some are even cheaper. Branches
of British Home Stores, Saxone Shoes, Olympus Sports and
the Body Shop exist within the Centre Department Store. The
air-conditioning in shops and restaurants can be icy. Many
younger Qataris are fluent in English.

Most goods are available, but fashionable clothes are very
expensive. Some bargains can be obtained during the sales
which are held twice a year.

There are numerous small boutiques for women, but prices
are high and the range is limited both in sizes and in styles.
Sandals for the beach are readily available in the souk. Sports
shops offer a wide range of clothing cheaper than in the UK.

A good supply of well-known brands of shirts, underwear,
ties and men's shoes is available as well as sandals. Prices are
generally higher than in the UK and larger sizes are sometimes
difficult to find. A good supply of lightweight suiting is available and local tailors can make suits of reasonable quality at
prices comparing favourably with those in the UK.

A good selection of British newspapers and magazines is
available, but they are censored and tend to be very expensive.
They are normally available a day or two after publication.
Magazines do appear, but are also censored. There is a reasonable
selection of English books is available, mostly paperbacks in light
reading vein, but they are a lot more expensive than in the UK.

EATING AND DRINKING
A wide variety of good quality cuisine is offered in hotels and
restaurants. The cost of meals out, particularly in the
better-class hotels, compares well with UK prices. No alcohol
is allowed in public places.

TRANSPORT

There is no public transport service. Taxis are numerous and cheap. All taxis have meters. Women should not use taxis after sunset. Some of the pavements are uneven and heels quickly become scuffed and damaged.

SECURITY

Public security is exemplary.

REUNION

ST-DENIS

The French influence is obvious, not just in the cuisine and in the use of francs. Shopping is expensive, with most shops on and around the Rue du Maréchal Leclerc at the western end and down towards the harbour. There are T-shirts and rum, and model ships are the most famous local craft. Little English reading matter is available.

ROMANIA

BUCHAREST

Language **Romanian**
Currency **leu (plural lei). £1=10733, Mar 1997**
Banks **0900–1200, 1300–1500 Mon to Fri,
    0900–1200 Sat**
Traveller's cheques **can be hard to cash**
Credit cards **accepted in hotels and up-market
    shops. Visa is the most widely accepted**
Cashpoints **yes, but daily limit of withdrawal is the
    equivalent of £10**
Tipping **under 10 per cent in restaurants; taxi
    drivers expect to be tipped**

It is very difficult to keep up to date with shopping in Romania because availability of produce and other things changes almost daily. There are many shops opening up with a wide range of merchandise and queues are diminishing. Frustrations are common, but there are also pleasant surprises.

For the short-stay visitor the only area really worth knowing is that between Piata Victoria and Piata Unirii. This includes Boulevard Magheru which becomes Nicolae Balcescu and then Bratianu before Piata Unirii. Calea Victoriei, still popular for an evening stroll and bit of window shopping, runs almost parallel to the main boulevard. Between these two streets are a number of smaller side-streets well worth a wander around. Lipscani, both a street and an area between Boulevard Mihael Kogalniceanu and Splaiul Independentei contains some of the most interesting shops, including art and craft outlets, for the patient shopper.

Shopping on Magheru starts around Piata Romana. Go down the side-street behind Magheru and you will come to Amzei, the largest of Bucharest's many open-air markets. This is mainly a fruit and vegetable market, with a profusion of fruit in summer. The covered area has an abundance of flowers which are inexpensive, but can be bargained for. A few stalls sell roughly-hewn wooden items and sometimes basketware. You will also find a good Turkish bakery, which is well patronised.

Back on the main street is where the up-market boutiques are situated. Clothes can be quite expensive and not necessarily well made, but some well-known international labels can be found there. Eva, an old-style department store, is worth a look for hand-sewn tablecloths and, occasionally, for fur hats – a popular souvenir and essential for Romanian winters. Just before the Hotel Lido turn right down Strada Franklin. Here at number 3 is Levintz and Dacoma which makes handmade shoes and bags and some evening wear.

On the opposite side of the boulevard are three bookshops. Libraria Mihail Sadoveanu is an old-style bookshop well worth a browse. Noi has a good antiquarian and arts section as well as novels in French and English, although it is a little expensive. Further on is a second-hand and antiquarian bookshop, Universitati Populara Bucuresti Sala Dalles. Books can be quite a good buy and there are some nice coffee-table books on Romania and Bucharest.

At Piata Universitatea wander down into the metro for a flash of Western influence, fast-food outlets and several small shops including a newsagent selling British magazines – foreign newspapers are rarer. Cross the road and walk a little up the street and you come to a good glass and art shop.

After Piata Universitatea the Boulevard changes face and the shops tend to sell more electrical and household items. At Piata Unirii is the gigantic department store Unirea. The core is a state shop and well worth a wander around. It is open on Sunday from 1000 to 1400. The outer units are privately owned, a real hotch-potch, including McDonald's.

A promenade down Boulevard Unirii towards the People's Palace can be impressive and rewarding. Along this tree-lined avenue are a number of artisanal shops selling tablecloths, other woven items, handmade rugs (get an export certificate), crystal (nice, but not up to the standard of Poland or the Czech Republic), other glassware, linen and some smaller craft items.

Once at Piata Unirii you might try a wander round the Lipscani area, although it is a little shabby and sensible personal security awareness is recommended. Try entering Lipscani from the bottom of Strada Selari, just off Splaiul Independentei. This street has several good glassware shops next to the courtyard where you watch glassblowers at work (Curtea Stictarilor, Strada Selari 9–11). There are also a number of shoe shops and furriers worth a look. Among the latter are Confecti Corona on Strada Covac, Blanaria Gaby on Strada Iulia Maniu and Blanarie on Strada Selari. On Strada Lipscani itself are a few shops of interest including the Agrimex arcade housed in a lovely old building near the top of the street by Calea Victoriei. This sells various items including leather and glass. Further down past the National Bank there is an old courtyard-cum-stables in which you will find a couple of antique shops (again, ensure you get export certificates for any such item) and craft and ceramic shops.

Calea Victoriei has long been a favourite for a promenade and has a variety of clothing, craft, antiques, glass and other shops. Starting from the Splaiul Independenti end there are several boutiques with various price ranges. Departmentul Copilor is good for children's clothing, especially good-value winter ski suits. The two artisanal shops near the start are good for little wooden boxes, some shaped like ducks, ideal as children's gifts. Further up behind the Continental Hotel is a Romarta shop selling tablecloths. There are several other Romarta shops and a number of glass and china shops. Collectors of little crystal animals should be able to find a few to add to their collection. The large Muzica shop has wooden crafts upstairs and also stocks some local instruments in wood and clay.

On a rainy day try the World Trade Centre shopping mall, still a new shopping experience for Bucharest. There are a number of boutiques, a good artisanal, a newsagent with foreign magazines, an excellent glass and gallery unit and several cafés.

There are two good bookshops on Magheru on the same

side as the Intercontinental Hotel.

EATING AND DRINKING

One can eat out to a reasonably high standard and at sensible prices, although these are rising rapidly. An acceptable three-course meal with wine at a decent restaurant will vary between US$15 and 25 a head, but could go as high as $40 – 50 a person.

For local cuisine try any of the following: Athenee Palace at Episcoepiei 1 is a small and cosy bistro serving good-value Romanian dishes, very popular; Boema behind the Lido Hotel off C.A.Rosetti has a nice screened terrace in summer; Casa Capsa at Calea Victoriei opposite Cercul Militar is one of Bucharest's oldest establishments, just renovated; Hanul Manuc at Strada Iulia Maniu 62 is an old merchants' inn; La Premiera is at Strada Tudor Arghezi 16, behind the National Theatre. For a beer and bowl of soup try Caru cu Bere at Str Stavropoles 3; the beerhall interior is worth viewing and there is usually live music in the evenings.

Along Calea Victoriei especially there are a number of pavement cafés in summer. Perhaps the swankiest is the newish Scala on Boulevard Magheru. Another favourite is the Casablanca further up and opposite the Effes pub and McDonald's.

There are some excellent red and passable white wines. Local people drink an amazing quantity of mineral water, which is very cheap. Always ask for Romanian beer, otherwise you will be given an expensive and average import.

Local honey is excellent and relatively cheap. Romania has specialist honey shops and there is an excellent one on Strada Xenopol near the Anglican church. Honey is also available in the local markets. Salamis, especially those from Sibiu, are excellent.

TRANSPORT

Provided you are staying in a central hotel and enjoy walking a little, you will not need to use transport, but pavements are in a poor state and get very icy in winter. There are buses, trams and a metro system which are cheap, but all become very crowded. Taxis can be called by telephone or hailed in the street. It is preferable to use the 941 state taxis. Most are fitted with meters and the fare is recorded. Some are not and drivers will try to get as much as possible.

SECURITY

Incidents of harassment and bag snatching are on the increase.

The area around the Intercontinental Hotel is particularly affected, but the visitor will probably feel no more threatened than in any other capital city.

RUSSIA

Language **Russian**
Currency **rouble (R) of 100 kopeks. £1=9136, Mar 1997**
Banks **US dollars are freely convertible; unmarked, post-1988 notes of $50 or below can be exchanged at banks or official kiosks. Black market exchange is illegal**
Traveller's cheques **not outside Moscow**
Credit cards **accepted by leading shops, restaurants and hotels in Moscow and St Petersburg, with passport as identification. Essential in joint venture and hard currency shops**
Cashpoints **a few, in Moscow and St Petersburg**
Shops **0900–2000**
Bargaining **in markets; shops have fixed prices**
Tipping **10–15 per cent in restaurants for good service, and for taxi drivers**
Export restrictions **items considered of cultural value such as paintings, books, carpets and antiques generally made before 1945 and religious artefacts must be declared to the State Customs Committee prior to export. If export is permitted, 100 per cent of the value, as determined by the Committee, must be paid at the border. Insist upon a receipt should any customs official confiscate any item. Electric samovars are permitted for export, as is 500g of caviar**

Warm winter coats are available from several outlets, but the price in some may come as a shock. Fur hats can be easily purchased locally, but are no longer the good buy they once were. Moon boots are very popular and available from all good sports shops.

Popular buys include Soviet memorabilia, matrioshka dolls or icons and samovars. There are hand-painted boxes and tin trays, china and porcelain and CDs. Other ideas include scarves and amber, items in lacquered wood, silver-gilt or enamelware. If the range of choice is too great you can always fall back upon vodka or caviar. All gift and souvenir items are widely available in tourist areas from shops, hotel shops or from street sellers.

The classic Russian restaurant is often an expensive establishment, sometimes with live entertainment. The word café is loosely used and can mean anything from an elegant restaurant to a coffee shop. They are generally smaller and less formal than restaurants. It is advisable to make reservations, especially for the larger and more popular restaurants. Payment is in roubles, although prices may be in US dollars. Check when booking if credit cards are accepted.

Although you can shop for drinks reasonably cheaply if you look around, spirits other than vodka can be expensive and the selection of wines is limited. Both local wines and beer are just about acceptable. Tea is a popular drink.

Russians working in shops, etc. do not normally speak English. Take a pencil and paper to write down prices and take your own shopping bag.

Footwear should be lined or insulated, with good ribbed soles for winter and waterproof for the thaw.

Muggers and pickpockets operate in all cities, particularly Moscow and St Petersburg. Criminal gangs also operate. Do not be ostentatious.

MOSCOW

The main shopping areas include Tverskaya, Old and New Arbat as well as Leninsky Prospect. GUM (the state department store) at Krasnaya Plosh 3 is world famous. It consists basically of a variety of different shops under one roof, including many designer names and several eating places. The nearest metro stations are Ploshad Revolutsii or Kitai Gorod. TsUM (central department store) at Ul Petrovka 2 is near Ploshad Revolutsii, Teatralnaya or Kuznetsky Most metro stations.

Petrovsky Passage, at Ul Petrovka 10 consists almost entirely of Western stores. The Valdai Centre and Europa Centre are both in Novy Arbat with a wide range of shops and boutiques including Adidas. Stockmann, the Finnish-based department store, has branches in Moscow. Stockmann's boutique is at Leninsky Prospekt 73/8 and sells designer fashion. Stockmann Fashion at Ulitsa Dolgorukovskaya 2 sells more affordable clothing. The Radisson Slanyanska Hotel has several boutiques. Well-known brand names represented around town include British Home Stores, Benetton, Galleries Lafayette,

Levi, Adidas and Reebok.

The Izmaylovo Market near Izmailovsky Park (Izmailovsky Park metro) is Moscow's largest flea-market, a must for tourists and only open at weekends. Craft stores sell matrioshka dolls, lacquer boxes, jewellery, fur hats, carpets, shawls, paintings and wooden toys. Definitely a place to bargain. There is also an arts and crafts market at Bittsa Forest (Yasenevo metro) where horse riding is also available. Sparrow Hills by the ski jump (Universitet metro) also has local arts and crafts and fur hats for sale. Try also the Art Gallery Market opposite Gorky Park (Kultury and Oktyabrskaya metros). Again be prepared to haggle. Gorbunov Collector's Fair (Metro Bagrationskaya) is open at the weekends between 0900 and 1500 and is a must for all music lovers.

All major hotels sell foreign newspapers and a few books. *Moscow Times* and *Moscow Tribune* are published Tuesday to Saturday and are free in some shops and hotels. An English bookshop, Zwemmers, is located at Kuznetsky Most and carries a good selection of mainly paperback books at prices about the same as in the UK. The English Language Bookshop is on Kaluzhskaya Ploshad. Shakespeare and Company at 1st Novokuznetsky Pereulok 5/7 sells new and second-hand books.

EATING AND DRINKING

Among Russian and Georgian restaurants, there is U Babushki at 42 Ul Ordynka Bolshaya which is quite expensive, but offers food "like Babushka used to make it". U Pirosmani at Novodevichy Proezd 4 is cheaper and popular with British Embassy staff, not least for its view of Novodevichy convent. Taganka Blues offers a range of live entertainment and is located at 15 Ulitsa Verkhnyaya Radishchevskaya, popular for parties and you can take your own drink. Specialities at Cyaapb in Zubovskiy Proesd include salmon with whisky and mushrooms with vodka. At Yar on Leningradskiy Prospekt they serve roast pig Gurman and veal Orlov.

TRANSPORT

Public transport is widely available. There are standard fares on buses, trolley-buses, trams and metros covering a single journey of any distance, but no transfers are allowed. Tickets can be bought in blocks of 10 from stations, kiosks and newspaper stalls; validate your ticket on entry. For the metro you will need a token purchased at the office at the station. This covers all transfers and unlimited distances. Taxi fares are whatever you can negotiate, either in roubles or dollars. Try to use a reputable company, such as Mosrentservice. Even the new yellow taxis do not seem to have meters which work. Wait your turn at one of the numerous taxi stands, but if taxis are free you can hail them on the street. Drivers assume that they are to keep the change.

ST PETERSBURG

There is now a complete spectrum of goods available, ranging from the cheap and cheerful to designer labels with prices beyond those even in London or Paris.

Local markets have the cheapest winter coats and shoes, as well as fur hats. Nevskiy Prospekt is the centre of the city and has most of the foreign shops such as Levi, Nike, Reebok and Adidas. There are three so-called shopping centres or department stores – Gostiny Dvor, Passage and DLT. Another famous landmark on Nevskiy Prospekt is the Eliseev food store. Littlewoods have their flagship store in Gostiny Dvor and another three around the city.

There are plenty of souvenir shops, stands and kiosks around the city centre and at each of the tourist attractions. Most local people agree that the souvenir market at the Church of the Blood is the best place. There you can get military memorabilia, crystal, St Petersburg porcelain and matrioshka dolls. Amber is also widely available. Ananov jewellery is available at the Grand Hotel Europe: it has been likened to Fabergé and has the price tag to prove it.

The main market in the city centre has a range of produce and fresh flowers in summer, silk flowers or other artificial arrangements in winter. Among supermarkets Stockmann's or the Super Babylon are popular.

The *St Petersburg Times* is the local English-language newspaper.

EATING AND DRINKING

Kiosks around the city sell everything from CDs to disposable lighters and are definitely cheapest for cigarettes. It is not advisable to buy bottled spirits from kiosks because it is highly probable that the contents are not the real thing: the best way to know with vodka is to put it in the freezer – real vodka does not freeze. Spirits and wine are expensive everywhere in the city. Georgian red wine is drinkable and will only cost about $5 a bottle: imported wine starts at double the price.

There are a number of good bars and restaurants. Local

cuisine tends to be meat-based, but there are menus to suit almost every taste and budget. Popular Western choices are Sadkos at the Grand Hotel, Milano, Tandoor, the French Bistro and the Tribunal Bar. On Nevskiy Prospekt Druzhba at number 15 offers Russian-style food. The Literature Café at number 18 is a favourite calling place for visitors.

TRANSPORT

The local public transport network is suffering at the moment. Some metro stations now have restricted opening hours and the tram system is being phased out. Trolley-buses and trams still run, but are packed at rush hours. There are two types of taxi: the Mercedes and Volvos that operate from outside hotels, and Russian cars which are a quarter of the price. You can hail a Russian taxi on the street, but do not be surprised when ordinary cars stop to offer a lift. They will charge even less, but it is not recommended to use them, expecially if you are on your own.

RWANDA

KIGALI

Language **Kinyarwanda, French**
Currency **Rwanda franc (Rf). £1=495**

Security is fragile, and the Foreign Office advises against all but essential travel. Most tourists have usually visited to see the gorillas, rather than Kigali. The countryside can be beautiful. Generally, what little is available to buy is expensive.

Saint Lucia

Castries

Language **English**
Currency **Eastern Caribbean dollar (EC$). £1=4.2, Mar 1997**
Traveller's cheques **dollar denominated**
Credit cards **major cards accepted in hotels, restaurants and big tourist shops**
Cashpoints **very few**
Shops **0830–late**
Refunds **possible if receipt kept**
Sales **Jun, Jul; genuine reductions**
Duty-free **at Pointe Seraphine, for souvenirs, perfumes and spirits; take airline or cruise ship ticket**
Tipping **10 per cent service charge added to bills in restaurants, 1–2 EC$ for ad hoc services**

As with most Caribbean islands, the cost of living is high. Most goods are imported from the UK or USA and are therefore approximately double the UK price. Almost everything is available some of the time.

Little serious shopping is done in the centre of Castries. Bridge Street has a small department store and a few fabric shops, etc. The main out-of-town shopping is at Gablewoods Mall on John Compton Highway at Sunny Acres. The markets are also near the harbour with a colourful range of produce, souvenirs such as spice baskets and clay pots and cheap clothing such as T-shirts.

Many of the souvenirs available come from other parts of the Caribbean. Steel-wire sculptures and pottery from Barbados are good. Tin and wooden painted artefacts are usually from South America or Haiti. Clay candle-holders are to be seen at Gablewoods Mall and Pointe Seraphine. There are local paintings at the Artsibit Gallery and Pointe Seraphine. Jill Walker coasters, mats and pictures of local scenes are available at Pointe Seraphine.

There are a number of good casual-wear clothing stores in Castries, but ranges and sizes are limited. Sarongs and tops of cotton, and silk Caribbean batik as well as imported sea-island cottons are in the Sea Island Cotton shop at Gablewoods Mall. Bagshaws at La Toc or in Reduit Beach Road is good not only for screen-printed clothing, but also for quality household linens and souvenirs. Good shoes and sandals in leather are sometimes obtainable, but are expensive.

British Sunday papers are on sale on Sunday evening or Monday morning, at a high price. There are several local newspapers, of which the principal one is the thrice weekly *Voice of St Lucia* which concerns itself chiefly with local events. Some American journals are on sale. A supply of paperbacks is available in St Lucia at prices approximately double those of the UK. The range of hardback books is limited. The best place to go is the Sunshine Bookshop.

EATING AND DRINKING

Food is seldom consistently good or bad in any particular hotel. Apart from the hotels there are several excellent restaurants providing local and international cuisine. Creole food is a local speciality to be tried. La Creole is on John Compton Highway just past the Marina. Jimmy's at Vigre Cove makes good seasonal use of local vegetables and offers a variety of ways to serve bananas. Tamarind balls and mangoes in season are recommended, as are the profusion of rum cocktails and green coconut water.

TRANSPORT

Only a few hotels are within walking distance of the centre. Most public transport consists of Combi vans driven by aspiring racing drivers and is not therefore recommended. Attempts are being made to regulate fares and to control standards and routes: route numbers are being introduced. Taxis are expensive.

SECURITY

There may be some hassle in the form of aggressive salesmanship, such as the Rastafarians on Reduit Beach, but relatively little from beggars.

ST MARTIN/SINT MARTEN

Language **French, Dutch**
Currency **French franc, Dutch guilder; US dollars accepted. Credit cards accepted**
Shops **0900–1800, with break for lunch**
Tipping **service usually included in bills**

The island is jointly owned by the French and the Dutch, hence the variation in style of name. It is rapidly becoming commercialised, particularly on the Dutch side, perhaps spoiling itself in the process. Cruise-ship passengers crowd the main street of Philipsburg looking for shopping bargains. The usual tourist trinkets and major international labels in a vast range of goods are all available, but to know if you are really getting a bargain you will need to know what the price would be in the UK. Jewellery and leather items are not at all bad. The French side in Marigot, by contrast, is less frenetic, relatively backward, and preferred by many.

Restaurants are expensive and better generally on the French side.

ST VINCENT AND THE GRENADINES

KINGSTOWN

Language **English**
Currency **Eastern Caribbean dollar (EC$). £1=4.2, Mar 1997**
Banks **0800–1200 Mon to Thur, 0800–1200, 1400–1700 Fri**
Tipping **appreciated, even where 10 per cent service charge added**

The cost of living is high and the range of food restricted. Visitors looking for gifts or souvenirs can do no better than start with St Vincent Craftsmen which has branches both at the airport and near the docks. Stecher's, a sort of Caribbean souvenir chain store specialising in luxury items, is also represented. Next door to each other on Main Street are Batik Caribe and Noah's Arcade, both well worth a look.

The fish market is on the harbour and the main market near by in Bay Street. This can be fun for a bit of local colour, particularly on Saturday.

EATING AND DRINKING

Eating out is expensive and an à la carte dinner for two might cost EC$200. A buffet lunch might cost EC$30 a head and a snack lunch perhaps EC$15. Hotels are fairly reliable for a taste of local cuisine, but the more adventurous will wish to try places like the Cobblestone. Drinks including wines and spirits are relatively cheap.

TRANSPORT

There are many Japanese-made minibuses so travel around Kingstown is cheap and buses are extremely frequent. Taxis are available; a journey of two or three miles would cost EC$ 20.

SAUDI ARABIA

Language **Arabic**
Currency **Saudi riyal (SR) of 20 qursh or 100 halala; tied to US$ at US$1=3.75. £1=6.00, Mar 1997**
Banks **0830–1200,1700–1900 Sat to Wed, 0830–1130 Thur; in Ramadan 0930–1400 Sat to Thur**
Credit cards **accepted, but cash preferred**
Cashpoints **yes**
Shops **0900–1200, mid-afternoon to late evening, 1800 and 2000; supermarkets open 24 hours. Closed Fri morning**
Refunds **exchanges possible**
Sales **yes; good bargains, especially at New Year**
Bargaining **yes, especially in souk**
Tipping **15 per cent service charge in hotels and some restaurants; 10 per cent where no service charge. 1–2 SR to taxi drivers**
Import/export restrictions **alcohol and pork are prohibited**

All products are freely available, except pork and alcohol. Opening hours are dictated by prayer times, which change by several minutes each week and are advertised in the local media.

Many items are imported and are expensive. Casual cotton tops, shirts, caftans, etc. are available in the souks and in some supermarkets. Larger sizes may be hard to find. Most men's shops sell either expensive designer clothing or extremely cheap clothing.

Good buys are gold and silver jewellery, both of which are sold by weight, Bedouin jewellery, pearls, carpets and rugs from all over Asia, antiques, Arabic coffee pots, hubble-bubble pipes, personalised perfumes, camel stools, ceremonial daggers, wall hangings and woven designs. Electrical goods, watches and cameras are sometimes cheaper than in the UK, but it can be difficult getting guarantees and the models are not always the most up-to-date.

British newspapers are available one or two days late, but they are expensive and subject to censorship. Local newspapers in English are the *Arab News* and *Saudi Gazette*.

Local food specialities include *sharwarmas* (shaved meat in pitta bread), various types of Arab breads, roasted chicken, fruit juices by the pint and cakes.

Visitors will find the level of personal security high and experience little hassle.

RIYADH

Shopping facilities are generally very good. There are several shopping malls as well as souks, but shopping may take time since there is no one single shopping area. The Body Shop and Mothercare charge about 50 per cent more than in the UK. Saudi House is a department store which sells some British Home Stores items at about 15 per cent more than in the UK.

EATING AND DRINKING
Riyadh boasts a good selection of restaurants including top-class continental restaurants, coffee shops and grills. Almost all these have separate sections for single men, families or any parties including women. Alcohol is prohibited on restaurant premises.

TRANSPORT
There is a public bus service in Riyadh, but it is not normally used by expatriates. Taxis are difficult to find off the main city thoroughfares. It is against the law for a woman to take a taxi alone or with a man to whom she is not related. It is recommended that passengers know where they are going. The most acceptable taxis are white with an orange stripe along the side and are known as limousines.

AL KHOBAR

There are very good shopping facilities in and around town, including shopping malls and supermarkets. Outlets include British Home Stores, French Connection, Next, Royal Doulton and Tiffany. The selection of wares such as electrical and luxury goods is wide ranging and good.

There is a good choice of restaurants, including many fast-food chains.

JEDDAH

Jeddah is a strict Islamic city due to its proximity to Mecca. Modest clothing is essential and women may feel more comfortable if they wear long, loose-fitting cotton dresses, skirts or caftans, which can be bought cheaply locally.

In the Balad (central) area are situated the gold souk, the Alawi Souk (various wares including electronics, toiletries, carpets and cloth) and the Bab Makkah Souk (spices and silks). Also in this area is the Mahmal Centre (camel souk) which is ultra-modern and features Body Shop, In Wear, T.J.Mexx and the Racquet Shop.

In the Medina Road area the International Market houses a supermarket as well as Mothercare, Body Shop and electronics shops. Al-Sholla, Jamjoom, Al Hefni, Mosadieh, Basateen and Hera are all smart, modern shopping centres with a huge variety of merchandise. They all tend to be more expensive than the souks. Fitaihi is famous as the "Harrods of Jeddah" and is wonderful for out-of-this-world delights at enormous prices.

EATING AND DRINKING
Restaurants are numerous with a range of tastes and standards of both service and quality including the very highest. The Green Island on the Corniche, the Moroccan Restaurant in Balad, Ciao in the Intercontinental, the Gulf Royal and Chinese restaurants in various locations are recommended.

TRANSPORT
Because of distances and the heat, transport is essential. Taxis and limousines are used by visitors. Women should not travel alone. Taxis are numerous, usually white Toyotas with an orange racing stripe. Agree the price before starting.

SENEGAL

DAKAR

Language **French**
Currency **Senegalese franc (CFA), tied to the French
    franc. £1=945, Mar 1997**
Tipping **10 per cent where no service charge;
    waiters expect a small tip added to service charge**

The cost of living is high, but most goods are available. Off-the-peg clothing, if French, is very expensive. There is no shortage of choice, but some items may be poor value for money in comparison with the range in Europe. Locally made leather sandals are cheap. Local caftans, or bou-bous, and tie-dye skirts are popular and not very expensive.

Galerie Antenna in Rue Felix Faure specialises in all kinds of African art, including jewellery, woodcarving, bronze, watercolours, silverwork, etc. Prices are very high, but even here bargaining is possible. The Kermel Market, which has just been beautifully restored after a fire, and the Village Artisanal in Soumbedioune have a complete range of African crafts. Touristy perhaps, but the choice is there and bargaining becomes easier the longer you spend in Dakar. High quality leatherware is available and books can be bound in leather at a reasonable price. There are "antique" sellers all along the Rue Mohamed V, their wares spilling all over the pavement. Bargaining is necessary. Robel in Rue des Essarts near Kermel sells glass, china, silver and pewterware. Galeries Orientales below the Hotel Independence and at 137 Lamine Gueye sells all manner of oriental items from rice bowls to trinkets. Art en Vie at number 178 is also worth a look. Air de Fête in the Place de l'Independence sells a range of ornamental and utilitarian, decorative pieces. There are many gold and silversmiths in town with attractive work at reasonable prices. La Parure D'Or on Lamine Gueye is a trustworthy goldsmith.

Sandaga is a very African market, alive with people, noise and colour. There are many side-streets and alleyways and many stalls of casual shoes and sandals. Tilene is similar, but smaller. Kermel is a market that caters perhaps more for the European. The interior has stalls with all manner of arts and crafts aimed to catch the eye of the tourist. Outside there is produce and fresh flowers. At all the markets bargaining is necessary. It is as well to have an idea of price and availability elsewhere to give yourself a bargaining base. Always have small change readily available, the vendors will not.

There are several boutiques where prices are generally high, but browsing may be worthwhile. In the Lamine Gueye between the cathedral and Ponty there are a number of boutiques such as Tiss Mag and Hana Salman. In the arcade opposite Laetitia's patisserie is Borsine Prêt à Porter. My Fair Lady is on Rue Jules Ferry opposite the Al Afifa Hotel. Line Senghor is in the Rue Pasteur and in the Teranga Hotel.

In the sidestreets between Ponty and the Boulevard de la République there are numerous tailors' shops. The area of Sandaga where Ponty meets Lamine Gueye is full of material shops, including Nosoca Textiles at the top end of Ponty.

There are several good patisseries in the French style such as La Palmerie at 29 Avenue Georges Pompidou, Laetitia at 180 Avenue Lamine Gueye and Gentina at Avenue Albert Sarraut.

There is a limited number of magazines and newspapers in English available at some hotels, bookshops and stands. The Librairie Universitaire at 26 Avenue Georges Pompidou has a varied selection of paperbacks in English.

EATING AND DRINKING

There are many restaurants and standards are high. The restaurant at the Croix du Sud Hotel in Avenue Albert Sarraut is good and offers an extensive choice. When in season it serves excellent shellfish platters.

Otherwise try Hostellerie du Chevalier de Boufflers on Goreé Island, L'Armatan on Pointe des Almadies, Le Dagorne on Rue Dagorne, Le Dionevar at Pointe des Almadies for good seafood, Almadies at La Récif, Le Bambou at 19 Rue Victor Hugo, or La Fourchette at Kermel. For a luxury meal, the Terrou Bi on the Corniche is well worth a visit.

Locally caught fish and shellfish are excellent. Kermel Market has stalls selling many kinds of shellfish and fish comes fresh off the boats at Soumbedioune at 1800 every evening.

Virtually every type of alcoholic drink and fruit juice is readily available. French wines are plentiful, but quite expensive. Cheaper North African and Spanish wines are also available. A full range of soft drinks and mixers is available.

TRANSPORT

There are private *cars rapides* which are invariably in a dangerous state of repair. Taxis are plentiful and cheap. The quality of both vehicles and drivers varies. Taxis cruise the streets in town and prices have to be negotiated for all journeys before getting into the vehicle.

SECURITY
Security is generally good, but sensible care needs to be taken and jewellery should not be worn in the street.

SEYCHELLES

VICTORIA

Language **Creole, English, French**
Currency **Seychelles rupee (R) of 100 cents.**
  £1=8.02, Mar 1997
Banks **0830–1230/1300, some also 1430–1630 Mon**
  to Fri, 0830/0900–1130 Sat
Credit cards **accepted by some, but not all**
  restaurants
Shops **0800–1200, 1330–1700; closed Sat afternoon**
Tipping **hotel and restaurant staff, even where**
  service charge added, and taxi drivers expect tips
Export restrictions **licence required for coco de mer**
  nuts

The Seychelles claims to be paradise, but it is certainly not paradisal for the shopper. What there is can be found mainly in the town centre, the hotel gift shops, the Craft Village and the various art galleries. Nearly everything is very expensive compared with European prices.

The best value in clothing is to be found at the Craft Village, Ron Gerlach's shop in Beauvallon and the hotel shops. Sunstroke in Market Street has good pareos. Diving gear and T-shirts are to be found at the Underwater Centre next to the Coral Strand Hotel in Beauvallon and at their other shops, next to the Reef Hotel and on Praslin next to the Paradise Sun. Diving shoes are a recommended buy for walking on rocks or beaches where there may be stonefish or rays.

Craft products are available at Codevar and at Memorabilia in Victoria, as well as at the Craft Village (Artisan des Iles) near La Plainte St André on the south-east coast road. Some of the shell and silver-plated jewellery is attractive and not outrageously expensive. There are street stalls in the centre of town, but many of the items they sell are imported. The purchase of seashells, or their removal from the beach, is strongly discouraged. Coco de mer nuts can occasionally be bought at considerable expense at the Craft Village, at the Botanical Garden or at the Valée de Mai on Praslin: an export licence is required. Small nuts in the unique female shape are usually fakes. Wooden models of traditional boats are available from La Marine at La Plainte St André and various other places.

Art galleries usually sell the work only of the proprietor. Hotel shops usually have a selection of artworks, as does the Craft Village. Best known is Michael Adams, who has his gallery in a pretty old Creole house at Anse au Poule Bleu near Anse à la Mouche on the south-west road. Interesting bronze sculptures can be seen and bought not far away at Tomi Bower's studio off Les Cannelles Road. On Praslin there is a good gallery at the Café des Arts, with crafts at the sister shop opposite.

A firm called Kreolfleurage on the Northcoast Road makes lovely perfumes and essential oils at reasonable prices. In the Victoria Market you can buy sticks of cinnamon, vanilla pods, cloves, spices, local tea, coconut butter soap and various chutneys and sauces.

The only daily local newspaper is the *Nation* which is government-controlled. Foreign newspapers, magazines and some books can be purchased when available at Antigone (in the arcade beside Temooljees supermarket), Espace and at the hotel shops. Antigone sells a few coffee-table books about the Seychelles.

EATING AND DRINKING

There are many restaurants. Some serve mostly Creole food, others are more cosmopolitan. Of those with generally good food the Auberge Louis XVII has a wonderful view of the inner islands. The Bagatelle on Sans Souci Road is an attractive old house with an interesting garden. The Scala at Bel Ombre has good Italian food and an attractive open-air restaurant. Chez Plume at Anse Boileau has a good reputation. On Praslin the Bonbon Plume beside the beautiful Anse Lazio beach serves good lunches and the Café des Arts on Grande Anse is popular. Fish is excellent, but not cheap. There are many local varieties. Exotic tropical fruits are available seasonally. The local lager, Guinness and soft drinks are all good. Wine, usually South African or French, is expensive in restaurants.

TRANSPORT
Public buses are acceptable, but may be infrequent. Taxis are
freely available at the hotels and in Victoria. Fares are reasonable and fixed. You can ask to have the meter turned on, but
it may be cheaper without it.

SIERRA LEONE

FREETOWN

Language **English**
Currency **leone (Le) of 100 cents. £1=1360,
    Mar 1997**
Banks **0800–1330 Mon to Thur, 0800–1400 Fri**
Credit cards **only at Mammy Yoko and Cape Sierra
    hotels and IPC travel agency**
Shops **supermarkets 0900–1900, shops
    0800–1200/1300, 1400–1630/1700 Mon to Fri,
    0800–1230 Sat, markets 0730–1930, street traders all
    hours**
Bargaining **everywhere, except supermarkets**
Tipping **200–500 leones for most services; some
    restaurants include service charge and 10 per cent
    tax, but a tip (dash) is appreciated**

Sierra Leone produces diamonds and gold, both of which can
be bought from licensed dealers. There are several dealers in
Howe Street. Alie jewellery shop opposite the German
Embassy is worth visiting, but bargain hard. The local
tie-dyed *gara* is popular for dressmaking and nice beach bags
of locally-dyed material can be bought cheaply on the beaches,
particularly Lumley Beach. European-style clothing is not
readily available locally. However a number of local tailors
specialise in safari suits, etc.

   Local woodcarvings and batik pictures are also available
on Lumley Beach. Cane, raffia and baskets are worth looking
at and there is a basket market on Wallace Johnson Street.
Victoria Park opposite State House is seething with stalls of
cloth, handicrafts and materials. The gift shop at the Cape
Sierra Hotel provides a smaller, but more accessible, range of
handicrafts. The Balmaya and Gaga galleries, both located in
Main Motor Road, are worth a visit for handicrafts as well as

gifts and souvenirs. East Street Market, opposite the mosque, is full of traders selling fruit and vegetables and a must for anyone who likes bargaining.

No overseas newspapers are available locally. Atson's Supermarket stocks a selection of out-of-date and expensive English-language magazines. New Horizons bookshop and gifts is in Howe Street.

EATING AND DRINKING

There are a few restaurants and eating places. The standard of cuisine is variable, and service is sometimes slow: expect to wait 45 minutes from time of ordering. Fish and chips and burgers and chips are widely available as are local dishes such as pepper soup, pepper chicken and groundnut stew.

Worth a visit are the Vendome at the Mammy Yoko Hotel and three restaurants opposite the hotel, Alex's Beach Bar, George's Spanish Restaurant and the Cape Club. Try also the Atlantic or Chez Nous in Lumley Beach Road, the Lagonda near the Cape Sierra Hotel and the Balmaya in Main Motor Road.

The local brewery produces a reasonable bottled lager (Star), a stout (Guinness) and a non-alcoholic malt beverage (Maltina). Several varieties of soft drink are produced locally under licence, including Coke and Pepsi.

TRANSPORT

Transport is necessary for shopping as the major hotels are beyond walking distance of the main market places. There is no public transport and taxis, identifiable by their yellow number plates, are not recommended. Fares should be agreed before starting the journey. There is never any problem obtaining a taxi in the town centre although one may have to share with other passengers.

SINGAPORE

Languages **Chinese, Malay, Tamil, English**
Currency **Singapore dollar (S$) of 100 cents.**
  £1=2.30, Mar 1997
Banks **1000–1500 Mon to Fri, 0930–1130 Sat.**
  There are also licensed money-changers
Credit cards **most accepted in larger stores,**
  surcharge may be added
Shops **1000–2100 Sun to Sat**
Refunds **possible in larger shops; some participate**
  in GST (Goods and Services Tax) refund scheme
Bargaining **yes, where no fixed price**
Tipping **not expected; 10 per cent service charge in**
  restaurants
Import/export restrictions **all weapons, including**
  swords bought as souvenirs, require licence from
  Singapore Arms and Explosives Branch

Singapore's reputation as a shopper's paradise is justified, although it is not as cheap as it once was. Just about everything is easily available. Prices are generally higher than in the UK, but values change with the fluctuating exchange rate. Cameras, videos, hi-fi and electrical items can be cheaper than in the UK, but it may be necessary to shop around.

The red and white Lion sticker shows an outlet recognised and recommended by the local Tourist Promotion Board and Consumers Association and offers some guarantee that goods are satisfactory. Complaints can be referred either to the Consumers Association of Singapore or, for S$10, to the local Small Claims Tribunals. You may have to specifically ask for, (and pay a little extra for) an international guarantee.

The prime shopping area is centred on Orchard Road. If you walk down Orchard Road from Tanglin Road to Park Mall, just past Edinburgh Road, you will come across no fewer than 30 different shopping centres. On side-streets such as Scotts Road there are designer boutiques including Toy 'R' Us, Isetan and Takashimaya from Japan; the local department stores Metro, John Little and Robinson's, as well as Yaohan Best for electrical goods and appliances.

The Raffles Hotel Arcade has something like 70 outlets. The Raffles City Shopping Centre over the road is also worth a visit, as is the massive Marina Square on Raffles Boulevard together with the neighbouring department stores of Metro and Tokyu.

Chinatown lies between New Bridge and South Bridge roads and between Upper Pickering Street and Cantonment roads. The newly renovated Tanjong Pagar area is on Tanjong Pagar Road just after the end of South Bridge Road. Little India is in Serangoon Road and its neighbouring side-streets. Arab Street and its neighbouring side-streets are also well worth a visit.

Fabrics and ready-made silk garments can be found in speciality Chinese silk stores in Tanglin Shopping Centre, Scotts, Lucky Plaza and in Chinese emporiums all over Singapore. Thai silk is also available. Larger sizes can be difficult to find in both shoes and clothing. Most casual clothing is cheaper than in the UK and there is more variety and choice. Cheap, locally made sandals are available and it is possible to have sandals copied in leather at prices comparable with those in the UK.

Generally prices for sports clothing and equipment are lower than in the UK. All books are available, but are a little more expensive than in the UK. Opticians are good and very reasonable in price. They are to be found in North Bridge Road, Tanglin Road and Orchard Road. New lenses can usually be supplied within hours.

Holland Village is good for Chinese art and handicrafts. Oriental carpets and rugs are to be found in Arab Street and Orchard Road. Ornate Chinese carpets are available from Peninsula Shopping Centre in Coleman Street. Magnificent Chinese Ping carpets can be seen in showrooms of Singapore Carpet Manufacturers in Haw Par Centre. Paris Silk Store in Transit Road, Nee Soon, is very competitive and helpful. Good places to look for jade, pearls, gold and diamonds are in South Bridge Road, New Bridge Road and People's Park. The largest range of wickerwork is in Arab Street.

EATING AND DRINKING

Chinese, Malay and Indian cuisines are readily available. Eating from street vendors is cheap and can be fun, but it is not particularly recommended. Cafés serving basic food are cheap enough. The visitor will need to be adventurous, although everyone will appreciate the quality of the fish and seafood. A steamboat is a Chinese-style fondu. Dim sum consists of steamed and fried dumplings in bamboo. Recommended restaurants which should not break the bank include the Cherry Garden in the Oriental Hotel, China Palace in the Wellington Building at 20 Bideford Road, Dragon City in the Novotel Orchid Inn and Garden Seafood in the Goodwood Park Hotel.

TRANSPORT
There is a bus network and a modern Mass Rapid Transit (MRT) rail system. The Singapore Trolley is an old-style tram-bus which covers the central shopping area. Daily tickets are available for all modes of public transport. Taxis are metered and inexpensive.

SLOVAK REPUBLIC

BRATISLAVA

Language Slovak
Currency slovenská koruna or Slovak crown (SK) of 100 halèfu. £1=53.12, Mar 1997
Banks carry passport as identification when changing money; do not buy other foreign currencies, e.g. schillings or forints
Credit cards Visa and Mastercard in some restaurants and hotels, not in shops or garages
Cashpoints yes, using Visa and Mastercard
Shops 0800–1800 Mon to Fri, 0800–1300 Sat; smaller shops close for lunch. Some Sun opening
Refunds only in Western-style shops
Duty-free yes, but no cheaper than town
Tipping round up restaurant bills if no service charge; taxi drivers SK10–20
Export restrictions Antiques, works of art, etc. should be made available for customs examination together with receipts. Check when purchasing if a licence from the Ministry of Culture is necessary

Bratislava and shopping are hardly synonymous and since tourism has yet to take off the range of goods likely to interest the visitor is limited. Basic goods are cheap and as the economy improves shops are becoming more Westernised and customer-orientated. However, traditional-style shops persist in a rather consumer-unfriendly unwillingness to allow browsing before buying. German is widely spoken.

It has always been a pleasure to wander in the Old Town and the increasing number of cafés and shops is bringing out the best in this pretty central area. The few shops of interest are mainly on Ventúrska, Michalská, Panská, Laurinská and

Sedlárska and in the main square (Hlavné námestie). These are generally up-market and cater for tourist traffic. They include attractive arts and crafts shops selling folk ceramics and other goods, a few jewellers, smarter bookshops and plenty of eating places.

Glass and porcelain are very reasonable – though do not be tempted to buy junk just because of that – and the craft shops carry some very attractive items. For glass, including Bohemia crystal, and porcelain try the as yet nameless shop on Hlavné námestie, Thun at Stúrova 7, Katka at Panská 24 or Bohemia Glass on Sedlárska. For local arts and crafts including Slovak ceramics and hand-embroidered white table-linen there are Ul'uv in Ventúrska and Námestie SNP and Folk-folk in Hlavné námestie, as well as a good outlet for Modrá ceramics on Klemensova at the Dunajská end.

There is an indoor market on the corner of Sancova and Krina which is uninteresting and a large outdoor market on Miletiova. This is good for produce and worth a browse. There are wonderful seasonal markets at Christmas and Easter on Hlavné námestie.

The modern part of central Bratislava clusters around the Kamenné námestie and Námestie SNP areas. The mix of shops is pretty functional. K-Mart represents the ultimate in Western sophistication. The Prior Department Store at Kamenné nám and the Ruinov department store at Tomásikova are old-style emporia. Among the cheap clothing shops reminiscent of former years some brave international labels such as Stefanel and Betty Barclay are beginning to be represented.

News stands carry a few out-of-date and expensive English-language newspapers and periodicals. The Big Ben Bookshop on Ventúrska stocks exclusively English-language titles. Prices are rarely if ever higher than in the UK and stocks are good.

EATING AND DRINKING

New restaurants and cafés are springing up everywhere and it is much easier than it was to find alternatives to the rather heavy Slovak diet – typical is meat with potatoes or dumplings. Slovak restaurants are usually cheap, something like £5 for a couple of courses and a glass of something. The biggest brewery restaurant, the Old Malt House, is in Cintorinska Street. Also Slovak in style are Modrá at Beblavého 14, Harmtoes or dumplings. Local wines are good and reasonably priced, even in restaurants. There are also some nice cafés such as Café Maximilian in Hlavné námestie.

TRANSPORT

Since Bratislava is so small, the visitor rarely has to worry about transport in the centre. There is, however, a good, reliable and cheap, though at times crowded, network of buses, trams and trolley-cars using a system of uniform fares per ride. Taxi charges are reasonable, although a visitor might be asked to pay an agreed fare rather than the meter rate.

SECURITY

Personal security is good, although petty crime is on the increase.

SLOVENIA

LJUBLIANA

Language **Slovene**
Currency **Slovenian tolar (SIT) of 100 stotin.**
   £1=247.29, Mar 1997
Banks **money can be exchanged at exchange**
   booths in the city
Traveller's cheques **Eurocheques**
Credit cards **most accepted**
Shops **0800–2000 Mon to Fri, 0800–1300 Sat; markets**
   0800–1300 Mon to Sat
Duty-free **several expensive foreign currency shops**
Tipping **10 per cent in restaurants**

Slovenia is a lovely country and one of Europe's best-kept secrets. Its tourism must surely take off in the new atmosphere prevailing. Contrary to popular belief, it is nowhere near the war zone in the former Yugoslav Republic.

The main shopping area is in the centre, on and around Nazorjeva ulica. New private shops are opening daily with firms such as Benetton and WFM now being represented. The majority of shops are small and many are branches of chains. There are a few department stores in the centre such as Maxi-Market on Trg Republike, Nama and Centromerkur.

Good quality crystal is produced at competitive prices. Otherwise cassettes of local music may be to your taste. Both are widely available. The best place for buying handicrafts and other gifts and souvenirs is the shop at the National Museum.

It is possible to buy books in English in many of the book-shops. Try also the big hotels such as the Grand Hotel Union.

EATING AND DRINKING
There are many restaurants offering a relatively good standard at reasonable prices. Local Slovene fare can occasionally be rather heavy. Fish and seafood appear regularly on the menu, but the selection is fairly restricted. Local wine is of good quality, but predominantly white. Local beer is also of good quality.

TRANSPORT
Taxis are usually stationed outside the principal hotels and at the main railway station. There are frequent bus services to all parts of the city.

SOLOMON ISLANDS

HONIARA

Language **English**
Currency **Solomon Island dollar (SI$) of 100 cents.
£1=5.87, Mar 1997**

Most things are available some of the time and some things are available most of the time. Shoes wear out quickly on coral paths.

Gold is mined in the Solomons and the best local item to buy is a *nguzunguzu* (pronounced nusu-nusu) head. This is the ancient God of War, who always adorned the prows of war canoes. Other interesting items include shell jewellery which is very cheap and wood carvings which are not so cheap.

A limited supply of clothing is available such as T-shirts, trainers and some canvas shoes. There are two European-type shops, OK Boutique and Tropicana, selling mainly Australian clothing, but occasionally clothing from Bali. There is a newly built Central Market.

Australian and UK weekly newspapers are regularly on sale as well as *Time* and *Newsweek*. There are two local news-papers, the twice-weekly *Solomon Star* and the weekly *Solomon Voice*. The *Pacific Island Monthly* magazine is also widely read and sold. A small selection of expensive imported women's magazines, comics and sporting magazines is available from time to time.

Eating and Drinking

Hotel and Chinese restaurant meals are reasonably priced. Of the latter, the Lei Lei some four kilometres from town is the best and most reliable. The Mendana Hotel is recommended and the Yacht Club serves inexpensive meals or snacks every lunchtime and evening. Other restaurants include the French-run La Pelouse, the Australian-run Hibiscus (which serves Thai food) and the Leilei, offering European food and efficient service.

Transport

Taxis are numerous, cheap and usually dilapidated.

Somalia

Mogadishu

Language **Somali, Arabic**
Currency **Somali shilling of 100 cents. £1=4057, Dec 1995**
Shops **0800/1000-1300, 1700-2000/2100 Sat to Thur, closed Fri morning**
Bargaining **in markets**
Duty-free **near Jubba Hotel, hard currency and credit cards accepted; 1500-1900 Sun to Thur Passport identification needed**
Tipping **up to 10 per cent in restaurants**

Due to the unstable security situation, the Foreign Office advises against travel to Somalia.

There are shops in the Savoy Centre and in the arcade opposite the National Theatre where there is a women's clothing shop with tie-dye dresses and a Government Shop where wrap-around skirts are available. The Via Roma usually has a selection of imported goods at reasonable prices. The Sinai Market has all sort of goods. Be prepared to bargain. The gold market is near the fruit and vegetable market in the centre of town. There is a stamp shop on the first floor of the post office, opposite the Jubba Hotel. It takes a day or two to order, but the beautiful stamps make an ideal gift for a stamp collector.

Samatur's Bookshop in the Savoy Centre sells *Time* and *Newsweek* plus paperbacks. British books and newspapers are not obtainable.

EATING AND DRINKING

Eating out is not always reliable, but try the Goat Restaurant at Km 13 towards Afghoi, a Somali-style restaurant in a unique setting under the trees, or Makka Al Makurama Hotel in Makka Road, which has a nice garden. You can take your own wine to the Croce del Sud Hotel. The Blue Marlin situated on the Lido serves Italian-style food. VIP, just past the Blue Marlin has some outside tables overlooking the sea and serves Italian food.

Fruit is good, but seasonal.

TRANSPORT

Taxis can be found in the vicinity of the hotels and cruising on the busier roads. Prices are negotiable and there are no meters. Local bus services are inexpensive, but very crowded and rarely used by tourists.

SOUTH AFRICA

Language **Afrikaans, English**
Currency **rand (R)of 100 cents. £1=7.10, Mar 1997**
Banks **0900-1530 Mon to Fri, 0830-1100 Sat**
Credit cards **widely accepted, but not at petrol stations**
Cashpoints **yes**
Shops **0830-1700 Mon to Fri, 0830-1300 Sat**
Tipping **10 per cent is usual**

The cost of living is roughly the same as in the UK, but anything imported can be two or three times the UK price. Locally made clothing can be cheap and there are local couturiers such as The Boys and Julian. Woolworths is almost identical to Marks and Spencer, both for food and clothing, and stocks many St Michael items.

Look out for Arts and Crafts including woodcarvings, ceramics, carpets and rugs or beadwork: particularly for craftwork and curios, pottery or hides and skins. Good lightweight suits can be bought off the peg more cheaply than in London. Other recommended buys include locally made clothing from department stores and boutiques, particularly casual lines. Sportswear and equipment can be good value.

The local English-language press is good and recommended. British newspapers and magazines are sold in a few shops, but are generally expensive and well out of date. Only a few English-language periodicals are available locally. English-language books are on sale at most bookshops, but are much more expensive than in the UK.

Meals out are cheaper than in the UK. Local wines, beers, sherries and brandies are substantially cheaper than imports and are of good quality. Most supermarkets have a wine department and stock a large variety of South African wines at competitive prices. Alcohol cannot be purchased at any type of shop on Saturday afternoons or Sundays.

Tropical fruit is good, but seasonal and not always available due to export priority.

The crime rate continues to rise and the incidence of mugging remains high. Particularly prone are Johannesburg and other major cities.

JOHANNESBURG

Shopping is excellent. Most shopping is in large malls or centres such as Bryanston Market, the Carlton Centre in Commissioner Street in the centre of town, the Eastgate Centre on Broadway Extension in Bedfordview, Hyde Park on Jan Smuts Avenue, Killarney Mall on Riviera Road, Rosebank Mall on Cradock Avenue and the Sandown Centre in Hill Street, Randburg.

For handicrafts and souvenirs there is the Rooftop Market at Rosebank Mall with 400 stalls offering a vast choice. There is also the Serendipity Gallery at Fourways Mall, Killarney Mall and at the Johannesburg Zoo.

EATING AND DRINKING

For a special meal at a moderate price try Harridan's in the Market Theatre Complex, Ma Cuisine at the corner of Seventh and Third Avenues in Parktown North or the Baytree at the corner of Hans Strydom Drive and North Road in Linden Extension. The Waterfront in Randburg offers a selection of 72 restaurants from which to choose.

TRANSPORT

The bus service cannot be relied upon and leaves much to be

desired. Taxis may not be hailed in the street, but may be telephoned in advance. They are expensive.

CAPE TOWN

The main central shopping area is on and around Lower Adderley Street and Strand Street. The Golden Acre shopping centre is in Adderley Street. St George's Street is now a pedestrianised mall. Long Street has some little shops which are quite interesting to browse through for things such as books or bric-à-brac. The Waterfront area is being developed as an area for shopping, eating and other entertainment. There is a good open market on the Parade where fabrics and other goods are sold quite cheaply. There is also a shopping centre at Cavendish Square in the suburbs.

EATING AND DRINKING

There are numerous restaurants in and around Cape Town to suit all tastes and pockets. Seafood is particularly popular, crawfish being a local delicacy when in season. Some restaurants are unlicensed and therefore customers may bring their own wine.

Try Champers at Deer Park Drive, Highlands Estate, Choices at 34 Loop Street, John Jackson in the Peninsula Hotel on Beach Road at Sea Point, Peers at Peerhead, the Waterfront, Bellinzona at the corner of Beach and Blauwberg Roads at Table View or Floris Smit Huis at 55 Church Street.

The Cape is world famous for its wines and no sensible visitor leaves before touring some of the vineyards, some of which serve excellent and reasonably priced food to complement the wines.

TRANSPORT

The main central area is easily covered for the most part by the pedestrian and the city likes to promote itself as a place suitable for sightseeing on foot. Buses are restricted both in terms of routes and frequency. Taxis are expensive and do not cruise.

DURBAN

The world-famous Golden Mile (more like four miles in fact) stretches from Rutherford Street northward along the coastline to Playfair Road. This and adjacent streets constitute the main shopping, eating and entertainment area.

Shopping is moving away from the centre of town, although among shopping centres the Workshop in Pine Street is still worth a look. The Pavilion at Westville is the largest and there are other fairly large centres at Musgrave and La Lucia. To the south around Victoria Street is the major centre of Asian influence in Durban, with shopping and eating to match.

Handicrafts for gifts and souvenirs are plentiful. Good places to buy are the BAT Centre in the Inkonkoni Building on Victoria Embankment and at the African Art Centre at 8 Guildhall Arcade, 35 Gardiner Street. Look out particularly for the Zulu influence in things such as woodcarvings and sculptures, pottery, beadwork, basketry and weaving. Good markets are Essenwood Road on Saturday morning and Point flea market at the North Beach area at weekends.

EATING AND DRINKING

For a meal out try the Colony at the Oceanic in Sol Harris Cresent, La Dolce Vita at Durdoc Centre, 460 Smith Street or the Royal Grill and Ulundi Restaurant at the Royal Hotel in Smith Street. There are some good restaurants at Umhlanga, north of Durban. Florida Road in Morningside also has a variety of good restaurants.

TRANSPORT

The Mynah shuttle bus covers the Golden Mile, which can be chaotic and difficult for motorists.

PRETORIA

The main shopping centres in town are De Bruyn Park at the corner of Vermeulen and Andries streets, the Sanlan Centre at the corner of Andries Street and Schoeman Street and Standard Bank Centre at the corner of Church and Van der Walt streets. In the suburbs there are the Arcadia Centre at the corner of Beatrix, Proes and Vermeulen streets, the Jacaranda Centre at the corner of Michael Brink Street and Frates Road; Menlyn Park in Atterbury Road and Sunny Park at the corner of Esselen and Mears Street in Sunnyside.

If you want to get out of Pretoria for a change, there is a good shopping centre at Centurion Park in Centurion (formerly Verwoerdburg) with most of the well-known shops such as Woolworths, Truworths, Edgars, Pick 'n' Pay, OK and CNA.

The main department stores are Edgars, Stuttafords, John Orrs and Milady. More trendy styles can be found at Queenspark (Waterkloof), Foschini and Truworths. There are branches of most of the above shops at Menlyn Park, Sunnyside and most of the shopping centres in town.

The State Theatre flea market is every Saturday morning at the corner of Prinsloo and Church Street. Sunnypark flea market is on Sunday mornings at Sunnypark Shopping Centre at the corner of Esselen and Beatrix. The Asian Bazaar in Boom Street has exotic spices, etc.

For ethnic crafts try Curio King in Shop 58 at Sancardia Centre and at 524 Church Street Arcadia or the National Parks Board Shop at 643 Leyds Street. Also try the street market outside Pretoria Zoo, every day of the week, Craft in the Park on the first Saturday of the month at Magnolia Dell, Queen Wilhelmina Avenue or Art in the Park on the last Saturday of the month. Art in the Sun is on Saturday mornings at Barclay Square and Rissik Street.

Good specialist sports shops are Varsity Sports at Menlyn, Hatfield and Brooklyn or Total Sports at Sunnyside and Menlyn. A good range of equipment at competitive prices is offered by supermarkets such as Hyperama, Pick 'n' Pay, Dions and Makro.

EATING AND DRINKING
For a special meal at not too outrageous a price try La Cantina at 895 Pretorius Street, La Madeleine at 258 Esselen Street, Sunnyside, La Perla at 211 Skinner Street or Stadt Hamburg in Brae Street.

TRANSPORT
Bus routes and timings are restrictive. Taxis are expensive and do not cruise. Prior booking may be necessary to avoid a long wait.

Spain

Language Spanish
Currency peseta of 100 centimos. £1=245, Mar
   1997
Banks 0900-1400 Mon to Fri
Traveller's cheques Eurocheque card not universally
   accepted as guarantee
Credit cards all major cards accepted
Cashpoints yes
Shops 1000-1300/1400, 1630/1700-2000;
   department stores 1000-2000. First Sun in month
   Commercial centres (malls) are open. Small shops
   close all or part of Aug
Sales Jan and Jul, large reductions on clothes, often
   discounts on non-sale goods
Duty-free not always cheaper than supermarkets
Tipping 10 per cent is standard; add 10 per cent tip
   at restaurants, a few pesetas after a cup of coffee.
   5-10 per cent to taxi drivers

Once Spain was considered a cheap country, but no more. The
cost of living has risen rapidly over the past few years. Food
prices are generally similar to those in the UK, but the price of
luxuries – including alcohol and imported tobacco – is, for the
most part, higher.

The clothing industry in Spain is large and growing and
produces goods of acceptable quality and style which are quite
competitive with UK goods at the lower end of the market.
However, the finer quality and imported goods are more
expensive than in the UK. Larger sizes of clothing can be difficult
to find. Locally manufactured shoes are available at reasonable
prices, but good-quality shoes are very expensive. Half sizes are
difficult to find.

Other leather items and ceramics are good value. CDs of
local music are a popular buy, but the easiest gifts and souvenirs are in the food and drink range, for example hams and
sausages or wines for which Spain is famous.

An average meal out costs about Pts3000 with wine, coffee,
VAT. Service is not included. In cheaper restaurants, a standard set *menú del dia* at lunchtime will cost about Pts1500.
Usually on offer at most restaurants is a wide variety of excellent fish which can be expensive depending on the venue. The
adopted national dish, *paella*, is readily available and well
worth trying. Less filling perhaps, but just as satisfying are

tapas, consisting of several small dishes of your choice.

Spanish table wines, Rioja and Ribera del Duero are good value, as are San Miguel and other beers. As a rule, red wines are generally of better quality than white. Liqueurs and spirits are sold in the supermarkets at good prices. There are two varieties of Spanish cigarettes, the "light" ones are called Fortuna and the ones made from black tobacco are Ducados. Both are quite cheap when purchased in special shops called *Estancos*. English cigarettes, the better known brands of Havana cigars and cigars from the Canaries (which are cheap and improving in quality) are also sold in Estancos.

MADRID

Without question, the best – and for some people – the only department store is El Corte Inglès. There are a number of branches throughout the city, the flagship is at Goya 76. Leading Spanish, Italian and British designer labels are all carried there. Head for the Serano/ Velazquez/Goya district if you are in the market for clothes and accessories in all price ranges. There are many big-name designer boutiques in this area as well as Zara (Princesa 45), which has wonderful clothes and accessories for the young and trendy at incredibly reasonable prices. In the same genre are Trucco (General Perón)and Globe (Padilla 4) which is a bit more expensive, but still good value. Acosta (Princesa 60) offers exceptionally good value for leather goods and accessories for women, and there are 12 branches in Madrid. The more exclusive Spanish designers are situated around Calle Jorge Juan where you'll come across some of Spain's most famous names: Sybilla (Callejon de Jorge Juan, 32), Adolfo Dominguez (Serrano 18) and Loewe (Serrano 26). Also in the area is Meye Maier (no. 12), a wonderful source for very elegant lingerie made of the finest materials. Further along Serrano is Don Carlos (Serrano 92). Another street worth exploring is Calle Almirante Ararat (no. 10), Berlin (no 20) and Enrique P (no.6) . For menswear stop at Massimo Dutti (Velazquez, 46), Pull and Bear (Goya 44) and Milano (Serrano, 29) has men's suits at unbeatable prices. Another area, Paseo de la Habana, has a very good shopping street for menswear. Moda Shopping (Calle General Peron) and Springsfield (Calle Concha Espina) are great sources for men's sportswear at low prices.

Unless you've recently won the lottery, or are desperate to window shop, avoid the area around Plaza Puerta del Sol and the adjacent Calle de Alcalá, Calle Major and Plaza Major. There are some wonderful shops but they are extremely pricey.

Two shopping malls worthy of a mention and a visit are the ABC de Serrano (Serrano 61) and La Esquina del Bernabeu (Plaza de los Sagrados Corazones).

There is a lively market life in Madrid. The Commercial Chamartin or Mola Market at the Calle Potosi and Bolivia is a good open market and El Rastro flea market (Ribera de Curtidores), is particularly popular on Sundays. For old books, go to Cuesta del Moyano and up Paseo del Prado. For stamps, go to the Plaza Major on Sunday morning. As with all markets worldwide, watch your bags and wallets, pickpockets are clever and very quick.

British newspapers and magazines are available on news stands and also at Vips y Bobs, open daily until 3am. Dailies are available in the evening of publication day and Sunday newspapers on Monday. Costs will be about four times that of the UK. Books in English are available, but are expensive. The Turner English Bookshop is at Génova 3. English Editions is at Plaza de San Amaro 5.

EATING AND DRINKING

There are many kinds of restaurants varying in price and quality. A simple meal with bread and wine in an unpretentious restaurant would cost about Pts3000. Lunch or dinner in a restaurant with atmosphere and well-cooked food costs double that. Some restaurants have flamenco dancing as a principal attraction. They are nearly always expensive and cater mainly for tourists. Despite the distance from the sea, there is an amazing variety of fresh fish and shellfish available daily. There are some very good eating places in and around the Plaza Santa Anna and Plaza Mayor.

TRANSPORT

All public transport is fairly cheap and services are frequent. The metro is the quickest way of reaching some parts of the city, but it is rather seedy and suffocating in summer. The network is in the process of being modernised and extended. The bus service is good. Predictably, the buses and metros become very crowded at peak hours. The yellow microbus is more comfortable and no more expensive than the big red bus. Ten journey tickets are available in newspaper kiosks and Estancos. There is no shortage of taxis within the city limits, where controlled tariffs apply, and they are cheaper than in the UK.

BARCELONA

Barcelona is one of the most expensive cities in Spain and is one of the world's greatest design and fashion cities. Certainly, it is a good place for shopping. Clothing and everything else tends to be more expensive than in the UK except at sale time. The prices for shoes are comparable to the UK, but one can pick up some very good bargains in the sales. By and large, leather handbags are no longer cheap but again, if you shop around you can uncover some bargains.

The main shopping area is on and around the Ramblas de Cataluña, Plaza de Frances Maciá, Calle Pau Casals, and Paseo de Gracia. The largest shopping mall is L'Illa Diagonal Shopping Centre 557 which has Marks & Spencer as its linchpin .

Just down the street is El Corte Inglès (Diagonal 617), Spain's foremost department store, which has an impressive cross section of goods at all price levels, including authentic flamenco costumes and mantillas. There are lots of boutiques in this area to explore; for women's shoes and handbags, try Cristina Castañer (Calle Maestro Nicolau 23), Las Maravillas (Calle Muntaner 356) and three outstanding shops (all on Calle Fernando Agullo) Santa Eulalia, Chosses and Charo. And do try and be in Barcelona when Adolfo Dominguez (89 Passaeig de Gracia) has a sale. Though they are rare, the bargains are well worth the wait.

The hands-down leader in design shops is Vincon, identifiable by its characteristic red neon sign. They have a wide selection of household goods and furniture and their cutting edge window displays have been known to stop pedestrian traffic.

The most famous and colourful market is Els Encants Flea Market (Placa de les Glories) where lamps, clocks, clothing and furniture all vie for space. Haggling is part of the ceremony and the fun. Market days are Monday, Wednesday, Friday and Saturday.

The Mercat de la Boqueria is a huge covered market with fresh fish, meat and produce which arrive at dawn. Don't miss the beautiful, 19th-century stained glass building with hectares of fruits, nuts and fish on display.

British and other international newspapers and magazines are widely available on the Ramblas. For English-language books, go to La Virreina (99 les Rambles).

EATING AND DRINKING

There are lots of places to eat around town. In the Ramblas and the Barri Gòtic district there is, for example, Amaya

(Rambla Santa M9 les Ra-24) for Basque cuisine or tapas. The Mercat San Josep nearby is the main food and produce market; it is good both for atmosphere and for snacks. The trendy places to go are Reno (Calle Tuset 27), La Balsa (Calle Infanta Isabel 4), La Vaqueria (Calle Deu i Mata 141) and Agua (Paseo Maritimo de la Barceloneta 30) which faces the sea.

TRANSPORT

There is a fairly frequent bus service covering the whole of the city, with a standard fare paid on entry, whatever the distance travelled. There are metro services from the centre of the city. Taxis are abundant and reasonable in price.

GRAN CANARIA: LAS PALMAS

A wide choice of shopping is available – if you're strictly window shopping, wander the pedestrian streets, Calle Triana, Calle San Bernado, Calle Malteses, and Calle Arena where Fendi, Loewe and the other designer boutiques are. One worthwhile stop in this very glitzy neighborhood is Maya, which specialises in watches, radios, and telephones at low prices. In Barrio de Vegeta, near the Old Town, purchase traditional crafts and make sure to spend some time around Luis Morote between the port and beach where there are duty-free shops and a branch of El Corte Inglés. Look out for a shop called 99 where you can find very cheap, but good quality cotton T-shirts, underwear, bathing suits, beach towels and tights. Just nearby is another good shopping area – which runs along the beach – called La Playa de las Canteras. Also, Visanta (Calle Ripoche) is perfect for radios, videos, televisions and sunglasses. Monica (Calle Ripoche) sells everything from clothes to furniture to linens and all at very good prices.

British daily newspapers are normally on sale in the afternoon of the same day. They are expensive. A few bookshops sell British books and magazines, but they are also very pricey.

EATING AND DRINKING

Eating and drinking out are cheaper than in the UK. Casa Grande (Triana 89), is an old palace which serves traditional food and has a lovely garden where you can dine. La Casita in the Hotel Santa Catalina (El Churchill, calle Leon y Castillo 272), serves delicious Catalan food in a gorgeous setting.

TRANSPORT

There is a good and frequent bus service, both in town and serving rural districts. Taxis abound.

MALLORCA: PALMA DE MALLORCA

Fear not, if the sun doesn't shine, there's always Palma's great shopping to fill your day. The Placa Major is the centre of the shopping district which extends from Plaza de Juan Carlos I, through Jaime III and Paseo del Borne – where you can find pottery, ceramics – to Rambla via Roma. Not to be missed are the pedestrian streets called San Miguel – a virtual shoe-heaven –, San Nicolas, Jaime II, Calle Colon and Plaza Cort. The best silverware can be bought either at La Pirne (Calle San Alonso) or Plateria San Alonso (Calle San Alonso).

Telas Mallorquinas are Mallorcan fabrics made on Balearic Islands, with hand-dyed threads of linen, cotton and silk. A beautiful selection of these can be found at Ribas (Calle San Nicolas) or at Juncosa just down the block. Breaking new ground in the area of design and merchandising is Canela (Calle San Jaime). This trendy boutique recently won an award called *Ciudad de Palma* for its design. There is a covered garden where you can have a drink and take a break from shopping. San Jaime (Calle San Jaime), is another decoration shop where you can purchase stunning accessories and furniture for the home. Also, not to be missed, is La Pajarita (Calle San Nicolas), which sells the unusual combination of the best chocolates, *ensaimadas* (spiralled flaky Mallorcan pastry) and *sobrasadas* (sausage).

EATING AND DRINKING

An à la carte meal with wine costs from about £25 at a reasonably good restaurant. However, all restaurants by law have to offer a menu del dia and these can be had in varying qualities from as little as about £5 each. Tapas are not necessarily cheap, but are recommended. For pastry and other sweets, which all the locals eat at teatime, try Can Joan de Saigo (Calle Bonaire at the corner of Jaime III). For tapas and *bocadillos* (hot and cold sandwiches on freshly baked bread), try Bar Bosch's outdoor café (Calle Jaime III) or La Boveda near La Lonja, where all the locals go.

SRI LANKA

COLOMBO

Language **Sinhalese, Tamil, English.**
Currency **Sri Lankan rupee (R) of 100 cents.**
  £1=92.25, Mar 1997
Banks **0900-1300 Mon to Fri**
Credit cards **major cards accepted at major hotels,**
  many shops and restaurants; imposition of
  surcharge is illegal
Shops **0800–1700**
Bargaining **expected in most shops and markets**
Export restrictions **the export of antiques over 75**
  years old is forbidden without the permission of
  the Commissioner of Archaeology

There is a vast range of different shops and goods in Liberty Plaza at the junction of Duplication Road and Dharmapala Mawatha. Colpetty Market is diagonally across the street. There are shops and street vendors from Liberty Plaza up to the junction with Galle Road.

Precious and semi-precious stones are worth looking at, but be on your guard against fakes.

Several shops sell end-of-lines of export garments bound for Marks and Spencer or C&A. Odel at 38 Dickmans Road is good for casual and sports clothing.

The local silk is beautiful, but quality needs to be checked; it can be quite coarse, since it is still woven on handlooms. Always wash it before making up. The Natural Silk Sales Centre is at 349 Galle Road and Janasai is opposite the Oberoi on Galle Road. Embroidery silks are very cheap, but of poor quality compared with those sold in the UK.

Paradise Road at 213 Dharmapala Mawatha has good-value picture frames as well as other ornaments and tableware.

Towels are produced at very competitive prices. Asian Fabrics has a factory on the way to the airport at 67 Attampolawatte. Barefoot on Galle Road has excellent, (but not cheap), linens and all sorts of other local fabrics including sarongs.

Several florists sell locally grown orchids and the bigger ones will do airpacks.

Some handicrafts, such as handwoven mats and baskets, brassware or carved elephants are still cheap, but the taste is sometimes questionable. For handicrafts and souvenirs try Crafts Gallery at 12 Ascot Avenue off Timbirigasyaya Road or Lakpahana at 14 Reid Avenue. Laksala at 60 York Street is a government handicraft shop with fixed prices. Enada Silva at 276 R A de Mel Mawatha near Liberty Plaza sells batiks.

For antiques try Collectors at the Galadari Meridian or Raux Brothers at 164 Galle Road.

Books and magazines are very expensive. English-language paperback books are freely available, but are variably priced. Penguin books for example are often sold below the UK price but the latest best-sellers often cost more than in the UK.

EATING AND DRINKING
For local-style restaurants try Alhambra at the Holiday Inn, Ibn Batuta at the Ramada, Palmyrah at the Hotel Renuka or Ran Malu at the Oberoi.

For seafood try the Harbor Room at the Oriental, Pearl Seafood at the Intercontinental or the Fish at the Meridien. Shellfish are very good and still reasonable in price. Local exotic and tropical fruits are excellent. Locally produced soft drinks and beer are available.

TRANSPORT
Buses of all types are ill-maintained, frequently overcrowded and often have accidents. Taxis and motorised trishaws are also poorly maintained and badly driven.

SUDAN

KHARTOUM

Language **Arabic**
Currency **Sudanese dinar (SD) of 10 pounds.**
  £1=2048, Nov 1996
Traveller's cheques **accepted in duty-free shops**
Credit cards **yes. American Express and Visa**
Shops **mornings only for shops, stalls and markets**
Duty-free **at the airport; supplies erratic. Traveller's cheques, cash sterling and dollars accepted**
Tipping **10 per cent in restaurants; taxi drivers are not tipped**

Modern Khartoum is not one city but three. It consists of old Khartoum, lying between the White and Blue Niles and rapidly expanding southwards, Omdurman, west of the White Nile, and Khartoum North, east of the main Nile.

There is a shortage of both food and clothing. Since September 1983 the import, sale and consumption of alcohol has been forbidden. Shoes for walking should be on the large side, flatter heels are more comfortable and practical; avoid glued soles in the heat.

The local *galabeya*, a style of long dress worn by men, is cool and comfortable and can be bought or made for both men and women. It is a popular gift or souvenir.

British newspapers and magazines are not available in Khartoum. There are a few shops which sell some English-language books, but these are expensive.

EATING AND DRINKING

Foodstuffs available locally are limited in variety, but include some good meats and fresh Nile fish. Local fruit is usually limited to mangoes, water-melons, oranges, guavas and grapefruit, but the last are among the best in the world. Locally bottled soft drinks are erratically available.

With the ban on alcohol, eating out is not such an attractive proposition as it once was. Basic meals for non-residents are available at most Khartoum hotels with the Hilton and the Meridien offering a better, but more expensive, choice. The Hilton's Friday brunch is popular.

TRANSPORT

Buses are mostly ancient and overcrowded and never used by expatriates. There are taxis, many as ancient as the buses, but they are not always easy to get and have no meters. Charges for foreigners are apt to be inflated, especially at night. Fares should be agreed before the journey.

SECURITY

The borders with Egypt, Eritrea and Ethiopia are closed (10/96), but Khartoum itself is generally quiet and crime levels are still relatively low compared with some other African countries. It is possible to walk fairly freely around the shops and souks even at night, provided sensible precautions are taken.

SWAZILAND

MBABANE

Language Swazi, English
Currency lilangeni (plural emalingeni) (E), at par
  with South African rand. £1=7, Mar 1997
Banks rand notes, but not South African coins, are
  generally accepted
Credit cards acceptable in most establishments
Shops 0830–1700 Mon to Fri, 0830–1300 Sat; some
  Sun morning opening
Bargaining expected in markets
Tipping 5–10 per cent to waiters for satisfactory
  service

Mbabane is only four and a half hours' drive from
Johannesburg, where some people prefer to do their serious
shopping. Local shops carry a limited range of ready-made
clothing. Apart from occasional shortages or erratic supply,
there are no problems with food. Local prices are reasonable
and on a par with those in the UK. Quality and branded goods
are generally dearer than in the UK or South Africa.

There are two modern shopping complexes, the Swazi
Plaza and the Mall which face each other across OK Road.
Both contain a range of eating places and shops, including
craft shops. The market has both a produce section and a
handicraft section.

International editions of British newspapers are generally
on sale and a good selection of books, comics and magazines
is available although at higher prices than in the UK.

EATING AND DRINKING
There is a limited number of reasonable restaurants. By UK
standards prices are cheap and the standard of cuisine and service is acceptable in most cases and very good in others. A
selection of spirits, South African wines and cigarettes is available.

TRANSPORT
Buses are crowded and unreliable and rarely used by visitors.
Taxis are not much better and charges are not regulated.

SECURITY
Muggings and burglaries are increasing. Do not walk in the town centre after dark.

SWEDEN

STOCKHOLM

Language Swedish
Currency krona (plural kronor) (Kr or SEK) of 100 ore. 31=12.42, Mar 1997
Banks 0930–1500 Mon to Fri
Credit cards accepted in most shops
Shops 0900–1800 Mon to Sat; some close earlier Sat
Sales after Christmas
Tipping service charge included in bill at restaurants; taxi drivers 10 per cent on metered fare

Sweden is not cheap. The cost of living is high because of high labour costs and taxation on domestically produced goods, while transport costs lift the prices of any imports. Look for things that the Swedes do best: stylish, well-designed modern livingware. Sweden is not only famous for its cutting edge furniture design, but also for a wide range of household and craft products such as glass (Orrefors, Kosta and Boda), ceramics, pewter, stoneware and wood. Local shops can meet all your needs for heavy winter clothing, so buy what you need to get you through the toughest of winters: fur hats with ear-flaps; warm and wind-proof sheepskin overcoats; fur or down duvets and gloves; and waterproof fur-lined boots with non-slip soles. Prices are high, but sales start just after Christmas. Other items which might interest visitors include traditional Lapp handicrafts made from wood, bone and reindeer skin. Most museums have souvenir shops for art and handicrafts. Alcohol is heavily taxed and generally a bad buy in this part of the world.

The main shopping area is in the centre of the city around Hamngatan. The largest department store NK (Nordiska Kompaniet,18-20 Hamngatan), is a beautiful turn-of-the-century building that now operates as a galleria with 100 separate boutiques. Some of the big Scandinavian design names to look for are Anna Holtblad known for her stylish knitwear, Filippa K's cleverly cut, "Joseph"-type clothing and Thalia's glamorous evening wear. British design is represented by Katherine Hamnett and Paul Smith. NK is also a great place to buy the glass and crystal made in Sweden. Asplund Design (Sibylle Gatan 31) is another great source for glass but also sells trendy furniture, lamps and textiles. Other department stores that are more low-key and less expensive are PUB (at the corner of Drottninggatan and Kungsgatan), and Ahléns (Karlbergvägen 50). Nybrogatan has some good smaller shops. The centre in the Old Town is around Vaterlanggaten and there are hundreds of small shops and restaurants that a visitor should see. The central outdoor market at Hotorget, off Svea Vagen, sells food Monday to Saturday and becomes a craft fair on Sunday. The Ostermalmshallen indoor market at Ostermannstorg is wonderful for Swedish caviar, seafood and game, especially elk and reindeer. Stockholm's largest flea market is held on weekends at the Skarholmen Centre, a 15-20 minute journey from the centre by the underground railway.

English is widely spoken in Sweden. British newspapers and magazines are normally available on the day of publication. There are a number of excellent bookshops which offer a large selection of books in English, but prices can be two or three times as much as in the UK.

EATING AND DRINKING

Stockholm has a wide range of restaurants offering most international cooking styles. Local delicacies such as meatballs, herring, reindeer, salmon pie or chopped meat and potatoes with fried egg and beetroot are readily available in local restaurants. Try Bafikan of Kungstradgarden, Nils-Emil at Folkungagatan 122, and Den Gyldene Freden on Osterlanggatan. Restaurant meals are expensive, particularly if you order alcohol with your meal. Best value is generally to be found on the mandatory daily lunch menu. Smorgasbord is a Swedish invention, and buffet dining remains very popular. For a mid-day break from the frenzy of shopping try either Sophie's Bar (Biblioteksgatan 5) or Opera Bar (Stromgatan 4). The national drink is Aquavit, traditionally drunk with herring and washed down with beer. Iced vodka is another favourite.

TRANSPORT

The public transport system is extensive and very efficient. Tickets are valid for an hour's travel on either bus or the Tunnelbanna (underground). A blue T indicates underground stations. Taxis are readily available and are metered by law, but drivers do not necessarily have the same knowledge of the city as their counterparts in London.

SWITZERLAND

Language **German, French, Italian**
Currency **Swiss franc of 100 rappen or centimes. £1=2.34, Mar 1997**
Banks **hours vary from city to city and between banks**
Credit cards **Mastercard and Visa most commonly accepted, but not in all shops and restaurants**
Cashpoints **yes, for both Swiss and French francs**
Shops **0900–1830 Mon to Fri, earlier closing Sat, late-night shopping Thur. Shops at airports and railway stations stay open later and on Sun. Many shops and restaurants close on Mon**
Sales **Jan and late summer; genuine reductions, good bargains**
Refunds **yes, except for perfumery**
Duty-free **at most large stores and at airport**
Tipping **15 per cent service charge included in hotel and restaurant bills and taxi fares; a small extra tip is customary, but not necessary**

Prices are high, considerably higher than in the UK, but the shops are still a pleasure to browse in. Clothing is expensive and of good quality. Casual clothing in particular can be competitively priced and in ski wear, for example, there is also a vast choice available locally at competitive prices. Shopping is very seasonal – you will not be able to buy a ski suit or fondue set in summer or a barbecue in winter.

Recommendations for gifts or souvenirs include Swiss penknives, Swatch watches or perhaps Calida and Hanro nightwear and underwear. Also worth considering are chocolates, better quality than in the UK, Swiss wine, a curiosity not to be found in the UK, cheese, abundant and tasty. Cow bells and cuckoo clocks are also available.

A reasonable selection of British newspapers is available from the main stations and from kiosks on the day of issue, but *The Times* costs £2.20 and the *Sunday Times* double that. Both books and newspapers cost several times more than the UK price.

Eating out probably provides the best value relative to the UK. The quality of restaurants is universally high. There is an extensive international cuisine with an emphasis on the French and Italian. You should try cheese fondue or raclette at least once. Set-menu luncheons or dinners can be good value.

Wine is relatively expensive considering that Switzerland is a wine-producing country, but it is well worth trying. Production is limited and very little is exported, but there are some excellent light reds and whites. The three regions most often represented are the Valais (pinot noir for reds, fendant for whites and the curious yet tasty Döle Blanche), Vaud (try expecially the whites from Epesses, St Sapharin, Luins and Rolle) and Geneva itself (the Chasselas whites, Gamay reds and Oeil de Perdrix rosé). Swiss chocolate is excellent and easily found. For real self-indulgence buy handmade chocolates from local confectioners.

The shopper will enjoy a high level of security and there will be no hassle with beggars.

BERNE

Most shops are within easy walking distance of the main railway station and located on or around Marktgasse and Spitalgasse. Both streets have many little passages containing a wide variety of shops. Some shops such as C&A, Laura Ashley and Benetton will be familiar, although prices can vary from those in the UK. Most of the other shops are Swiss. Globus in Spitalgasse provides the equivalent of Harrods food hall. Loeb, also in Spitalgasse, is Berne's largest department store. Quality clothes are expensive, casual clothing is more reasonably priced. There are many boutiques in and around Gerechigkeitsgassse, Spitalgasse, Marktgasse, Schauplatzgasse and Schwannengasse. A wide variety of discount shops sell reasonably priced perfumes and cosmetics. The produce market is on Bärenplatz. There is a market on Tuesday and Saturday in Waisenhausplatz which sells antiques, clothing and arts and crafts. Areas for ethnic produce and other things include Munstergasse for Italian, Kramgasse for Hungarian, Duranstrasse in Muri for Indian, Breitenreinstrasse for Thai. Shoppyland is a large shopping centre about 15 minutes' drive from Berne just off the Zurich/Basel autobahn at Schönbuhl.

British newspapers arrive at the main railway station on the afternoon of the day of publication. *The Times* costs SF4. Stauffacher in the Neuengasse also has a good choice of glossy English-language magazines.

EATING AND DRINKING

There are many restaurants in the town and near by. A set menu in an ordinary restaurant will cost something like SF20 each, dinner SF45 including service. A special meal in a good restaurant could cost four times as much. Some of the most formal and expensive restaurants are in hotels. For special ambiance, particularly in summer, try Schwellenmätteli at Dalmaziquai 11, Kirchenfeld at Thunstrasse 5, FähriBeizli in Muri or Moostinte in Münchenbuchsee.

TRANSPORT

There is an excellent system of public transport involving trams, buses, trolley-buses and a suburban railway service. Passengers must always purchase a ticket before boarding and there are on-the-spot fines for those who do not. One ticket is necessary for one journey in a particular direction, but is interchangeable between trams and buses. Multiple-use tickets are available. Taxis do not ply for hire, but can be obtained at a taxi rank or by phone. They are expensive and although service is included in the price, a small tip is customary.

GENEVA

Geneva is a modern cosmopolitan city with excellent shopping facilities and international tastes. The main shopping areas lie on both sides of the Rhone, where large department stores such as Grand Passage and Placette are to be found as well as familiar chain stores and small boutiques. Bon Genie is also on the Rue du Rhône, up-market, high quality and with prices akin to Harrods. The Old Town is a maze of galleries, antique shops, bookshops, restaurants and cafés.

There are three large shopping centres close to Geneva. Balexert is a large, covered shopping centre approached from either the Route de Meyrin or the Avenue Louis Caswai; there is a supermarket and department store as well as other shops. Chavannes Centre is at the Coppet turn-off of the Geneva Lausanne motorway, and among others Body Shop, Mothercare and Benetton are here. Meyrin is off the Route de Meyrin.

There are open-air markets all over Geneva on different

days of the week. There is a flea market at the Pleinpalais on Wednesday afternoon and on Saturday from 0700 to 1700. The French border towns of Ferney Voltaire and Divonne have open-air markets on Saturday and Sunday mornings respectively. Selling mainly food, they are picturesque and fun.

Nyon is an ancient town on the lakeside about 30 minutes from Geneva, which can be reached by train. There is a compact shopping area centred around the La Combe Centre and many smaller shops in town waiting to be discovered.

Antique books and prints can be found in the Old Town of Geneva and in Nyon and are surprisingly reasonable. There are lots of local artists and many scenes of lakes and mountains are available. Decorated porcelain is a speciality in Nyon. There is an excellent toy shop called Pinocchio at 10 Rue E. Dumont in the Old Town of Geneva with lots of wooden handmade toys.

The shopping area at Geneva Airport is open seven days a week.

The *Geneva Post*, a daily English-language newspaper, was launched in 1994 with quality local and international news coverage. For English-language books try Elm Books at 5 Rue Versonnex near the Jardin Anglais or Payot SA, one of whose main branches is just off the Rue Mont Blanc oppposite the Gare Routière. The Bookworm in Rue Sismondi near Cornavin Railway Station deals in second-hand English language books.

EATING AND DRINKING
A number of restaurants serve fish from the lake, most common being *filets de perche*. If you visit in the autumn the *chasse* or game season is not to be missed. Try the Rendezvous des Chasseurs at La Batie, Versoix, but dine early. You will not get a table after 2130.

TRANSPORT
The centre of Geneva is relatively small and distances between most hotels and shops can be easily walked. There are excellent fixed-price bus and tram services. Plenty of taxis are available, but they are expensive except for short journeys in town.

ZURICH

The Old Town on the banks of the Limmat with its narrow alleyways, numerous antique shops, restaurants and bars is worth exploring. There is a Thursday and Saturday handicraft market in this area, but prices are not cheap. There is a flea market on Saturdays between May and October at Burkliplatz at the lake end of Bahnhofstrasse.

The Bahnhofstrasse itself is a famous shopping street with many designer shops such as Chanel with prices to match. It also contains a number of large department stores such as Jelmoli, Manor and Globus. Migros City just off the Bahnhofstrasse offers a range of cheaper clothing and toiletries. So do ABM and EPA in Bellevue near the Quai Brucke.

Heimatwerk is the local handicraft shop and stocks wooden toys and ornaments, quality glass and embroidery. Best duty-free buys at the airport include chocolate, penknives and schnapps.

There is an English bookshop, Stahelis, on Bahnhofstrasse, but prices are higher than in the UK.

EATING AND DRINKING

Visitors must try at least one of the many coffee-houses to eat, or at least to look at, the variety of cakes available. Sprungli in Bahnhofstrasse is good. The Zunfthauses (Guildhouses) offer daily menus at reasonable prices for the standard of cuisine. A number can be found on the Limmatquai such as Saffron, Ruden and Zimmerleuten.

TRANSPORT

Tram, trolley-bus and bus services are good. Tickets must be purchased before boarding and a range of travelcards is available. Fines for travelling without a ticket are severe. Taxis are reputedly the most expensive in the world.

SYRIA

DAMASCUS

Language **Arabic**
Currency **Syrian pound (S£) of 100 piastres.**
  £1=67.20, Mar 1997
Banks **currency other than US dollars is difficult to exchange; hotel bills are quoted and normally paid in dollars**
Traveller's cheques **dollar denominated**
Credit cards **occasionally useful, especially for airline tickets**
Shops **1000–1400, 1700–1900**
Sales **occasionally in clothes shops**
Refunds **possible**
Bargaining **yes, in markets**
Tipping **waiters expect small tips; amount depends on number being served and standard of restaurant. 10-20 per cent to taxi drivers**

Damascus is a city crammed with shops, many of which you do not realise exist until after dark, as in the daylight they blend in with the buildings and seemingly disappear. No addresses and hardly any street names are used so directions are difficult to give. Check with your hotel porter if in doubt. Excellent English is spoken at shops in the souk and others selling principally to visitors.

Damascus souvenirs lend themselves to home decoration. Carpets, rugs, brass, copper, silverware, embroidered table-cloths, inlaid furniture, the famous Damascus silk brocade and local wall decorations are easily obtainable in the souk. These are of varying quality and price. It is customary to bargain and always wise to go initially with somebody who knows the market.

The souk is a renowned and absolutely fascinating ancient shopping area, and visitors will wish to make this the first stop for shopping. The Souk al Hamadiyeh runs from near the Citadel to the Omayad Mosque. Its traders make an excellent living from tourists and their prices are generally grossly inflated. The Street Called Straight is to the south and runs parallel to Souk Al Hamadiyeh. Between these two is a labyrinth of tiny streets and alleyways. There is an area in the souk for just about everything including kitchenware, rugs, toys, haberdashery, gold, spices, paper, plastics and other merchandise. You can find beautiful inlaid boxes, pearl necklaces, silver old and new as well as a myriad other things in this veritable Aladdin's cave. Tony Stephan's, a shop located about half-way down Souk al Hamadiyeh, where the roof is uncovered, sells virtually all Damascene handicrafts and a fine range of silk brocade. Prices are reasonable and quality is good. The Cave is an excellent fixed-price tablecloth shop which also sells a few boxes, caftans, T-shirts, etc. To get there turn up to the right just before the pillars before the neon Cave Exhibition sign. If you want to buy gold, ask for directions to Garo's in the new gold souk. The sign reads G.Oustayan. For new silver try Michael at Saladdin's. Facing the Omayad Mosque you turn left and left again. Look for the shop on the right with the old wooden chest outside (and the best loo in the souk inside!).

The handicraft souk is located just before the Semiramis Hotel, on the opposite side of the road to the Meridien Hotel, but towards the main souk. (Look for the Military Museum.) It is worth a look, but prices tend to be a little high. There are pottery and glass shops as well as the usual Damascene craft shops.

Saliyeh, a pleasant pedestrianised area, is parallel to Hamrah Street which runs up from the Cham Palace Hotel. In both streets you will find a good selection of fairly up-market clothing and some shoes.

Best buys popular with tourists include silver, pearls, backgammon sets, marble and other items mentioned above as well as sewing notions and materials for dressmakers, silk brocade ties, waistcoats and the brocade itself. All these items can be found in the souk and elsewhere.

If you wish to see glass-blowing, the factory is located near Bab Sharqi. Cross the dual carriageway, turn to the left, then take the first right and first right again. Only one colour of glass is blown at a time. Prices are cheap, but the quality is poor. It is possible to see many other items such as inlay work and silk brocade being made. Your hotel porter should be able to give more information.

A two- or three-day-old copy of the *Daily Telegraph* will cost about £2 at a hotel bookshop, but few British magazines and newspapers are available. The English-language daily *Syrian Post* costs S£5. The Sheraton, Cham and Meridien hotels all have good bookshops. Prices are higher than in the UK.

EATING AND DRINKING

Every visitor should sample at least one Arab meal. This normally comprises mezze, a selection of cold hors d'oeuvres and dips with pitta bread, followed by chicken and/or meat on a skewer, and salad. Many restaurants serve no alcohol. In Abu el Ezz, off Souk Al Hamadiyeh (mosque end) you can be assured of good Arab food at a reasonable cost, served in a mock Bedouin tent. On Thursday evenings at 2230 you will be treated to a performance by whirling dervishes. Restaurant Square south of the canal between Malki Street and Abu Rumaneh has many good restaurants, including the Chevalier and Chaumière. The Zeitoun (Street Called Straight, right before Bab Sharqi) serves excellent Arab food in a beautiful courtyard setting. Al Fursan, beside the American School in Malki, and the Snobar near the Habitat sign on the Autostrade in Mezzeh, should also be mentioned. Some Syrian delicacies are prepared with uncooked meat, which some people may prefer to avoid. Local soft drinks and mixers are satisfactory. Syrian beer and wine are cheap, but of middling quality. Lebanese beer and wine are popular. Local cigarettes are very strong.

TRANSPORT

Most shopping areas are within walking distance of the main hotels, but sensible clothing and shoes should be worn and a bottle of water carried during the summer, when walking can be particularly exhausting. The bus and microbus services are cheap, but can be overcrowded. Yellow taxis are metered and no fare should be more than 50 pence around town. Many drivers will speak only Arabic and the cab might be quite dilapidated.

SECURITY

Damascus is a relatively safe city, and even women, modestly dressed, should be safe enough walking around alone.

TAHITI

(SEE FRENCH POLYNESIA)

TAIWAN

TAIPEI

Language **Mandarin Chinese**
Currency **new Taiwan dollar (NT$) of 100 cents.**
£1=44.10, Mar 1997
Traveller's cheques **dollar denominated**
Credit cards **accepted in big hotels, department**
stores and shops catering for Westerners
Cashpoints **cash can be drawn with Visa cards at**
Bank of America
Shops **1000/1100–2000/2200**
Sales **not genuine**
Bargaining **yes, in markets and small shops**
Duty-free **not recommended**
Tipping **only hotel and airport porters**

Shops stretch far and wide and there are many markets scattered all over the city. Few people in shops will speak English and no one in the markets will: few street signs are in English and hardly any taxi-drivers speak the language. Several staples in the Western diet are hard to come by or expensive. Electrical goods and tailored clothing are cheaper in Hong Kong. Ready-made clothing in Western styles and sizes is reasonably priced, but fashions tend to be in small sizes only. Locally made silk, cotton and straw slippers for house wear are attractive and inexpensive. Larger shoe sizes may be hard to find. Pirated books and tapes used to be cheap, but the government has now clamped down on copyright infringement. Standard CDs will cost less than in the UK. Golf clubs are well priced and available in most sports shops such as Benny's at 669 Lin Sen North Road, Golf Store at 151 Chung Shan North Road Section 7 and Nevada Bob's at 113 Szu Ping Lu.

A good shopping overview is given by the larger department stores such as Mitsukoshi at 12 Nanking West Road, Pacific Sogo at 45 Chung Hsiao East Road Section 4, Sunrise at 15 Fu Hsing North Road, Shinkong Mitsukosi near the Hilton and Takashimkaya at Tien Mu.

Traditional favourites with visitors are the export stores (also known as outlet stores). These are mostly clothing stores that stock seconds or over-runs from export factories in Taiwan. They still exist although in smaller numbers than before and stocks tend to come and go. The prices are attractive and you will see many well-known labels. Check the items for faults. Try Ding Hau off Chung Hsiao East Road or Chungshan North Road Section 7 in Tien Mu.

The Taipei World Trade Center gives a comprehensive view of all products manufactured in Taiwan. Although many of the stores deal only with trade enquiries, some are able to provide shoppers with samples at attractive prices, but these are strictly for export only.

The ancient art of cloisonné is practised in Taiwan. Pendants on silk cords, thimbles, napkin rings, stick pins and pill boxes can be found in many handicraft and jewellery stores. Try China Cloisonné at 10–6 Lane 49, Shuang Cheng Street, items range from inexpensive gifts to large floor-standing vases. The quality is excellent. Try also the government-sponsored Chinese Handicraft Mart at 1 Hsu Chou Road or Taiwan Crafts Centre in the Rebar department store at 14 Nanking West Road.

Taiwan jade and coral are plentiful and can be fashioned into rings, pendants, earrings, beads and carved figures. Try the Jade Market under the Chien Kuo Highway at Chung Hsaio East Road Section 3 or Jade Alley at Alley 3, Lane 89, Nan King East Road Section 3. Check all jade items for cracks or flaws.

Calligraphy items such as brushes are obtainable at Ta Chang Painting Supplies at 104 Chang An West Road or Ta Lib Stationery at 138 Tai Yuan Road.

Reproductions of National Palace Museum porcelains, bronzes and ceramics can be purchased at the museum and at many other outlets. Copies of blue and white Ming and early Ch'ing dynasty porcelain seem to be most popular. Reproductions of T'ang horses and other figures are also popular. Most hotel shopping arcades have shops which will make your own "name chop" for you with the astrological sign for the year of your birth incorporated in the seal.

Sanyi is two hours south of Taipei. On the main street, Chung Cheng Road, there is a great selection of woodcarvings at lower prices than can be found in other major cities. Yingko is one hour south-west of Taipei and is the centre of the pottery trade. There are hand-painted replicas of elegant Ming and Ch'ing vases. The narrow streets are lined with shops selling a variety of reasonably priced porcelain.

There are dozens of markets in Taipei, including excellent large open-air food markets. Be watchful for spoiled goods. The East Gate Market has handicrafts and a wide range of other goods. It is on both sides of Chin Shan South Road. In Ding Hua Street, apart from the fabric market, there are temple stores and Chinese herbal medicine shops. The Kuang Hua Market under the bridge of that name sells antiques and old books, handicrafts and electronic goods. The Kung Kuan Market at Ting Chou Road Section 3 has a wide variety of goods. The Cheng Chung Market sells clothing and produce. It is in the area at the intersection of Wu Chang Section 1 and Chung King Road Section 1. The Szu Ping Market in the street of that name has clothes, shoes, jewellery and accessories. The Tai Yuan Market in the road of that name has clothing, jewellery and other goods. The Ching Kuang Market has a wide variety of goods. It is off Chung Shan North Road Section 2 near Nung An Street. There is also the Pin Chiang flower and produce market at 366 Nin Tsu East Road. The fresh produce in the local markets is of high quality. Many local fruits are available only in season, but the variety is so great there are always several to choose from. There are many varieties of vegetable not obtainable in the West. The markets are closed for two variable days each month, listed in the local newspapers, but your hotel should also be able to advise you.

Two English-language newspapers are published daily, the *China Post* and the *China News*. The *Financial Times* is the only British newspaper obtainable, apart from weekly editions of the *Express*, *Telegraph* and *Herald Tribune*. There are many Western magazines, always American. The various branches of Caves or Eslite bookstores have a limited range of English-language books, which are expensive.

Eating and Drinking

Seafood, pork, fruit and noodles are all excellent. Every style of Chinese food may be tried at reasonable prices. English is not normally spoken. Try Tong Men restaurant at 37, Lane 31, Chin Shan Road, Section 2; San Hsi Chin Chi at 83 Yen Ping South Road or North Sea Fishing Village Restaurant at 8 Han Chou South Road Section 1. Mongolian and Korean barbecues are available cheaply, but most other foreign food restaurants tend to be very expensive. Depending on the season, fruit can be expensive or cheap, but the selection is amazing, much of it not available in the West. Try a shot of mao tai, a fermented rice wine. The Shihlin Night Market in the area bordered by Wen Lin Road, Chi Ho Road and Chung Cheng Road sells a wide range of goods and many food stalls sell Chinese delicacies.

Transport

Transport will probably be required to the main shopping areas. There is a price difference between air-conditioned and other buses; all have their destinations marked in Mandarin. Buses accept pre-paid cards, not cash. Taxis are ubiquitous and cheaper than the London variety although the driving can be hair-raising. All have meters and many carry a sticker 'please pay NT$ 15 extra'. This is legitimate because of a new government tax.

Security

Shop with the usual care and attention for personal security. Beggars are normally no problem.

Tanzania

Dar es Salaam

Language **Kiswahili, English**
Currency **Tanzanian shilling (sh) of 100 cents.**
 £1=810, Sep 1994
Banks **only hard currency cash or traveller's**
 cheques can be exchanged for shillings
Credit cards **only accepted by European airlines**
Shops **0800–1200, 1400–1715/1800 Mon to Sat**
Tipping **expected for usual services, e.g. hair-**
 dressers and taxi drivers

For souvenirs and craftwork try Nyumba ya Sanaa (House of Art) at the Upanga/UWT roundabout or Ebony Carvers on University Road. There are also plenty of shops and street traders on Samora Avenue selling carvings and other crafts. Makonde carvings can be bought from street sellers outside the Palm Beach Hotel. For souvenirs try also the shops in the Oyster Bay Hotel and Kilimanjaro Hotel. Tinga Tinga paintings and painted trays are popular. Zanzibar carved furniture such as chests, coffee tables, backgammon and chess boards can be bought at the Zanzibar Curio Shop off Samora Avenue near St Joseph's Cathedral and at shops in the Kilimanjaro Hotel and the Bahari Beach Shop. The Zanzibar Silver Curio Shop in Mansfield Street and Silver Curio Shop in Samora Avenue are good for gold and precious or semi-precious stones as well as silver. There are also many jewellery shops around the Market Street and Aggrey Street area.

Kinondoni Market in Kinondoni Road has not only produce, but other goods such as kangas and occasionally birds and animals. Kariakoo Market behind Msimbazi Street is the wholesale and retail covered market. Security can be a problem here. The fish market is at the harbour entrance end of Ocean Road.

There are many shops around the Morogoro Road area and in Zanaki Street with a wide selection of fabrics and there are some excellent and cheap local tailors, for example Rathod at the corner of Aggrey and Jamhuri Street. For local ready-made casual clothing you could try Afro Fashion or Sun City in Samora Avenue. Liberty Leather Shoes on Pugu Road just past the end of Nkrumah Street has good locally produced shoes. There are numerous other shoe shops along Samora Avenue.

There is an English-language newspaper, the *Daily News* and its Sunday edition, the *Sunday News*. It is owned and controlled by the government. The best magazines include the *Business Times*, the *Express* and the *Family Mirror*. Novel Idea at the Casanova shopping centre has a reasonable supply of imported books, at a price. International newspapers and magazines are obtainable along Samora Avenue and Maktaba Street.

EATING AND DRINKING
There are a few reasonably good restaurants and others where the standard is acceptable. Popular eating places are the New Africa Hotel, Motel Agip, Palm Beach Hotel and the roof-top restaurant in the Kilimanjaro Hotel (recommended for the view rather than the food). Also recommended are the Alcove in Samora Avenue and the Bushtrekker at the Upanga Street/UWT Street roundabout.

TRANSPORT
There is a very limited bus service. Buses are generally crowded and badly driven and little used by expatriates. Taxis are obtainable in the city and charges are subject to bargaining. They are in a run-down condition and should be used only as a last resort.

SECURITY
Vigilance is needed. Burglaries and muggings are not uncommon.

THAILAND

BANGKOK

Language Thai, Chinese
Currency baht of 100 satang, freely convertible and
  tied to US dollar. £1=41.57, Mar 1997
Banks 0830–1530 Mon to Fri
Credit cards accepted in major stores; some give
  discount for cash
Cashpoints yes
Shops 1000–2200, markets 0900–1930, Mon to Sat
Refunds possible in major stores with receipt
Sales yes, with genuine bargains
Bargaining for most purchases, but not in major
  stores
Duty-free at airport, in World Trade Centre and
  Ploenchit Road, but not good value
Tipping 10 per cent in restaurants without service
  charge, otherwise 20 baht. Taxi drivers are not
  tipped
Export restrictions licence needed from Fine Arts
  Department (obtainable from reputable shops) for
  antiques and works of art

You can buy anything in Bangkok if you know where to look
for it. The standard of local produce is high and prices tend to
be cheaper than similar imported articles. Many consumer
goods and durables are now produced locally under licence.
English is the first Western language in Bangkok.

Bangkok has many different shopping areas, but most visitors
will get to know only the areas around Silom Road, Sukhumvit
Road, Ploenchit Road, Ratcha-Damri Road and Ratcha-Prarop
Road. Here there are many shops and air-conditioned malls. On
Ratch-Damri Road there are two shopping malls – the World
Trade Centre and Gaysorn Plaza - both selling a wide range of
local and imported goods. Opposite the World Trade Centre
is the Narayana Phan Pavilion which sells traditional Thai arts
and crafts, antiques and jewellery on the top floor. The base-
ment is full of stalls selling fake designer clothes, jeans, videos,
CDs, silk clothes and arts and crafts. Central City Mall is very
good out on Bang-na Trat. There is a large well-stocked
Central Department Store plus many other smaller shops.
Central has a Marks and Spencer outlet on the ground floor.

You will find many well-known Western names such as Next and Body Shop represented in the malls, but at prices usually higher than in the UK. Seacon Square, a little further out, has masses of shops. Pratunam Market is a good place to buy locally made clothing such as T-shirts and jeans, which are much cheaper than anywhere else.

Ready-made clothing is available, but sizing is small. If you are over size 10 you may have problems. Imported clothing attracts a high import tax. Casual fake designer clothing of an acceptable standard can be purchased cheaply from market stalls. Trousers, suits and shorts can all be made to measure satisfactorily in a few days. There are many good-value tailors along Sukhumvit Road. Made-to-measure shirts from cheaper tailors may have ill-fitting collars. Made-to-measure and ready-made shoes are available from 1000 baht. Sports clothing and equipment can be cheaper than in the UK. Spectacles and frames are good value.

The best bargains are Thai silk and locally made casual wear. Thai silk ranges from 260 baht a yard for lightweight material up to 500 baht for Jim Thompson fabric. Thai handicrafts include woodcarvings, jewellery, silk picture frames, cutlery, pewterware, silk artificial flowers, pottery and hand-painted umbrellas or fans. Ceramics include blue and white pottery as well as Bencharong porcelain decorated exquisitely in multi-coloured enamels. Jewellery is available in the World Trade Centre, Central Department Store at Bangna, Maboonklong Shopping Centre and Chinatown (Yaowarat Road). Craft items can be bought at Sports in Pratunam Rachaprarop Road, Narayana Phan Pavilion or in the weekend market at Chatuchak.

The *Financial Times* and the weekly editions of the *Telegraph* and *Express* are available locally. The *Weekly Telegraph* costs 95 baht. There are three locally produced daily English-language newspapers of quite good quality which cost 15 baht. Asia Books Store has nine branches in Bangkok and stocks an excellent range of books and magazines. There is a large DK bookstore at Seacon Square, just outside Bangkok.

EATING AND DRINKING

Eating out is no problem. It is possible to eat good Thai food for 250 baht upwards. Popular Thai restaurants include Lemongrass in Sukhumvit Soi 24, Whole Earth in Soi Lang Suan and Cabbages in Sukhumvit Soi 12. There are many other restaurants with international cuisines from sushi to spaghetti, soufflé or steak. All budgets are catered for from fast-food outlets to some of the world's finest hotels.

TRANSPORT
You can walk from most central hotels to the main shopping centres. Flat comfortable shoes are essential for walking on the dusty broken-up pavements. There is a public bus service which is cheap, but it can be very crowded at rush hour. Taxis are plentiful and inexpensive. Most taxis now have meters, but ensure that they are switched on. Traffic is notoriously bad and it may be quicker to walk anyway.

SECURITY
Security is not a problem and beggars are not troublesome, but watch out for pickpockets.

TOGO

LOME

Language **French**
Currency **franc CFA West African. £1=798, Sep 1996**
Shops **0800–1200, 1500–1800 Mon to Fri, closed Sat afternoon**

Togo is a small country which enjoys a deservedly big reputation. It is an attractive place and has good food and things worth buying.

The centre of town is in and around the Rue de la Gare towards the ocean end. Towards the northern end is the SGCT department store. The market lies just to the east of the Rue de la Gare and is good for fabrics, handicrafts and sandals. The fetish market is in Akodessewa about five miles from the centre and entails a taxi ride. It is touristy and not without hassle, but worth a visit, probably to enjoy the atmosphere rather than to buy.

Sandals are good quality and plentiful. Crafts worth looking out for include brasswork, carvings, jewellery and textiles.

There are one or two decent bookshops in Rue du Commerce, off Rue de la Gare, but French books and newspapers sell mostly.

EATING AND DRINKING
There are good food and good restaurants. French cuisine and seafood are particularly recommended. Look in the area on and around Boulevard du 13 Janvier. Local beer is excellent.

TRANSPORT
Taxis are plentiful, but not metered. Establish the fare before starting.

SECURITY
There is a high level of street crime. Do not venture out after dark.

TONGA

Language **Tongan, English**
Currency **Tongan pa'anga (T$) of 100 senifi.**
£1=1.95, Mar 1997
Tipping **not customary, but welcomed**

Ready-made casual clothing, mainly imported from Asia, is available locally, although it is not always to European taste, size or quality. There is a duty-free shop at the Dateline Hotel.

EATING AND DRINKING
There are two European restaurants serving mainly seafood and steak, and one Chinese restaurant of acceptable standard and reasonable price. At the best restaurant a large lobster dish will cost about T$25 and a decent bottle of wine the same or a little more although some restaurants allow you to bring your own wine. Tongan Royal beer is good.

TRANSPORT
Buses are not reliable. Taxis are available except on Sundays at a reasonable price.

SECURITY
There is no pestering and security is not a real problem.

TRINIDAD AND TOBAGO

PORT OF SPAIN

Language **English**

Currency **Trinidad and Tobago dollar (TT$) of 100 cents. £1=9.92, Mar 1997**

Banks **0800–1230 Mon to Thur, 0800–1200, 1500–1700 Fri**

Credit cards **Visa and Mastercard widely accepted in main centres and hotels**

Cashpoints **yes**

Shops **0900–1700, suburban malls till 1900 Mon to Sat, some Sun opening; markets 0500–1000 Wed to Sun**

Bargaining **most prices fixed; discounts possible from street vendors**

Duty-free **at airport and Stechers in Long Circular Mall and West Mall; take passport and departure ticket; spirits and cigarettes at airport are good value, otherwise not always cheaper than in town or in UK**

Tipping **service charge normally included in bills; small extra tip appreciated**

Shopping in the centre of town can be a very hot, sticky affair. The main shopping area lies to the north of Independence Square and is roughly bounded by St Vincent and Abercromby streets to the west, Henry Street to the east and Park Street to the north. The centre is a good place to look for cheaper goods such as cosmetics and textiles; roadside vendors sell locally made leatherware (such as sandals and handbags), music tapes (calypso, reggae, soca and steelpan) and ethnic jewellery.

The cruise ship terminal is open to the general public and has souvenir and gift shops, including a branch of Stecher's, a Caribbean chain store. Most of the big hotels such as the Hilton also have decent shops. The Central Market is on Wrightson Road and opens every morning Wednesday to Sunday inclusive from 0500 to 1000. Saturday is good for fish and shrimps.

Away from the centre, to the north and west, are several good shopping malls – Long Circular Mall in St James near the American Embassy, West Mall at Westmoorings and Ellerslie Plaza in St Clair. Further afield are Valpark Shopping

Plaza on the Churchill-Roosevelt Highway at Valsayn and the latest addition to the retail scene, Grand Bazaar about twenty minutes' drive east of Port of Spain at the junction of the Churchill-Roosevelt and Uriah Butler Highways.

There are several places to look for local gifts and souvenirs such as the Normandie Hotel complex in Nook Avenue, St Ann's. Inn Side is at Coblentz Avenue, St Ann's. At the Long Circular Mall there are Cocoyea, Jackie Smith, the Signature Collection, Roukou and Cattleya. At West Mall are Maca Fouchette, Pop-In, Precious Little and Niftees. At Elleslie Plaza are Poui Batik and Niftees.

Niftees and B-Tees brands of T-shirts are quite good buys. Local pottery such as Ajoupa and Make or batik from Ellerslie Plaza also make nice gifts and souvenirs. There is a local equivalent to the David Winter/Lilliput Lane cottage ranges made by Llanos and Maingot and available at quality gift shops in the malls and elsewhere. Some locally made jewellery and copper or bronze items from places such as the Signature Collection are also popular. Budding musicians can buy steel pans at Lincoln Enterprises at 68 Ariapita Avenue, Woodbrook. Jane Albert watercolours are popular among local art items. Most portable are bottles of hot pepper sauce or Angostura.

The flowers sold in the shops and by roadside vendors are quite magnificent. The Caribbean Flower Shop in Abercromby Street will do travel packs.

Tobago has limited shopping with the focus on crafts. All the large hotels have small boutiques. The Cotton House in Scarborough has batik and tie-dye items as well as other gifts; you can also see batik being made. Stecher's has a branch in Scarborough.

There are three local daily newspapers and some mainly American imported dailies and magazines are available. There are bookshops at all the malls as well as in the town centre. Most of the big hotels have paperbacks on sale, but they are imported and expensive.

EATING AND DRINKING

There are many restaurants offering all types of food. Generally they are of good standard and are value for money. For a culinary experience try local Creole food from Veni Mange in Ariapita Avenue in Woodbrook or the Verandah at 13 Rust Street, St Clair. The Breakfast Shed at the Cruise Ship Complex is basic, but with original, fresh and mainly good local cuisine. Otherwise for Chinese try Singhoo at the Long Circular Mall (which also has a fast-food area), Tiki Village at the Kapok Hotel or Imperial Garden in Saddle Road, Maraval. For Italian food there are the Gourmet Club at Ellerslie Plaza, Trees at 58 Frederick Street and Pavio's at the Shoppes of Maraval. For international cuisine try Solimar at 6 Nook Avenue in St Ann's or Rafter's at 6a Warner Street.

For eating on the go there are some tasty and addictive local foods such as roti (curried meat or vegetables in an unleavened bread chapati) and shark 'n' bake (grilled shark in a roll). The quality of locally grown tropical fruits is good.

TRANSPORT

Minibuses and route taxis are privately operated, cheap, but not recommended. Taxis are expensive, but relatively safe. Fares to out-of-town tourist sights are quoted in US dollars.

SECURITY

Port of Spain is no worse than any other large city, provided normal rules of personal security are observed. Do not be ostentatious. Avoid the centre of town after dark. Also avoid lonely beaches.

TRISTAN DA CUNHA

Language **English**
Currency **pound sterling; US dollars, Deutschmarks and South African rands accepted**
Banks **none**
Traveller's cheques **change at Government Treasury Office**
Shops **0830–1230, 1330–1600**
Refunds **defective goods can be exchanged**
Sales **occasional**
Tipping **not expected, but acceptable**

Sophisticated shopping is unlikely on an island which received its first incoming mail since January 1996 – via fishing boat – in late June 1996!

Tristan is the world's most remote inhabited island and is only accessible by sea. Shopping is restricted to essentials. Short-stay visitors will return to their ship by night.

The only shopping area is in the settlement of Edinburgh of the Seven Seas. There are only three shops (no chain stores or designer boutiques as yet, maybe because the resident population of only 290 is insufficient incentive). They are the Supermarket, the Agriculture Shop and the Handicraft Shop. The Supermarket is known locally as the Canteen and is recommended more for casual gazing than for serious window shopping. Some island T-shirts may interest the visitor.

Best local buys are all available from the Handicraft Shop, which is located in the museum. Souvenirs include woollen articles ranging from jumpers to knitted penguins, model longboats and bullock carts as well as a range of coasters, plaques and table mats. The post office sells a range of first-day covers and loose stamps as well as postcards.

There are no British papers or magazines available, apart from the *Tristan Times*, published quarterly and available from the Administration Office.

EATING AND DRINKING
There are no hotels, restaurants, boarding houses or bed-and-breakfast establishments. There is a private enterprise café which sells beer and spirits on Sunday mornings. A slice of Tristan crayfish pie in the café is recommended while you are there. The café is open all day when ships are visiting. The annexe to the village hall is the pub, open daily in the evening except Sunday.

TUNISIA

TUNIS

Language **Arabic, French**
Currency **dinar of 1,000 millemes. £1=1.73,
    Mar 1997**
Banks **0800–1100, 1400–1600 Mon to Thur, 0800–1100,
    1300–1500 Fri in winter; 0730–1100 Mon to Fri in
    summer**
Credit cards **accepted by most hotels, airlines and
    banks**
Bargaining **yes, in souks and antique shops**
Tipping **10–15 per cent service charge in hotels
    and restaurants; round up bills by small
    amounts; extra for good service not expected, but
    appreciated**
Export restrictions **it is illegal to export antiques**

Imports are expensive and the local products are of variable
quality and availability. Olive oil is a famous Tunisian product,
but the first pressing is exported.

Knotted carpets and flat, woven rugs called kilims are sold
in the Medina and in Sidi Bou Said. Prices vary tremendously
according to style and quality. The ONAT, the official state
crafts organisation, grades carpets and the tags show the
materials used as well as the number of knots and the weight
of the carpet. La Rachidia at 11 Souk Ettouk has antique carpets upstairs. The Musée des Turcs carpet shop is in the Souk
el Trouk. It is worth remembering that Tunisian carpets,
although attractive, are not particularly prized internationally.

The ONAT has its own shop on Avenue Mohammed V
with a wide range of good quality items of all sorts: although
it tends to be expensive, it provides a good starting point for
the shopper who wishes to see what is available and at what
sort of price. The Rue Djema Zitouna next to the Great
Mosque is overpriced and aimed squarely at the tourist market.
Prices are better in the Medina.

Jewellery available in the Souk des Orfèvres includes coral
as well as silver and gold. There are some interesting carvings
such as salad bowls in olive wood as well as some attractive
articles in hammered metal like trays and plates. Copper pots
are a good buy. Try the Central Market or the Rue de Cuivre.
For lamps try Inter Equipment at 5 Rue d'Alger, Meublentub

at 40 Avenue Bourguiba or Habib Basly at 31 Avenue de la Liberté. Leather goods are not particularly recommended, but those interested should go to Atelier Gaiasse at 24 Rue Salah Ben Mrad near Le Jardin metro station. Embroidery is a speciality. Try Fathia Djemali at 14 Rue de l'Argentine. Soft-toy camels are immensely popular, but hardly traditional.

There are flea markets at Ariana on Thursday and Friday mornings, daily at the Rue Zirkoun in the Medina and daily near le Bardo and Place de la Hafsia in the Medina.

For antique shops try the Rue Zirkoun or the Rue des Glacières, as well as the Medina. Recommended shops include Antiques in Rue Autriche, Au Fil du Temps at 5 Rue de la Clinique in Mutuelleville, Marché de la Brocante at 8 Rue Youssef Rouissi, near Cité Saba, Musée des Arts Antiques in a side-street near Le Passage el Menzah, Atyka Antiques next to Sidi Bou Said railway station, L'Antiquaire in Avenue Bourguiba in Le Kram.

There are department stores in all parts of Tunis. The major ones are Magasin General, Monoprix, and Touta. Local clothing is available in the Souk al Khachachine, but is not recommended.

British newspapers are available on the bookstalls, usually a day or two after publication. English-language periodicals are not generally available. Few bookshops sell books in English, and the range is very limited.

EATING AND DRINKING

There are many reasonable restaurants although the fare offered by the majority is very similar. Fish and seafood are popular and often very good. The national dish is couscous – semolina with vegetables, meat or fish served with a piquant sauce. There is an ethnic restaurant in the Medina itself. Most restaurants are licensed, serving acceptable local wines and beer and (more expensive) spirits. There is a good selection of soft and fizzy drinks.

For restaurants try Le Regent behind the Africa Hotel car park or Le Cabestan at 33 Rue el Aziz. In the suburbs there are also Au Bon Vieux Temps near the TGM station at La Marsa, Restaurant l'Atlantide on the Corniche at La Marsa and Le Golfe on the beach at La Marsa.

TRANSPORT

There are regular bus services which can be crowded and uncomfortable.

TURKEY

Language Turkish
Currency Turkish lira (TL) of 100 kurus. £1=49,
  Mar 1997
Banks 0830–1200, 1330–1800 Mon to Fri
Credit cards accepted in many shops and hotels,
  though surcharge may be imposed, and in cash-
  points
Cashpoints yes
Shops 0900–1300,1400–1900 Mon to Fri, 0900–1200,
  1300–2000 Sat
Sales Jan and Jul; good bargains
Bargaining in all but the most up-market shops
Tipping expected in addition to 15 per cent service
  charge in hotels and restaurants; taxi drivers are
  not tipped
Export restrictions antiques are subject to strict
  regulations

Turkish carpets and kilims enjoy a high reputation. Basically
you get what you pay for, silk carpets being the most expensive.
Gold, silver and semi-precious stones are sold by weight rather
than according to workmanship. Other best buys include traditional products such as flutes and other musical instruments,
hand-beaten copper and brassware, inlaid wood such as
backgammon boards, water ewers, onyx or hookah pipes.
Turkish towels are excellent quality and good value. Caviar is
often smuggled into Turkey, but do not be tempted: it could be
awful.

Good leather, suede and sheepskin jackets and coats can be
bought as well as women's shoes, although larger sizes are difficult to find. Ready-made clothing is freely available in styles
modern and European, but it is of varying quality. There is
quite a good selection of casual clothes.

Pirated records, tapes and CDs can be found, but must not
be imported into Europe or the USA.

Local wine is inexpensive and perfectly acceptable for
everyday drinking, particularly the white. Locally produced
Efes and Tuborg beers are available. Local raki (aniseed) and
liqueurs are good and cheap. Fruit squashes are syrupy and
sweet, but pure fruit juices are good.

Lokum is Turkish delight. Baklava is a mille-feuilles pastry.
Ayran is a yoghurt drink mixed with water and salt.

ANKARA

Facilities are reasonably good, with a plentiful supply of buses and taxis around the city and fairly easy shopping. Most goods and services are now available and the range is increasing all the time. Hills, traffic and the habit of using the pavement for parking discourage walking. Many streets are badly lit with holes in the pavements. Winter can be very cold and icy, slushy or muddy. Moon boots are available and advisable.

Visitors should go to the old shops in Cikrikcilar Yokusu, near Ulus. Bakircilar Carsisi is the street of copper-workers. As well as copper, both old and new items of jewellery, carpets, antiques and embroidery are to be found. On the way from there up the hill to Citadel Gate you pass other shops selling spices, dried fruits, nuts and other produce. Modern shops including the Karum shopping mall are to be found on Tunali Hilmi Avenue in Kizilay. There are other modern shops in the Atakule Tower shopping centre in Cankaya. The Cankaya Market is open on Saturday all day from early morning. There is a flower market on Sakarya.

There are bookshops catering specifically for the English-speaking market, but prices of books are very high. These bookshops also sell British newspapers and magazines. Some papers can be bought the day after publication in the UK, but they are very expensive. There is one English-language newspaper produced locally, the *Turkish Daily News*.

EATING AND DRINKING
You can enjoy a good meal out at a reasonable price. There are some good restaurants serving Turkish food. Try Mangal at Farabi Sok 34 in Cankaya, Pineapple at Köroglu Cad 64B, Gopor or Yakamoz at Tunali 114/J2-3.

TRANSPORT
Taxis are plentiful and all have meters. They can be flagged down in the street or summoned by pressing a bell on the telegraph poles (warning – these are frequently out of order). *Dolmus* (small minibuses) run on regular routes and are cheap and reasonably comfortable. Buses are cheap and can be convenient although they are often crowded.

SECURITY
Security in Ankara and most tourist areas is not usually a serious problem.

ISTANBUL

Everyone who gets as far as Istanbul will want to see the *Kapali Carsi* (covered bazaar) in the Old City. A veritable labyrinth of alleys and passageways, the bazaar has more than 4,000 shops and 2,000 workshops. Each trade has its own area, and street names tend to reflect the trade in question: Goldsmiths' street, Carpet-Sellers' street, and Cotton-Printers street are just a few examples. Best buys while in Turkey include antiques, hand woven silk and wool carpets, ceramics, leather goods and jewellery. All of these can be found in the bazaar, but be sure to shop around, and be prepared to bargain before you buy. Behind the Yeni Mosque is the *Misir Carsisi*, or spice bazaar (do stop at Ucuzcular, No 51, and purchase one of a selection of aphrodisiacs that come in pretty tear-shaped bottles), and next to it there is a wonderful flower and bird market. Both the Istanbul Sanatlari Carsisi (Bazaar of Istanbul Arts) and the Caferaga Medrese sell local arts and crafts, and are located near Sultan Ahmet Square. The copper market is near Nuruosmariye Camii. On Sunday, there is an Arts and Crafts market on the waterfront in Ortaköy.

For more up-market, modern shops, try the shops in the Rumeli Caddesi in Nisantasi, the Istaklal Caddesi in Beyoglu and Cumhuriyet Caddesi near Taksim. Shopping malls can be found on both the European and Asian sides of Istanbul – perhaps the most popular are Akmerkez at Etiler on the European side, and the Galleria in Ataköy near the airport. All the best-known international designer shops, such as Benetton, Lacoste, Max Mara, Mondi, Ralph Lauren and Stephanel are represented in the malls. Beyman (Galleria, Ataköy) and Vakko (Istiklâl Cad 123-125, Beyoglu) specialise in stylish men's and women's fashions, while clothes by Nesilihan Yarguci, one of the country's leading designers, can be found in the Galeria or at Kuyulu Bostan Sokak 6 in Nisantasi. The Home Shop is a must for furniture and design items and Mudo Design sells both clothing and soft goods for the home.

There are several bookshops and kiosks which sell British or American newspapers and magazines. Daily and Sunday newspapers are normally available on the day following publication. They are expensive. The only English language newspaper is the *Turkish Daily News*. English-language books are hard to find, but try ABC Kitabevi at Istiklal Caddesi 461 in Beyoglu or Librairie de Pera at Galip Dede Caddesi, near Tunel. Book lovers will enjoy browsing in the old book market in Beyazit.

Eating and Drinking

Turkish cusine is considered by many to be one of the world's finest. Given Turkey's geographical location between Europe and the Middle East, there are unmistakable links between Turkish, Greek, Lebanese, and Israeli cuisine. Those comfortable with any of the latter will find something they know in the former. Food is generally cheap by UK standards, except in restaurants that cater to the high end of the tourist trade. The best restaurants tend to be found in Taksim or Galata. Try hotel chains like the Sheraton or Hilton for more international dishes. There is a great range of less sophisticated restaurants all over the city with plenty of sidewalk cafés to choose from in the *Balik Dazari* (fish market).

Local cuisine can best be found in areas like Haci Baba and Baribaldi in Iistiklal Cad. Kebabs are perhaps the best known feature of Turkish cuisine, but the mezzes or appetisers are also well known. Fish and seafood are generally good, but can be expensive. Baklava and other pastries are made from local ingredients like pistachios, honey, nuts and filo, and are more than enough to satisfy the sweetest tooth. Turkish coffee is not well known or much appreciated in the west, perhaps due to its mud-like consistency. It is served in small cups, grounds and all, and is very concentrated. A nice light alternative is a glass of tea, usually served sweetened to taste. A 10% tip is usually included in the bill, but it is customary to leave an additional 5% on the table.

Transport

Public transport is often crowded and although buses are cheap and run frequently, they tend to move slowly through the dense traffic. Taxis are sometimes difficult to get at rush hour, but are otherwise easy to find and reasonably priced. All yellow cabs have a meter. The dolmus travel on recognised routes at a fixed rate for set distances, and are a quick and effective way of getting about once you know the routes. A new underground light railway line links Aksaray to Serhatpasa in the old city, and there is an ancient single stop connection between Tunel and Karakoy. Ferries provide one of the most pleasant ways to move around the city, and the name of the pier indicates the destination of the boats that leave from it.

Security

Violent crime is rare in Istanbul, and one is generally safe on the street at any time of day or night. Street crime is on the increase, however, and precautions against pickpockets are advised.

TURKS AND CAICOS: GRAND TURK

Language **English**
Currency **US dollar of 100 cents**
Credit cards **Visa and Mastercard widely accepted**
Shops **0900–1800**
Refunds **possible, but credit notes sometimes given instead**

Many shops are scattered around the town within walking distance of each other and the Salt Raker Hotel, the Turks Head Inn and the Sitting Pretty. The one mall is called Sarah's. There are dive shops and hotel shops, but they sell mainly T-shirts and items for the beach, all aimed at the tourist trade and expensive. T-shirts, for example, might cost $20. Most people prefer to do their serious shopping in Miami.

All foodstuffs are imported from Miami and are very expensive. Most essentials can be obtained, but not necessarily specific brands. There is little in the way of fresh foodstuffs, farming being at subsistence level. The islands produce frozen lobster and conch for export. Clothing and shoes are not easy to obtain locally and are expensive and limited in choice.

One local speciality worth considering as a souvenir or a gift is the maps of the Turks and Caicos Islands drawn by the manager of the Turks Head Inn. They cost $15 each.

EATING AND DRINKING

Conch and chips from the Regal Begal in Hospital Road is a lot cheaper than in the main hotels, and much nicer in the opinion of many locals. The fried chicken is exceptional at the Poop Deck in Front Street. Rum punch is best drunk at the water's edge at – the Water's Edge, of course, in Duke Street.

TRANSPORT

Apart from a few very expensive taxis (the charge is per person in the cab) public transport is non-existent.

SECURITY

No precautions are needed on Grand Turk, the only slight hassle from the occasional harmless beggar, but exercise common sense.

UGANDA

KAMPALA

Language **English**
Currency **Uganda shilling (Sh).£1=1,620, Mar 1997**
Banks **0830–1400 Mon to Fri**
Duty-free **at the Nile Conference Centre, mainly drink and cigarettes**

Shopping in Kampala is a chore. Reading material, good shoes and tailored clothing are all in short supply. Imported items cost about two to three times UK prices. There are no large supermarkets like those in the USA or UK in Kampala, and shoppers tend to go from one small shop to another – although there are now some modest supermarkets which are reasonably well stocked. More and more boutiques are opening, but not with a great variety of goods.

The main thoroughfare is Kampala Road. There are many small to medium-sized shops of all types here and in Bombo Road. The Sheraton and Grand Imperial have reasonable shopping facilities for gifts. Daisy's Deli Arcade and Pioneer Mall are recommended. Nakasero Market is the place to go for produce. Try the shops in the Sheraton, the Equatorial Hotel or in the Pioneer Mall.

Most handicrafts are imported from Kenya or Tanzania, but there are some local items available such as drums, baskets, woodcarvings and mats. Try Uganda Crafts in Bombo Road or the craft market behind the National Theatre. The Furnishing and Craft Shop on Kampala Road opposite Biblous and Uganda Arts in Bat Valley are also worth a look. On the road to Entebbe there are several stalls with drums, baskets and plant-pots. The RSU Vocational Training Centre at Nakulabye-Kiwumya near SDA Church sells weaving and textiles. Cheap rattan items can be bought in Gaba Road.

The most popular English-language daily is the *New Vision*, which is government owned. There are some foreign newspapers and magazines available. Books "R" has a wide selection at reasonable prices. The Family Bookshop in Nkrumah Road has a variety of paperbacks. The Sheraton Hotel also has a bookshop.

EATING AND DRINKING

For meals out, try one of the restaurants in the Sheraton, Nile or Equatorial Hotels. There is a variety of places on Kampala Road itself such as the Nile Grill, the Red Bull, Bat Valley, the Slow Boat, the China Palace or the China Great Wall. An average lunch costs about 8,000 shillings. An evening meal for two with local beer or soft drinks would cost from 20,000 shillings to perhaps twice that and even more with wine. Soft drinks and local beer are available.

TRANSPORT

There are buses and route taxis, but it is not advisable to use them. Taxis should be taken only from one of the major hotels, but negotiate the price before hiring.

SECURITY

Although the situation has improved, criminal activity remains a major consideration, particularly after dark.

UKRAINE

KIEV

Language **Ukrainian**
Currency **hrivnya of 100 kopeks. £1=2.95, Dec 1996**
Traveller's cheques **not advised; bring clean US dollar bills, and exchange at money-changers**
Credit cards **accepted in larger hotels and restaurants**
Shops **1000–1400, 1500–1900/2000**
Bargaining **possible in markets**
Duty-free **at the airport, both arrivals and departure; good but limited stock. Vodka, champagne and cigarettes cheaper in town**
Export restrictions **controls on export of antiques**

Kiev is a large city, with its old part to the west of the River Dnipro, its modern tower-block part to the east. Economic reform is slowly changing things. Summers are hot and a street café culture is developing, but you will need to wear plenty of layers for winter visits.

The main shopping areas are Khreshchatyk and Podil. Unreformed state shops stand alongside expensive Western imports. A visit to Tsum, the state department store on Khreshchatyk, is a worthwhile experience. In the same street are Benetton, Reebok and other Western designer names. Recommended markets are Besarabska, Podil and Volodymyrs'ka. They sell wonderful fruit and vegetables in summer. They all, particularly the last, also sell imports such as clothing.

Local specialities obtainable at the markets and elsewhere include caviar, vodka, champagne, smetana, antiques and art. There are interesting crafts in the daily street market at Andriyivsky as well as at shops in Khreshchatyk, at the hotels or around town. Look out particularly for papier-mâché boxes, painted eggs, reproduction icons, embroidered cloths and amber jewellery.

Little or no English is spoken in shops and restaurants and it is worth while at least knowing the Cyrillic alphabet. Foreign newspapers are obtainable at the large hotels. The local English-language paper is the *Kiev Post*, a weekly free-sheet from the hotels.

TRANSPORT
It is sensible to bring a pair of practical walking shoes for general use around town. Taxis are plentiful, but not always available especially at night. The metro, trolley-buses, trams and buses are cheap and efficient, but they can be overcrowded.

SECURITY
The city remains on the whole a safe place. However muggings and thefts are on the increase and common sense should be exercised. Do not be ostentatious.

UNITED ARAB EMIRATES

Language **Arabic**
Currency **dirham of 100 fils. £1=5.90,**
  Mar 1997
Banks **0800–1200 Sat to Wed, 0800–1100 Thur in**
  Abu Dhabi; 0800–1200 Sat to Thur in Dubai
Credit cards **only in larger stores and shops**
Cashpoints **yes, with Visa and Connect; exchange**
  rate may be lower than elsewhere
Shops **0800–1300, 1600–1700/2100; some shops close**
  Fri
Bargaining **yes**
Duty-free **best in Dubai**
Tipping **not prevalent; service charge in restaurants**
  and hotels. Taxi drivers are not tipped

There are excellent shops as well as traditional Arab souks. Shopping is done primarily using cash and is expensive. English is commonly spoken and bargaining is widespread.

Best buys are electronic and camera equipment, watches, rugs, antiques and jewellery. There is almost nothing in the way of local crafts and souvenirs; even the Bedouin jewellery will come from Oman. Cotton caftans and wrap-around skirts can be bought cheaply in the souk and make useful beach wraps. Labels such as Cardin, Levis or Wranglers may not always be authentic, but can be very cheap.

Alcoholic drinks are expensive and available only in hotel bars and restaurants. (Sharjah is the only Emirate where the sale of alcohol is not permitted in hotels.) A good range of spirits, wines, liqueurs and canned beers is available from licensed stores. Liquor licences must be produced.

English cigarettes are inexpensive and there is a fair range of tobacco and cigars.

Personal security is generally good.

ABU DHABI

The main shopping area is around Hamdan Street, Al Nasr Street and Zayed First and Second Streets. The Abbas Ismael Hypermarket is at the corner of Baniyas and Zayed Second Streets and has some Boots own-brand goods. Dana Plaza is a supermarket/department store in Zayed First Street. It is good for clothing and footwear and less expensive than many dress shops and boutiques. There is also a British Home Stores in Hamdan Street, where many of the dress shops are situated. Prisunic is a supermarket/department store on Airport Road in Khalidiya. Spinney's Department Store is in Zayed First Street.

The fish souk is now in modern air-conditioned premises in the Free Port area. Everything from kingfish and sardines to crab, shrimp and squid is usually available. The vegetable souk, also modern and air-conditioned, is between Al-Nasr and Istiqlal Streets by the Otaiba Mosque. The New Souk is between the Corniche and Khalifa Street and the Old Souk opposite, between Khalifa and Hamdan streets.

There are several antique shops in Al Nasr Street behind the Arab Monetary Fund Building. Watches and other jewellery can be good value. Try Khalifah Jewellers on Khalifa Street. There is a good selection of Indian silks at Elson's in the TV Building in Hamda Street. For dressmakers and tailors try Beauty Tailors in Zayed Second Street, Gulf Tailors in Zayed First Street or White Castle opposite the fort.

Most British newspapers can be bought locally the day after publication, but they are very expensive and sometimes censored. A large selection of English-language magazines can also be bought, but again they are very expensive. All books are expensive. Recommended bookshops include the Family Bookshop in Zayed Second Street, All Prints at the corner of Tarriq bin Zayed and Al Nasr streets, the Oxford Bookshop opposite the International Hotel, the Star Bookshop near the Sheraton Hotel and the Al-Muttari Bookshop in Zayed First Street.

EATING AND DRINKING

There are numerous restaurants, but only hotels have liquor licences. Prices vary enormously. Hotels worth trying are the Hilton (Pearl and Japanese Restaurants) or Sheraton (Mexican and La Mamma) The Chinese restaurant in the latter is excellent, but expensive. Other hotel restaurants recommended are the seafood restaurant at the Holiday Inn, Chinese food at the Centre Hotel, the Meridien Hotel for Lebanese food, the Corniche Residence for Friday brunch and the Khalidiya Palace Hotel for good Japanese and Italian food. For local cuisine try the Golden Fish in Khalidiyah Street, L'Auberge in Mina Zayed Road, Al Safeena or Abou Tafish dhow restaurants off the Corniche.

There are also good pastry shops with coffee and tea areas, such as La Brioche behind Prisunic on the Corniche, which has good croissants, Charlotte's Patisserie at the corner of the

Corniche and Khalidiya, Arlequin in Khalidiya, extension of
Zayed First Street and Bavaria Pastries in Khalifa Street.

TRANSPORT

There are buses and minibuses which are cheap, but little used
by Europeans. Taxis are numerous, fitted with meters and
inexpensive.

DUBAI

Dubai is an Arabic Hong Kong and well known as a duty-free
outlet. Shops selling luxury items such as cameras, watches,
hi-fi, TV and video equipment, electrical goods, jewellery, perfumes and fashionable clothes are abundant. Cameras and all
electrical items can usually be obtained at slightly lower prices
than VAT-free in the UK. The range of choice can, however, be
restricted. Dubai is also one of the best places to buy Persian
carpets outside Iran itself.

The town of Dubai is divided by a salt-water creek, the
southern side of which is called Bur Dubai and the northern
Deira. Deira is in fact the central area with its heart between
Beniyas Road which runs along the waterfront and Naif Road
about 500 metres too the north.

The main area for duty-free goods is Beniyas Square.
Dubai's traditional wealth was built on gold and the gold souk
is situated around Sikkat Al-Khail Street. The covered souk is
behind the Shatt Al-Arab Hotel, with a smaller souk on the
Dubai side, near the docks.

There are now several large shopping centres with new
ones opening all the time. One of the most popular is City
Centre in Deira, where many familiar names are represented.
Another popular centre is Bur Juman on the Bur Dubai side.

Designer clothing abounds and many famous names have
boutiques in Dubai, including Dior and Gucci. There is a
Jaeger shop and you can also buy Jacques Vert fashions.

Casual clothing can be found in the boutiques and the
souks. Smart casual clothing and sportswear for men is available
and good value. Cheaper ranges are available in the shops and
in the souks, and there is a British Home Stores and Next. On
the whole, however, clothing is cheaper and best bought in the
UK. Excellent silks are plentiful and reasonably priced.

British newspapers and periodicals are available in the big
hotels and elsewhere, but are expensive. There are three local
English-language newspapers which have good coverage of
world news. There are several bookshops which sell a wide

selection of novels. They are, however, expensive.

EATING AND DRINKING
The major up-market restaurants are in the big hotels and expensive. As well as Arab restaurants there are others offering cuisines from all over the world. There are some independent, cheaper restaurants in the town centre which are acceptable, although these do not sell liquor.

TRANSPORT
Public transport facilities are minimal. Taxis are plentiful, but relying on these alone would be expensive.

UNITED KINGDOM OF GREAT BRITAIN AND NORTHERN IRELAND

Language **English**
Currency **pound sterling (£)**
Banks **0930-1550 Mon to Fri; some open Sat morn**
Traveller's cheques **at banks and exchange booths**
Credit cards **all major cards accepted in most shops, hotels and restaurants**
Cashpoints **at banks, shopping malls and supermarkets**
Shops **0900/0930-1730, London: late-night Wed (Knightsbridge) or Thur (Oxford Street); some supermarkets open earlier and close later. Some Sun opening**
Refunds **yes, with receipt. Value Added Tax (VAT) can be reclaimed by non-EU visitors exporting goods within three months; most large, central shops operate this scheme**
Sales **controlled by law; good bargains in Jan and Jul; some special promotions and early sales**
Bargaining **possible in flea markets, but not elsewhere**
Duty-free **at international airports. Heathrow and Gatwick have shopping malls in which many famous British and international names are represented; VAT can be deducted for those about to board a plane**
Tipping **10 per cent in restaurants if no service charge; 10 per cent to taxi drivers and hairdressers**

LONDON

Shopping in London can be exhausting, and it is recommended that the visitor concentrates on the central area. Most serious or window shopping can be achieved within the area bounded by Piccadilly to the south, Oxford Street to the north, Bond Street to the west and Regent Street to the east. On the south-east corner of this quadrilateral is Piccadilly Circus, once the centre of an empire and now the centre usually of a traffic jam. On one corner is the giant specialist sports store Lillywhite's and on the other corner Tower Records.

Along the elegant curve of Regent Street are other famous designer shops such as Aquascutum on the right (now owned by the Japanese, with small sizes a speciality) and Austin Reed (now for both women and men) on the left. Next is Garrards, the court jeweller. Jaeger and Liberty (famous for exotic carpets as well as fashion) and Hamleys, the world's leading toyshop, are a little further ahead. Dickens & Jones, just beyond, has undegone an extensive facelift and is definitely worth a stop.

Turning left into Oxford Street we see why "nobody shops in Oxford Street any more"; some recent additions have been pretty tatty, but Marks & Spencer's flagship store (458 Oxford) alone make the street a must for the visitor. It's ideal for those wanting to take home woollens, including mohair and cashmere. M & S's other claim to fame is its ladies' knickers, without question the best quality and selection for the fiscally responsible. Oxford Street's grande dame department store is Selfridge's, (which since 1994 has undergone renovation costing £70 million). John Lewis and Debenhams are two other reliable names, especially in their respective homewares departments.

Then there is the serious shopping street. New Bond Street which becomes Old Bond Street at its southern end. This has been a veritable hotbed of designer activity for the past few years with every big name designer staking his or her claim. Calvin Klein (55 New Bond), Emporio Armani (111 New Bond), Nicole Farhi (158 New Bond), Donna Karan, Mulberry (41 New Bond)) and Versace (34-36 New Bond) have all opened new or renovated existing stores. The antiques and fine arts connoisseur will enjoy popping in to Asprey, the Fine Art Society and Sotheby's and if you're feeling peckish, get a bite to eat at the Café at Sotheby's. Savile Row, the name synonomous world wide with top-class English tailoring is nearby.

Turn left along Piccadilly, past the Ritz and Royal Academy for the Queen's grocers, Fortnum and Mason(181 Piccadilly), and the royal bookshop, Hatchard's (187

Piccadilly). To the left and right are elegant Georgian shopping arcades and parallel, on the right, is historic Jermyn Street with Paxton & Whitfield (93 Jermyn) for cheeses, Czech and Speake (39c Jermyn) for bathroom accessories (including some of the most intoxicating – and expensive – bath oils made) and many shirtmakers. At Jerymn Street and St James's is Davidoff of London (35 St James's) the prestigious cigar maker which has the Royal warrant. Also in Piccadilly, there is Simpson's (202 Piccadilly), another label for quality British fashion.

The main addition to this core area is Knightsbridge, two bus or underground stops to the west, and home not only to world-famous Harrods, but also to Harvey Nichols, just two hundred yards up the road. Harrods remains expensive, but still provides one of London's best and most comfortable free mornings out, ideal for window-shopping and admiring the pets on the second floor. Sales time is excellent for bargains and the fresh fish display in the Food Hall is breath-taking. Many locals now rely upon "Harvey Nicks" for their designer-wear. Nearby is the Scotch House (2 Brompton Road) for tartans and cashmeres, and several trendy, if variable, boutiques. Just a little further west is Walton Street, Beauchamp Place, and "Brompton Cross". For the most part, this area is very expensive but the window shopping is incomparable and there are even a few good values to be found. The Conran Shop (81 Fulham Road) is an impressive showcase of innovative contemporary design in furniture, homewares, lighting. Jewels One (101a Fulham Road) is a minute boutique chock-a-block with an enormous selection of stunning and reasonably priced earrings, necklaces and bracelets. Further down Fulham Road at 163 is Jerry's Home Store, two fabulous floors of anything you could ever want for your home. There's also a Seattle Coffee Company on the lower ground floor. Habitat and Heals, both big names in furniture design are just down Sydney Street at 206 and 234 Kings Road respectively. Covent Garden is another good place for a (potentially) free and enjoyable excursion, particularly in the early evening. The old fruit and flower market immortalised in the opening sequence of *My Fair Lady* has been converted into boutiques and food and drink outlets aimed very much at the younger market, with an array of stalls selling fashions and souvenirs and entertainment provided by some excellent buskers. There is an antiques market here on Monday, and a craft market Tuesday to Friday.

Carnaby Street belongs to the past, and is now an insult rather than a monument to those wonderful years of the

1960s. Tottenham Court Road also belongs to the category of streets to forget. Traditionally the place for best value hi-fi, and more recently for computers, it has in recent years seen some new and down-market additions.

Those wishing to go further afield to get a hint of the collection of villages which London once was, can do no better than go to Hampstead, whose beauty and wealthy residents have attracted boutiques, bookshops and restaurants.

There are now few street markets worth visiting other than for a bit of fun. Of possible interest to the antique collector is Portobello Road (underground Notting Hill Gate) on Friday or Saturday, if only for the pubs and the fact that it is near Kensington Church Street which has many antique shops.

The best places for good quality gifts and souvenirs are the shops at the main art galleries, museums and other tourist attractions. The National Gallery basic catalogue, for example, for well under £10 is both attractive and informative. Worth remembering is the London Transport shop at St James' underground station or in the Visitor Information Centre at Victoria Station.

Shops such as Harrods or Fortnum and Mason are experts in gift-packaging almost any item for the souvenir trade, from English breakfast tea upwards. For the shopper on a budget, any good supermarket such as Waitrose, Tesco or Sainsbury, will have teas, local cheeses, chocolates and even English wines.

Booklovers will wish to visit Charing Cross Road, a short walk from Piccadilly Circus and traditionally the home of books old, new and antiquarian and, for the academically inclined, Dillon's University Bookshop at 82 Gower Street WC2 are worth the detour.

British newspapers vary widely in their standards and their news coverage. Broadsheets (as opposed to tabloids) such as *The Times* and the *Daily Telegraph* provide reasonable coverage and at least some food for thought. The international press is widely available in profusion in central areas, even from the smallest outlet.

EATING AND DRINKING

In the central theatre areas there are good value pre-theatre suppers, and for the serious diner things then become quieter for a few hours. Wherever you are going, at whatever time, it is always safer to reserve a table in a restaurant in advance by telephone. Remember also that some restaurants will insist on jacket and/or tie even at the hottest times of year and will not always have garments to lend. Fixed-price, fixed-menu lunches give a value for money opportunity to sample the food at some of London's better restaurants.

Pubs are a British institution that face you on almost every street corner. Two recent changes are that they offer food, and can now stay open all day. In addition to which, many still offer quite genuine English draught beer.

Riverside and old traditional pubs are particularly recommended. Many of them have proper restaurants as well as just bars serving old-style cottage pie, shepherd's pie or ploughman's lunch. Try the Dove at Hammersmith, the Anchor at Bankside SE1, the Angel on Bermondsey Wall East SE16, the George off 77 Borough High Street SE1, the Lamb and Flag off Rose Street WC2, the Mayflower at 117 Rotherhithe Street SE16 or Ye Olde Cheshire Cheese in Wine Office Court off 145 Fleet Street EC4.

Even Britons now rarely have time for afternoon tea and the meal is almost entirely preserved for the benefit of the tourist trade. Around 1600 all the biggest and grandest hotels such as the Savoy, Ritz and Waldorf – as well as the biggest department stores – wheel out the white grand piano and the full works for the benefit of the American visitor. The menu will probably be fixed, and will include sandwiches and cakes, no matter how hungry you are.

For a good-value British breakfast, try only the biggest hotels or the smallest English (now more frequently Italian) cafés.

TRANSPORT

The underground and bus systems are comprehensive and perhaps a little confusing at first, but even in the centre they are useful for hopping on and off, particularly if you have a Travelcard for the day. These are available from underground booking offices, but not on buses, for travel after 0930 on both underground and bus plus some main-line trains for those wishing to use this service. The cost will vary according to how many zones, measured in concentric circles from the middle of London, you wish to use. If traffic is bad, favour the underground, or "tube" as Londoners call it. If trying to find somewhere difficult or unusual, use a traditional black taxi – not cheap, but a great saver of time and hassle. The drivers are trained to know everywhere in London. All fares are metered and the system is rigidly controlled by the Metropolitan Police.

SCOTLAND

EDINBURGH

Language **English**

Currency **pound sterling of 100 pence; Scotland has its own banknotes, not always accepted in the rest of the UK**

Banks **0930–1600 Mon to Fri; some open Sat**

Credit cards **widely accepted**

Cashpoints **plentiful**

Shops **0930 to 1730 Mon to Sat, late night shopping Thur. Some shops now open on Sun**

Sales **Jan and Jul, genuine and good value**

Refunds **yes, with receipt. Value Added Tax (VAT) can be reclaimed by larger and smarter shops participating in the VAT refund scheme. Ask for details**

Tipping **10 per cent in restaurants where service has not already been added, and in taxis and hairdressers**

Edinburgh is proud to project itself as the capital city and important financial centre which it is. Its image is quite distinct from that of urban and industrial Glasgow.

The heart of Edinburgh and the only part of the city which many visitors will see is on and around Princes Street and the Royal Mile. Princes Street is built up on only one side and is watched over by the castle. Just to the south the Royal Mile proceeds from the castle to Holyroodhouse, changing its name as it does so from Castle Hill, to Lawnmarket, to High Street, to Canongate. These constitute the main central shopping areas.

Almost anything you care to mention comes gift-wrapped in tartan, but there are lots of sensible things to buy. High on the list comes Edinburgh crystal, widely available and in many different designs. The factory is a few miles away to the south at Penicuik. There are fabrics such as tweeds and tartans, or knitwear; these will come from different areas of Scotland such as Fair Isle, Harris or Shetland. Celtic silver and other jewellery is worth looking out for.

Local food and drink provides plenty of ideas for gifts and souvenirs. Foremost, of course, is Scotch whisky, particularly malt whiskies from the different areas of Scotland. Then there are the liqueurs such as Drambuie. All of them are to be found in chocolates for the benefit of chocaholics. Edinburgh rock can be found in presentation boxes. Any supermarket should be able to provide you with biscuits such as shortbread or oatcake, Dundee cake, local honey or cheeses, haggis, venison, kippers, smoked salmon or even fresh salmon (if you are not travelling too far).

Princes Street is the home of the leading department store, Jenner's, and of most of the main British chain stores, including Marks and Spencer and a branch of the Scotch House. The Royal Mile is a bit touristy, but worth a look. So is Rose Street, one block north of Princes Street, not only for its pubs, but also for its individual shops and boutiques. One block further north still is George Street, also good for shopping. Dundas Street is a magnet for the antiques enthusiast.

There are shopping malls at the St James Centre in Leith Walk and Waverley Market at the end of Princes Street.

Jenner's is a good place for a general look around. For knitwear try the Shetland Connection at 491 Lawnmarket and for kilts and tartans Geoffrey at 57 High Street. The Whisky Shop in Waverley Market has a vast choice. MacSween's at 130 Bruntsfield Place is world famous for its haggis.

The local press is good, and quite distinct from that in England. The *Scotsman* likes to consider itself the national quality newspaper. Foreign newspapers are widely available from central shops and kiosks. Waterstone's in Princes Street is a good general bookshop. A little further afield are Bauermeister's on the George IV Bridge and James Thin on South Bridge.

EATING AND DRINKING

A Scottish breakfast is even more filling than an English one, the essential added ingredient of porridge and the option of kippers. Pubs are now open all day and many offer quite adequate meals of such fare as shepherd's pie or salads to keep you going through the day. The heart of Scottish drinking lies in Rose Street, an ideal place to sample the different local brews. Scottish cuisine is traditionally ample rather than exotic, with fish and game as specialities, but plenty of ethnic restaurants are also to be found in the main tourist and central areas. Popular places for local cuisine include Howie's in St Leonard's Street, Jackson's in High Street, Kelly's in West Richmond Street and Martin's in Rose Street, North Lane. At the very top of the market, not least in price, is the Pompadour in the Caledonian Hotel.

TRANSPORT

The centre of town is sufficiently compact to make use of public transport unnecessary, but there are plenty of buses: pay the driver as you get on or get a day pass for better value. Taxis are to be found at stands or can be hailed on the street. Fares are metered.

SECURITY

Sensible personal security precautions are necessary, but your most difficult problem is likely to be an over-boisterous pub on Friday or Saturday night.

UNITED STATES OF AMERICA

Language **English**
Currency **US dollar of 100 cents.£1=1.60, Mar 1997**
Banks **0900-1500 Mon to Fri**
Traveller's cheques **sterling can be difficult to change; declare large amounts of cash dollars on entry**
Credit cards **essential when hiring cars or booking hotel rooms; internationally recognised cards American Express, Diners Club, Visa, Access**
Cashpoints **in most supermarkets**
Shops **1000-2130 Mon to Sat, 1200-1800 Sun; some supermarkets open 24 hours**
Refunds **yes, with receipt**
Sales **frequent, especially at holiday times; good reductions**
Bargaining **only in flea markets**
Duty-free **at airports; alcohol and perfume may be cheaper in town**
Tipping **15 per cent in bars and restaurants; 10-15 per cent to taxi drivers; $1 per item to airport and hotel porters and cloakroom attendants; not necessary for supermarket porters**
Export restrictions **on antiques of exceptional value or government property**

Shopping facilities are excellent. All you normally need do is to find a favourite neighbourhood mall, which might be some miles away, given that America is such a car-borne society.

The aphorism that America and Britain are two nations

divided by a single language should always be borne in mind. Everyday functions such as visiting a garage can be confusing when a bonnet is a hood, a boot is a trunk and petrol is gas. Spanish is widely spoken, particularly in the southern states. Measurements are not metric and there are other peculiarities; for example, the US pint is 16 fluid ounces, not 20 as in the UK.

Sales tax is levied on top of retail sales prices at the register on all items except non-prepared food and medicines. Prices for formal clothing and footwear are higher than in the UK, even when account is taken of the many sales. Top quality shoes and woollens, for example, are expensive. The cost of imported and designer items can be prohibitive.

Casual and sports clothing for everyone is an especially good buy, and there is an excellent range in all the department stores and other shops. Lightweight men's suits are good value. Those with narrow feet will have no difficulty in getting shoes; many shops stock a range of triple A fittings.

Familiar names will confront you in almost every shopping mall. Saks, Neiman Marcus and Bloomingdale's cater for the luxury market. Hecht's or Nordstroms equate to John Lewis. Sears or J.C.Penney equate to British Home Stores or Littlewoods. Neither Marks and Spencer nor Boots the Chemist have a direct American equivalent. There are many single designer stores such as Liz Claiborn, Ann Taylor and Banana Republic. Laura Ashley, Next and the Body Shop are also to be found.

Factory outlet stores offer savings on retail for name-brand merchandise and clothing. They carry production over-runs, seconds and old as well as new stock. Merchandise is not always cheaper than in stores, particularly when stores are having sales.

Best buys are what you fancy. You will be sure to find it. Sports and leisure goods are particularly good.

There is an extensive and good-value English-language press. British newspapers are available. The *Daily Telegraph* costs $3.50 and a day-old copy of the *Sunday Times* $6.

Food is plentiful and generally good value at all levels. Standing in line (queueing) is commonplace, particularly at peak times, since many restaurants do not take table bookings.

The best Californian wines are outstanding and even the cheap ones are drinkable, and American beer has made huge progress. Although the fizzy tasteless stuff abounds, hundreds of micro-breweries have arisen producing delicious beer. Anchor Steam Beer and Samuel Adams are the best known of the good beers.

WASHINGTON

Though the Washington DC area is considered one of the most expensive in the USA, it is very competitive for consumer goods. Washington is an international city and the most exclusive brands all have an outlet somewhere.

There is no single, main, town-centre shopping area, although both Georgetown and Alexandria have shopping areas on UK lines. Shopping is convenient, mainly in purpose-built shopping centres (malls or plazas) with abundant parking.

Georgetown Park Mall at 3222 Main Street, Washington DC has over 120 major and up-market stores. Union Station at 40 Massachusetts Avenue, Washington DC is equally large. The shops at National Place at 13331 Pennsylvania Avenue, Washington DC number about 80. The Pavilion at the Old Post Office at 1100 Pennsylvania Avenue, Washington DC is about the same size. The Fashion City at Pentagon City in Arlington has 160 stores and a good food court. Tysons II the Galleria is more up-market than its sister Tysons Corner Center, both are at McLean Virginia. Springfield Mall at Springfield Virginia has all the major stores among its 230 outlets. Montgomery Mall and White Flint Mall are both at Bethesda Maryland.

The nearest factory outlet mall in the Washington area is Potomac Mills on the I-95, 15 minutes' drive from the Beltway at Dale City. You could easily spend a whole day there, with so much choice.

Recommended best buys to take home include linens such as sheets and towels, all excellent quality and sometimes at half the UK price; all sorts of sportswear and sports equipment from branches of Sports Authority; denim jeans such as 501 Levis for around $39 from County Seat in Tysons Corner Center or the Levi store at Potomac Mills; CDs at about $13 each and computer books and software at about two-thirds the UK price.

There are excellent local newspapers such as the *Washington Post*, *Washington Times* or the *Washington Business Journal*, and good bookshops such as Borders and Supercrown in DC, Maryland and Virginia.

EATING AND DRINKING

There are something like 500 restaurants with a wide variety of meals at all prices and a good selection of wines from around the world at reasonable prices. Fresh seafood comes from Chesapeake Bay, crabs abound, hence the famous Maryland crabcakes, which are wonderful. Starbucks Coffee

Shops have every type of coffee imaginable. Chesapeake Bagel Bakeries specialise in different types of bagels with hundreds of fillings.

TRANSPORT

The metropolitan transport facilities include Metrorail and Metrobus – a subway train and a bus system. The trains are safe, clean and efficient and operate daily until midnight. There are discounted transfers from rail to bus, but not vice-versa.

There is usually no difficulty in hailing a taxi. In DC fares are set to a zone system, not by meter, and are reasonable, probably about $10 downtown.

SECURITY

Shopping is generally safe with the exception of areas where most sensible people would not venture anyway.

NEW YORK

New York is expensive, particularly in Manhattan. Manhattan is only a small part of the city in area, the island being 14 miles long and only two and a half miles wide at its widest point. It is one of the most densely populated districts in the world. It has thousands of restaurants and its shopping facilities vary from department stores to one-man businesses, some of the latter functioning around the clock.

New York deals in instant fashion; quality and finish are not always satisfactory. There are many shops where designer clothing may be bought at discounts and unlike the UK, where sales are rare apart from the traditional January or July ones, in New York any excuse is used to have a sale.

It is surprising that in a country which invented the mall there are only three on Manhattan - Manhattan Mall at Sixth Avenue and 33rd Street, World Trade Center Mall bounded by West-Church-Vesey-Liberty and South Street Seaport at Fulton and South Streets. What distinguishes these malls is location rather than content. The South Street Seaport is a historical area with lots to offer the tourist besides shopping (though the shopping is very good) while the World Trade Center Mall and Manhattan Mall are more geared to the business community. For instance, the Manhattan Mall has 91 boutiques on nine floors, including Ann Taylor, Nine West shoes, The Limited and Foot Locker, a food court on Level 7, and a Stern's department store. For general browsing, the city breaks down into four general areas, the East side (42nd-94th Streets), the West side, (59th-86th Street), Greenwich Village and downtown areas known as Soho and Tribeca (south of Houston Street and north of Chambers Street).

A good setting off point is mid-town as that is where the majority of hotels are located. What better place to start than at Tiffany & Co (Fifth Avenue at 57th Street), one of New York's most famous institutions thanks to Audrey Hepburn in the film, *Breakfast at Tiffany's*. This a requisite stop even if you're only window shopping. Once you've recovered from the sticker shock of what the world's finest jewels will set you back, gather your wits about you and do a promenade of Fifth Avenue, one of the city's finest shopping neighbourhoods. Large, elegant department stores are every few blocks: Lord and Taylor at 424 Fifth (39th Street) and then Saks Fifth Avenue at 611 (50th) then Henri Bendel at 712 (54th) then Bergdorf Goodman at 754 (58th) and finally Barneys New York at 660 (61st). Other important department stores not on Fifth Avenue are Macy's at Herald Square (151 West 34th Street), the largest department store in the world which covers a full city block and Bloomingdale's at Third Avenue and 59th Street. If you prefer to steer clear of the department stores, Brooks Brothers (346 Madison Avenue) is a leader in business clothes for men and women but also carries classic sportswear and of course there are branches of Gap or Banana Republic all over the city. Chain stores for women include Ann Taylor, Talbots or Eileen Fisher and for men Eddie Bauer or Dockers. There is great bargain shopping in Manhattan, but you must know where to go and always be discriminating. The heaviest concentration of discounters is downtown with one notable exception: Daffy's on 57th between Lexington and Park Avenues. Century 21 at 22 Cortlandt Street (in the financial district) is a name everyone knows and trusts, though that's not to say that all the merchandise is top-quality. The women's lingerie department is usually a reliable bet and it buzzes with activity as Christian Dior, Jessica McClintock, and Natori labels are deeply discounted. The men's and women's clothing departments also stock and sell many well-known designer names. Filene's Basement and T.J. Maxx are two other notable fashion discounters, both at 620 Sixth Avenue (between 18th and 19th Streets). Stories about women wrestling each other to the ground over a pair of leopard print lycra tights are legendary but most days the ambiance is more mild-mannered. Also in the same building is Bed, Bath and Beyond, a vast space filled to capacity with good quality sheets, towels, linens, candles, gadgets for the kitchen and bathroom and on and on. As you travel further downtown, the bargains tend to be hit or miss. Canal Street shopping can be good – Ezra Cohen (307 Grand Street) or Harris Levy (278 Grand Street) specialise in linens and sheets – but more often it's not. Beware of the fakes: never buy a Rolex or Cartier watch regardless of how authentic it looks or how sincere the vendor seems. There are acres of imitation Hermès, Prada and Gucci handbags and scarves, don't be taken in. Remember, this is a place where you can and must haggle or you will get ripped off.

The one market not to be missed is the Annex (Sixth Avenue at 26th Street) where hip New Yorkers and Europeans converge on weekends to scour the antiques market on one side of this parking lot and the flea market on the other. What to buy in New York depends on your expendable cash and personal tastes. Compact discs from the Virgin Megastore (Broadway between 45th and 46th Streets) are much better value than in Great Britain and the Continent. Sportswear, outdoor wear and equipment, trainers and running shoes, jeans whether Levis, Calvin Klein or Gap, Walkmans, souvenir T-shirts and sweaters, computer and photographic equipment, souvenirs from Warner Brothers or Planet Hollywood, Clinique cosmetics and American sweets such as Reese's pieces or Butterfingers are all less expensive in the States than in the UK. Though there are no "local" arts and crafts, the museum shops offer an excellent choice of American and ethnic wares. The Museum of Modern Art shop (53rd Street between Fifth and Sixth Avenues) and the Metropolitan Museum Shop at Rockefeller Center are two standouts.

Local newspapers such as the *New York Times* enjoy international recognition and are cheap. Various chains such as Doubleday, Dalton and Barnes & Noble, the world's largest bookstore, all have an excellent range of books and magazines at reasonable prices and often the added facility of a coffee shop. Barnes & Noble (Sixth Avenue between 21st and 22nd Streets) has large couches to lounge on without being hassled and is open until 2300 every night. The biggest and best second-hand bookstore is The Strand (828 Broadway at 12th Street), a must for book lovers.

EATING AND DRINKING

Musts include bagels and muffins, iced coffee and tea, root beer, pecan pie, New York cheesecake, brunch at the weekend, eating in ethnic areas such as Little Italy or Chinatown and sampling the clam chowder at the Oyster Bar in Grand

Central Station.

There are probably more restaurants to the square mile than in any other city. Eating out can be as cheap or as expensive as you like, starting at about $4 for a hamburger or sandwich with several times the content of British ones. A meal at a reasonable restaurant can be had for between $20 and $30 per head. For a full meal in the evening, when prices are usually increased, at one of the better New York restaurants you must expect to pay from $40 upwards.

TRANSPORT

Conditions underfoot can be unpleasant and even dangerous during wet and snowy weather. Paved areas are often uneven and comfortable walking shoes are advisable. Snowboots are much cheaper in the US than in the UK.

The subway and bus systems have a standard $1.50 fare. Use tokens, change or a Metrocard which comes in value from $5 to $20. The subway system is extensive; most of it is shabby, appallingly noisy and crowded in rush-hours. Travel on the subway, and subway stations, can be dangerous late at night. Taxis are yellow and plentiful except during the rush hour and when it rains. They are hailed in the street. Fares are metered.

SECURITY

Crime is common in New York, but given reasonable common sense the risk should not be greater than in any other major US city. Beggars are not particularly aggressive.

ATLANTA

Metropolitan Atlanta is a shoppers' paradise and has 16 regional shopping malls. Every neighbourhood will have at least one mall. There are even antique malls (for anything over 75 years old).

Dominating the town centre is Underground Atlanta on Martin Luther King Jr Drive: this is a combined shopping and entertainment centre with lots of eating places. Otherwise the nearest mall is Lennox Square, one of the largest in the south-east, complemented by its newer and grander neighbour, Phipps Plaza, which is more expensive, but beautiful to browse through.

Perimeter Mall, Northlake Mall, Cumberland Mall, Gwinnett Mall and Town Center Mall are all within 30 minutes' or so drive of downtown and each has from 100 to 200 shops including the major department stores – Macy's, J.C.Penney, Rich's and Sears.

Jaeger are at Phipps Plaza and Laura Ashley in Lennox, but prices are high.

The *Atlanta Constitution and Journal* is the leading local newspaper. Other local and national newspapers are widely available at hotels and kiosks.

EATING AND DRINKING

Eating out is cheaper than in the UK. Apart from the usual fast-food outlets there are numerous middle-of-the-road restaurants – Grady's, Steak 'n' Ale, Shoney's, Denny's, Houston's and Mick's. High-class restaurants abound, especially in Buckhead and Downtown – the big hotels, the Peasant, City Grill and the Pano and Paul's group. Consult Yellow Pages for locations.

TRANSPORT

The MARTA (Metropolitan Atlanta Rapid Transit system) system is clean and cheap, but still largely confined to the downtown area. It offers an overground and underground rail system with connnecting bus service. The flat-rate charge is $1.50 including connecting bus. Metered taxis are available in the town centre and at all large hotels.

SECURITY

Atlanta has been named the most violent city in the United States, but with common sense precautions this need not be a problem.

BOSTON

The effects of Boston's Puritan origins are still felt today. Some suburban areas are still dry, with alcohol only available in restaurants for those over 21. Liquor stores close all day on Sunday.

After New York, Los Angeles and San Francisco, Boston has one of the highest costs of living in the continental United States, although there are many places to shop inexpensively.

Faneuil Hall Marketplace and Quincy Market are situated in three restored nineteenth-century buildings between North Street and State Street. There are over 150 outlets here, many of them especially good for creative and unusual gifts and souvenirs. The Quincy Market building specialises in every kind of food you can think of.

Newbury Street is expensive, but worth a look. The shopping area stretches from Arlington Street to Massachusetts Avenue and comprises more than 300 outlets including galleries, boutiques, eating places and exclusive stores.

Copley Place at 100 Huntington Avenue is pricey, but convenient, with over 100 outlets serving the major hotels. It includes Neiman Marcus.

The shops at Prudential Center at 800 Boylston Street, include Saks Fifth Avenue and a food court.

Downtown Crossing is a central, outdoor, pedestrianised area based on Washington Street which includes the famous Filenes Basement for fashion bargains at 426 and Macy's Marsh at 450, New England's largest department store, as well as street vendors.

Beacon Hill is a charming old cobble-stoned area whose Charles Street is well known for its antique shops. Also for antiques are the Boston Antique Center at 54 Canal Street and Brodney Gallery of Fine Arts at 811 Boylston Street

Recommended best buys include clothing such as Levis from Filenes, CDs from HMV at 24 Winter Street or Tower Records in Newbury Street, local foods such as maple syrup from Quincy Market and gifts and souvenirs from Faneuil Hall.

Good newspapers are available locally, such as the *Boston Globe,* which costs 50 cents daily. British newspapers are available at locations such as Copley Place. Recommended bookshops include branches of Barnes and Noble, Waterstones and Borders.

EATING AND DRINKING

Boston boasts a good selection of restaurants. The North End is little Italy and is a must for lovers of that cuisine. Chinatown, between Kneeland and Summer streets, offers a wide variety of oriental cuisine. Back Bay offers everything from trendy American *nouvelle cuisine* to long-established ethnic restaurants.

Boston and the New England area have a justly proud reputation for seafood such as lobster and clam chowder. Legal Sea Foods has a claim to be the best seafood restaurant in the US. There are eight branches in Greater Boston.

TRANSPORT

The Massachusetts Bay Transportation Authority (MBTA), known as the T, provides very good service to just about anywhere in metropolitan Boston. Trains start early and run late. The bus service is good. The flat-rate fare is 85 cents and the correct change is required when boarding. Daily passes are available. Taxis may be hailed on the streets and there are stands throughout the city. Cost is about $4 per mile.

SECURITY

Boston proudly promotes itself as America's walking city and it is indeed possible to walk from downtown hotels to the main shopping areas, although it is not sensible to do so alone late at night. There are street beggars, but they rarely cause any hassle.

CHICAGO

There are lots of things worth looking at in the malls and plazas. Long, down-filled coats are popular at $200 upwards. Fur hats and ear-muffs are equally popular, overshoes or boots are useful for the slush and snow. Almost every type of fur, from rabbit to sable, is available at reasonable prices. Mink is a particularly good buy, as there are many varieties often at prices well below those in the UK.

Chicago's stores contain a wide variety of women's clothing of all kinds and cater for all ages, sizes, tastes and incomes. Bloomingdale's. Henri Bendel, Saks Fifth Avenue, Neiman Marcus, Marshall Field's, Lord and Taylor and most Michigan Avenue stores carry clothes with international and exclusive labels. These can be expensive, but good quality moderately priced clothing can also be obtained. There are also discount houses such as Loehmanns, Handmoor and T.J.Maxx which sell name-brand clothing at lower prices.

Downtown Chicago is compact and coverable on foot for the most part. It is defined by the area of the Loop, or elevated railway, which surrounds it. Within the Loop on State Street are the Marshall Field department store and Carson Pirie Scott; these provide a comfortable and convenient overview of what is available. There is a shopping mall just to the west of the Loop in the Sears Tower.

More fashionable now for shopping than the traditional downtown area is the "Magnificent Mile" stretching north of the Chicago River along Michigan Avenue.

EATING AND DRINKING

Eating out is popular and there are literally thousands of restaurants providing a good selection of international menus at a wide range of prices. An adequate daily lunch in a cafeteria or cheap restaurant can be obtained for $10 or so. A business lunch for two at an acceptable restaurant will cost around $30 per head including drink and a tip. A dinner for two in town, including wine and tip, will cost at least $50 per head at a reasonable restaurant, but the price can go much higher. Visitors wishing to mark Chicago's meat-eating and meat-packing tradition should try Eli's at 215 East Chicago Avenue.

TRANSPORT

Public transport is reasonable and more extensively used than in many other US cities. Bus services in the city are good and cost $1 plus 25 cents for transfer. There are several underground routes at the same cost. Taxis are numerous; you should check that the meter is on when entering.

SECURITY

Despite its reputation, Chicago is a safer place to live than many other US cities.

CLEVELAND

The city centres on Public Square. Malls in the area include the Tower City Centre in Terminal Tower.

The only British newspaper readily available is the *Financial Times* which can be bought in the city centre on the morning of publication.

EATING AND DRINKING

There is a considerable price range in eating out. Few restaurants have dress requirements. At weekends, even in summer, many downtown restaurants are closed. There are some reasonable restaurants on the waterfront, just west of Public Square.

TRANSPORT

There is a better than average bus service, but it covers only a small area of the city. Outside the city centre and the airport there are no taxi stands. Suburban taxis do not always have meters.

DALLAS

The centre of Dallas is on Main Street, where the original Neiman Marcus is still to be found. To the north of the western end of Main Street, the West End Historical District is a magnet for tourists and has some interesting shops and eating places. Equally fashionable now is Deep Ellum which also centres on Main Street, but is to the east of downtown.

Many reasonable eating places can be found in Deep Ellum, such as the Deep Ellum Café on Elm Street.

HOUSTON

Houston society is very fashion – and label-conscious; women generally seem to own a fur coat or two for winter use.

Despite the city's ungainly sprawl, downtown Houston, basically defined by the area of Loop 610, can be largely accessed on foot. The main shopping mall, the Galleria, is situated on Westheimer to the west of the Loop.

EATING AND DRINKING
Houstonians are said to eat out more often than the citizens of any other US city. There is something in the region of 500 restaurants with a wide variety of meals at all prices and a range of ethnic foods on offer. There is a wide selection of good wines at reasonable prices. With the arrival of a number of "micro-breweries", good beer can also be found on draught.

TRANSPORT
The bus service is fairly limited compared with other US cities. Taxis are not too expensive, but they are not allowed to cruise for fares.

SECURITY
Houston has a high crime rate and although things have improved few people venture out on foot after dark.

LOS ANGELES

The only way for a visitor to successfully "shop" LA is to concentrate on just one or two parts of this massive city. If you try and take on too much you'll be overwhelmed. As in most other US cities, one secret of shopping is to find the nearest mall. There you will normally find all the choice you need. Should you prefer to be adventurous, there are other options. Los Angeles is not a "walking" city, but there are areas that you can drive to, park your car and actually spend the day strolling, window shopping and stopping for a light bite or a cappuccino.

If you were planning a rough itinerary, West Hollywood is a logical setting off point with one of Los Angeles's most famous names: Fred Segal (8100 Melrose at Crescent Boulevard) as a first stop. If Fred Segal didn't coin the phrase "one-stop shopping", he certainly capitalised on it. For a price, you can have alligator cowboy boots with silver tips, purchase a bottle of Estée Lauder self tan, and enjoy a delicious lunch, all under the same roof. The Melrose Avenue area is akin to the King's Road in London, a mix of trendy and funky and lots of great vintage clothing stores. Not to be missed are American Rag (150 South La Brea Avenue, between First and Second Streets), Aardvark (7579 Melrose Avenue) and Time after Time (7425 Melrose Avenue between Martel Avenue and Vista Street). If you've always wanted to dress like Winona Ryder at the Oscars, you should visit Lily et Cie, (9044 Burton Way). This is where she buys her vintage gowns.

A quick drive down La Cienega is the Beverly Center (8500 Beverly Blvd). The mall – which covers an entire city block, has over 150 shops, 14 movie theatres and a Hard Rock Café – is a challenge for even the most indefatigable shopper. And just across the street is the grande dame of all discount stores, Loehmann's. Further west towards Beverly Hills, you could park the car and visit LA's elegant department stores, Neiman Marcus (9700 Wilshire Boulevard.), Saks Fifth Avenue (9600 Wilshire) and Barney's New York (9570 Wilshire Boulevard). While at Barney's, don't forget to go to Barney Greengrass, on the fifth floor, it's a favourite lunchtime haunt for celebs. Just around the corner is Rodeo Drive. On Rodeo, shopping is an "experience" and one you need to dress for. Shorts, t-shirts or running shoes are considered inappropriate attire, the locals dress up for Rodeo and so should you. Considered by many the glitziest shopping block in the world, Rodeo has everything – from mink-trimmed eyeglasses to $45,000 dresses.

Beyond Rodeo Drive is Century City Shopping Center and Marketplace, a vast mall covering eighteen acres and offering close to two hundred shops, the second largest movie theatre in the US with an unbelievable 14 screens, a supermarket and valet parking. Now it's time to head out to Santa Monica where you can either shop, take in a little culture or do both. Santa Monica is an art lover's nirvana. The Bergamot station, (2525 Michigan Avenue) was formerly a trolley station and is now the hottest destination on the beach. A small settlement of tin sheds which cover 5.5 acres (2.25 hectares), this complex consists of 21 galleries which exhibit and sell paintings, sculpture, photography, furniture, glass and collectibles. If clothes, not crafts, are your thing, try Montana Avenue which is where the beautiful people shop. It's less expensive than Rodeo but still pricey. There's a mix of designer names, antique shops, and the original Shabby Chic shop (1013 Montana Avenue, between 10th & 11th Streets) where British country style meets Californian dreaming

From there, head north on Pacific Coast Highway to Sunset Boulevard, through Brentwood, Bel-Air, Beverly Hills. and then you reach Sunset Plaza which in the last five years has become Los Angeles's flashest shopping area with outdoor cafés and tons of boutiques. Among these are Oliver Peoples glasses, A/X Exchange, Laura Urbinati for women's fashion, and BCBG. There's also the Mondrian Hotel, celeb hotelier Ian Schrager's hottest new property.

In a culture that embraces mall mentality, you might wonder who bothers with markets. However, with 9.3 million people in Los Angeles County, the markets, like the shops are always booming. The best are the Santa Monica's Third Street Promenade, an open-air, pedestrians-only zone which runs four city blocks and should not be missed. On offer: restaurants, shops, bookstores, and every Wednesday and Saturday, a farmers and flower market. The Farmers' Market (6333 West Third Street at Fairfax Avenue) is a market which the locals flock to as much if not more than the tourists. There are over 160 stalls selling every kind of food imaginable, from fresh fruit and vegetables to ethnic specialities. There are also stalls with Arts & Crafts, jewellery, candles, clothing and accessories as well as tourist souvenirs.

The Rose Bowl flea market (1001 Rose Bowl Drive at Arroyo Blvd, Pasadena), held on the second Sunday of the month, is without question the best in town. Angelenos in the know never plan brunch for the second Sunday as everyone goes to the Rose Bowl. While you're there, do wander through Pasadena's Old Town (on Colorado Blvd and Raymond Avenue), a 12-square block area which feels like a small village, makes for a delightful change after all the hustle and bustle of the mega-malls.

EATING AND DRINKING
Restaurants are of paramount importance in Tinseltown.

Where the studio big guns choose to chow down is as important as who they put on contract. Remember, two worldwide institutions: California cuisine and Superchefs, began here. Dress codes are very casual and the standard tipping is 15% of the final bill. Like shopping the key is to decide where and what you want to eat. Some of the big flash names on the restaurant circuit are Chinois on Main (2709 Main Street, Santa Monica), Border Grill Citrus (6703 Melrose Avenue, West Hollywood), Matsuhisa (129 North La Cienega Boulevard., Beverly Hills) and Joe's (1023 Abbot Kinney Boulevard, Venice), but this is barely scratching the surface.

TRANSPORT
Local bus services are restricted to a few main arterial streets, but they are certainly worth exploring as taxi services are limited and fares are high.

SECURITY
In many areas it is not safe to walk, particularly at night. However, reasonable precautions and the application of common sense greatly reduce the risks.

MIAMI

Miami has a large catchment area for shopping, including many countries in the Caribbean and Latin America which can be reached by plane from Miami. Miami itself is also large, stretching geographically from Homestead in the south to Fort Lauderdale in the north, about 50 miles. From the sea to the westernmost suburbs is some 25 miles. Fortunately the airport is centrally situated and little more than 10-12 miles from the places most visitors to Miami usually head for. Obviously with such huge distances the use of a car is a necessity. Miami is the home of the indoor shopping mall and those visiting with serious shopping in mind would do well to stay in a hotel near a mall.

Miami's biggest and best mall is Dadeland, which has a number of department stores as well as many shops and cafés. The Dadeland Marriott is on the Metrorail which links to Miami Airport. Omni Mall is smaller than Dadeland, but it has a reasonable selection of shops and is also very close to the scenic Bayside where there are further shops and cafés. Two other good shopping malls, quite a way out of town, are Sawgrass Mills on Sawgrass Expressway, West Sunrise Boulevard and Aventura Mall at 19501 Biscayne Boulevard,

North Miami Beach. Near by and good for electrical goods is Brands Mart at 4900 NW67 Street.

Most people in Miami prefer to shop in a mall, but there is shopping downtown which is good for electronic goods and there is also a department store. The nearest city centre mall is Bayside Marketplace on Biscayne Boulevard.

Miami Beach has quite a good selection of shops, but no mall as such. Key Biscayne has only a few shops. Coconut Grove is just south of downtown Miami and its shops, restaurants and hotels are popular with the younger set. A UK equivalent would be Covent Garden.

Fort Lauderdale is a reasonable alternative to Miami as a vacation spot with some quite good shopping. Las Olas Boulevard has a mixture of fashionable and trendy boutiques, galleries and restaurants.

EATING AND DRINKING

Hotel MIA in the Miami International Airport has arguably one of the best restaurants around, and the airport has plenty of good if pricey shops.

For meals at moderate prices, try Café Bistro at 10121 SW 72nd Ave, Miami, Café Med at 3015 Grand Avenue, Coconut Grove, Greenwich Village at 1001 S Miami Avenue, Miami or Benihana's (see Yellow Pages for address).

More expensive are Christy's at 3101 Ponce de Leon at Coral Gables and Rusty Pelican at 3201 Rickenbacker Causeway, Key Biscayne.

There are also several cheap restaurants in Miami such as El Pub at 1548 SW 8th Street, La Caretta (see Yellow Pages), the Big Fish at 55 SW Miami Avenue, the Big Cheese at 8080 SW 67th Avenue and Villa Habana at 3398 SW 22nd Street. Also cheap and worth trying are Bayside Hut at 3501 Rickenbacker Causeway, Key Biscayne, News Café at 800 Ocean Drive, Miami Beach, Bennigan's (see Yellow Pages) and Bayside Mall at 401 Biscayne Boulevard.

TRANSPORT

The Metromover which circulates downtown is excellent value at 25 cents. Taxis are plentiful, speedy, safe and somewhat expensive. Most visitors who want to get around, particularly those with limited time, will need a hire car.

SECURITY

Crime is a problem. Taking standard precautions will contribute towards a safe and pleasant stay.

SAN FRANCISCO

Even by US standards, San Francisco is an expensive city, more so than New York and Washington DC.

Though San Francisco covers only 47 square miles and seems tiny compared to Los Angeles, it is a shopper's nirvana. The city is centred around Market Street, but Union Square, just a couple of blocks to the north, is the shopping hub. There's the usual mix of department stores and boutiques on or near the square – Macy's (170 O'Farrell Street at Stockton), Neiman Marcus (150 Stockton at Geary), Hermès (1 Union Square), Saks Fifth Avenue (384 Post Street), Brooks Brothers (201 Post Street), Cartier (231 Post Street), Tiffany & Co (350 Post Street) and Gump's (135 Post Street) world famous for its collection of jade, pearls, Asian treasures, china and crystal. If you adore exquisite linens, pop into Scheuer Linens (318 Stockton) next door to Gump's. Around the perimeter of the square are plenty of boutiques as well as branches of some of the nation-wide retailers like Williams-Sonoma (150 Post Street), Crate & Barrel (125 Grant Avenue), Banana Republic (256 Grant Avenue) and Emporio Armani (1 Grant Avenue). Don't miss Wilkes Bashford (375 Sutter Street), one of San Francisco's most prestigious retailers of clothing for men and women. They are renowned for their striking and innovative window displays.

The SoMa district (South of Market) is a bargain hunter's paradise with lots of outlets and warehouses. Yerba Buena Square (899 Howard) has the Burlington Coat Factory Warehouse, The Shoe Pavillion and many clothing and accessory discount shops for the entire family. Gunne Sax Factory Outlet (35 Stanford Street) and Six Sixty Factory Outlet Center (660 Third) both have big names at discount.

If you're looking for that special something and are willing to pay full-price wander through The San Francisco Shopping Center (65 Market Street), a $140-million vertical shopping mall with the department store Nordstrom – famous for its incomparable service – as its anchor. There are 90 boutiques in the Center with the usual high-quality, good value names such as J. Crew, Ann Taylor, and Adrienne Vittadini.

Chinatown, few blocks north of Market, is vast and spreads out around Grant Avenue. This is more of a tourist attraction than a shopper's destination as most of the shops sell cheap reproduction ceramics, lace and other mass-produced Asian objects. At the extreme northern end, a mile or so away from Market Street are more tourist attractions which should be considered by the visitor, (whether to visit or to avoid is debatable). If you decide to take the plunge then Ghirardelli Square, once a chocolate factory, is now a very attractive complex of over 75 shops and restaurants and home to the Folk Art International, The California Crafts Museum, The Green Peace Environmental Store and Ghirardelli Chocolate Manufactory, an old-fashioned ice cream parlour and candy store.

Next door is The Cannery, originally the Del Monte Fruit Company built in 1909. It was remodelled in 1968 and turned into a three-story complex of shops, restaurants and galleries. There's a comedy club, a movie theatre, and the San Francisco Museum. It has very much the same feeling of the Ghirardelli complex but its bigger and busier. Finally, there's Fisherman's wharf and Pier 39, one of the most-visited tourist attractions in America. Pier 39 is full of knick-knack shops, nothing particularly original but relatively inexpensive, though downmarket.

Pacific Heights is one of the best residential areas in the city and has three exceptional shopping streets; Fillmore, Union and Sacramento near Laurel Village. Haight Ashbury of flower-power fame, a couple of miles west, has interesting, quirky shops, a good many of which still retain the hippie orientation for which this area was known in the 60s and 70s. Revisit the 60s at Buffalo Exchange (1555 Haight), a vintage clothing store which specialises in the funky psychedelic threads that were cutting edge then.

San Francisco is a city with a distinguished literary past, so its no surprise that there is a plethora of bookstores. City Lights Booksellers & Publishers (261 Columbus) became the city's most famous bookstore in the 1950s when the writers of the Beat generation were first emerging in San Francisco. There's an entire section devoted to the works of Jack Kerouac, Allen Ginsburg and Ken Kesey. The shop is often packed well until its doors close at midnight. Just a few blocks away immerse yourself in authentic Victorian ambiance while browsing through an impressive selection of maps, globes and atlases at Thomas Brothers Maps (550 Jackson Street at Columbus). Borders (400 Post Street) is the largest bookstore in the city and is located close to Union Square.

EATING AND DRINKING

Food is a serious business in this city though you don't necessarily need to pay serious prices to eat well. Because there are so many diverse neighbourhoods in the city, you are spoiled for choice – from Californian *nouvelle cuisine* to Chinese. Some of the big name, trendy spots are Postrio (545 Post), Stars

(150 Redwood Alley) Fournou's Ovens (905 California), Bix (56 Gold), Greens (Fort Mason Center, Bldg A). More mainstream are Perry's (1944 Union), Prego (2000 Union), Sam's Grill (374 Bush) and Kuleto's (221 Powell). Dinner for two at a reasonable restaurant costs from $50 up, not including drinks or sales tax. A business lunch will cost from $35 per head.

TRANSPORT

The public transport system works well. A network of buses, trolley-buses, trams and cable-cars criss-cross the city. The cable-car system, built by a Scotsman in the 1870s and completely renovated in 1983-4, is still an essential part of the city's public transportation system and a popular tourist attraction. All services run to a reasonably late hour. There is a standard fare with the facility for free transfer from one line to another. There is a good taxi service. Taxis can either be flagged down in the street or ordered by telephone. From the airport there is an excellent door-to-door van service called SuperShuttle which operates 24 hours a day and guarantees no more than three stops, except during busy holiday periods.

SECURITY

Although it is not without its fair share of crime, San Francisco is one of the few American cities where it is generally safe for people to walk on the streets after dark. As with most large cities, however, certain areas, like the Tenderloin (near Union Square-Theatre District) Western Addition (near Japantown) and some blocks in SoMa (south of Fifth Street) should be avoided.

SEATTLE

The main shopping areas in downtown Seattle are the Westlake Centre and Pike Place Market. Pike Place is fun with its small shops – many of them selling craft items – eating places and buskers. Pioneer Square, about a half mile southwards and a couple of blocks from the waterfront, is another restored area with galleries and bookshops.

In the suburbs there are Bellevue Square, South Centre Mall, Auburn Mall and numerous others. There you will find the usual range of shops such as Sears, Nordstrom, J.C.Penney, Bon Marché and labels such as Gap and Eddie

Bauer among the customary vast range of goods.

Indian handicrafts make popular gifts and souvenirs. They are available downtown, at most tourist sites and at the airport. Otherwise salmon, pre-packed for the UK, or Starbucks coffee are recommended.

There is a wide range of local newspapers available at reasonable prices. Barnes and Noble has a good range of books.

EATING AND DRINKING

Seafood is particularly recommended. In Pike Place Market, for example, there is the Athenian Inn. Otherwise a trip out to Capitol Hill in the area around Broadway might be worth while for a meal that will not break the bank.

TRANSPORT

Buses are reasonable, but slow – and free downtown. Taxis are ubiquitous, but expensive – airport to downtown will cost $35.

HAWAII

HONOLULU

Language **English**
Currency **US dollar of 100 cents. £1=1.60, Mar 1997**
Shops **0930–2100 Mon to Sat; more restricted times Sun**

The islands of Hawaii form a state of the USA. Nowadays it is packed with tourists and far from idyllic, but much of the hassle is confined to Waikiki. In central Honolulu the shopping area around King Street is fairly compact and Chinatown is near by, around Maunakea Street. Fort Street Mall is recommended. Shopping hours in central Honolulu are earlier than elsewhere, and are geared to the business community. The island's major mall is the Ala Moana Centre situated on Ala Moana Boulevard between the airport and Waikiki. The Bishop Museum shop has a wide range of artefacts from all over the neighbouring area of the Pacific. Hotel shops tend to be expensive.

For the dedicated tourist desperate to look like one, there are always aloha shirts at a wide range of prices. Other trivia include T-shirts, leis and hula music. The more serious will find interesting arts and crafts to buy such as bone or wood carvings, coral jewellery or a lau hala hat.

EATING AND DRINKING
Good food is to be found in the famous Restaurant Row near the harbour on Ala Moana Boulevard. *Luan* is a sort of Hawaiian buffet and is well worth a try, usually good value at a set all-in price.

TRANSPORT
There is a good bus network which operates on a single fare basis.

URUGUAY

MONTEVIDEO

Language **Spanish**
Currency **Uruguayan peso of 100 centesimos.**
£1=14.38, Mar 1997
Banks **1300–1700 Mon to Fri**
Shops **0900–1200, 1400–1900 Mon to Fri,**
0900–1230 Sat
Tipping **10–15 per cent expected in addition to cover charge and VAT in hotels and restaurants; tips expected for all services, and by taxi drivers**

Although a virtually complete range of clothing is available in Montevideo, much of it is of indifferent quality and finish. Furs are worn during the winter months and a fair selection is available at reasonable prices. It is possible to buy inexpensive leather, and good leather handbags and shoes are often cheaper than in the UK. There are also bargains to be had in wool and suede.

No English–language newspapers are produced locally, although the *Buenos Aires Herald* is readily available. British newspapers are not available. English-language books are, but very expensive.

EATING AND DRINKING
A lunch or a simple meal at a barbecue restaurant (*parrillada*)

will cost about £10. A three-course business-style lunch or dinner with local wine would cost about £20 a head. Beef and fish are both excellent. Uruguayan wines are relatively inexpensive and have improved considerably in recent years. Local beer is good and cheap. Imported spirits are expensive and the locally produced ones are poor.

TRANSPORT
All public transport is very cheap by European standards. Bus services are frequent and reliable, though not particularly comfortable and often overcrowded. Taxis are plentiful and are fitted with meters. They are generally safe, and recognisable by their yellow roofs.

UZBEKISTAN

TASHKENT

Language **Uzbek**
Currency **sum, not yet convertible**
Banks **exchange currency booths will change new (pre-1990), unmarked US dollar bills, in denominations under 20 dollars**

Tashkent has a large number of markets selling local produce at prices cheap by UK standards. In the summer a succession of high quality fruit and vegetables is available.

There is a Turkish-Uzbek joint venture which sells a small number of Tesco home products. A small selection of Western-style goods, including cigarettes and drinks, is sporadically available at high prices from a number of specialist stores. Almost no clothing is available, except in a small number of expensive and poorly stocked private shops.

EATING AND DRINKING
Restaurants tend to be expensive, the menus limited and the music deafening. Perhaps the most satisfactory way to eat out is to go to an unofficial restaurant in a private house or flat. An introduction is usually necessary, especially for the Korean establishments in south Tashkent. There is one evening club which foreigners can attend by invitation which offers music, drinks and sometimes food in a converted art gallery.

TRANSPORT

The city is spacious, distances are large and relatively few places are within walking range. Local transport is still relatively cheap by foreign standards. The underground is efficient, but it has only three lines. There is a good, if slow and crowded, tram, bus and trolley-bus service during the day, but few vehicles run late in the evening or during the night. Taxis are few, but metered: most drivers are happy to offer lifts to people standing by the road at an agreed price.

VANUATU

VILA

Langauge **Bislama, English, French**
Currency **vatu of 100 centimes. £1=179,**
   Mar 1997
Shops **0730–1130, 1330–1700 Mon to Fri 0730–1100 Sat**
Tipping **no; can cause offence**

Vanuatu has the third most expensive economy in the Pacific after New Caledonia and French Polynesia. The country exports cocoa, coffee and beef. Almost all consumer goods are imported and subject to high import duties. Food in particular is expensive. There are three local supermarkets stocking mainly French, Australian and New Zealand products. Availability of items is dependent on the arrival of supplies by ship, but by and large there are few shortages. Cyclones can affect the supply of local produce. Prices generally are high.

Clothes are either of poor quality or expensive and the choice of footwear is poor. There is a limited and rather expensive range of slacks and shirts available although most shops do not get beyond the T-shirt and shorts level.

The market opposite the Government Buildings is open on Wednesday, Friday and Saturday mornings and has handicrafts and shells as well as flowers and produce.

For local arts and crafts go to Art Blong Yumi at Melcoffe, Goodies Store or Handicraft Blong Vanuatu next to the library on the main street.

The British *International Express* and *Weekly Telegraph* and Australian newspapers and magazines are available from Stop Press and Chew Store. The only local newspapers are the government owned *Vanuatu Weekly* and the independent bi-weekly *Trading Post*. A limited and expensive range of books can be bought locally.

EATING AND DRINKING
There are a number of good restaurants. The general standard is high and prices are similar to or dearer than those in the UK. There is an emphasis on French cuisine. A good selection of soft drinks and squashes is available, although they are rather expensive. There is also a wide choice of wine from France and Australia at prices only a little higher than in the UK. Kava a non-alcoholic drink made from the root of a plant, is the national drink.

Most international cigarettes are on sale and are cheaper than in the UK.

TRANSPORT
Buses are used infrequently by tourists. There is a good number of taxis and fares are relatively cheap.

SECURITY
There are few serious problems of personal security.

VENEZUELA

CARACAS

Language **Spanish**
Currency **bolivar (B) of 100 centimos. £1=763, Mar 1997**
Banks **0830-1130, 1400-1630 Mon to Fri**
Credit cards **widely accepted**
Shops **0900-1300, 1500-1900 Mon to Sat**
Tipping **general and generous; tip in addition to 10 per cent service charge in restaurants**

There are no serious shortages, although imports are rather expensive. Most men's clothing, including tropical suits, is available, though neither quality nor variety is as good as in the UK, nor is there any price advantage. Shopping centres are full of boutiques selling women's clothing at every price level and locally made clothes have improved greatly in quality in recent years. However styles available will not always appeal to European taste. Shoes are a good buy, with a wide variety of colours, styles and fittings, although larger sizes may be difficult to obtain. Gold is very good value and there are several workshops which make jewellery on request.

British newspapers are almost impossible to find, apart from the *Financial Times*, which is available at the Tamanaco Hotel, usually the day after publication.There is an English-language daily newspaper printed locally. There are almost no bookshops which sell books in English.

EATING AND DRINKING
There are over 800 registered restaurants in Caracas, in which quality can vary as much as price. Wine in restaurants tends to be expensive, although local beer and soft drinks are good. There is an excellent supply of locally produced gin, rum and liqueurs.

There is a good selection of citrus and other fruits and year-round strawberries.

TRANSPORT
With perhaps the exception of the metro, public transport is not regularly used by visitors. There is an excellent metrobus system, linking with the metro, which is frequent, cheap and clean.Other buses are rather dilapidated. Collective taxis and minibuses ply a fixed route at a fixed price. Ordinary taxis are reasonable in price, although not advisable for women alone at night.

SECURITY
Because of the difficult economic conditions, crime is increasing, particularly in Caracas.

VIETNAM

Language Vietnamese
Currency dong. £1=18,630, Mar 1997
Traveller's cheques dollar denominated; cash
  US dollars widely used, though not legal tender
Credit cards accepted in hotels and restaurants
Cashpoints in banks
Shops 0700/0900-1800/2200, lunchtime closing
Refunds considered unlucky, but exchange possible
Bargaining yes
Duty-free at airports; perfume and drink worth
  buying, handicrafts cheaper in town
Tipping included in taxi fares, service charge added
  in restaurants and hotels, but small tip in addition
  appreciated
Export restrictions antiques (anything over 20 years
  old) cannot be exported

A dual pricing system operates and the cost of living for
Westerners is high, with high duty on imported goods. Hotels,
for example, are on a different scale from that used for
Vietnamese and transport costs might be double the
Vietnamese price. French can be useful when speaking to older
Vietnamese, but English is increasingly widely spoken.
Customers are encouraged to examine goods before making a
purchase and while they may come under pressure to buy,
mere handling is no commitment.

There is an increasing number of smart shops as more and
more overseas Vietnamese return home, although their claim
to sell imported designer goods should be discounted. The
copy trade in fashion, CDs and videos, gems and paintings is
booming.

The Vietnamese are justifiably famous for their handicrafts.
Recommended as gifts or souvenirs are lacquerware or tortoise-
shell goods, Hanoi stone ornaments (a Northern speciality),
ceramics, blue painted dishes and crockery, ginseng (genuine),
gold and silver jewellery, leather and snakeskin items, amber,
jade and gem-stones (watch out for fakes), silk goods including
kimonos, which are cheap, and artificial flowers, embroidered
napkins and tablecloths, wooden wall plaques inlaid with
mother of pearl, brass and bronzeware and carpets. For collectors there are old currency notes and coins, stamps, paintings
and sketches. All are widely available.

There are plenty of flowers, including orchids, available.

They are all beautiful and inexpensive, particularly in the markets.

There is an increasing number of restaurants and cafés. Vietnamese food is generally mild and quite palatable to European taste, but facilities and hygiene may not always be up to Western standards. Particularly worth trying is a steamboat, Vietnam's answer to the fondue. Snake and dog restaurants exist for those with stronger constitutions.

Beer, soft drinks and some liqueurs can be purchased locally, but the Johnnie Walker bottle will not necessarily contain the original distillation. The beer is good. Snake or gekko wine is not for the squeamish.

Seafood is recommended, including seafood pancakes (*ban sao*). Noodles and spring rolls are musts. Try also Vietnamese pepper, coffee, peanut brittle, sesame-seed brittle and dried fruits.

It is increasingly dangerous to show any ostentation in personal possessions, since you may become a target. Look out particularly for the motor-bike boys when crossing the road. Also the local women who will pursue foreign men. Beggars are persistent.

HANOI

There are no modern arcades, Western retailers or designer shops–although good imitation designer-wear is readily available at fair prices. Local markets sell a range of basic goods, but supplies and quality are erratic.The main area for shopping is a triangular area in Northern Hanoi known as the Old Quarter. In days gone by, the original 36 streets were each named for the craft practised there. However as tourism increases, shops of all types are opening all over town.

The *Vietnamese News* is the local daily English-language newspaper. A limited variety of foreign newspapers and magazines can be found at the Metropole Hotel at 15 Ngo Quyen Street.

EATING AND DRINKING

You can sample a steamboat at the Piano Bar in the Old Quarter or at the Purple Rain in Giang Vo Street. The Cha Ca Fish Restaurant in Cha Ca Street is a very special experience. At the top end of the market, the best local cuisine restaurants are the Indochine at 16 Nam Ngu, Club Opera at 59 Ly Thai To and Restaurant 202 at 202A Pho Hue.

TRANSPORT
There is no usable public transport other than taxis, readily available, particularly from any of the larger hotels, or cyclo- (bicycle rickshaws). Fares are negotiable, but hotels and bar owners are often willing to advise.

SECURITY
Hanoi is a particularly safe city and can be travelled on foot at almost any time. Beggars are only a minor nuisance.

HO CHI MINH CITY

Roads and pavements were not made with high heels in mind. Local artists sell their oil paintings on the street or in one of the numerous art galleries. There are also many charcoal sketches on Dong Khoi Street and elsewhere. Framing is available, which is good and cheap. You will also find impressive detailed hand-carved varnished wooden models of galleons, sampans and other old boats at prices ranging from US$5 to 50. Wooden Disney figures cost only a few dollars.

The main tourist and shopping area is within District 1 and all references here unless otherwise stated are to District 1. For Vietnamese silk and silk clothing, lacquerwear or other souvenirs or gifts try the shops in Dong Khoi Street and Le Loi. For example, try Prestige or Viet Silk in Dong Khoi for silks. For jewellery try Saigon Jewellery Company at 2D Nguyen Trung Truc or Saigon Jewellery Centre at 68 Le Loi. For leather and snake or crocodile skin try Tran Quoc Lan at 97 Le Thanh Ton. For ceramics try Nga in Ngo Duc Ke or Van Hien in Pasteur Street.

English-language books and newspapers are two or three times their price in the UK. Newspapers can be found in hotel shops or at Xunhasaba at 25B Nguyen Binh Khiem Street. For books try the Foreign Bookshop on Dong Khoi Street. Several cheap second-hand bookshops will be found in Pham Ngoc Lao, a favourite area for backpackers.

EATING AND DRINKING
New restaurants are opening all the time. They can be inexpensive and excellent for those who like local food. Many bars also serve food. Finding somewhere to eat is not a problem and prices vary according to standards. At the top end of the market for local cuisine is the Hoa Mic in the New World Hotel. Reasonable are the Lemon Grass in Nguyen Thiep Street, Vietnam House in Dong Khoi Street and Thanh Nien in

Hai Ba Trung Street. In District 3 are Blue Ginger or Ngoc Suong Saigon, both in Nam Ky Khoi Nghia Street, the latter specialises in seafood. The Nha Hang Ban Seo in Nguyen Trai Street in District 3, specialises in pancakes, oily, but tasty and cheap.

TRANSPORT

Most buses are old and dirty. There are now thousands of taxis and they are cheap. Use one of the better known taxis such as Saigontaxi for preference, but still take a local map to show your destination – the driver may not speak English. Motor-bike taxis are becoming more common. You ride pillion and pay a small fee. Cyclos are a pleasant way to get about, but they are now often forbidden from operating in many parts of the town centre. Hiring a bicycle can be dangerous.

BRITISH VIRGIN ISLANDS

ROAD TOWN TORTOLA

Language **English**
Currency **US dollar; also £ sterling and East Caribbean dollar(EC$)**
Banks **0900–1400 Mon to Thur, 0900–1400, 1600–1800 Fri**
Tipping **10–15 per cent in restaurants and bars**

The British Virgin Islands are at the very top end of the tourist market. Thanks to the need to service the up-market yachting holiday makers, local supermarkets and other shops are very well stocked. However almost everything is imported and so is expensive with the exception of alcohol and cigarettes which are virtually duty-free. St Thomas in the US Virgin Islands is only 45 minutes away by regular ferry service and offers a K-Mart, Woolworths, supermarkets and duty-free speciality shops at prices which are often half of those in British Virgin Islands.

The nearest to local produce worth looking at include some casual clothing such as T-shirts or rum.

Two local newspapers are published weekly.

EATING AND DRINKING

Life in Road Town centres on Main Street, both for shopping and eating. Purser's Country Store and Pub is popular. There are many restaurants with international cuisine and high prices.

TRANSPORT

There is no public transport system, but there are plenty of taxis. Agree the fare before starting the journey.

YEMEN

SANA'A

Language **Arabic**
Currency **riyal. £1=210, Mar 1997**

North Yemen is in the bottom league of underdeveloped countries. Improvements in the supply of foreign goods are due largely to the influx of foreigners, mostly in the oil industry. Good clothing is not available, nor are alcohol or pork. Because of dust, dryness and the poor state of pavements and roads, trainers are most suitable for outdoor wear.

The town centre around Tahrir Square is the main shopping area. The Old City is a fascinating complex of ancient mosques and other buildings with souks.

Some paperbacks can be purchased from the two international hotels, but the choice is limited.

EATING AND DRINKING

Restaurants at the two major hotels cater for Westerners and are of a relatively good standard, but beer and wine, when available, are expensive. Fish generally is one of the better food options. Imported meat is usually available, though expensive. The supply of fresh fruit and vegetables is seasonal. Qat chewing has the same social position for nearly all Yemenis that alcohol has in the West. *Qat* is a shrub, the leaves of which are mildly euphoric and stimulating. Westerners may find it difficult to sleep, or experience mild constipation following a qat-chewing session.

TRANSPORT

Taxis are expensive, but reasonably reliable. There is no telephone taxi service. Shared taxis are available.

Yugoslavia (Serbia)

Belgrade

Language Serbo-Croat
Currency new dinar (ND) of 100 paras, fixed to the
  Deutschmark. £1=8.64, Mar 1997
Banks 1730-1200 Mon to Fri
Traveller's cheques no; bring hard currency,
  preferably Deutschmarks
Credit cards American Express only; limited outlets
Shops 0900-1200, 1600-2200 Mon to Fri in summer,
  0800-1200, 1600-1900 in winter; state department
  stores and supermarkets 0900-1500 Sat; markets
  close 1200
Sales New Year, spring and summer
Tipping 10 per cent in restaurants, round up the
  fare in taxis
Export restrictions certificate from Department of
  Antiquities needed for antiques

Yugoslavia now comprises two of the six republics that con-
stituted Yugoslavia before 1991: Serbia and Montenegro.

Trade sanctions have now been suspended (10/96). Shops
are mostly state-owned, but in recent years an increasing number of smaller privately owned boutiques has opened up. They
often have a better selection of goods and are open for longer
hours. More goods likely to interest visitors are appearing,
such as Sirogojno sweaters and crystal. Belgrade is very continental in atmosphere, with outdoor cafés in abundance. Knez
Mihailova is not only the main shopping street, but also a
place to see and be seen: it is busy every evening until quite
late.

There is a pedestrian precinct on Knez Mihailova and
another main shopping street is Srpskih Vladara. A reasonable
shopping mall is the Sava Centre next to the Hotel
Intercontinental; the state-owned Beograd department store is
on Teraziije. Mothercare is opposite Trg Republika, Rifle
Jeans on Srpskih Vladara and both Stefanel and Benetton in City
Passage (behind Knez Mihailova). There are outdoor markets,
mainly for produce, all over the town. The Zelena Vranac or
Turkish Market is situated on Naradnog Fronta below the
Hotel Moskva.

Sirogojno, where the famous sweaters come from, is a

four-hour drive and a living museum of folk architecture. It is well worth a visit, but the sweaters are also available at Beogradski izlog on Trg Republika. This shop also sells good-quality hand-crafted souvenirs. There are branches of Traditional Handicraft Shops at Terazije 43-45, Knez Mihailova 2-4 and Knez Milosa 17. For crystal, glassware and ceramics try Genex Kristal at Terazije 37 or one of the shops on Knez Mihailova such as Staklarna Boris Kidric. Zaric Antiques at Vuka Karadzica 9 is an exclusive shop in the middle of town with many rare items, mostly eighteenth and nineteenth century. Galerija 12+ at Vuka Karadzica 12 represents younger artists. Singidunum at Knez Mihailova 40 is a picture gallery which also sells objets d'art.

For newspapers go to the large hotels or the Central Railway Station. The *Financial Times* costs ND 13. Bookstores include Jugoslovenska Knjiga at Knez Mihailova 2 which has some English-language books.

EATING AND DRINKING

For a meal out, try the Metropole, Moskva or one of the other large hotels. Fish and seafood can be good. Dva Ribara at Narodrog Fronta 21 is a fish restaurant with a pianist; the Restaurant Reka at Key Oslobodenya 73b in Zemun is similar. For local atmosphere try the Skadarlya area off Francuska Street, where there are plenty of restaurants and outside cafés to sit and watch the world go by.

TRANSPORT

It is 20 minutes' walk from the Hyatt or Intercontinental to the main shopping area. However, walking is not always easy because of the bad state of repair of the pavements. Flat shoes are recommended for sightseeing.

Trams and buses run regularly, day and night, but can be very crowded. Tickets for five rides cost ND15 and can be bought at kiosks near the stops. Taxis are good, although drivers do not always know the routes. Check the clock: setting 1 is the daily rate, setting 2 the evening rate and 3 is after midnight. Some drivers like to charge Sunday rates.

SECURITY

Muggings and car thefts are increasing.

ZAIRE (REPUBLIC OF CONGO)

KINSHASA

Language **French**
Currency **new Zaire (NZ) of 100 makuta**
  £1=130,000, Oct 1996
Banks **0800-1130 Mon to Fri**
Shops **0800-1200, 1500-1700 Mon to Fri,**
  0800-1200 Sat

Kinshasa is a sprawling and run-down city with a population of around five million. There is little new development and the transport infrastructure is poor. The spine of the city is the Boulevard du 30 Juin, the artery of the shopping and business area with its open-air markets, supermarkets and restaurants. Most things are available provided you are not fussy about particular brands, but everything is expensive.

EATING AND DRINKING
There is a good selection of restaurants. Arguably the best are the Café Conc and L'Etrier, but they are very expensive. Otherwise try the Étoile at the Intercontinental or La Devinière, Lolo la Crevette, the Greek Club, the Mandarin and the Big Steak. None is cheap.

TRANSPORT
There is a desperate need for public transport. Buses are crammed to bursting point. Taxis are available, but shared more often than not, and not recommended. Be aware if you do use them that drivers often do not know the route. Meters are almost non-existent, so settle the fare in advance.

SECURITY
There is a high level of crime and lawlessness. Care should be taken when travelling around at night. Beggars are persistent, but not usually aggressive. The current civil war (May 1997) means that travel plans should be suspended.

Zambia

Lusaka

Language **English**
Currency **kwacha (K) of 100 ngwee.£1=2064, Mar 1997**
Banks **0815-1245 Mon to Wed and Fri, 0815-1200 Thur, 0815-1100 Sat**
Shops **0830-1630 Mon to Fri, 0830-1300 Sat**
Refunds **not common, but exchange possible**
Bargaining **at stalls and markets**
Duty-free **cigarettes and drink in Cairo Road and at airport**
Tipping **illegal, but expected; 10 per cent is standard**
Export restrictions **licences needed for trophies, skins, etc. are arranged by hunt companies**

Many tourists come just for the game parks, and business people often see only the inside of their hotel and office, but Lusaka is quite a comfortable place, having improved dramatically over the last three years or so, helped by increased imports from South Africa. New shops are opening all the time, mostly selling foodstuffs. There is a huge gap in the market for good clothing and footwear, but the present economic and political climate does not encourage investment. Any shortfalls are easily made up in Zimbabwe or, better still, in South Africa.

Lusaka is a fairly small city with few shopping centres as such. Instead, there are individual shops dotted over town.For supermarket and general items there is a branch of the South African chain Shoprite Checkers in Cairo Road, but security can be a problem in this area.

Local specialities include silverwork – jewellery and small ornaments – and gem-stones. It is best to price them at home first, to ensure that you are getting a bargain. Never buy gems on the street – they will be glass.There is no such thing as a cheap gem. The Intercontinental and other big hotels have reasonable shops to try. There is also a jewellery shop with a good reputation in Cairo Road, but again be aware of security. There is a good silver jeweller in the Castle Shopping Centre in the south-west of the city.

Also popular, but not always easy for the tourist to take home, are carved wooden giraffes from six inches to six feet in height. These can be bought from roadside stalls in Kafue Road.

Malachite figures can be bought in the shops in the hotels or in the market at Northmead. The quality of the work is not good, but prices are better in the market. Woodcarvings can be bought in the same places or by the garage at Longacres roundabout. Carved local chairs are interesting and sturdy, but tend to be too heavy for tourists to take home. Silver animals made of driftwood are interesting and unusual and can be bought in jewellers or at the craft fair at the Dutch Reformed Church in Kabulonga on the last Saturday of each month.Prices there are good and hand-printed lengths of batik cloth and made-up clothing can also be purchased.

Local shopping baskets are strong and cheap and some are attractive. Woven basket trays and bowls are cheap, pretty and practical. There is asmall art gallery where local artists exhibit and their paintings are usually for sale.

Zambia grows an increasing number of roses, mainly for export, but available locally outside most shops and supermarkets at cheap prices by UK standards.

There are six local English-language newspapers, three daily, two Sunday and one weekly. International newspapers can be bought at supermarkets and hotels – at a price. There are a few bookshops with a limited choice of books at high prices. Mary's Bookshop on Leopards Hill Road is perhaps best. Bushcraft in Mwlwa specialises in books on plants, birds and wildlife.

EATING AND DRINKING

There are several restaurants in Lusaka.There are three good hotels which also providea reasonable restaurant service. Meat, beef in particular, is excellent and there are good seasonal fruit and vegetables. Local mushrooms come in an amazing range of varieties, sizes and colours and are well worth trying. A good range of South African wines is available in supermarkets and elsewhere.

TRANSPORT

Public transport is not a realistic option for the visitor. Taxis are expensive, unreliable and often dangerous, but walking is hardly practical except in areas such as Kabulonga. The doorman at your hotel will negotiate a price for you, since there are no meters.

SECURITY

Security is a problem in Lusaka. Try to avoid doubtful areas, do not dress ostentatiously or make yourself otherwise conspicuous. Try to avoid carrying large amounts of cash – although only a few restaurants will accept credit cards. There are few beggars, but plenty of people trying to sell you goods such as fruit or music cassettes.

ZIMBABWE

HARARE

Language **English**
Currency **Zimbabwe dollar (Z$) of 100 cents.**
   £1=17.90, Mar 1997
Banks **0830-1300/1400 Mon, Tue, Thur, Fri,**
   0830-1200 Wed, 0830-1100 Sat
Credit cards **accepted in shops, hotels and**
   restaurants; Visa and Mastercard preferred
Cashpoints **yes**
Shops **variable; closed Sat afternoon and Sun;**
   many close Wed afternoon
Refunds **yes, or credit notes**
Bargaining **in People's Markets and at stalls, not in**
   shops
Duty-free **at airport; cigarettes, tobacco, cigars and**
   wine more expensive than local varieties in town
Tipping **10 per cent maximum for services, and in**
   restaurants without service charge

Lifting of import restrictions has led to a dramatic improvement in the availability of imported goods, but they tend to be expensive.

The main shopping area is compact and easy to reach on foot from most central hotels. There are a number of small arcades and shopping malls. Two of the best are situated to either side of Meikle's Hotel. The newest is Eastgate on Third Street, pleasant and modern and specialising in clothing and curios with plenty of eating places. There are a number of department stores in town including Barbours and Greatermans along Jason Moyo Avenue and Meikle's on Robert Mugabe Road. Casual clothing is widely available and although not up to UK quality it is often considerably cheaper. Safari clothes are usually good quality and readily available. Men's casual suede boots and also excellent elephant-skin boots are good value.

The choice of curio shops in the city centre is wide, with a large selection of interesting and unusual handicrafts. For woodcarvings and the famous Shona sculpture, the cheapest source is at the People's Markets. There is one on the roadside of Unity Square opposite Meikle's Hotel and another on Enterprise Road about five kilometres from town. Also in the suburbs is the modern and pedestrianised Borrowdale shopping area, where there is a People's Market, and also a market every Sunday morning. Mbare Market on Chaminuka Street near Rufaro Stadium has a great atmosphere and a real feel of Africa. It includes a curio market with a wide selection of crafts at reasonable prices.

Curios and sculpture are generally of high quality, as are crocheted garments, semi-precious stones, basketware and batik or *sadza*-dyed fabrics.There are a number of sculpture parks around Harare, and for those interested in purchasing Shona sculpture a visit to one of these might be worth while. Bear in mind that sculpture can be very heavy, and so difficult to take home. Chapungu Sculpture Park is in the Msasa Industrial Estate about eight kilometres from Harare. The N'thaba Sculpture Gallery has a beautiful setting 30 kilometres away in Umwinsidale, home also of silver craftsman Patrick Mavros who specialises in silver models of wild animals.

Most British newspapers are available at a price – the *Daily Telegraph* costs Z$50. The locally published *Herald* costs Z$2. English-language books are readily available in the many bookshops, but are usually more expensive than in the UK.

EATING AND DRINKING

There is a wide selection of restaurants serving European, Indian, Chinese and other cuisines. The food is good, but not epicurean and relatively cheap by UK standards. Seasonal produce is delicious and beef is plentiful and of high quality. Sadza, a maize porridge, is the traditional basic food, but it is too tasteless for most Western palates. Non-alcoholic Malawi Shandy is widely available and thirst-quenching.

Local tobacco, cigarettes and cigars are acceptable and cheap, as is local wine. They will cost less in the town than their international equivalents do at the airport.

TRANSPORT

The bus service is infrequent and unreliable and not used by foreigners. "Emergency taxis" should also be avoided. Regular taxis are generally fairly reliable. Some have meters, but if not you should establish the fare before embarking on any journey. Fares are similar to those in the UK.

SECURITY

Muggers and pickpockets are prevalent in city centres especially near hotels, banks and the airport.

CONTRIBUTORS

LOUISE AKHURST, BARBARA ALCOCK, AURIOL ALMOND, CHARLOTTE AMALIA, CAROLYN ANDREWS, PLAXY ARTHUR, CHRIS AVERY, LAURAINE BAINES, PATRICIA BALDWIN, LIZ BANKS, ANDREA BATEMAN, COLETTE BATES, SHARON BEAN, JILL BECKINGHAM, YOLANDE BEDWELL, CHRISTINE BEETHAM, MARYLYN BENNETT, STEPHANIE BENNETT, SUZANNE BERGNE, LINDSEY BLAKE, JOAN BLAKEMORE, JANE BOWDEN, JENNY BREAR, JANE BRIGHT, BRENDA BROWN, SHEILA BROWN, HENRIETTA BUCKNALL, AISLING BULL, HILDA BURNHAMS, MARINA BURNS, JACQUI BUSHE, MURIEL CALLE, MARILYN CAMERON, AILSA CAMPBELL, MAUREEN CAMPBELL, ALICE CANNON, LESLIE CANNING, MARIA DEL CARMEN-WEBB, LISA CARR, ANDREA H CARTER, CATHERINE ROSE CARTER, JANE CARTWRIGHT, SHEILA CASE, LINDA CASEY, FIONA CASSELLS-BROWN, M.M. CATON, JANE CHILCOTT, JANICE CHUN, AGNES CLARK, LIZ CLARK, LINDA CLARKE, LOUISE CLEGG, MARY CLEPHANE, CAROL COLE, LORETTA COLE, ANN COLLINS, TERRIE CONNELLY, BERNIE CONNOLLY, LYNN CONNOR, MAUREEN COOK, DONNA COOPE, DAVID COTTON, ELIZABETH COX, BETTY CREES, STEVE CROSSMAN, HILDEGARD CROUCHER, MARGARET CULVER, BRENDAN DALLEY, ELIZABETH DALTON, MRS DALY, GRISELDA DAVIES, PURI DAVIES, CAROLINE DEAR, JANINE DEARDEN, LIGIA DENT, JENNIE DEWAR, JACKIE DIAS, MARIANNE DICKERSON, FIDELMA DRAYTON, DEBRA DREW, JOAN DRURY, PAUL J. DRYDEN, DIANE DUCKETT, SHAN DURHAM, DEIRDRE DYSON, ANN EASTBURN, BETTY ENGLAND, LIZZIE EVANS , HEATHER EVERARD, CLARE EVERSON, GWENDOLYN FALL, G. FAURE, CLAIRE FELL, JENNY FENTON, S A FERGUSON, KATHRYN FIELDEN, SYLVIA FLUCK, CHRIS FORD, JOANNA FRANKLIN, NADE FRASER, CORINNA FREEMAN, ANNE GALE, CHRIS GARDINER, LISA GARN, DJIHAN GIRDLESTONE, RUTH GLASS, CLARE GOODALL, HEATHER GORDON, ADRIENNE GORDON-MACLEOD, MARINA GOWAN, JOANNA GREENSTREET, DOTTIE GREENWOOD, AVRIL GROWCOTT, LORNA GUCKIAN, MARGARET HALL, PENNY HANNANT, TESSA HARRIS, SARAH HASWELL, SALLY HAY, YVONNE HAZLEWOOD, VALERIE HEAD, LESLEY HEDLEY, JULIA HENDERSON, JANICE HENTLEY, THELMA HIGGINSON, LISA HILL, MELANIE HIMMER, ERENDIRA HOBBS, ANNE HOLLAND, ANNE HOLMES, JENNY HOLMES, ELIZABETH HONE, PAULINE HOOK, ANNMARIE HUMPHREY,

JANE HURLEY, IAN HUTCHISON, JACQUI HUTCHISON, NIDDY HUXLEY, RICHARD HYDE, SUSAN INNES, MARIKO JACK, MAUREEN JACKSON, SUSIE JACOBSEN, MARY JAMES, ANNA JARROLD, HEATHER JESSOP, GINNY JOHNS, BARBARA JOHNSTON, AMANDA JONES, SYLVIA JONES, CLARE KENNEDY, LESLEY KERLY, IRENE KERRISON, ANNONG KERSHAW, I KINGSTON, ELLEN KNIGHT SMITH, BERNADETTE LAMBE, CATHERINE LAMPORT, SALLY LARNER, BRIGITTE LAVERS, JOANNE LAWRENCE, PAULA LEAHY, LESLEY LEE, PENNY LEGG, MELANIE LEGGE, LESLEY LIDDELL, KATIE LLOYD, JOANNA LOWIS, SUE McADAM, JANET MACAN, GILL McCARTHY, ALEXANDRA McGREGOR, TRICIA McKELVEY, MARGARET McKENZIE, IAN McKINLAY, RACHEL McLOUGHLIN, AMANDA MARSHALL, BOBBY MARSHALL, AILEEN MARTIN, ELISABETH MATHERS, MAGGIE MILBURN, DAVID MILES, JULIAN MILLER, THE HON MRS A MONCKTON, SHEILA MOON, AGNI MOREY, CLARE MORRICE, ANN MORRIS, MARGARET MORRIS, JOAN MURAS, FIONA MURRAY, NORMA MURRAY, MADELEINE MUSGRAVE, SONIA NEWTON, SUZANNE NICHOLS, JENNY NORMAN, YOLANDE O'BRIEN, BRIDGET O'SULLIVAN-KEMP, EVA OWEN, DAVINA PALMER, JANE PARKER, DIANE PARKINS, MARGARET PATERSON, ANNA PATTEN, ROGER PATTEN, PHILIPPA PATTERSON, MARGARET PATTERSON, SEGOLENE PAXMAN, JULIAN PEARSON, HELENA PEART, PAM PEERS, NEIL PORTER, TRICIA POWELL, CORIE PRYCE, EILEEN REBECCHI, SIOK BOI REDDICLIFFE, ANDREA REILLY, SAMANTHA RISELEY, SISI ROBBINS, KIM ROBERTS, HELEN ROBERTSON, KAY ROISSETER, MAUREEN ROSS, MARGARET ROTHWELL, VALERIE RUDDLE, JEAN RUSSELL, KAREN RUTHERFORD, GILL RYAN, JENNY SCARBOROUGH, CAROL SCRAFTON, MONICA SEDDON, LIZ SELLEN, TRICIA SHARP, GEORGINA SHIELDS, TINA SHINGLER, VICKEY SHORT, CAROLINE SIMMONS, JENNY SIMPSON, LISE SIMPSON, ADELE SIMS, JANE SINTON, JUNE SLOANE, ALETHEA SMITH, DELYTH SMITH, SUZANNE SMITH, SUSAN SOMERSET, LAILEEN SPRINGGAY, VALERIE STOREY, SUSAN SWIFT, VALERIE TATHAM, JOAN TAYLOR, FIONA THOMAS, GILLIAN THOMAS, BARBARA THOMPSON, LUCINDA THOMSON, DAVID TUCK, SUSAN TUCKER, MARGARET TUNNELL, KATHY TUNSLEY, M TWIGG, MIKE UPTON, BEVERLEY WALLACE-HANDFORD, JEANNIE WEINRABE, DEBORAH WHITE, JUDY WHITE, MELANIE WIELD, JEANETTE WILDE, ELIZABETH WILLIAMS, G J B WILLIAMS, JOHN WILLIAMS, CAROLINE YARNOLD, ELISABETH YOUNG, SARAH YOUNGER